Ruling America

RULING AMERICA

A History of Wealth and Power in a Democracy

Edited by

Steve Fraser & Gary Gerstle

Harvard University Press
Cambridge, Massachusetts
London, England
2005

Library of Congress Cataloging-in-Publication Data

Ruling America : a history of wealth and power in a democracy /
edited by Steve Fraser and Gary Gerstle.
p. cm.
Includes bibliographical references and index.
ISBN 0-674-01695-5 (cloth : alk. paper) — ISBN 0-674-01747-1 (paper : alk. paper)
1. Elite (Social sciences)—United States—History.
2. Social classes—Political aspects—United States—History.
3. Power (Social sciences)—United States—History.
4. Democracy—United States.
I. Fraser, Steve, 1945–   II. Gerstle, Gary, 1954–

HN90.E4R85 2005
305.5′2′0973—dc22
2004059769

For Emma and Sam

Contents

Ruling America

Introduction

❧

STEVE FRASER AND GARY GERSTLE

This book is founded on a paradox, one that has baffled historians and citizens generally for as long as there has been a United States of America: How can a nation consecrated to freedom and equality nonetheless give rise to great hierarchies of power and wealth that undermine the very foundations of that extraordinary promise? The paradox is more pointed than that. The country is a democracy. The people rule. And yet the people do not rule; elites, patriciates, castes, classes have ruled in their stead. Sometimes they seem to rule with the people's interests in mind, sometimes not.

Phrases like "ruling class" or "ruling elite" sound a discordant note. They do not feel as though they belong in the vocabulary of American politics and its history. After all, the very openness, fluidity, and social heterogeneity of American society defy anything as exclusive, ongoing, and inaccessible as a "ruling class." There is something ineffably alien about such notions, stepchildren imported from the lingua franca of the Old World and its sedimentary layers of titled aristocrats, landed gentry, military castes, and dynastic families. It is a cherished

American folk belief, after all, that classes do not exist or, if they do, are always going out of existence. Democratic political institutions, whatever their defects, will not tolerate a continuous monopoly of power by a tiny clique of self-anointed overlords. And even if such usurpation might be attempted, the sheer overwhelming tidal force of the American economy would wash it away in an onrushing flood of new enterprise, new technology, and new sources of wealth that would inundate the old ruling groups and either force them open to rising elements of the middle classes or dissolve them entirely. So, too, the ethnic promiscuity of American society, its open invitation to people from every country and culture to come aboard and grab a share of the American dream, inexorably wears away at the internal cohesion, that vital complex of shared traditions, beliefs, and customs that any ruling milieu depends on for its élan and its sense of entitlement.

Over the last quarter-century, historians have by and large ceased writing about the role of ruling elites in the country's evolution. Or if they have taken up this subject, they have done so to argue against its salience for grasping the essentials of American political history. Yet there is something peculiar about this recent intellectual aversion, even if we accept as true the beliefs that democracy, social mobility, and economic dynamism have long inhibited the congealing of a ruling stratum. This aversion has coincided, after all, with one of the largest and fastest-growing disparities in the division of income and wealth in American history. We have all grown used to characterizing the 1980s and 1990s as the second coming of the Gilded Age. "Crony capitalism" has reentered our everyday political vocabulary, a term carrying unsavory associations, suggesting the cross-fertilization of privileged economic and political circles in open defiance of the normal protocols of democratic politics. Since historians, like everybody else, are hardly immune to the subtle influence of the pressing issues of their own day, even as they burrow deep into the distant past, it is noteworthy that so few have felt the urge of late to explore the class dimensions of power in years gone by. Some have, of course, and the editors of and contributors to this volume are among them.

That this recent neglect of the way ruling groups formed, exercised their power, and came to an end has followed the "social history revolution" of the 1960s also seems peculiar. That revolution generated a remarkably fertile outpouring of historical research and writing that focused on the experience of oppression going all the way back to the colonial origins of the New World and beyond. But this meticulous examination of the lives of slaves, immigrants, industrial workers, Native Americans, impoverished underclasses, women, disenfranchised minorities, and others has, for the most part, not concerned itself with the social and political history of those presumably responsible for their oppression. Most of this writing has exhumed the underground histories of peoples whose lives—family organization, religious behavior, community relations, work experience, and diverse forms of racial, ethnic, and political solidarity—had remained virtually invisible to historians for generations. "Invisible" is the operative word here. The tacit assumption informing so much of this history from below was that, precisely because these were subordinate populations, they had been robbed of their own histories; indeed, the hidden nature of their distinct pasts was itself a cardinal symptom of that subordination. To recover those pasts, to bring them into the light of day, was to help restore long-effaced identities. For some historians this became a way of asserting those identities in the political present. Moreover, what might be called "identity history" naturally enough tended to channel its energies inward, that is, toward uncovering the internal social metabolism of a group's coherence and endurance, how it defended its fragile and imperiled existence against a whole array of forces—economic upheavals, cultural suasion and coercion, mass prejudices, and paranoid scapegoating—and not merely on those menacing it from above, from the ranks of the putative "ruling class."

However valuable and innovative such historical detective work on the experiences of the subordinate often was (and is), it drained intellectual attention away from the collective lives of the superordinate. Of course, these histories treated as axiomatic the power and exploitation exercised by upper classes, master races, and patriarchs. Beyond that, any more intimate examination of how ruling groups coalesced, how they exercised their authority in an ostensibly democratic political environment, how they formulated the ideological justifications for their empowerment, how they faced up to crises and challenges to their supremacy—these and a dozen other similarly intriguing questions about the world of American hierarchs often fell from view.

Neglecting the powerful had not been characteristic of historical work prior to World War II. To the contrary, the story of the ruling elites had preoccupied historians for a very long time. Moreover, to talk about classes and the struggles between them was common parlance. Indeed, for the first 150 years of the nation's life, the language of ruling and subordinate social groups defined the contours of one of the grand narratives of American history. Measured by the long sweep of that history, stretching back into the colonial era, it is the recent muting of these concerns about the concentration and exercise of power that seems odd. This does not mean that those who once stressed such matters were right. But it does mean that a whole set of historical metaphors and categories of analysis once taken for granted have lost much of their legitimacy.

Beginning sometime after World War II, and with increasing force in the wake of the Reagan "revolution," a gathering consensus concluded that events, "History," the impersonal forces of the market, or some other analogous abstractions rule, not classes or elites. Certainly the cultural Cold War helped stigmatize notions of "class struggle" and "ruling classes" as so much communist verbiage, a purely propagandist rhetoric that failed to capture the more centerless, polymorphous, and pluralist makeup of American politics and social organization. Yet precisely the opposite conviction runs likes a red thread through much of the nation's past. It is virtually impossible to make sense of any of the great epochs in American political history or of the grander chronicle of democracy in America without coming face to face with "Tories," "moneycrats," "the Monster Bank," "the slaveocracy," "robber barons," "plutocrats," "the money trust," "economic royalists," "the Establishment," the "power elite," or the "military-industrial complex." All these colorful variations echo a single theme: that, the fluid and anarchic character of the American experience notwithstanding, organized political and social groupings have arisen at key junctures in the country's history and have succeeded for more or less extended periods of time in exercising broad dominion over the nation's political economy and even its cultural and social life.

One might view this rich imagery of the pursuit of power either as a reproach or as a vindication of the pursuit of happiness—a reproach insofar as it suggests that the American promise of freedom and equality has been a sham and a delusion, a vindication inasmuch as it implies that democracy has been a permanent revolution, forever embattled against those who have tried to abrogate that promise. Either way, America is depicted as densely populated with an assortment of social groups that all seem to behave suspiciously like ruling classes or elites.

Survey the landmarks of the national drama. Every president of enduring reputation up to John F. Kennedy is remembered for some vital crusade against a usurping or entrenched elite. Washington and Jefferson overthrew the minions of the British monarchy and then fended off attempts at aristocratic counterrevolution by home-grown Tories. Andrew Jackson waged war against a "Monster Bank" that presumed to monopolize the credit resources of a fledgling nation and turn enterprising citizens into its vassals. Lincoln purged the nation of its mortal sin by extirpating the "slaveocracy." Teddy Roosevelt unleashed rhetorical thunderbolts against those "malefactors of great wealth" whose gargantuan corporate combines showed no regard for the public welfare and bought and sold senators and congressmen like so many pigs at a market. Woodrow Wilson promised, if swept into office, to take on the "money trust," that financial octopus whose tentacles were stran-

gling to death the economic opportunity and democratic independence
that were every citizen's birthright. In the midst of the greatest calamity since the Civil War, FDR chased the "money changers from the
temple" and declared that his New Deal would henceforth police and
punish the "economic royalists" who had brought on the Great Depression. Even the mild-mannered Dwight Eisenhower left office cau-
tioning the country against the overweening power of the "military-industrial complex."

Just because specters of self-aggrandizing power have time and
again haunted presidents and ordinary citizens, that doesn't make them
real. Nor does it necessarily follow that scholars would naturally have
taken them up as the dramatis personae of historical narratives. Many
have not. Beginning with the earliest chronicles of the national saga,
historians have adopted alternative scenarios for capturing the essence
of the American story. Some have talked about Manifest Destiny, nation building, modernization, the taming of the West, the social and
political alchemy at work on the rolling frontier, the extraordinary impact of the American melting pot, the moral vision of the "city on a
hill," or of the world's longest-surviving experiment in government by
Everyman. Most of these syntheses of the country's experience reduced internal economic, social, and political inequities and relations
of domination and subordination to secondary issues, speed bumps on
the highway to national greatness or malfunctions of an otherwise self-
correcting social order.

Still, it is noteworthy that questions about the distribution of wealth
and power have formed the thematic core of the writings of some our
most distinguished historians. Charles Beard, who deeply influenced
American history writing during the first half of the twentieth century,
became most famous for his economic interpretation of the Constitution.[1] He argued that the nation's founding document expressed the
material interests of a dominant alliance of merchants, planters, and
financial speculators. Despite the weightiness of his historical research,
Beard was criticized as an economic reductionist, blind to the impact of

culture and ideology; by World War II, many dismissed him as a cranky leftist because he clung to widely unpopular isolationist sentiments even after war broke out in Europe. Arthur Schlesinger, Jr., by contrast, was always strictly mainstream. His seminal writings on Jacksonian America (*The Age of Jackson* won the young scholar a Pulitzer Prize) and the New Deal explored these turning points in American political history as great struggles between propertied elites and the common workingman.[2] One of the founding fathers of American intellectual history, Vernon Parrington, deployed the Progressive Era's fascination with concentrated wealth and its social reverberations to interpret the work of a diverse array of intellectuals, theologians, novelists, and essayists. Parrington depicted American thinkers locked in cerebral combat, wrestling with the forces of invidious social and material distinction and a contrary egalitarian impulse.[3]

Louis Hartz and Richard Hofstadter, also pathbreaking historians of liberal political culture, pushed their scholarship in a different direction. They dedicated their work to the proposition that the kind of class antinomies characteristic of European society were stillborn in the New World. Their argument for the one-dimensional nature of American political life rested on what they concluded was an indigenous universal preference for private property that tended to suffocate all outbreaks of more radical social and political experimentation. Outbreaks there were, however, and so Hofstadter, for example, was compelled to come to grips, at least within the American mind, of what he chastised as the "paranoid imagination." Hofstadter's treatment of populism, and what he considered its post–World War II McCarthyite analogues, acknowledged the salience, if not the palpable reality, of popular beliefs, whether paranoid or not, in the existence of ruling classes and their machinations.[4] David Potter, a contemporary of Hofstadter, wrote a prizewinning analysis of the coming of the Civil War that worked out the intricate interconnections between ideology, political disunion, and economic interests. His classic meditation *People of Plenty* wrestled, like Hofstadter's work, with whether or not the amazing cornucopia of American economic resources and output could continue to function the way it had for generations, as the lubricant for incipient class abrasions.[5] The African American scholar and radical activist W. E. B. Du Bois authored a remarkable study of Reconstruction that captured the organic connection between racial and class exploitation and subordination and how these developments imprinted themselves on post–Civil War America.[6]

More historians of great accomplishment could be added to this gallery. But pondering the relationship between power and wealth in the United States has by no means been confined to scholars trained as historians. To be sure, many American intellectuals have not expended much effort on deciphering the internal social and cultural cohesion and external mechanisms of domination characteristic of ruling elites. No doubt they considered such explorations an arid exercise in a society famous for its social fluidity. But some of the country's most original social thinkers thought otherwise.

John Adams was ambivalent. He candidly voiced his doubts that the vox populi could be trusted to identify a truly honorable and meritorious elite dedicated to public service, so easily was it led astray by quacks, hypocrites, flatterers, and bald-faced knaves. Fearing the "tyranny of the majority," Adams nonetheless accepted the revolutionary principle that the "people" were sovereign. But to abolish, as the French revolutionaries talked of doing, all distinctions of rank and order based on wealth, tradition, and family lineage struck him as a road to certain disaster. How to forge a workable balance? Allowing wealth alone to determine who reigned would encourage the most selfish instincts and weaken the impulse to win social distinction through disinterested public service. Yet there was no question in Adams's mind that social stability would always require "that every man should know his place and be made to keep it." At bottom he believed that "the great question will forever remain, who shall work?" The answer was obvious: most would, and they would envy that tiny privileged percentage of their "betters" who remained at leisure to think or govern. For this

Founding Father and future president there was no escaping the historically inevitable: "The controversy between the rich and the poor, the laborious and the idle, the learned and the ignorant . . . will continue and rivalries will spring out of them."[7] The art of good government consisted of striking the right balance of power between them, not in misguided attempts to do away with these intractable social divisions altogether.

Jefferson, Madison, Hamilton, and other political thinkers of the revolutionary generation all understood, like Adams, that republican government was no foolproof prophylactic against conflict between popular forces and various elites—landed, commercial, and financial. Madison feared that economic power would one day try to seize political power, and he was convinced that the anti-republican party "was more partial to the opulent than to the other classes of society."[8] Much of the *Sturm Und Drang* that raised political temperatures during the 1790s pitted Jacobin levelers against moneyed aristocrats—or at least that is how the Hamiltonians and Jeffersonians maligned each other. The Adams family itself carried this intellectual tradition into the nineteenth century, albeit adjusted for the change in historical context. Charles Francis Adams, and the brothers Henry and Brooks, responded to the advent of industrialism and the rise of the corporation and financial capital with a pitiless critique of the new order. Dyspeptic, harboring an inbred patrician disdain for the money game (and in Brooks's case an intellectual grandiosity and *Götterdämmerung* pessimism), the Adamses nevertheless were discerning observers of what they viewed as a new ruling elite. Its power over the country's basal economy, they warned, made these new corporate behemoths muscular enough to overwhelm the rickety institutions of democratic government.[9]

Plutocracy was a preoccupation of the Gilded Age. Some intellectuals, Yale professor William Graham Sumner most prominently, were fully prepared to deploy Darwinian thinking to naturalize and justify the emergence of this band of business tycoons. Thus Sumner treated the titans' stupendous wealth, social prestige, and political authority as proof of their fitness to survive and thrive in a social world subject to the same principle of natural selection that governed all life on earth.[10] Thorstein Veblen, by contrast, found this new ruling caste unfit. In a series of surgical dissections of the era's plutocrats—most memorably in his 1899 *Theory of the Leisure Class* and a quarter-century later in *Absentee Ownership*—Veblen viewed them as an alarmed anthropologist might. He depicted them as an exotic atavism, aping the customs and mores of outmoded warrior cultures, consumed by insatiable cravings for invidious social and cultural distinctions. They were utterly out of touch with the forces of modern science and industry that made the modern world run. The "leisure class" possessed a toxic power. Rule they did, but at enormous social cost to the rational processes of technological progress and general economic well-being. Moreover, their cultural influence was pernicious, since their practices of "pecuniary emulation," in Veblen's phrase, and status-seeking seeped downward, demoralizing those who looked up to them as exemplars.[11]

Irascible, contrarian, and full of irrepressible disdain for conventional thinking, Veblen was a highly original and idiosyncratic thinker. But a wide array of writers and intellectuals shared his underlying conviction: that the country was more or less at the mercy of a tiny body of enormously wealthy men endowed with a supervening political influence earned without the benefit of public, democratic decision making. This same conviction animated the magazine exposés, political treatises, and utopian and dystopian novels written by Henry George, William Demarest Lloyd, Edward Bellamy, and Ignatius Donnelley during the Gilded Age. These writers were generally not practitioners of high theory like Veblen, but they captured the attention of broad audiences, for whom they articulated a creeping suspicion that something other than democracy had arisen and was threatening the land.[12] During the twentieth century, through the era of the Great Depression, jurists such as Louis Brandeis (the most prominent and inde-

fatigable foe of "the money trust"), popular muckrakers like Charles
Edward Russell and Upton Sinclair, and such novelists of the left as
Jack London, Theodore Dreiser, and John Dos Passos continued to
fire away at the hubris, appetite, and tyrannical instincts of Morgan,
Harriman, Rockefeller, and other ruling dynasts.[13] When the old order
finally fell apart in the Crash of '29, intellectuals surveyed the damage
and looked to the future. References to Ferdinand Lundberg's voluminous *America's Sixty Families*, which attempted to map the genera-
tional interconnections of the country's ruling elite, found their way
into FDR's presidential addresses.[14] Matthew Josephson published *The
Robber Barons* at this time, coining an analytic rubric that seemed made
to order to sum up the moral character of those oligarchs most blamed
for the disaster of the Great Depression, even though Josephson's
book was a history of their nineteenth-century predecessors.[15] And
New Deal brain-truster Adolf Berle and Columbia University economist Gardiner Means produced a classic analysis of the usurpation of
the economy by a clique of corporate insiders, recommending in its
stead a more democratic management of industry and finance.[16]

Only after World War II did this long cultural tradition become less
robust and begin to peter out, though not all at once. C. Wright Mills,
like Veblen an anti-academic inside the academy, published *The Power
Elite* in the mid-1950s, in which he traced the interlocking and cross-
fertilization of military, industrial, and political hierarchs. The notion
of a "ruling class" was already in bad odor in Cold War America, and
Mills did not use that term. Not that he was afraid to, but he drew back
from more rigid Marxist conceptions that seemed to him to imply
greater coherence, more single-mindedness, and less contingency than
his own more loosely configured "power elite." Nonetheless, Mills argued passionately that a closed community of power-meisters either
formulated or influenced all the key decisions affecting the nation's fate
in war and peace as well as its critical economic choices. Most occupied
non-elective political or civil positions and tended to have graduated

from the same select circle of preparatory schools and Ivy League universities, to frequent the same social gathering places, and to swap offices with casual regularity.[17]

By Mills's day, however, notions of a "power elite" or "ruling class" had fallen out of fashion. Some intellectuals, like Schlesinger, did allude to "the Establishment." This was a more benign version of the "power elite," allegedly composed of a self-effacing group of international financiers who had created the Marshall Plan, the International Monetary Fund, the World Bank, NATO, and the democratic, anticommunist reconstruction of war-torn Europe. Even those willing to take the idea of an Establishment seriously, however, were more impressed with its wisdom, its prudence, and its apparent lack of self-interested motivation than with its aloofness and immunity from public accountability.

Moreover, the dominant intellectuals of the postwar era—including Daniel Bell, David Riesman, Robert Dahl, and others—did not recognize even this degree of hierarchy. They celebrated instead the classlessness, or homogeneous middle-classness, of American society. In this pluralist idyll no social interest lorded it over all others, but rather each contended for influence with a dozen other well-organized power blocs, arriving at rolling compromises that left authority in a permanent state of flux. Bell declared this historical moment the "end of ideology," meaning that the old categories of a suppressed proletariat and a domineering bourgeoisie no longer had any traction in the postwar world, at least in the United States. America was simply too decentralized a society to support anything as centripetal and enduring as a "ruling class." A whole new academic cross-discipline, American Studies, was invented to explore a national experience that had managed to elude the rigid hierarchies and maldistributions of power typical of other industrial societies.[18]

The downfall of the Establishment during the tragic debacle in Vietnam reignited passionate inquiries into the uses and abuses of power,

past and present. New histories appeared, treating the social and economic fissures in colonial America, the internal class dynamics of the
American Revolution, the political economy and cultural coherence of
the "slave power," the "non-paranoid" resistance to the advent of corporate capitalism. Thus, notwithstanding the triumph of the postwar
consensus, a once honored countertradition lived on in the writings
of Eugene Genovese, Eric Foner, William Domhoff, Michael Harrington, Noam Chomsky, Barbara Ehrenreich, Kevin Phillips, and others.
Genovese, for example, produced a revolution in southern historiography with his meticulous re-creation of the political economy and cultural identity of the slave-owning "master class." Foner, another historian of the generation following Potter and Hofstadter, argued that a
main engine driving the new Republican Party's determination to keep
slavery out of the western territories, even if that meant civil war, was
the deep anxiety that opportunities for landed independence were van-
ishing. Without free land, Republicans asserted, class divisions would
harden and make America like the Old World. Foner's subsequent
monumental work on Reconstruction traced the conversion of that Republican Party into a vehicle of national rule for the rising industrial
bourgeoisie.[19]

In the wake of the conservative intellectual ascendancy that accompanied the rise of Ronald Reagan, however, what had once been a main
current of the country's historiography became little more than a trib-
utary. It is true that plenty of books have appeared over the last decade
or so revisiting the lives of legendary business titans such as Morgan,
Rockefeller, Gould, and Harriman.[20] But nearly without exception they
steer clear of treating these figures as emblematic of some ruling elite.
Nowadays, it may seem old-fashioned, against the American grain, or
even subversive (*pace* President George W. Bush's warning that to crit-
icize his tax cuts for the wealthy was to indulge in "class warfare") to
talk about classes, about the struggles between them, about something
as exotic and alien as a ruling elite. But it is not. The corpus of think-

ing about hierarchy and democracy that extends all the way back to the days of John Adams has left behind a series of questions still worth pondering. That is what we aim to do in this book.

From the moment we began conceptualizing *Ruling America*, we were determined to produce a volume that surveyed ruling elites in America from the Revolution to the present. With the exception of Kevin Phillips's 2002 book *Wealth and Democracy: A Political History of the American Rich*, no effort has been made to produce such a comprehensive work in half a century. Our book, while complementary to Phillips's work, has a different emphasis. It stresses the variety of economic elites that have ruled, or attempted to rule, the nation. It demonstrates the different ways in which elites have constituted their political, ideological, and social worlds; it examines the internal fissures and external challenges that have threatened and sometimes undermined those worlds; and it explores the special problems facing elite pretensions to political power in a democracy. Its focus is on instability and change as integral features of elite rule in America.

One fundamental transformation involves the etiology of power. In the era of Adams and Jefferson, government seemed the principal incubator of elite aspirations to overweening authority. By the time of the industrial revolution, however, civil society, in particular the centers of greatest economic power, had supplanted government as the breeding ground of aristocratic hubris. Government had become either the servitor of powers greater than itself or the inspirational hope of those who saw it as the only mechanism capable of wrestling the country's illicit ruling cliques to the ground. This great sea change in where power was rooted and on whose behalf it might be deployed arose in most societies undergoing the transition from precapitalist to capitalist mechanisms of wealth creation. Moreover, it was itself organically connected to an equally profound change in the way elites organized and conceived of themselves.

In the late eighteenth and early nineteenth centuries, elites configured themselves as an aristocratic caste whose position rested on lineage, inbreeding, and various forms of social exclusivity. Even apart from their real and personal property, their inherited cultural capital commanded deference from those not so blessed. Over time, those boundaries blurred along with the explosive expansion and differentiation of the economy. Those occupying the commanding heights of the economy and the political system began to look more like a class, open to—even forced open by—newcomers of more plebeian origin. This new social fluidity further complicated attempts to discern just who ruled and how. This was emphatically the case, moreover, as rising corporate industrial and finance capital overcame or merged with more settled and dynastic forms of landed and mercantile wealth.

This proliferation of power centers, in turn, generated internal divisions that could take on cultural and political as well as economic shape. Most significantly, it produced a fissure within the "leisure class" between those absorbed by their own self-interest and self-regard, psychologically and politically deaf and blind to the economic mayhem and social antagonisms accumulating around them, and a fraction of that same universe—people such as the Roosevelts, for example, or those to-the-manner-born Establishment figures of the next generation—who self-consciously took up the challenge of ruling on behalf of the whole commonwealth, even if that meant now and then risking the enmity of their social peers. Within these circles, a sense of social trusteeship subdued the instinct for self-indulgence. Here the possibility of collaborating with subordinate segments of the body politic— the labor movement, for example—was actively explored, leaving the makeup, not to mention the verifiable existence, of a ruling group even more intriguing to ascertain. Fissures this profound took on measurable, visible form only during mortal crises. One thinks of the constitutional period, the Civil War, the political firestorm ignited by populist and antitrust passions at the turn of the century, the Great Depression, and the defeat in Vietnam and the end of U.S. world economic supremacy in the 1970s.

What is fascinating about these occurrences is that they show how dominant groups faced up to the challenge and either succumbed in war or public ignominy or else surmounted it, whether through pure self-assertion or shrewd political compromise. The road from omnipotence to superannuation or omni-incompetence has by no means been a straight one. Whatever the outcome, the life and death of ruling elites is one of the enduring themes that run through the long literature of wealth and political power in America. It remains so today as the country witnesses the tribulations of its latest ruling group, born at the dawn of Reagan's "morning in America" and now struggling to master what may be either the high noon or the twilight of the new American Century. The contributors to this volume examine these and other dimensions of the ways in which distinct social groups grasped and then lost their hold on power over the course of the country's history.

We are aware that American history is populated with numerous kinds of elites—some regional, others national; some that staked their prestige solely on wealth, others that derived their preeminence from politics; some grounded in professional, religious, or educational expertise, others in the influence they exercised in particular ethnic or racial communities. Here we are concerned principally about those elites who sought to use their economic wealth to achieve national political power.

What does it mean to aspire to rule the nation? Sometimes it has meant literally becoming one of America's political rulers: one thinks of the Federalist elite who wrote the Constitution and dominated political life through the 1790s, or of the southern plantation owners who controlled the Senate in the 1830s, 1840s, and 1850s and, by perpetuating slavery, drove national economic policy. But, more commonly, economic elites have not been able to rule in such a direct manner. They had to fight to establish their dominance in a political system that was formally democratic and frequently hostile to their wealth and their pretensions. Often they could achieve their ends only through political representatives who did not share their class origin and who might or might not be open to persuasion or bribery. Thus, few elites have been

able to assume that political rule naturally gravitates to them by virtue
of their wealth or social station. On the contrary, they have had to fight
to establish their legitimacy and to hold off challengers, both from below and from ascendant elites who sought to displace them. For this
reason, the history of ruling elites is an exceptionally dynamic and
complex story. All of the contributors wrestle with three salient features of that dynamism: the vulnerability and even mortality of elites,
the drama of elite succession and adaptation, and finally the instinct for
counterrevolution.

There is no denying that America has always been a highly fluid society. Nothing has ever been able to assume its own permanence, not
even ensconced centers of wealth and power. In terms of political influence, hierarchs have led a precarious existence. The tension between
presumptions to domination and the undermining of those presumptions informs every chapter of this book. In "The Dilemmas of Ruling
Elites in Revolutionary America," Gary J. Kornblith and John M.
Murrin explore how quickly the "natural aristocracy" of the Founding
Fathers who led the Revolution and devised the Constitution fell to
pieces and gave way, in the North, to a more plebeian politics. Sven
Beckert, in "Merchants and Manufacturers in the Antebellum North,"
argues that by 1830 the great merchants were already losing their grip
to middling and lower orders whom the Jeffersonians, thirty years earlier, had invited onto the political stage. Of course, the "slave power"
held on the longest and remained essentially unchallenged in its regional domain until its defeat in the Civil War. For sheer longevity, no
other ruling group in American history matches it. But, as Adam
Rothman makes clear in "The 'Slave Power' in the United States, 1783–
1865," as early as 1820 the slaveocracy, in national politics, felt itself to
be under siege.

While the political landscape changed dramatically as a result of the
Civil War, the underlying sense of elite vulnerability did not. As David
Nasaw argues in "Gilded Age Gospels," the nouveau riche industrial-
ists of the Gilded Age at first had no interest in government (as long as

public institutions kept their hands off corporate affairs and opened their coffers to capitalist enterprises). Soon enough, however, they felt compelled to exert their will in the political realm in order to fend off attempts by farmers and laborers and smaller businessmen to limit their prerogatives. They succeeded, but it was a hotly contested struggle whose outcome was hardly foreordained. The more politically engaged circle of Wall Street financiers and corporate executives who supplanted the "robber barons" seemed to put matters on a firmer footing. In "The Abortive Rule of Big Money" and "The Managerial Revitalization of the Rich," Alan Dawley and Jackson Lears, respectively, analyze the consolidation of this industrial-financial elite and its search for cultural authority and political influence in what might be called the Age of Morgan. This was a formidable elite indeed that held sway for a long generation. But as Dawley emphasizes, its members were compelled to limit their power in response to democratic challenge. The Progressive Era bubbled over with proposals to reach some political compromise between elite desire and popular demands: a capitalism supervised by the state that would ensure profitability for the owners of capital but also impose democratic checks on the ability of the wealthy to influence politics and dominate the economy. Yet the substance of the compromise never materialized, as post–World War I elites chose to roll back democracy's encroachments on their customary prerogatives.

Events since the Second World War offer additional evidence about the vulnerability of ruling groups. In "The Foreign Policy Establishment," Godfrey Hodgson dissects the anatomy of a mandarinate that presided over the postwar reorganization of Europe and directed the Cold War. Men of impeccable social credentials, socialized at the toniest prep schools and educated at Ivy League colleges, managers of distinguished Wall Street banks and law firms, apparently impregnable to democratic dissent, they nonetheless crashed and burned in a disaster of their own making in Vietnam.

Dominant ruling groups have felt the heat not only from below but also from the energies radiated by the dynamic U.S. economy as it repeatedly generates opportunities for individuals to launch capitalist enterprises and assemble new fortunes. Indeed, the challenge to the rule of particular elites has come as much from other elites as from democratic pressures. Thus, in the 1830s, the merchant grandees of the North found themselves confronted by rising artisan-manufacturers, men who proudly called themselves "mechanics" and constituted, in embryonic form, an industrial bourgeoisie. By the 1850s and 1860s, this bourgeoisie sought to displace not only the northern merchant elite but the slaveocracy as well, a group whom industrialists regarded as dessicated and, even worse, as a drag on the expansion of capitalist markets, trade, and accumulation. A century later, as Michael Lind demonstrates in "Conservative Elites and the Counterrevolution against the New Deal," the descendants of this industrial bourgeoisie, whose power was concentrated in industry and finance in the Northeast and Midwest, found themselves under political siege by a new elite rooted in the raw material/energy/military-industrial complex of the Southwest.

Looking back, then, we find that the political power of ruling groups has proved perishable. The different elites share that in common. The vulnerability of individual elites, however, should not blind us to the resilience and adaptability of elite power in general. New elites have always seemed ready to take the place of those in decline and to adapt themselves to changing economic and political realities.

The first moment of crisis and succession occurred in the decade following ratification of the Constitution. America's Revolution of 1776 did not settle the issue of whether the new nation would be a democracy. As late as the 1790s, a powerful group of Anglophiles, calling themselves Federalists and led by Alexander Hamilton, wanted to establish a British-style aristocratic republic in the United States. And they might have succeeded had they not overreached themselves and, panicked by the French Revolution, imposed repressive measures that, ironically, caused a democratic opposition to coalesce. That strategic error opened the way for Thomas Jefferson's election in 1800 and

made what Kornblith and Murrin call a "decentralized and . . . democratic structure of power" an enduring feature of American politics.
By 1820, the Federalists had all but disappeared as a political force.
Subsequent elites had to accommodate themselves to a democratic politics that had become a defining feature of the American republic.

This did not mean that these new hierarchs had fully embraced democratic behavior, however. On the contrary, the successors to the Federalists, the Jeffersonian planters in the South and the mercantile elites
in the North, still evinced a rather Federalist degree of caste exclusivity
and superiority. They expressed a sense of entitlement and with it a
readiness to accept social obligations. As Rothman and Beckert both
demonstrate, the antebellum southern and northern men of power
styled themselves respecters of the traditions they were born to, and
they sought to preserve them rather than invent new ones. Moreover,
they believed that their economic independence and cultural breeding
made them society's natural overseers. Indeed, the proportions of
these groups who held public office at all levels, from local officials and
state legislators to presidents, senators, and Supreme Court justices, exceeded those of all subsequent ruling groups. In short, they thought of
themselves as public men who were uniquely fit to rule. They expected
to be deferred to by others and, in return, to shoulder the burden of
maintaining a rightly ordered society. But the Civil War precipitated
their downfall and a second moment of elite crisis and succession.

The sheer scale of upper-class upheaval triggered by the destruction
of the planter class and the eclipse of New England's mercantile elite
was bound to generate alternate forms of elite ascendancy. But the economic transition from a society of slave-based plantation agriculture
and smallholder family capitalism to a society of impersonal corporate
industry and finance magnified the impact of the war. The buccaneer
industrialists and financiers who emerged during and after the Civil
War did not think of themselves as public men, and they were deeply
unsure of just what constituted their social responsibilities. This change
in the character of elites had something to do with the shift from an

agrarian society to one based on the less fixed interactions and perpetual arrhythmias of industrial and finance capitalism. Under the rule that "all that is solid melts into air," even the most imposing bastions of wealth and power may be disoriented and live anxiously with a looming sense of their own mortality

As Nasaw demonstrates, the new Gilded Age elite was both ignorant and contemptuous of the public realm. As adept as its members were at purchasing political favors or simply looting the public treasury, they had no desire to take on the responsibilities of public administration. The ideology of social Darwinism to which they subscribed only aggravated that predicament by raising their instinctual political absenteeism to the level of moral and natural law. Nevertheless, these Gilded Age tycoons were increasingly compelled by the anti-corporate measures passed by state governments during the 1870s and 1880s to embroil themselves in struggles with workers, farmers, and their supporters over the legitimacy of capitalist institutions. Nothing in the experience of these nouveau riche industrialists prepared them for negotiating the increasingly dangerous terrain of mass politics, and in the 1890s they came perilously close to losing their control altogether, as the People's Party, an anti-corporate, anti–Wall Street grassroots organization of poor farmers and their allies, convulsed national politics.

The Populist challenge triggered a third moment of elite crisis and succession, as new leaders emerged from the upper-class ranks to regain economic and political control. Those who directed this consolidation, in particular the circle gathered around J. P. Morgan, were indubitably readier to rule than the commanders of the Gilded Age had been. Lears paints a portrait of a revitalized ruling class, a hybrid mixture of the patrician and the parvenu, whose social élan, managerial self-confidence, spiritual athleticism, and careful grooming of the young for a life of social privilege and public responsibility gave this new elite a resiliency and an interest in the commonweal that the robber barons had never possessed. So, too, Dawley demonstrates how this elite gained an embracing sovereignty over the nation's political economy. Its members were unlike those earlier, more provincial captains of industry who lorded it over their particular fiefdoms and cared about nothing beyond their borders. From their redoubts on Wall Street, the new men of power at the turn of the twentieth century took a more global view of their hegemonic responsibility for ensuring the stability and orderliness of the new corporate economy, and even extended their superintendence beyond the boundaries of the United States.

But they could never entirely eliminate the disorderliness of the capitalist order or of the democratic political process they wanted to control. And as Lears observes, self-doubt and self-absorption occasionally peeked through the self-assurance this elite sought to project. Still, upper-class Americans of F. Scott Fitzgerald's Jazz Age were far more poised than their predecessors had been in the 1890s.

But then the Great Depression undermined the confidence and power of the ancien régime. The stock market collapse shrank or destroyed economic fortunes. The misery caused by mass unemployment and the inability of capitalism to right itself stripped economic elites of their legitimacy. Popular protest helped chase the Morgan-centered group of financiers and industrialists from key cabinet positions, the Federal Reserve, and other government posts and brought to the presidency a man of patrician breeding, Franklin D. Roosevelt, who refused to rule in the sole interest of the class from which he came. Moreover, Roosevelt's New Dealers subjected strategic economic institutions—banks, utilities, and capital markets—to the kind of public regulation and surveillance that they had never experienced before. Roosevelt attracted to his New Deal hard-pressed workers and farmers and struggling homeowners, of course, but also new elites drawn from mass-consumption sectors of the economy—mass merchandisers, urban real estate moguls, men from the newer investment houses, clothing and appliance manufacturers, and bankers catering to small depositors—that stood to gain from Roosevelt's regulatory and redistributionist policies. This alliance of popular social movements and reform-minded elites together erected a New Deal order in which the state managed capitalism to ensure corporate profitability, high wages, and social welfare for those unable to live off their own labor.[21]

Other, older elites also accommodated themselves to the New Deal and found ways to exercise political influence in this liberal age. The most celebrated was the Establishment, a fragment of the Progressive Era plutocracy that kept its wealth and its wits during the Great Depression. These circles did not fall into the rabid hostility to the New Deal that characterized the plutocracy in general. Instead, its members found a way to demarcate themselves from the Roosevelt haters, to nurture links to the New Dealers, and, when war came in the 1940s, to exercise extraordinary influence in foreign affairs.

Where the "robber barons" had no tradition to speak of, and the Morgan milieu still gave precedence to private over public concerns, the Establishment came closer than anything else since the first fifty years of the republic to defining itself in terms of public service. As Lears and Hodgson make clear, its members were patricians in the manner of the antebellum merchant grandees and Virginia planters, convinced that their wealth, education, and disinterestedness had endowed them with a special capacity for rule. They disliked the messy world of mass politics but found ways to tolerate or circumvent it. Ultimately, however, the arrogance of the Establishment, and its disdain for popular politics in an age infused with democratic desire, not just in the United States but throughout the disintegrating European colonial world, did it in.

While this remnant of the Morgan-era ruling group prospered during the New Deal, so too did a regional southern elite. Its rise not only exemplifies the cycle of elite succession and adaptation, but also brings us face to face with the latest incarnation of that penchant for counterrevolution that forms so distinctive a part of the story of elites throughout American history. As Lind demonstrates, Roosevelt needed southern support to bring his New Deal order into being; in return, liberal New Dealers agreed to allow prevailing class and racial hierarchies in the South to stand. Moreover, the New Deal undertook a vast program of state capitalism to provide water, electricity, and a transportation infrastructure to the South, Southwest, and West. This program tied Roosevelt and his Cold War Democratic successors even more closely to southern landlords and raw materials producers. Meanwhile, the Cold War incubated a new elite of weapons manufacturers that President Eisenhower so famously described as the military-industrial complex. Few members of either of these two groups ever demonstrated the commitment to social welfare and government regulation of business (not to mention racial equality) of their northeastern and midwestern partners in the New Deal alliance. Those political contradictions exploded in the 1960s and 1970s.

Defeat in Vietnam, the U.S. loss of global economic supremacy in the 1970s, the election of Ronald Reagan in 1980, and the difficult transition to a postindustrial computer and information economy together constitute the nation's most recent moment of elite crisis and succession. Lind surveys the changing landscape of wealth and power during this time and shows how the petroleum, agribusiness, raw materials, and military elites in the South and Southwest that had been nurtured by the New Deal shook free of this liberal political formation and coalesced around a party (the Republicans) and an ideology (conservatism) dedicated to freeing capitalism from state regulation. Lind alerts us to the possibility of ideological and cultural reversion among rising centers of power for whom the naked pursuit of self-interest is synonymous with the general welfare. Compound that self-regard with fundamentalist religious zealotry, and the story of this ruling elite's formation takes a strange, unexpected turn indeed. Lind explains how a counterrevolutionary impulse, already detectable in the 1940s, eventually succeeded in undermining the ethos of social responsibility that once animated the New Deal coalition. This impulse also damaged the labor movement, widened the gap between rich and poor, and weakened the welfare state.

Elite rule in a nominally democratic political system seems to generate counterrevolution in recurring waves. By counterrevolution we mean elite campaigns to roll back or contain democratic advances. American counterrevolution is not to be understood in the classical European sense, in which dominant social groups are assumed to exist already, to govern for more or less long stretches of time, to be challenged from below, and then to fight back. Here, by contrast, as often as not, ruling groups seem to cohere in the first place in order to stave off democratic advances. We see this logic at work as Kornblith and Murrin explain the coming together of the new country's regional ruling groups in their joint creation of the American republic. The Constitution, in particular, was meant to arrest the devolution of power downward and outward into the middling ranks of the postcolonial world. Gilded Age industrial titans were likewise driven into the political arena only by social upheavals on the land and popular eruptions in the great cities. It was, moreover, the challenge of populism in 1896, more than the giant corporate amalgamations at the turn of the century, which implanted a nationwide class consciousness among the people Dawley and Lears write about. The ideological conviction and cultural self-consciousness of today's conservative elites derive, Lind tells us, from their determination to reverse what they regard as the revolutionary momentum of the New Deal.

Counterrevolution is far from the whole story. Jefferson's accommodation with popular rule was real, not simulated, as Murrin and Kornblith note. The conservative temperament of the Morgan elite does not cancel out the reorganization and modernizing of the economy that took place on its watch, as Dawley makes clear. "Old money" patricians such as the two Roosevelts attempted to police and humanize the marketplace and, in the process, earned the undying hatred of their peers as "traitors to their class." While the Establishment, in Godfrey Hodgson's view, worked to constrain or defeat revolutionary movements for national independence all over the world, it also erected a framework of multilateral relations whose recent dismantling is lamented by millions in America and abroad. U.S. elites, then, have shown a capacity for reform as well as for an enduring reaction against reform.

Beginning with Jefferson's election in 1800, those who seek to govern, whatever their elite provenance, however devoted to the distinct interests of their own milieu, have felt it increasingly necessary to defend what they are doing as a form of general liberation. Further complicating our ability to understand American patterns of democratic containment is the tendency of those ruling groups to rely on a language of democracy and freedom. This fills the political air with the sounds of cultural dissonance. At no time, perhaps, has this been clearer than at present, when every overture to dismantle the apparatus of public surveillance over the business system is presented as a form of emancipation from the tyrannical hand of bureaucracy. In America, even ruling elites have learned to live, if reluctantly, by the democratic imperative. No matter how extravagantly populist their language may become, however, the footprint of wealth and power is clearly visible across the whole span of American history.

1

The Dilemmas of Ruling Elites in Revolutionary America

❧

GARY J. KORNBLITH AND JOHN M. MURRIN

The American Revolution became a battleground between two powerful, rising forces: the growing exclusivity and sense of entitlement of colonial elites, and the emerging egalitarianism, especially of the "middling sort" who were just beginning to master the new language of natural rights. Both the aspirations of the elites and the hopes of those who resisted them derived in large part from Great Britain. Much of what these settlers from very different colonies had in common stemmed from their willingness to anglicize their culture and society throughout the eighteenth century.[1]

In 1760 there was no "America," no "South," and no "North." The rice planters of South Carolina and Georgia seldom interacted with the tobacco planters of Virginia and Maryland. In North Carolina, the one colony in which those cultures coexisted, the result was bitter conflict between them, not a recognition of a common identity among slaveholding planters. Because slavery existed in all the colonies, contemporaries did not yet see a sharp contrast between slave and free societies.

The Revolution would create not just a new nation but distinctive regions within that nation. The elite families who survived that struggle would also have to discover whether they could become a ruling class. Did they share enough in common to cohere as a national governing elite despite the sectional differences that were becoming ever more obvious? In the 1790s a mostly northern elite seemed close to achieving this goal, only to lose its power in 1800, but not its economic resources, to a coalition of southern planters and northern middling people. That coalition largely defined what America would be until the Civil War. In the North, which began to generate much greater extremes of wealth than had existed in the colonial period, economic and political power were increasingly exercised by different elites. In the South, great planters retained power in both spheres, especially on the stage of national politics.

But in 1760, following the British Empire's conquest of New France, the colonists looked forward to a future of peace and prosperity, and many settlers rejoiced in the accession of a new, youthful king, George III, whose pronouncements in favor of virtue and piety elicited a warm response. Virtually none of them anticipated that, within fifteen years, they would be engaged in a desperate struggle against the same British army and navy that had led them to victory against France.[2]

Anglicization

Since England's Glorious Revolution of 1688–89, the British state had achieved a level of military might unparalleled in the previous history of its island peoples. The Royal Navy was the strongest in the world, and while the army was much smaller than those of France, the Hapsburg Empire, Russia, or even Prussia, it more than held its own in the overseas struggle that began in North America in 1754 and engulfed even distant India before it was over. The British fiscal system, anchored in the Bank of England, made these triumphs possible. At a more basic level, what held everything together was the British ruling class, firmly rooted in the monarchy, with its ability to elicit deference, distribute patronage and honors, and command the armed forces; in the titled aristocracy, organized politically in the House of Lords; and in the gentry, wealthy landowners who lived on their rents and dominated the House of Commons while sharing some seats with affluent merchants, lawyers, army and navy officers, and even a few colonials, mostly absentee West Indian planters. By 1760 the British ruling class was one of the most dominating forces in the entire world.[3]

Over the same seven decades the North American colonies had grown from perhaps 210,000 people to nearly 1.6 million. In 1690 colonial officeholders lacked the resources and prestige to set themselves apart as a ruling class, even on a local level. Almost none of them lived in anything more than a modest house, and many of them still worked with their hands. The colonies possessed almost nothing that a later generation would recognize as refinement, although for that matter England too lagged far behind its continental rivals in nearly all forms of artistic expression except literature. But by the 1760s, Georgian architecture and English painting and music had soared ahead, while in North America every colony could boast that it possessed some elegant houses, that polite letters were definitely taking hold, and that a few American painters had become so talented that they could thrive in London, as did Benjamin West and, a few years later, John Singleton Copley. Because the size of the legislatures in most colonies grew much more slowly than the population at large, many of the people who occupied those seats were much more affluent and refined than their predecessors had been in 1690, but they were still far short of levels of wealth concentration in Britain. There the top 1 percent controlled almost 45 percent of the wealth, and the top 10 percent controlled 82 percent. In the colonies, the comparable figures were 13 percent controlled by the richest 1 percent, and 51 percent by the wealthiest 10 percent. Despite this contrast, in the middle decades of the eighteenth century, family, social prominence, wealth, education, officeholding, and pretensions to gentility were beginning to converge more closely upon a fairly small number of families in each colony than at any other time in the history of the American people, and by 1760, free colonists were more overtly loyal to Britain than they had ever been before.[4]

As of 1760 the colonies were still quite diverse. Their modes of production set them apart from one another. The rice and indigo planters of the lower South dominated a population most of whom were enslaved Africans. In Virginia and Maryland, where tobacco had all but defined both colonies well into the eighteenth century, slaves were a majority in some tidewater counties but not in either colony as a whole, and the rise of wheat as a second crop and the growth of shipbuilding were bringing greater economic diversity to the region. Pennsylvania, New York, and New Jersey thrived on the export of wheat and flour. New England, by some measures the poorest region of British North America, built more ships than the rest of the colonies combined, sustained a very active fishery, and turned the region's dependence on West Indian trade into an opportunity to create a sizable rum distilling industry, but could not raise enough cereal crops to feed the region's population.[5]

If modes of production highlighted how the colonies differed from one another, patterns of consumption revealed ways in which they were becoming more alike. Between the Glorious Revolution and the 1730s, population grew more rapidly than the ability of individual settlers to consume British goods. After 1730 or 1740, while population continued to expand at an explosive rate, the per capita consumption of British goods also began to rise. As their wealth increased, elites throughout the colonies actively emulated the standards of Great Britain's polite society. Newspapers kept them informed of events in Europe, and newspaper ads reminded them what enticing goods were available to those who could afford them. Much of this sort of conspicuous display also began to affect the middling classes. A passion for Georgian architecture meant that refined colonials by 1760 were living in houses that were far more alike than anything available to their ancestors, who had developed quite distinct vernacular styles. The eighteenth century also witnessed a dramatic rise in the number of professional men—educated lawyers, physicians, and ministers of the gospel. For the most part, until mid-century, southern colonies imported their professionals from Britain or sent their young men across the Atlantic to acquire a professional education. New England, with two colleges after 1701 and four by the 1770s, overwhelmingly trained its own. The Middle Colonies, where three colleges were founded in the decade after 1746 and a fourth shortly before independence, were shifting from the southern pattern toward New England's.[6]

In short, even though the population of the colonies was becoming ethnically and racially much more diverse throughout the eighteenth century, these provinces anglicized in striking ways. Their elected assemblies emulated the British House of Commons. Even the language of politics was mostly borrowed from Great Britain. Two strains of thought critical to the Revolutionary generation came rather late to North America. Country ideology, or what a later generation would call "republicanism," was borrowed mostly from British opposition spokesmen who thrived between 1700 and 1740, who warned, often in shrill language, that liberty cannot survive for long in a society that allows its government to become hopelessly corrupt. The language of natural rights arrived even later, in the middle decades of the eighteenth century. Seventeenth-century colonists had spoken of their "liberties," and only occasionally of their rights. After 1760 the colonists would become almost obsessed with defining and protecting their rights. John Locke's *Second Treatise of Government* had attracted little attention in the colonies when it was published after the Glorious Revolution, but its day was coming. In many important ways, the colonies had to become more self-consciously British before they would be able to recognize one another as "American."[7]

The sharp increase in consumer goods, the improvement of communications and education, and the determination of the "better sort" to set themselves off from the "meaner sort" did create an incipient class

system in the colonies. No province had a hereditary peerage comparable to England's, Scotland's, or Ireland's, but in Virginia the office of
councillor often did pass from father to son in the eighteenth century,
provided the Crown approved. In many New England towns the most
important offices were controlled most of the time by a small number of families, and by the third quarter of the century those who sat in
colonial assemblies were usually wealthy or at least well-to-do and
thought of themselves as gentlemen. The class system remained fluid
enough to admit some newcomers to the emerging elite classes, such as
John Adams in Massachusetts and Benjamin Franklin in Pennsylvania.[8]

Societies acquire a class structure when they develop a significantly
asymmetrical distribution of wealth and power, and especially when
the wealthiest people also control the most important political offices.
In all of the colonies some men had been wealthier or more powerful
than others, but quite often other asymmetries had been equally important or even more significant. In seventeenth-century Massachusetts,
whether a man was a member of the Congregational Church mattered
more than his wealth. By the 1650s a growing number of affluent
Boston merchants were ineligible for colony-wide office because they
had never had a conversion experience that would qualify them as full
church members. After the Glorious Revolution, wealthy merchants
exercised far more political power. In New York, ethnic and religious
loyalties often counted for more than wealth alone. Pennsylvania by
the middle of the eighteenth century had two elites. One was Quaker,
and its members dominated the colony's assembly. The other was
mostly Anglican, with some Presbyterians, and its members increasingly dominated executive and judicial offices. The two elites seldom
socialized and did not intermarry.[9]

Slaveholders presided over the most asymmetrical power relationships in North America. Virginia's great planters came as close as British America could get to a true ruling class, but because Virginia remained a colony, many important decisions were still made in London
or by governors sent from London. Relations between great planters

and lesser settlers grew more cordial from about 1720 to 1740, partly because great planters took their magisterial responsibilities quite seriously but seldom made any severe demands on small planters. Virginia had become, in effect, a participatory oligarchy in which, every seven years, the gentlemen candidates proclaimed themselves the servants of the people, and the people then elected (or reelected) them to the House of Burgesses. Small planters had almost no chance of winning high office, but many who voted were rewarded with lesser positions.[10]

South Carolina's Low Country planters were wealthier than their Virginia counterparts but exercised little control over the growing backcountry settlements where most white people lived by the 1760s. The planters' relationship with their field slaves was more distant than similar relations between planters and slaves in Virginia, which were actively and often oppressively paternalistic. Planters and overseers closely supervised the gangs that toiled to raise tobacco, but white men who spent much time in the rice marshes were likely to catch malaria. By the Revolution, rice was grown through the task system, in which each laborer had a daily quota to fulfill, after which his time was his (or her) own.[11]

Around mid-century, signs of class tensions began to multiply in the mainland colonies. Extensive land riots broke out in both northern New Jersey and New York's Hudson Valley. In Boston, New York City, and Philadelphia, poverty increased markedly during and after the mid-century wars with France, and the tone of political debate became much sharper and more contentious in British America's three largest cities.[12]

Revolution

North America's elite families believed that they served the people but derived much of their legitimacy from the Crown. In royal colonies, public offices conferred titles on the gentlemen who held them. "His Excellency," "Honorable," and "Esquire" all derived from the Crown, the ultimate source of public honors throughout the empire. Open resistance to British policy could cost a colonial leader any further chance of royal favor. Complete acceptance of royal demands, however, could arouse the wrath of the populace. Between 1763 and 1776, nearly every public official was compelled to choose between these unpleasant alternatives. Those who became loyalists were nearly always forced to resign their offices and were often driven into exile. Those who became patriots had to appeal to the people for the kind of legitimacy the Crown had once provided and hope that their own wealth and social position would allow them to continue to enjoy public respect.[13]

The Stamp Act Crisis of 1764–1766 demonstrated that gentlemen, the "middling sort," and even the "lower sort" could cooperate effectively to achieve a political goal they all shared, but it also revealed how perilous these attempts could become. Colonial gentlemen wrote closely reasoned pamphlets and resolutions of protest against the Stamp Act. By 1765 they agreed that Parliament had no constitutional power to tax the colonists without their consent. Nearly all of them also agreed that, once Parliament had spoken, the colonists must obey. They could petition for a redress of grievances but not resist openly. Boston's "middling sort" (especially the "Loyal Nine," who would soon take the name "Sons of Liberty") and the "meaner sort," in particular a mob led by Ebenezer McIntosh, a shoemaker from the South End, showed them otherwise. On August 14, 1765, McIntosh and his followers leveled a new building (rumored to be the stamp office) belonging to Andrew Oliver, who had been appointed stamp distributor for the province, then marched on Oliver's home, where they did enough damage to convince him that they were serious. He resigned his position, and this example soon spread to the other colonies. By the time the Stamp Act was supposed to take effect on November 1, no one was available to distribute the stamps in any of the thirteen colonies except Georgia, and that colony soon joined the other twelve after its distributor also fled. Mob violence, or the threat of violence, nullified the Stamp Act and forced the British government to choose between repeal and civil war in North America. Using mostly economic justifications, Parliament repealed the act.[14]

Violence could achieve spectacular results, but it could also get out of control. On August 26 McIntosh's mob virtually demolished the Boston mansion of Lieutenant Governor and Chief Justice Thomas Hutchinson, at a loss to him of several thousand pounds. Most Bostonians believed, mistakenly, that Hutchinson was one of the authors of the Stamp Act, when in fact he had argued against its passage in letters to British officials. The flagrant destruction of Hutchinson's property shocked respectable opinion, and the militia finally took to the streets to restore order. Nevertheless, the town also made it clear that it would tolerate no judicial retribution for the August 14 riot, which meant, in effect, that McIntosh would never be prosecuted.[15]

The Boston riot that destroyed Hutchinson's house triggered an equally violent outburst in Newport, Rhode Island, where a mob destroyed the homes of two defenders of the Stamp Act, who soon fled the colony; but after forcing the stamp distributor to resign, the mob threatened to turn against the city's elite, who had been organizing resistance to the Stamp Act. For several days class war seemed a real possibility, until the mob leader was arrested.[16]

In New York, after the Stamp Act was repealed, angry tenant farmers adopted the rhetoric of the city's Sons of Liberty, many of whom were artisans, when they launched a massive protest against the great landlords of the Hudson Valley, even threatening to kill the lord of Livingston Manor and to march on New York City to attack others. Some of the Sons of Liberty were connected politically to the great landlords, and they demanded the use of redcoats to suppress the rioters. One of the Sons, John Morin Scott, even served on the jury that condemned William Prendergast to death as the leading rioter, although George III later pardoned the man. Urban artisans and tenant farmers often had reason to resent their social superiors, but persuading them to work together in a common political cause was no easy matter. Many tenants had learned to expect more sympathy from

George III than from such patriot leaders as the wealthy Livingston clan.[17]

Charleston, South Carolina, also discovered that popular demonstrations could be dangerously contagious. After whites marched through the streets chanting "Liberty!" they were later shocked to witness slaves also parading through the streets shouting "Liberty!" More than a hundred slaves then tried to escape. Resistance to British measures did indeed create strong criticisms of slavery. Between independence and 1804, every northern state would take steps to abolish slavery, either immediately or gradually.[18]

In the late 1760s both Carolinas were rocked by what contemporaries called "regulator" movements. (A century later such men would be called "vigilantes.") In South Carolina, rural turbulence almost led to an armed clash between two groups of several hundred men, each with its own formula for restoring order, before the provincial government intervened by promising to create a circuit court system for the entire colony. North Carolina's discontent revolved around the corruption of magistrates and sheriffs in several interior counties, and violent protests against them finally led to a pitched battle at Alamance Creek in 1771, when a mustering of about two thousand poorly armed regulators was overwhelmed by a smaller but better-armed force from the eastern counties, commanded by the royal governor.

From New York through the Carolinas, rural discontent seethed dangerously as the colonies lurched toward the final imperial crisis with Great Britain. As that crisis unfolded, most colonists decided, many after prolonged hesitation, that the danger from Crown and Parliament outweighed what the colonists had to fear from one another. Yet roughly one-sixth of the settlers chose to remain loyal to George III, and south of New England, more enslaved Africans—when given a political choice—saw British soldiers, not the American revolutionaries, as their potential liberators.[19]

Royal authority broke down in 1774–75 after most governors dissolved their assemblies and refused to summon new ones. The settlers responded by electing what they called "provincial congresses" or "conventions," which were usually much larger bodies that contained sizable contingents of the "middling sort." Potential sectional differences failed to predominate because Virginians joined with New Englanders in leading the transition from resistance to independence, while the five colonies from New York through Maryland displayed the most reluctance to leave the empire. There still was no "South" and no "North," but "America" was in the making.

Class antagonisms were also muted, except when aimed at wealthy loyalists. The First Continental Congress, which met in Philadelphia in the fall of 1774, created the "Association"—elective committees at the local level that were charged with enforcing trade sanctions against Britain and purging or disciplining those who refused to support the emerging Revolutionary cause. During these months the American countryside mobilized politically with an intensity never seen before. As in the seventeenth century, the "middling sort" once more began to hold significant public offices, this time with a new sense of entitlement provided by the language of natural rights, but they were also willing to accept the leadership of men from prominent families who successfully articulated their grievances and their goals. Patriot elites approached independence confident of their ability to lead and inspire a society of freemen committed to asserting their natural rights. Gentlemen patriots were delighted and pleased with the way public order held together in their colonies between the collapse of royal power and the assertion of independence. But once the British war effort became grimly serious after August 1776, some of this confidence evaporated. As the colonies became states with formally organized governments, and as the imperatives of war impinged upon them, tensions again emerged between gentlemen and lesser citizens. In both New York and Maryland, for example, the wealthy discovered that they could not lead politically unless they accepted new taxes that soaked the rich.[20]

A famous incident during the Revolutionary War revealed the different assumptions about class that separated the emerging elite, in this case mostly officers of the Continental Army, from less privileged Americans, such as Continental enlisted men and ordinary civilians. In 1781 General Benedict Arnold almost managed to betray the American fortifications at West Point to the British, but instead a few American militiamen captured Major John André, the British officer who had been negotiating with Arnold and was trying to return to British lines. Arnold learned of André's capture just in time to escape to a British warship on the Hudson River, thus leaving André to face alone a military tribunal that condemned him to death as a spy who had clearly been behind American lines while out of uniform. On the American side, everyone joined in the ferocious condemnation of Arnold as a traitor who deserved to hang, but assessments of André's plight followed class lines. American officers greatly admired André's family credentials, his gracious manners, his artistic talents (he sketched an impressive self-portrait while awaiting execution), and his calm acceptance of his fate. Some of them wept when André was hanged. Ordinary soldiers, by contrast, believed that André got exactly what he deserved. "I have seen several men hung," noted eighteen-year-old John Shreve, with no sense of compassion for the condemned victim, "but he flounced about more than any one I ever saw." Another soldier, informing his wife that André would be hanged at 5 P.M., added, "This is the way we keep the sabbath, I wish we could employ every day to as good advantage."[21]

Between the collapse of British authority in 1774 and the ratification of the federal Constitution in 1788, the sensibilities of ordinary citizens seemed to be carrying the day in most states most of the time. State politics became an arena of conflict between two loose coalitions of "cosmopolitans" and "localists." Former Continental Army officers, most great planters, most merchants engaged in Atlantic commerce, most lawyers, physicians, ministers, printers, and urban artisans made up the cosmopolitan bloc. They were richer than their opponents, and they yearned for recognition as a respectable ruling elite. They favored sound money, debt collection, and decent salaries for executive officials and judges, but low compensation for legislators, presumably so that only men of means could serve in that capacity for long. Localists included most ordinary farmers, former Continental soldiers, many militia veterans (both officers and men) who had served in the war, and small-town or rural artisans. They often favored paper money, "stay" laws to postpone the collection of debts, and low salaries for governors and judges (positions that few of them yet aspired to hold), but sufficient compensation for legislators to permit middling people to serve. They were highly suspicious of the class aspirations of men in the rival coalition.[22]

During the 1780s the localists won so often at the state level that cosmopolitans began to despair of their own success unless they could somehow create a more powerful central government and place themselves in a position to dominate it. Even when cosmopolitans were able to crush Daniel Shays's armed rebellion in western Massachusetts in 1786–87, Shays's sympathizers elected enough representatives to the Massachusetts legislature a few months later to pass many of the reforms he had advocated.[23]

Cosmopolitan elites also discovered that sectional quarrels could destroy their unity and undermine their class aspirations. During the same months, John Jay tried to negotiate a treaty with Spain that would have granted commercial concessions to northern states in exchange for closure of the Mississippi to Americans for twenty-five years. This proposal split Congress along strictly sectional lines. Northern states voted to approve, but all five southern states opposed the treaty and thus blocked ratification under the Articles of Confederation. The struggle was fierce enough to provoke calls for breaking up the Union into two or more smaller confederacies. While confronting both class and sectional conflict, elite men in several states got Congress to endorse their call for a Constitutional Convention, which finally met in Philadelphia between May and September 1787.[24]

The Constitution: From Counterrevolution to Revolution

At Philadelphia, America's aspiring elites flirted with several reactionary ideas before drafting a form of government that they believed could legitimize their desire to rule by successfully appealing to the shared values of the Revolution.

Two-thirds of the fifty-five delegates who gathered in Philadelphia were rich; three-fifths either came from genteel families or, like New York's Alexander Hamilton, had married into one. Most had served in Congress, and three had been generals in the Continental Army, including George Washington, who presided over the convention's deliberations. The delegates agreed to meet in secret sessions with no outsiders present, which allowed them to be far more candid about the dangers of popular rule than they would have dared to be in an open forum.[25]

On May 31, the third day of actual debate, Connecticut's Roger Sherman, who had helped to draft the Declaration of Independence, opposed the election of any part of a national legislature "by the people, insisting that it ought to be by the [state] Legislatures. The people he said," according to James Madison's notes, "[immediately] should have as little to do as may be about the Government. They want information and are constantly liable to be misled." Elbridge Gerry of Massachusetts, a future Jeffersonian Republican, agreed. "The evils we experience flow from the excess of democracy," he insisted. "He had . . . been too republican before: he was still however republican, but had been taught by experience the danger of the levilling spirit." By contrast, Pennsylvania's James Wilson, considered by many historians to be quite conservative, championed popular elections. "He was for raising the federal pyramid to a considerable altitude, and . . . wished to give it as broad a basis as possible," he explained. "No government could long subsist without the confidence of the people."[26]

Profound doubts about the capacity of ordinary people to participate in government except as voters and jurors help to explain the early proposals for a new central government. All of them flirted with what the French, in the 1790s, would begin to call "counterrevolution." James Madison's Virginia Plan contained almost no effective separation of powers such as had become hallmarks of the New York and Massachusetts constitutions. After a vicious war in which Americans had defeated parliamentary sovereignty, Madison was proposing something close to a sovereign parliament for the United States, a bicameral legislature with broad, loosely defined powers, including a veto over state laws. In both houses the states would be represented according to population. Small states responded with William Paterson's New Jersey Plan. It proposed to amend the existing Articles of Confederation by giving the unicameral congress, in which each state had a single vote, the power to levy import duties and a stamp tax, the reforms that Parliament had tried to impose on the colonies with the Sugar and Stamp Acts of 1764 and 1765. If any state resisted an act or a treaty adopted by Congress, Paterson proposed that "the federal Executive . . . be authorized to call forth ye power of the Confederated States . . . to enforce and compel an obedience to such Acts, or an observance of such Treaties," a provision uncomfortably close to Lord North's Conciliatory Proposition, adopted by Parliament in 1775 and rejected out of hand by the Second Continental Congress.[27]

Even more explicit was Alexander Hamilton, who laid out a detailed plan of his own but never offered it as a formal motion, probably because no other New York delegate would have supported him. He was almost ready "to despair that a Republican Govt. could be established over so great an extent" of territory as the United States. He added that "the British Govt. was the best in the world: and that he doubted much whether anything short of it would do in America." He proposed a bicameral legislature in which senators would be chosen by electoral colleges and serve for life; the executive, similarly chosen, would also serve for life but would be subject to impeachment and would appoint all state governors, who in turn would have an absolute veto over all legislation. In short, his model for America was royal government pretty much as it had existed in North America before the Revolution.[28]

Beginning in July, several major compromises reshaped the existing plans of union, resolved the rift between large and small states, and persuaded most delegates that elites from different states and regions could settle their differences and work together. Under the Connecticut Compromise, the House of Representatives would be apportioned according to population, but all states would be equally represented in the Senate. Free and slave states resolved their principal difference by agreeing that, for purposes of apportioning both representatives and direct taxes, a slave would count as three-fifths of a person. At about the same time, the Confederation Congress, sitting in New York, passed the Northwest Ordinance of 1787, which prohibited slavery north of the Ohio River. Every southern congressman present for the vote supported the ban, which may indicate that North and South had reached a compromise negotiated by both the delegates in Philadelphia and the congressmen in New York, who were in touch with each other.[29]

Many delegates to the Philadelphia Convention recognized that, in Madison's words, "the States were divided into different interests not by their difference of size, but by other circumstances; the most material of which resulted . . . principally from . . . their having or not having slaves." The biggest difference "did not lie between the large & small States: it lay between the Northern & Southern." These differences of interest, moreover, had taken on moral implications in the wake of the Revolution's celebration of liberty and the equality of natural rights. Although slavery remained legal across most of the United States when the delegates gathered in Philadelphia, over the previous decade the legislatures of three northern states (Pennsylvania, Rhode Island, and Connecticut) had initiated gradual emancipation schemes, courts in Massachusetts had found slavery incompatible with the state's new constitution, and a similar process was apparently taking hold in

New Hampshire. Basing his enumeration on social rather than legal conditions, Madison counted five southern and eight northern states in 1787. When Gouverneur Morris, Rufus King, and other northern delegates boldly questioned whether republican principles could be reconciled with the perpetuation of slavery, delegates from South Carolina made clear that the protection of chattel bondage in the lower South was a nonnegotiable prerequisite for continental union. Prominent Virginians may have felt uneasy about the ethical basis of the institution, but South Carolina delegates acknowledged no qualms. "If slavery be wrong," Charles Pinckney declared, "it is justified by the example of the world . . . In all ages one half of mankind have been slaves."[30]

The size of congressional districts provided another potentially contentious issue. At a time when the Massachusetts House of Representatives had over two hundred members and Virginia's House of Delegates had more than one hundred, the convention agreed that the First Federal Congress, representing the entire nation, would have only sixty-five men in the House and that, after a federal census had been taken, the House would be apportioned with one congressman for every thirty thousand people. The delegates believed that this requirement would almost guarantee a federal legislature composed of gentlemen. In 1787, when Boston and Baltimore combined had scarcely thirty thousand people, the names of very few "middling men" would even be recognizable by people living in an area that large. Gentlemen would be able to vie with other gentlemen for the honor of serving their districts.[31]

In the ratification struggle, both sides understood what that clause meant. Madison was trying to shift power from the middle toward the top of the social pyramid, but as Melancton Smith, an articulate New York Antifederalist, insisted, "Those in middling circumstances," not the elite, "have less temptation; they are inclined by habit, and the company with whom they associate, to set bounds to their passions and appetites." So "when the interest of this part of the community is pursued, the public good is pursued," he explained, "because the body of every nation consists of this class, and because the interests of both the rich and the poor are involved in that of the middling class."[32]

In their last two months of deliberation, the delegates paid far more attention to what the voters would accept than to their own formulas for a perfect plan of government. Madison's nearly sovereign parliament for America gave way to a government with a clear separation of powers, a legislature with carefully specified powers, and a much gentler "Supreme Law of the Land" clause to replace his proposed veto over state laws. The Constitution, most delegates now insisted, grew out of the central values of the Revolution.

The delegates also incorporated a truly revolutionary proposal into the new Constitution, the ratification clause. The Articles of Confederation could be amended only with the unanimous approval of all thirteen state legislatures. In the two most serious attempts to amend the Articles—the proposed imposts of 1781 and 1783—Rhode Island had defeated the first one, and the New York Senate by a margin of eleven votes to seven had scuttled the second. Eleven states had bicameral legislatures; only Pennsylvania and Georgia were unicameral. This meant that, as mandated by the Articles, the Constitution, which was far more controversial than the impost proposals, would have to be approved by twenty-four distinct legislative houses. Under the existing rules, it had no chance of ratification.[33]

Accordingly, the first draft of the Virginia Plan called for ratification by popular conventions specifically chosen for that purpose alone. Within a week James Wilson went much further. According to Madison, he hoped the ratification clause would "admit of . . . a partial union, with a door open for the accession [of the other states]." Charles Pinckney then suggested that ratification by nine states be sufficient to launch the new government.[34]

Incorporated into Article VII of the Constitution, this ratification procedure was indeed revolutionary. It amounted to an illegal overthrow of the existing legal order. In the Northeast between September

1787, when the convention finished its work, and the summer of 1788, popular majorities against ratification existed in, among others, New Hampshire, Massachusetts, Rhode Island (where hardly anybody favored it), and New York. The Wilson-Pinckney strategy might have produced a very different American union, one that left out New York and nearly all of New England. Or, to put the question more provocatively, supporters of ratification were willing to risk destroying the Union in order to save and strengthen it. They did not think that the bankrupt Confederation could survive much longer. They believed that the collapse of the Union would be a catastrophe, one that would "Balkanize" American politics, to use a phrase not then current. Their revolutionary step seemed worth the gamble. As risky as the strategy undoubtedly was, nothing else held an equal promise of success.[35]

As the delegates left Philadelphia, they began to call themselves Federalists, a word that until then had referred to advocates of decentralized government and that they hoped would disguise the degree of centralization they were proposing. Their ratification strategy worked because they possessed a tremendous asset: they could appeal to the highest values of the Revolution and proclaim them as their own. They invoked the sovereignty, not of government at any level, but of the people themselves, who had already bestowed specific powers on each of their state governments and now would be similarly endowing the new federal government. Ratification by special conventions, which had a strong precedent in the popular acceptance of the Massachusetts Constitution of 1780, made this principle concrete and effective, and it gave the federal Constitution a legitimacy that the Articles of Confederation had never achieved. But if ratification was a truly revolutionary process, it was also nonviolent. The Federalists knew that they had to *persuade* the broad American public to give their new system a fair chance. These efforts succeeded. Indeed, Wilson's strategy of establishing the new government before all the states had ratified worked as he had hoped. The federal government was organized after eleven states ratified, and then North Carolina and Rhode Island also signed on. By 1790 the federal Constitution had finally achieved the unanimous ratification by the states that the Articles of Confederation required.[36]

In the ratification struggle, most urban artisans and printers supported the Constitution, while most ordinary farmers remained suspicious or hostile. The separate elites of America were uniting behind the Constitution in a manner that they hoped would pull them together while keeping the middling and lower orders divided among themselves. But the men about to take charge of the new government never did cohere into a true ruling class, even though, after adoption of the Bill of Rights, they could claim a degree of popular support they had not enjoyed since 1774–1776.

Federalist Vision and Elite Division

To the surprise and disappointment of the framers, soon after the Constitution took effect, the compromising spirit of the Philadelphia convention gave way to a fierce partisan struggle within the new central government. Each side—Federalist and Republican—viewed the other not only as wrong on matters of policy but as unpatriotic and subversive of the entire republican enterprise as well. At issue, above all, was Hamilton's system of national finance based on British precedent. For Hamilton, the promise of the American Revolution was the creation of a strong and wealthy United States able to compete successfully on the world stage against other great powers. By means of his fiscal and economic program, he sought to speed the anglicization of American society and thereby to accelerate the nation's rise to global prominence. Against Hamilton's vision, Madison, Jefferson, and other self-styled Republican critics offered a counter-paradigm of agricultural expansion in the context of free trade, westward migration, and decentralized federalism. They believed that the British model of political economy was fundamentally incompatible with a republican society. During the 1790s, partisan and sectional interests became increasingly intertwined until the contest over who should rule at home threatened to break the nation apart at the outset of the nineteenth century.

Although he had been a fervent patriot from the beginning of his political career and a leading American nationalist during the 1780s, Hamilton made no secret of his continuing admiration for Great Britain and its time-tested institutions. For him, the greatest dangers confronting the United States in the aftermath of the Revolution were the destabilizing forces of fragmentation and democracy, both reflected in the growing power and irresponsible policies of popularly elected state governments. He turned to the history of the British nation-state for strategies that would achieve the immediate goal of political stability and advance the long-term aim of American greatness. To the extent possible within the federal system of government established by the Constitution, he envisioned a national ruling class like Great Britain's combination of landed grandees and merchant-financiers that would promote elite hegemony and the public good at the same time.[37]

At the core of Hamilton's fiscal program was his belief that the public debt of the United States—as incurred both collectively by the Congress and separately by the various state governments—could be converted into circulating capital by a national promise to fund the debt at par and to issue interest-bearing government securities that would enjoy the confidence and attract the funds of both foreign and domestic investors. "It is a well known fact," Hamilton observed in his "Report on Public Credit," "that in countries in which the national debt is properly funded, and an object of established confidence, it answers most of the purposes of money." Furthermore, "trade is extended by it; because there is a larger capital to carry it on, and the merchant can at the same time, afford to trade for smaller profits," he explained. "Agriculture and manufactures are also promoted by it: For the like reason, that more capital can be commanded to be employed in both."[38]

Hamilton argued further that, by assuming responsibility for funding state debts as well as the debts of the Confederation Congress, the new national government would unite men of capital behind it and gain political power and economic leverage at the states' expense. "If all the public creditors receive their dues from one source, distributed with an equal hand," he wrote, "their interest will be the same. And having the same interests, they will unite in the support of the fiscal arrangements of the government." A fully funded consolidated debt would energize the economy, strengthen the national government, and promote mutual cooperation between prominent private investors and public officials.[39]

Madison, however, had his doubts, which he raised openly on the floor of the House of Representatives in the spring of 1790. Appalled by the rage of speculation in public securities since ratification of the Constitution, he called for discrimination in the treatment of original purchasers and current holders of such certificates. Original purchasers deserved full payment in reward for their patriotic commitment at a time of national crisis, he argued, but wily investors who had bought government securities at huge discounts—and perhaps with the advantage of inside information—should not benefit unduly from their devious behavior. Of paramount concern to Madison was the moral legitimacy of the new government, not the stability of the fiscal system. There simply was no place for financial speculators in Madison's concept of an enlightened republican elite, in his vision of governance by a natural—as opposed to an artificial—aristocracy.[40]

For similar reasons, Madison fought Hamilton's plan for the federal assumption of state debts. States that had struggled to pay off their debts should not be required to subsidize those that had shirked their patriotic responsibility. To some extent, his position on assumption may have been influenced by local concerns—Virginia stood to gain much less from assumption than either Massachusetts or South Carolina—but the deeper source of Madison's opposition to Hamilton's program on funding the debt was his different view of how the political economy of the American republic should operate.[41]

The full extent of ideological division within elite circles became evident in the wake of Hamilton's other major reports to Congress. In December 1790 Hamilton proposed the establishment of a national bank to house federal deposits that would be governed by a board elected mainly by private shareholders. By making loans and issuing banknotes in amounts greater than their actual holdings of specie, banks could create new working capital out of thin air so long as investors maintained confidence in the bank's long-term financial commitments. This additional capital would spur economic growth for the benefit of all Americans, Hamilton believed, though he knew that those benefits would not be spread evenly throughout society. The generation of national wealth, not its internal distribution, was his primary concern.[42]

In December 1791 Hamilton issued his "Report on Manufactures," which recommended a series of federal measures to encourage the development of the nation's industrial sector. Citing Adam Smith as an authority, Hamilton argued that manufacturing was no less—and probably more—productive than agriculture. He contended further that a diversified economy would expand more rapidly and more steadily than one heavily weighted toward agriculture and agricultural exports. Manufacturing lent itself to technological improvement and could convert otherwise underemployed capital and labor into national wealth. Equally important, growth of the manufacturing sector would help stabilize demand for agricultural commodities. "Foreign demand for the products of Agricultural Countries," Hamilton observed, "is, in a great degree, rather casual and occasional, than certain or constant." The remedy was to create a reliable home market for the nation's agricultural surplus by "detach[ing] a portion of the hands, which would otherwise be engaged in Tillage," and employing them instead in manufacturing. By Hamilton's logic, diversification would enhance productivity across all sectors of the economy.[43]

The more Hamilton elaborated his vision, the more alarmed grew Madison and Jefferson. To them, Hamilton's program heralded a return to the monarchical social order that the patriots had rebelled against. By their analysis, debt was the wellspring of British corruption, and financial speculation was the enemy of republican virtue. Madison and Jefferson had no objection to the pursuit of national greatness, but they conceived of that goal in terms profoundly different from Hamilton's vision. They did not want the United States to become a new Great Britain. They sought instead to create a different kind of social order and a different kind of nation, one based on modern republican principles and uncontaminated—as far as practical—by the corruptive practices of the former mother country. They were not utopians, but they believed that the American Revolution had opened up New World options that were far more promising than Hamilton's Old World aspirations.[44]

For Madison and Jefferson, the proper basis of American political economy was liberty and land, not public debt, paper securities, and banks. As members of the Virginia gentry, they viewed agriculture as a way of life intrinsically—morally—superior to any other. In his *Notes on the State of Virginia,* penned in 1781–82, Jefferson famously proclaimed, "Those who labour in the earth are the chosen people of God . . . whose breasts he has made his peculiar deposit for substantial and genuine virtue." A dozen years later Madison echoed, "The class of citizens who provide at once their own food and their own raiment . . . are the best basis of public liberty, and the strongest bulwark of public safety." The agriculturalists Jefferson and Madison had in mind were clearly not plantation slaves, though by strict logic they could have been. In the Virginians' worldview, the ideal republican citizen was a yeoman farmer possessed of his own freehold of arable land.[45]

Although on occasion Madison and Jefferson celebrated the yeoman farmer as if he relied on nobody but himself and his own labor (understood to include that of family members), they had a keen appreciation for the role of markets and commercial exchange in the operation of American agriculture. That was why Madison stood firm against any renunciation of American rights to the Mississippi River in the 1780s and advocated a national policy of commercial discrimination against

Great Britain in the early 1790s. The goal in both cases was to open up new markets for American agricultural exports. Farmers with no place to sell their surplus production could achieve only a primitive form of independence and autonomy. Madison and Jefferson, like their nemesis Hamilton, appreciated the human desire for material betterment, and they were prepared to adjust commercial policy to promote republican prosperity in a market environment. Their ultimate aim was a world of free trade without mercantilist tariff barriers—a global market where Americans would supply foodstuffs in return for manufactures produced by other, less free and less fortunate peoples.[46]

Although liberal in its celebration of property rights, private enterprise, and free trade, Jefferson and Madison's conception of a proper republican economy was structurally different from capitalism in its modern form. They envisioned a republican social order devoid of "stockjobbers," large-scale investors in public or private securities, and other agents of high finance—in effect, a form of capitalism without capitalists. Their code of republican conduct could accommodate speculation in land, even in slaves, but not speculation in intangible paper instruments. "All the capital employed in paper speculation," Jefferson wrote George Washington in May 1792, "is barren & useless, producing, like that on a gaming table, no accession to itself, and is withdrawn from commerce & agriculture where it could have produced addition to the common mass." According to Jefferson, "the ultimate object of all this is to prepare the way for a change, from the present republican form of government, to that of a monarchy of which the English constitution is to be the model."[47]

Hamilton won most of the early congressional battles over economic policy, gaining full funding of the national debt without discrimination between primary and secondary holders, achieving federal assumption of state debts (in return for the designation of the District of Columbia as the nation's future capital), and establishing a national bank with continental reach. As a result, the United States embarked on a financial revolution similar in historical significance to those of the

Netherlands and Great Britain. The advent of regularized securities markets and a reliable banking system greatly reduced the "information asymmetry" that had plagued the colonial economy for the previous century. Notwithstanding the personal bankruptcies of such major speculators as William Duer and Robert Morris, the nation's fledgling financial institutions achieved monetary stability and global credibility in the 1790s. One need not embrace Hamilton's vision in its entirety to acknowledge that his program was a major factor in America's escape from the kind of economic dependency that has plagued most other postcolonial societies over the past two hundred years.[48]

Whatever their long-term benefits, Hamilton's policies in the short term deeply divided the nation's political leaders. Having come together in support of ratification of the federal Constitution in 1787–88, representatives of the various state elites separated into two distinct parties within the federal Congress by 1792. The sectional cast of this division was obvious for all to see. Most representatives from New England and the mid-Atlantic states stood behind Hamilton's Federalist agenda, while those from the southern states—with the important exception of South Carolina—tended to join the Republican opposition. By 1794 there was once again talk of sundering the United States along geographical lines. In a private conversation that may have been staged for political effect, Rufus King told Virginia's John Taylor of Caroline in May 1794 "that it was utterly impossible for the union to continue. That the southern and eastern people thought quite differently. . . . That when I[zard] and S[mith] of S.C. were out, the southern interest would prevail. That the eastern would never submit to their politicks, and that under these circumstances, a dissolution of the union by mutual consent, was preferable to certainty of the same thing, in a less desirable mode."[49]

As an alternative to disunion, Madison, Jefferson, and their Republican allies developed a three-pronged strategy to prevent the consolidation of a national ruling class along Hamiltonian lines. First was the argument for "strict construction" of the federal Constitution, particularly in regard to the powers of the national government. In response to Hamilton's proposal for a national bank, Madison argued that "the power of establishing an *incorporated bank*" was simply not included "among the powers vested by the constitution in the legislature of the United States." Rejecting the view that such a power was *implied* by clauses authorizing Congress to raise taxes and borrow money, he warned that the "doctrine of implication" lent itself to abuse and to the potential loss of all meaningful restraints on government. He failed in 1791 to convince either his fellow congressmen or President Washington that the national bank was in fact unconstitutional, but his argument for strict construction would become an effective weapon in future struggles against the concerted exercise of power at the national level.[50]

The second and most important prong of Madison's and Jefferson's opposition strategy was the coordinated mobilization of voters to support Republican candidates in state and federal elections. In Federalist no. 10, Madison had warned against the dangers posed by factious majorities, and he had championed a far-flung polity with large electoral districts as "a republican remedy for the diseases most incident to republican government." But now he and Jefferson sought to rouse a *virtuous* majority by means of direct appeals to public opinion in the *National Gazette* and other partisan newspapers. Building on a strong regional base in the upper South, they cultivated political alliances with former Antifederalists, including New York's Melancton Smith, and with a variety of ambitious men excluded from local establishments across the country. Most strikingly, Madison was prepared to stoke feelings of class resentment to promote his cause. In an essay published in September 1792, he denounced Federalists as "more partial to the opulent than to the other classes of society." Members of the "antirepublican party," he wrote, believed "that government can be carried on only by the pageantry of rank, the influence of money and emoluments, and the terror of military force." Against this wicked faction stood the patriotic Republicans, firmly committed to "the doctrine

that mankind are capable of governing themselves, and hating hereditary power as an insult to the reason and an outrage to the rights of
man." Between these two parties there could be little cooperation or
compromise because fundamental values and the very survival of the
United States were at stake.[51]

Although Madison expressed confidence that "the mass of people in
every part of the union, in every state, and of every occupation must at
bottom be with" the Republicans, rallying the populace at large proved
difficult—especially after the French Revolution and the war in Europe
increasingly impinged on American politics. In the rapidly growing
mid-Atlantic cities, Republicans successfully exploited the anger felt by
mechanics and middling merchants toward the grandees who dominated Anglo-American trade and major financial institutions. Elsewhere Republicans appealed to farmers both as the moral pillars of the
nation and as fellow members of the landed interest. But President
Washington's angry denunciation of Democratic-Republican societies
for supposedly fueling a tax revolt by farmers in western Pennsylvania
(the so-called Whiskey Rebellion) did not help the Republican cause,
nor did his endorsement in 1795 of the Jay Treaty with Great Britain,
which Madison, Jefferson, and their allies fiercely opposed. Still, in
1796, Republicans came within three electoral votes of making Jefferson president. In the early months of John Adams's administration, partisan acrimony subsided, but then came a major diplomatic crisis with France (the notorious XYZ Affair) and the outbreak of an
undeclared "quasi-war" between French and American vessels in the
Caribbean. Popular opinion turned sharply against the Francophile Republicans, and in the summer of 1798, congressional Federalists, with
Hamilton's encouragement, pushed through the Alien and Sedition
Acts aimed at silencing the government's critics in the Republican
press.[52]

Out of desperation, Jefferson and Madison in the fall of 1798 formulated the third prong of their opposition strategy: the assertion of
residual sovereignty in the states and of the rights of states to defy fed-

eral laws they deemed unconstitutional. In his draft of the Kentucky Resolutions, Jefferson declared "that whensoever the General Government assumes undelegated powers, its acts are unauthoritative, void, and of no force." He elaborated, "Every State has a natural right in cases not within the compact, (casus non fœderis,) to nullify on their own authority all assumptions of power by others within their limits." Likewise, in the Virginia Resolutions, Madison affirmed "that in case of a deliberate, palpable and dangerous exercise of other powers not granted by the said compact, the states who are parties thereto, have the right, and are in duty bound, to interpose for arresting the progress of the evil, and for maintaining within their respective limits, the authorities, rights and liberties appertaining to them."[53]

For Madison, the assertion of states' rights in 1798 represented a dramatic reversal of his position a decade before. In the 1780s he had repeatedly decried the vicious behavior of state governments, and at the Constitutional Convention he had sought to endow the national government with the power to veto state laws. Now he decried the vicious behavior of the national government and, in effect, sought to endow state governments with the power to veto national legislation. But no other states endorsed the Kentucky and Virginia Resolutions, and in 1798–99 they probably damaged the Republican cause more than they strengthened it. What really undermined the Federalists was the Sedition Act itself. It angered printers so greatly that they established new Republican newspapers faster than Federalist courts could shut down the older ones. Between 1798 and 1800, the number of Republican papers rose by over 50 percent nationwide. The Federalists' attempt to silence their opponents did just the opposite: it energized them and prepared the way for a Republican victory in 1800.[54]

Democratization, Decentralization, Disintegration

Jefferson's accession to the presidency serves as a "Rorschach test" for American historians. For some scholars it signifies the first peaceful transfer of executive power from one party to another in American history and provides proof that, notwithstanding the inflammatory rhetoric of the 1790s, there existed an underlying ideological consensus in post-Revolutionary America regarding fundamental principles. Other scholars take more seriously Jefferson's own assessment that "the revolution of 1800 . . . was as real a revolution in the principles of our government as that of 1776 was in its form." We belong to the latter camp. In our view, Jefferson's election marked the end of anglicization in American politics and ushered in a new, more decentralized and more democratic structure of power—one much closer to that envisioned by the Antifederalists than by the Federalists during the debates over ratification of the Constitution.[55]

Under this new structure, members of the middling sort exercised far greater political influence in the United States than anywhere else in the Western world. In the early decades of the nineteenth century, the right to vote in most states was extended to nearly all adult white men. Equally important, the culture of politics shifted. Ordinary citizens increasingly expected their elected representatives to reflect, rather than refine, their views when making government decisions. Candidates for public office presented themselves as the people's "friends" rather than as their "fathers." Yet democratization in the political realm did not produce an egalitarian social order. Even as they lost political hegemony, the elites grew richer, and class hierarchy remained an important feature of American life. In the North, enterprising merchants—most famously the coterie of Bostonians who erected the nation's first integrated textile mills at Waltham and Lowell—pioneered new forms of business incorporation to protect property rights and to promote capitalist development in lieu of direct federal assistance. In the South, large planters responded with alacrity and impressive economic efficiency to skyrocketing global (particularly British) demand for cotton. In ways not anticipated by the framers of the federal Constitution, political democracy proved highly compatible with the preservation and accumulation of private wealth and with the persistence of economic inequality.[56]

If the implications of Jefferson's accession to the presidency were large, his margin of electoral victory in 1800 was not. Despite a fierce split within Federalist ranks between followers of Hamilton and President Adams, Adams received a total of 65 electoral votes compared to Jefferson's (and Aaron Burr's) 73. As in 1796, the geographical pattern of partisan behavior was striking, with Republican support concentrated in the South and Federalist support in New England. The mid-Atlantic states were again the "swing" region, but their role should not obscure the essential part played by the three-fifths clause in shaping the final outcome. Had not the southern states possessed 14 additional votes as a result of the inclusion of slaves (albeit at a discount) in the calculation of their populations for electoral purposes, Adams would have won reelection. From the beginning, a subtext of the "Revolution of 1800" was the preservation of chattel slavery in the South.[57]

Slavery went unmentioned in Jefferson's famous inaugural address of March 4, 1801. That speech is rightly celebrated for its inspiring and conciliatory presentation of the democratic side of Jefferson's political vision. While he affirmed that "the will of the majority is in all cases to prevail"—a precept profoundly at odds with Madison's approach to majority factions in Federalist no. 10—Jefferson proclaimed as a "sacred principle" that the will of the majority, "to be rightful, must be reasonable; that the minority possess their equal rights, which equal laws must protect." He envisioned a "wise and frugal government" that would barely act on society, serving mainly to "restrain men from injuring one another, which shall leave them otherwise to regulate their own pursuits of industry and improvement, and shall not take from the mouth of labor the bread it has earned." Within this context, he characterized "the general government . . . as the sheet anchor of our peace at home and safety abroad," yet he called for "the support of the state governments in all their rights, as the most competent administrations for our domestic concerns and the surest bulwarks against anti-republican tendencies." In short, Jefferson limned in his own graceful words the Antifederalist alternative to the Federalist synthesis of 1787–88: a continental confederation of sovereign states whose central authority would possess enough power to repel foreign intrusion, sell public lands to eager farmers, and deliver the mail, but play no other major role in the lives of ordinary American citizens.[58]

Jefferson and his Republican supporters repudiated the British model of government in both style and substance. As president, Jefferson went out of his way not to appear monarchical—to the point of personally answering the front door of the White House in slippers and other casual attire. He considered himself a natural aristocrat but also a true embodiment of the people's will. Because he possessed abiding faith in the virtue of the nation's agricultural majority, he was sure that, once freed from Federalist deceptions, the citizenry would recognize as self-evident the same political principles and governmental policies that he, as their president, knew to be right.[59]

Under Jefferson's leadership, the Republicans abolished internal taxes, shrank the military, and slashed annual expenditures of the federal government. Although they did not dismantle the national bank or quash financial markets, by reducing the size and scope of the federal government, they transferred much of the responsibility for ruling the country to the separate state legislatures, where men of modest fortunes and middling status held more sway than they did in Congress. As a result, the locus of political power shifted downward in the social order, though not below the ranks of propertied white men.[60]

The devolution of political power from natural aristocrats to men of the middling sort had begun during the 1780s, when localists wrested control from cosmopolitans in many state legislatures. The process was interrupted, even reversed, in the 1790s, when Federalists dominated the national government and promoted a program of national integration, if not full-fledged consolidation. With the Jeffersonian victory in 1800, state governments once again became key battlegrounds in political disputes over fiscal policy and economic development. In the North, upwardly mobile Republicans openly challenged their social betters, and voter turnout in state elections rose dramatically during the first decade of the nineteenth century. Political upheaval was more limited in the South, where Republicans usually represented the local establishment and continued to enjoy the support of yeoman farmers not only as fellow members of the landed interest but also as fellow members of the white race with a mutual concern to keep blacks in subjugation. Among white southerners, racial solidarity fueled democratic rhetoric and vice versa. Augustus John Foster, the English minister to the United States in 1811–12, observed that the Jeffersonian gentry could "profess an unbounded love of liberty and of democracy in consequence of the mass of the people, who in other countries might become mobs, being there nearly altogether composed of their own Negro slaves . . . who form no social check upon their masters' political conduct."[61]

In Jefferson's mind, the Revolution of 1800 was more than a victory for majoritarian principles. It also was a triumph of agrarian virtue over the anti-republican forces of speculation and corruption. With the purchase of Louisiana in 1803, Jefferson believed he had ensured the agrarian character and hence the civic health of his "Empire for Liberty" for generations to come. Yet his vision of an expansive agricultural republic remained tethered to the institution of racial slavery in ways he hated to acknowledge. Not until the controversy over Missouri's application for admission to statehood broke out in 1819 did he and other members of the South's Republican elite confront the full implications of the Faustian bargain they had made in joining with plebeian northerners to defeat their Federalist foes.[62]

A comparison of how national leaders handled the Missouri Crisis with the framers' approach to sectional differences at the Constitutional Convention three decades earlier demonstrates the erosion of elite control over American politics. At Philadelphia in the summer of 1787, genteel delegates spoke frankly and struck hard bargains behind closed doors with remarkable efficiency. They then presented a united front in public on behalf of the compromises they had reached, deliberately downplaying the competing sectional interests at stake. By contrast, during the Missouri Crisis the process of intersectional negotiation extended well beyond the natural aristocracy to include the press and the electorate at large. The drama took place largely in public view, and the openness of the decision-making process made a compromise over Missouri much more difficult to achieve. Not coincidentally, the Missouri Crisis lasted more than two years—longer than it took for the federal Constitution to be drafted, ratified, and put into operation.

The persons most responsible for converting Missouri's application for statehood into a large-scale political crisis were northern Republicans, not Federalists. They turned the rhetoric of democratic rights and majority rule against the southern Republican elite that had wielded that same rhetoric so effectively against the Federalists for the previous quarter-century. Take, for example, James Tallmadge, Jr., the representative from New York who proposed the amendment to make gradual abolition a condition for Missouri's admission to statehood. Explaining to Congress the reason for his provocative action, he portrayed himself not as an enlightened refiner of public opinion but instead as the reflexive, democratic agent of his constituents' antislavery views. "Whatever might be my own private sentiments on this subject, standing here as the representative of others, no choice is left me," he declared. "I know the will of my constituents, and regardless of consequences, I will avow it." In keeping with Jeffersonian principles, Tallmadge further insisted that his amendment abided by a strict construction of the Constitution, and he invoked the Declaration of Independence's assertion "that all men are created equal" for ultimate ideological support.[63]

Southern leaders reacted with horror to the campaign against Missouri's admission as a slave state. In his famous letter to John Holmes, dated April 22, 1820, Jefferson claimed to detest slavery as much as ever, but, in a reversal of his previous pronouncements on the subject, he rejected any effort to restrict the peculiar institution's expansion. Prohibiting slavery in Missouri or in federal territory would only aggravate sectional tensions and cause more trouble, he now insisted. "A geographical line, coinciding with a marked principle, moral and political, once conceived and held up to the angry passions of men," he warned, "will never be obliterated; and every new irritation will mark it deeper and deeper."[64]

Jefferson viewed the restrictionist campaign of 1819–20 as a stratagem engineered by desperate Federalists and hence not a legitimate expression of the people's will. So did Madison and James Monroe. But the wave of public meetings over the Missouri question and the defeat of "dough-face" congressmen in 1820 indicate that politically mobilized northerners did care deeply about curbing the spread of slavery. In this context, the principle of majority rule—a central tenet of the Revolution of 1800—threatened the long-term viability of the South's peculiar institution, the economic basis of the planter elite.[65]

The Missouri Compromise—which coupled the admission of Missouri as a slave state with that of Maine as a free state while prohibiting slavery in the remainder of the Louisiana Purchase north of 36° 30' latitude—ended the immediate crisis but left unresolved critical questions about the future of republican government in the United States. On the one hand, by 1820 it had become evident that, contrary to the Federalist vision of 1787–88, the natural aristocracy could not rule the nation effectively from the top down—in large part because northern and southern elites could not agree on fundamental issues of political economy. On the other hand, it appeared that the Antifederalist alternative of a loose confederation of states coordinated by a weak central administration could neither defend Americans against foreign depredations—the main lesson of the War of 1812—nor satisfy the expansive ambitions of either northern or southern leaders.

Over the next generation the democratic implications of the Revolution of 1800 would continue to unfold. To an extent that would have shocked the framers, ordinary citizens abandoned their faith in rule by a natural aristocracy and embraced instead a concept of government by representatives much like themselves in talents and training. The foremost symbol of this process was Andrew Jackson, who—though a wealthy slaveholder—presented himself as a candidate for president in 1824 and again in 1828 and 1832 as the common man writ large, emphatically not as a natural aristocrat. At Jackson's side by 1828 stood Martin Van Buren, the "Little Magician," who promoted party competition as a means both to enhance popular participation in politics and to curb sectional antagonism. The Jacksonian denunciation of the "money power" in the 1830s echoed the attacks by Madison and Jefferson on Hamilton's fiscal plan in the 1790s, and, to a significant extent, the Democrats reunited the nation's agricultural majority in opposition to elite financial interests centered in the Northeast. Yet Jacksonians could not erase the issue of chattel slavery from national politics any more than Jeffersonians had been able to before them. By mid-century what had once been a subtext of the Revolution of 1800 surfaced as the main subject of debate at both state and federal levels of government. During the 1850s, fear of the "money power" gave way to fear of the "slave power" in the North, and in 1860 Abraham Lincoln was elected president on a platform firmly committed to the containment of slavery. Before he even took office, leaders of the lower South—citing the Jeffersonian doctrines of 1776 and 1798 but defying the principle of majority rule—fulfilled the threat made by South Carolina's delegates at the Constitutional Convention of 1787: they took their states out of the Union.[66]

The outbreak of the Civil War confirmed Hamilton's darkest forebodings about the dangers of fragmentation and democracy. In the absence of a national ruling class, the American republic imploded. During the secession crisis, many of the richest and most prestigious men of both the North and South sought alternatives to open warfare, but they lacked the influence and power to impose a solution from above upon the wider citizenry. In the North, political control rested with the upstart Republican Party, which represented the interests of the section's growing middle class, not those of the largest merchants and most illustrious gentlemen of New England and New York. Likewise, in the South, the state conventions that voted for secession were made up mainly of middling men, not—outside of South Carolina—the great planters. At the outset, at least, the Civil War was not a "rich man's war and a poor man's fight." It was instead, as Lincoln observed, "a People's contest" of huge and unprecedented proportions—the glorious yet horrific culmination of the Jeffersonians' remarkable Revolution of 1800.[67]

2

The "Slave Power" in the United States, 1783–1865

ཚ

ADAM ROTHMAN

How is it possible for a minority of citizens to get their way time after time in an ostensibly democratic polity? That question became central to northerners' discovery of a "slave power" in the United States beginning in the mid-1830s. The slave power signified not the power of slaves but the power that accrued to slave owners by virtue of their owning slaves. Antislavery critics charged that slave owners exerted power far out of proportion to their numbers, and that they used their power to enlarge the realm of slavery in violation of the country's founding tenets of liberty and equality. The enlargement of slavery, critics argued, threatened the rights of free people and corrupted the republic.[1] As John Gorham Palfrey of Massachusetts wrote in 1846, the founders of the United States would have been appalled to learn "that a vast majority of the high offices in all departments [of government], including nearly three-fourths of the offices in the army and navy, had been held by slave-owners, that slavery had been the great dictator of its policy, foreign and domestic, and that at this moment none but slaveholders were ministers of the nation at any foreign court, though there are more than three millions of voters in the country, and only one hundred thousand of them hold slaves."[2]

There was more than paranoia in Palfrey's lament. Slave owners wielded power in the United States from the American Revolution to the Civil War. The slave power originated in the combination of terror and succor that slave owners used to rule over enslaved people and compel them to labor. The wealth, standing, and reputation that slave owning gave to slave owners enabled them to assert political leadership among the broader free population throughout the southern United States. Then constitutional, partisan, and ideological mechanisms translated slave owners' regional power into national power, resulting, as Palfrey observed, in the conspicuous presence of slave owners in the highest echelons of American politics. Slave owners disagreed among themselves on many important political issues, yet they formed a dominant element in the constellation of political forces that governed the country and protected slavery through the first half of the nineteenth century.

Slave owners' power across different levels of political life allowed them to expand remarkably in the decades that followed the American Revolution. Attaching themselves to economic development taking place in the emerging industrial centers of the capitalist world, the slave-owning population spread from the southeastern seaboard to the lower Mississippi Valley and beyond. Their commercial basis shifted from tobacco and rice to sugar and, especially, cotton, which seemed capable of nearly limitless increase owing to the transatlantic revolution in cotton textile production. As slave owners' numbers grew, their aggregate wealth also increased in spectacular fashion. They became confident that, if let alone, slavery would allow them to profit from their connections to the Atlantic economy without suffering the social degradation that seemed to plague industrial society in the northern United States and Europe. They thought they had it made, except for one problem.

Southern slave owners' socioeconomic expansion coincided with their relative political decline in the country as a whole. From the early 1820s to the late 1850s, a growing antislavery movement, and more robust free population growth in the northern United States, sharpened sectional tensions. One consequence was to force southern slave owners into overt conflict with the basic principle of majority rule in the country as a whole. While couching their position in the unique idiom of U.S. constitutionalism, they increasingly relied on the most undemocratic aspects of American politics to preserve their interests within the Union. The South Carolinian John Calhoun offered the most sophisticated expression of the slave owners' political dilemma in his formulation of the "concurring majority," an innovative theory that used the federated structure of the American republic to guarantee the interests of influential propertied groups. As the northern antislavery threat grew in the 1840s and 1850s, proslavery politicians struggled to preserve a de facto concurring majority in national politics and even to formalize it in the U.S. Constitution.

Abraham Lincoln's election to the presidency in 1860 finally convinced southern slave owners that the only way to protect slavery, and with it their whole way of life, was to have their own country. The self-defense of slavery culminated in the secession of eleven southern states and the formation of the Confederate States of America; but secession turned out to be the downfall of the slave power. It precipitated a war that ultimately linked the fate of slavery to the survival of the Confederacy, and as the Confederacy fell, so too did the slave system it was formed to protect. This outcome was not part of some grand design but was accomplished piecemeal during the war and in its wake as a consequence of complex military and political pressures. In the end, defeat and emancipation destroyed slave owners as a ruling class and forced the vestige of that class to reconstitute itself in a new world of "free labor" and black citizenship.

❧ The slave-owning class in the United States was forged through its evolving relations with other people in American society and the broader Atlantic world. It was not frozen in time but was a fluid and dynamic entity. There were approximately eighty thousand house-holds with slaves in the United States in 1790, making up around 15 percent of all American households. Although slave owners lost tens of thousands of slaves during the Revolution, they retained al-most 700,000 slaves, or roughly 18 percent of the total population of the United States, under their dominion. Slavery was legal in every state except Massachusetts, but slave owners were largely concentrated in the southern states of Maryland, Virginia, North Carolina, South Carolina, and Georgia. In none of these states were slave owners a ma-jority. Even in South Carolina, the state most thoroughly identified with slavery, slave-owning households constituted only one-third of all households.[3] Tobacco, rice, and indigo—the three major commodities grown by slave labor—accounted for almost one-third of the value of the new country's exports, but foreign markets were uncertain in the new era of independence.[4]

Slave-owning planters throughout the British mainland colonies provided crucial leadership for the cause of independence during the Revolution, and they were a vital element of the nationalist coalition that pushed for a new federal Constitution at the end of the 1780s. George Washington's election to the presidency in 1789 symbolized slave owners' political and cultural authority in the new United States. In addition to being the hero of the American Revolution, Washington was one of the largest tobacco planters in Virginia, the most populous state in the Union and the one with more enslaved people than any other. Despite his status as a big planter, Washington was ambivalent about owning other human beings, and he signaled that ambivalence to his countrymen by providing in his will for the eventual manumission of his human property.[5] The qualms exhibited by some of Virginia's leading tobacco planters suggested that Enlightenment ideas of natural rights and the American Revolution had unsettled slavery in the very center of its power. Most famous were the words of Thomas Jefferson, who confessed in *Notes on the State of Virginia,* "I tremble for my country when I reflect that God is just."[6]

Political, economic, and demographic forces combined over the next half-century to reconfigure the slave-owning class in the United States. The old image of American slave owners as backward and static—an image fostered by critics and defenders alike—contrasts sharply with their actual history as avatars of change. Geographic expansion was the first important transformation. Planter-politicians engineered the key phases of the country's western push from the 1790s to the 1840s: the Louisiana Purchase, Indian removal, the annexation of Texas, and the Mexican War.[7] Expansion was never solely a southern dream, but it is telling that most of the vocal opponents of expansion were New Englanders who recognized that the addition of new territory in the South and West would augment the slave power.[8] They were not wrong. Nine slave states were added to the Union between 1789 and 1860 (in order of admission: Kentucky, Tennessee, Louisiana, Mississippi, Alabama, Missouri, Florida, Arkansas, and Texas), and by 1860, more than half of the 395,000 slave owners in the United States, including a majority of those with twenty or more slaves, lived in these new slave states. Diplomacy, conquest, and migration shifted the weight of the slave-owning class to the South and West. At the same time, gradual emancipation in the original northern states and the prohibition of slavery in the newer northwestern states made slave owners an increasingly sectional, as opposed to national, class.[9]

Western expansion dovetailed with a tremendous expansion of the transatlantic cotton economy. Cotton was a minor crop in the United States until the 1790s, when technological and managerial innovations in Great Britain's textile industry began to generate enormous demand for raw cotton. Slave owners took advantage of the new market by turning their attention—and their slaves' labor—to the cultivation of short-staple cotton. Cotton production in the United States increased from about 50 million pounds in 1800 to 180 million pounds in 1820 and 650 million pounds in 1840. In 1860 the U.S. cotton crop exceeded 1.6 billion pounds—about two-thirds of the world's cotton. One traveler touring the South in 1827 saw cotton everywhere, even in his sleep. "I dreamed of cotton," he wrote to a friend. The Deep South eventually came to dominate the country's cotton production. More than half of U.S. cotton in 1860 was grown in Louisiana, Mississippi, and Alabama, most of it on land that had been purchased or simply taken from indigenous people, then surveyed and sold by the government of the United States at public auctions.[10]

Cotton planters produced mostly for the transatlantic market. More than three-quarters of the U.S. cotton crop was exported, accounting for more than half the value of all U.S. exports. Two-thirds of U.S. cotton exports went to Great Britain, the world's leading manufacturer of cotton textiles. British textile manufacturers bought almost all of their raw cotton from the United States, thus relying on slave labor for decades after slavery had been abolished in Britain's own plantation colonies.[11] Cotton planters were fervent advocates of free trade and consistently opposed protectionist policies for manufacturing interests. (On this point they clashed with Louisiana's sugar planters, who were unable to compete in the world sugar market and required a protective tariff to shield them from foreign competition in the domestic market.) Despite episodic downturns in commodity prices, the cotton planters' success in the international market gave them confidence that they were indispensable to the American and Atlantic economy. "No, you dare not make war on cotton," South Carolina's James Henry Hammond famously declared in the Senate in 1858. "Cotton is king."[12]

If cotton was king, other sectors of the southern economy formed a respectable court. Tobacco, rice, and sugar markets sustained the livelihoods of perhaps one in every five American slave owners, including some of the most prominent and prosperous planters from the Carolina-Georgia Low Country and the lower Mississippi Valley.[13] Another 10 percent of slave owners lived in cities.[14] Thousands of slaves worked in mills, mines, workshops, factories, and refineries and on railroads.[15] Although the pace of urban and industrial development in the slave states trailed that of the free states, it matched development in several "advanced" European nations and far exceeded that of Brazil.[16] Not even a prolonged decline in cotton prices from 1818 to 1845 damp-

ened southern slave owners' faith in slavery. During these years many
southern reformers urged economic diversification to lessen the region's reliance on the world cotton market, but few advocated a turn to
free labor. The range of activities amenable to slave labor gave many
southern boosters confidence that slavery was compatible with a diverse, modern economy.[17]

Along with the westward push and the rise of the cotton economy, a
quintupling of the number of slaves increased slave owners' wealth
and boosted their moral confidence. By 1860 there were almost 4 million slaves in the United States, out of a total population of 30 million
people. The slave population grew by the accretion of new slave territories; the legal importation of foreign slaves until 1808 and illegal
smuggling thereafter; and, most important, natural reproduction. Unlike the slave populations of Cuba and Brazil (the two other major
slave societies in the Americas that endured until the second half of the
nineteenth century), the slave population of the United States increased from 1810 onward without continual massive replenishment
from Africa. The prohibition on slave importation meant that slave
owners in the United States had to provide enslaved people with food,
clothing, and shelter adequate for biological and social reproduction.
Slave owners elevated that economic necessity into a moral principle.
For instance, Andrew Flynn, a cotton planter in the Yazoo-Mississippi
Delta, instructed his overseer in 1840 to pay special attention to the
slave children, "for rearing them is not only a Duty, but also the most
profitable part of plantation business."[18]

Crucial to slave owners' transformation in the first half of the nineteenth century was the emergence of a massive forced migration of
slaves within the United States. The historian Michael Tadman estimates that roughly 1.1 million slaves were transported from slave-exporting to slave-importing regions of the country between 1790 and
1860. Some were transported by migrating owners, others by professional slave traders. They trekked over land, floated down the Mississippi and its tributaries, and sailed on coasting ships from Baltimore,

Norfolk, and Charleston to Savannah, Mobile, and New Orleans.[19] Forced slave migration had many benefits for slave owners. Although smuggling of foreign slaves into the lower South did occur after 1808, the vigorous internal commerce reduced its scope and allowed slave owners to adhere to a national political consensus against foreign slave importation—at least until the 1850s. It permitted them to shift slave labor from less profitable to more profitable sectors of the southern economy, boosting the price of slaves throughout the southern states and linking the slave-exporting and slave-importing regions of the South in a mutually advantageous trade. Moreover, forced migration terrorized enslaved people and extended the transatlantic process of deracination that rendered them vulnerable and powerless. One can sense Harriet Newby's desperation as she penned a letter to her husband in August 1859. "The last two years has been like a trouble dream to me," she lamented. "It is said Master is in want of money. If so, I know not what time he may sell me, an then all my bright hope of the futer are blasted . . . for if I thought I shoul never see you this earth would have no charms for me."[20] Newby's letter poignantly reveals that American slave owners participated in a commercial system with devastating consequences for enslaved people.

The expansion of slavery meant more laborers and greater capital for slave owners, who had the legal right to use physical punishment to compel slaves of all ages and both sexes to work under conditions that free people would not tolerate for themselves. Slavery's advocates argued that only coerced labor could transform the southern wilderness into civilized society. University of Virginia professor Thomas Roderick Dew recognized slavery's labor-generating and wealth-producing effects in his 1832 essay "Abolition of Negro Slavery." Abolish slavery, wrote Dew, "and Virginia will be a desert."[21] Moreover, slaves embodied capital that increased over time as slave prices rose. In 1860 the average value of an American slave was $900, an increase that boosted slave owners' wealth and gained them access to precious credit.[22] The capital embodied by their slave property elevated big planters to the top of the wealth pyramid in antebellum America. A few statistics illustrate the point. In 1860, 7,000 Americans owned wealth valued at $110,000 or more, and 4,500 of them lived in the South. The richest 0.1 percent of southerners were more than twice as wealthy on average as the richest 0.1 percent of northerners. Moreover, the twelve richest counties in the United States in 1860 in terms of total wealth per free man were all in the South, and nine of them were located in Louisiana and Mississippi. Finally, the overall inequality of wealth among free men was somewhat greater in the South than in the North in 1860, and if one includes slaves in the calculation, then wealth inequality was substantially greater in the South than in the North.[23]

It is the wealthiest slave owners who generally dominate the image of American slavery. Many of their mansions still stand for tourists to view. Their voluminous personal papers occupy libraries and archives, where scholars now study them. Their stories have been famously represented and misrepresented in film. The historian William Scarborough has written a collective biography of 339 slave owners, each of whom owned at least 250 slaves in 1850 or 1860. His book, *Masters of the Big House*, is a rich trove of information about this elite group. Altogether they owned more than 100,000 enslaved people in 1860. Almost half lived in Alabama, Mississippi, and Louisiana, while more than one-quarter called South Carolina home. The biggest of them all was Nathaniel Heyward, who owned 1,834 slaves in 1850, most of whom worked on his rice plantation in South Carolina's Colleton–St. Bartholomew Parish. Heyward's total estate was valued at more than $2 million when he died in 1851. From this super-elite came five U.S. senators, seventeen U.S. representatives, fifteen governors and lieutenant governors, and seventy-three state legislators. Most of these planter-politicians lived in South Carolina, where politics was especially beholden to the grandees.[24] Of course, most American slave owners did not live quite so high and mighty. Only 3 percent of all slave owners in 1860 owned fifty or more slaves. One-quarter owned from ten to forty-nine slaves. Around 70 percent owned fewer than ten slaves.[25] Yet the differences between the middling majority of slave owners and the super-elite should not be exaggerated. Slave owners were a diverse lot, but fundamental commonalities united them. Most were southern-born, Protestant white men who absorbed slavery into the other elemental aspects of their personality. They understood the northern assault on slavery not merely as an attack on their property but also as an attack on their region, their manhood, their race, and their God. All slave owners shared a fundamental class interest in protecting slavery, which was a basis of their way of life.

Precisely how to characterize that way of life has involved historians in a long-standing debate. Some insist that slave owners were capitalists because they were fully involved in transatlantic networks of commodity production and exchange. They argue that making money was the southern slave owners' overriding concern, and that they were relatively indifferent to nonpecuniary values. Others insist that capitalism is a historically specific social system that requires wage labor as its prevailing form of labor, so, by definition, slave owners cannot be capitalists. These historians tend to emphasize the aspects of slave owners' behavior and values that emerged directly from the master-slave relationship, especially their allegiance to a culture of honor and obligation commonly known as "paternalism."[26] My own view, closer to the latter, is that American slave owners constituted a profiteering class that arose and evolved within the transatlantic division of labor, and whose behavior and values were not identical with those of other profiteering classes, such as the industrial bourgeoisie, but were firmly rooted in their own local attempts to secure and justify their power over enslaved people. Thus the crucial questions about southern slave owners' class character can be answered only by a close examination of their various struggles for power.

Like charity, power began at home. Or in other words, the household formed the basic unit of slave owners' rule.[27] Many of the aspects of sovereignty that are generally associated with state administration were delegated to slave owners who governed the human property collected in their households. The slave owners were the ultimate authorities within their households, punishing slaves for violating written and unwritten laws. As James Henry Hammond argued in his 1845 *Letter to an English Abolitionist,* "We try, decide, and execute the sentences, in thousands of cases, which in other countries would go into the courts."[28] Assisted by members of their own families, overseers, and drivers, planters regulated the daily lives of their slaves. Andrew Flynn instructed his overseer to "visit the negro houses every morning by daylight" and at least one night per week "after horn blow."[29] The purpose of such visits was to keep enslaved people within the plantation's boundaries and subject to its many forms of discipline. Whipping, extra work, reduced rations, and selling were just some of the lawful methods that planters used to punish insubordinate slaves.[30]

Slave owners used the carrot as well as the stick. They met minimum standards in providing food, clothing, and shelter. They offered bonuses for good conduct and hard work, or simply to demonstrate largesse. They paid for overwork, for Sunday labor, and for crops that the slaves grew on their own time. Some slaves even managed to amass property of their own—recognized as such by custom if not in law. It was not that slaves were treated well, or that they were convinced that slavery was right and just. Rather, in these and many other ways, slave owners gave enslaved people something to lose. Such allowances were central to American slave owners' managerial technique and moral defense of slavery. Proslavery theorists argued that masters and slaves were bound together in a system of reciprocal obligation. Masters were obliged to protect and uplift their slaves, and in exchange, slaves were obliged to submit to and labor for their masters. Law enforced the slaves' part of the bargain, while masters were, for the most part, regulated solely by their own personal regard for honor and desire for profit.[31]

An array of neighborhood police institutions buttressed slave owners' authority. Slaves who visited nearby plantations, or who went to town for work or pleasure, or who dared to run away entered into pub-

lic spaces regulated by slave patrols—a ubiquitous presence in slave societies. These spread the task of protecting slavery throughout the
adult white male population and even to free people of color. The patrols figure prominently in autobiographies written by fugitive slaves in
the antebellum period as well as in the memories of former slaves recorded in the 1930s by the Works Progress Administration. "If you
wasn't in your proper place when the paddyrollers come," one North
Carolinian recalled, "they lash you til' you was black and blue."[32]
When slaves were formally accused of crimes, special public courts ad-
judicated their cases with an eye toward protecting slave owners' property rights. Slave owners presided over these courts, and several southern states limited the number of non-slave-owners who could serve as
jurors in criminal cases involving slaves.[33]

Enslaved people tested the authority of their owners in many ways,
ranging from running away to sabotage to homicide, but these forms
of everyday resistance only rarely congealed into collective, armed resistance on a scale that actually threatened the plantation system. Many
real and alleged conspiracies were squelched before they ripened into
outright rebellion—usually with the help of slaves who betrayed their
fellows' plots. ("Servile deceit" was what the free black abolitionist
David Walker called the pattern of collaboration.)[34] The rapid, effective suppression of the two major slave revolts that did occur in the
United States in the first half of the nineteenth century—one in the
sugar parishes above New Orleans in 1811 and the other in Virginia's
Southampton County in 1831—demonstrated the overwhelming military strength available to southern planters in moments of crisis. The
little-known slave revolt of 1811, the largest in the country's history, is
particularly notable because federal troops contributed to its suppression. Their commander, General Wade Hampton of South Carolina,
happened to be one of the largest slave owners in the United States at
the time of the rebellion, and he would shortly become Louisiana's
richest sugar planter.[35]

Slave owners' power over slaves ultimately depended on mustering

support from the majority of white southerners who did not themselves own slaves. About two-thirds of all southern households headed
by white people in 1860 did not include slaves, a proportion that appears to have held more or less constant throughout the first half of the
century.[36] Had these non-slave-owning white southerners leagued with
the slaves, the slave-owning minority would not have been able to
maintain its rule. But that is not what happened. As the acute Frederick
Law Olmsted observed in *The Cotton Kingdom*, "The security of the
whites is in a much less degree contingent on the action of the 'patrols'
than upon the constant, habitual, and instinctive surveillance and authority of all white people over all black."[37] It is easy but inadequate to
assume that the southern white yeomanry supported slavery because
they were racist, or because they earned some vague psychic benefit
from lording it over black people. Most white Americans of the era
were racist, but not all endorsed slavery. Olmsted himself suggested
that the yeomanry's apparently spontaneous support for slavery derived from an implicit law of self-defense against slave insurrection.
That is a reasonable start toward an explanation, but it must be allowed
that the non-slave-owning majority of white southerners supported
slavery for other solid reasons as well. Mutual interests, shared values,
and the suppression of dissent led most white southerners to accept
slavery and the leadership of the planter class.[38]

Many white southern men who did not own slaves nevertheless materially benefited from the plantation system. Some hired or borrowed
slaves. Some took their cotton to wealthier neighbors, who ginned it
and sold it for them. Thousands worked as overseers and craftsmen
on plantations. Young, slaveless white men often looked forward to
owning slaves as they made their way in the world, and indeed, the
likelihood of white southern men owning slaves increased with age.[39]
Equally important were the indirect effects of slavery in preserving the
white yeomanry's independent and relatively self-sufficient communities. The plantation system bypassed large regions of the South because the land was not fertile enough or transportation costs were too

high for profitable commercial agriculture. The southern yeomanry occupied these interstitial places, where commercial society remained relatively undeveloped, and yeoman households sustained traditional agrarian and patriarchal mores. The circumstances of their lives gave non-slave-owning white people little reason to oppose slavery or slave owners' leadership, and good reason to be suspicious of abolitionists' more progress-oriented, bourgeois values.[40]

Those few free white men and women who dared (or appeared) to challenge slavery faced social pressure, intimidation, and even violence. Antebellum southern slave codes allowed for the prosecution of free people who engaged in unauthorized contact with slaves. Eight South Carolinians, for instance, were convicted of abolitionism between 1847 and 1852.[41] Extralegal coercion also suppressed antislavery dissent. Vigilance committees throughout the South blocked the dissemination of abolitionist propaganda through the mail in 1835.[42] A committee in Lexington, Kentucky, closed down Cassius Clay's antislavery *True American* in 1845 and shipped his printing press to Cincinnati.[43] Nobody knows exactly how many people were run out of southern towns and communities, as was the Connecticut-born Nathan Bird Watson in 1851, for "promulgating abolitionist sentiments . . . at war with our institutions and intolerable in a slave community."[44] The extent of such repression among southern white people cannot be measured precisely, but it surely muted antislavery organization in the slave states. Perhaps opposition to slavery is one reason why thousands of native-born southerners emigrated to free states and territories. For instance, approximately 390,000 free people born in Virginia were living outside the state in 1860, and more than half of these were living in free states or territories. Seventy-five thousand had emigrated to Ohio. Migration may have eased antislavery pressures within the South while strengthening them elsewhere.[45]

Southern political institutions did require slave owners to take the interests and values of non-slave-owning white people into account. The formal sphere of southern politics widened in the first half of the nineteenth century. Constitutional reform in the slave states generally ran toward eliminating property qualifications on suffrage and officeholding, equalizing representation, and subjecting more offices to popular election.[46] Competition between the Democratic and Whig parties in the 1830s and 1840s brought more white men into the political process and increased turnout at elections.[47] These changes enhanced the influence of the yeomanry, who generally opposed state banks, costly subsidies for canals and railroads, and the taxes these entailed. The yeomanry's opposition to an activist government derived from a fear of political corruption and an indifference to the benefits of market expansion. These same preferences reinforced their hostility to schemes for emancipation and abolition, which also seemed to use the power of government to disrupt artificially the natural economic and social order contained within their households. In the era of two-party competition beginning in the 1830s, non-slave-owning white farmers' anti-statist outlook tended to direct them to the Democratic Party, while more commercially oriented southerners tended to identify with the Whig Party, but both parties in the South were led by slave owners.[48]

There is little doubt that political leadership in the mid-nineteenth-century South remained safely in the hands of slave owners despite the march of "democracy." Slave owners had more education than other men, and they moved more easily into public life. They were able to mobilize sprawling connections of kinship, friendship, and patronage to win appointment or election to office.[49] One study of antebellum Texas determined that 68.3 percent of the state's political leaders in 1860 were slave owners, as opposed to just over a quarter of all household heads.[50] Two-thirds of all southern state legislators in 1860 were slave owners, and the only two slave states where they did not hold a majority of seats in 1860 were Arkansas and Missouri.[51] Slave owners were even more overrepresented among southern congressmen, but there are few available statistics on slave owning among national politicians. One study of Mississippi found that at least forty-eight of the state's fifty-two representatives and senators before 1861 owned slaves, and two-thirds of them were owners of more than ten slaves.[52] Similar studies of other southern states are unlikely to show that slave owners were much less dominant elsewhere.

An important aspect of southern slave owners' struggle for power was their increasingly sophisticated effort to justify slavery. The emergence of a transatlantic antislavery movement in the late eighteenth century stirred the formidable intellectual resources of American slave owners into an ever more rigorous and thorough analysis and defense of their way of life. They were fascinated and appalled by the slave revolt in St. Domingue, compensated emancipation in the British West Indies, and the slow decline of slavery in the northern United States. Proslavery intellectuals interpreted these processes to show that emancipation retarded economic progress and harmed freed people. The rise of the organized abolitionist movement in the North during the Jacksonian era intensified the national debate over slavery. Southern intellectuals offered speeches, sermons, reviews, pamphlets, treatises, and novels demonstrating the morality of slavery. One need only read Louisa McCord's review of Harriet Beecher Stowe's *Uncle Tom's Cabin* to grasp the southern intellectuals' unrelenting effort to defend slavery. "Again and again have we, with all the power and talent of our clearest heads and strongest intellects, forced aside the foul load of slander and villainous aspersion so often hurled against us," McCord protested in the pages of the *Southern Quarterly Review*.[53] This circulation of proslavery ideas strengthened the solidarity of southern slave owners in the 1840s and 1850s. It armed them intellectually with a formidable critique of bourgeois social relations.

The proslavery argument came to rest in the 1850s on a characteristic contrast between slave and free society. Whereas slave society was cooperative, peaceful, and God-fearing (so the argument went), free society was competitive, anarchic, and secular.[54] The proslavery contrast between slave and free society reconciled two cherished values, freedom and obligation, in tension with each other. Freedom largely prevailed in the relations among white southern men, obligation in the relations between white southern men and others in society, including women, children, and slaves.[55] If freedom and obligation were slave owners' major values, then dependency (the negation of freedom) and alienation (the negation of obligation) were their antitheses, the slave owners' nightmare. The proslavery contrast between slave and free society drew its logic from the combination of these four values: freedom, obligation, dependency, and alienation. The industrial bourgeoisie embodied freedom without obligation—a corrosive social force associated with duty-dissolving ideas including transcendentalism, feminism, and abolitionism. The monstrous offspring of the bourgeoisie, wage workers, occupied the most degraded position in the proslavery structure of values. Wage workers, especially free black people, appeared to be both alienated and dependent. Oppressed by poverty, they threatened to tilt the social order toward anarchism or socialism. If enfranchised, they reduced democracy to mob rule. Like wage workers, slaves were dependent rather than free, but from the proslavery perspective they were rescued from the despair of free society by immersion in the mutual obligations of slavery. Only slave owners and their allies, the southern yeomanry, embodied an ideal synthesis of freedom and obligation.[56]

The logic of the proslavery argument resonated in an 1857 speech by Jefferson Davis, the wealthy Mississippi planter who eventually became the president of the Confederate States of America. He declared that slavery provided "the most humane relations of labor to capital which can permanently subsist between them, and the most beneficent form of government that has been applied to those who are morally and intellectually unable to take care of themselves." Like other advocates of slavery, Davis argued that black people were incapable of self-government. They had to be protected from the competitive pressures of free society, and they needed moral guidance to prevent them from regressing into barbarism. Moreover, he declared that the presence of black slaves "elevated the white man, and gave our social condition that freedom from humiliating discrimination and dependence among individuals of our own race, which, where they existed, would leave but the name of political equality."[57] Slavery alleviated relations of exploitation among southern white men and allowed them to face one another as equals. In a far cry from the ambivalent antislavery of Washington and Jefferson, Jefferson Davis now argued that black slavery made white freedom possible.

The proslavery argument helped to solidify the internal cohesion of the slave-owning class, but most northerners were not convinced of its logic. While slavery disappeared as a mode of labor in the North, it reappeared there as a key symbol of savage cruelty, economic stagnation, and political corruption.[58] The slave owners' major political dilemma was that northerners lay beyond the reach of the intensive networks of power that smothered opposition to slavery in the South. In the country as a whole, therefore, slave owners had to rely on more extensive networks to protect their interests. These included constitutional rules, partisan alignments, and ideological affinities, which all needed the acquiescence of sufficient numbers of free northerners to be effective.[59] Until the late 1850s, slave owners were an indispensable part of every national administrative and legislative coalition, and they used their leverage to protect the slave-owning interest in direct and indirect ways.

The federal Constitution protected slave owners without ever mentioning slavery by name. Article 4, Section 2 (the fugitive slave clause), prevented slaves from becoming free by escaping to free states. Article 1, Section 9 (the slave trade clause), prohibited the national government from banning the importation of slaves until 1808. Article 1, Section 2 (the three-fifths clause), based apportionment of seats in the House of Representatives on free population plus three-fifths of "all other persons," meaning slaves. The three-fifths clause was particularly significant for slave owners' national power. It boosted the slave states' representation in the House, though not as much as the southern delegates to the Constitutional Convention would have liked. The southerners wanted apportionment based on the total population, while northerners wanted it based on free population alone. The three-fifths ratio emerged as a compromise derived from the ratio that the Continental Congress had used to apportion direct taxes among the states.[60] Their representation augmented by the three-fifths clause, the slave states enjoyed near-parity in the House of Representatives in the 1790s and the first decade of the nineteenth century, when 47 percent of congressional representatives came from the South. Although the three-fifths clause never gave southerners an outright majority in the House, it lessened the number of northern representatives that southern congressmen had to win over to their side on any question respecting slavery—for instance, when antislavery congressmen tried to block the admission of Missouri as a slave state in 1819–20. It also augmented the influence of the slave states in the electoral college and national party caucuses. Thomas Jefferson owed his narrow margin of victory in the 1800 presidential election to the additional electoral votes awarded to the South by the three-fifths clause. This clause eased the task of protecting slave owners' interests.[61]

But as population growth in the free states outran that of the slave states, the three-fifths clause lost its potency. The proportion of southern representatives declined in every decade until it reached 35 percent in 1860. The shifting balance substantially reduced the original southern states' influence in the House. By 1860, Maryland, Virginia, North Carolina, South Carolina, and Georgia accounted for only 17 percent of representatives in the House. The three mid-Atlantic states of New York, New Jersey, and Pennsylvania alone accounted for 26 percent.[62] Their declining influence in the House forced southern politicians to focus on preserving slave state parity in the Senate, a bastion of the slave power in the first half of the nineteenth century. The equal rights of states became a counterweight against the equal rights of citizens. Time and again, antislavery legislation that passed in the House died in the Senate. The Wilmot Proviso, which would have prohibited slavery in territory won during the Mexican War, is a good example. Though endorsed by the House of Representatives several years in a row, it never survived the Senate's proslavery gauntlet.[63]

Southern slave owners found influential allies among conservative northern businessmen whose economic endeavors linked them to the plantation system. New England's cotton textile manufacturers had a clear interest in preserving a steady supply of cheap cotton from the slave states. As a dominant element in the leadership of Massachusetts's Whig Party in the 1830s and 1840s, they tried to hold back the rising antislavery tide while reassuring the southern wing of their party that there was nothing to fear. "Cotton thread holds the union together," wrote a disapproving Ralph Waldo Emerson.[64] New York's mercantile elite also supported slavery. They were the middlemen of the Atlantic cotton trade. A substantial proportion of southern cotton passed through New York on its way to Liverpool and Le Havre, while many of the consumer goods purchased and consumed in the South were manufactured in New York and shipped by the city's merchants. These linkages made New York fertile ground for proslavery apologists such as the newspaper editor Thomas Prentice Kettell, who published an anti-abolitionist treatise in 1860 titled *Southern Wealth and Northern Profits*.[65] The antislavery movement thus confronted entrenched conservative elites in the North as well as in the South.

Competition between national political parties further protected slave owners' interests from the Missouri Compromise until the Mexican War. The polarizing issues of partisan conflict in the era of the second-party system—Indian removal, internal improvements, tariffs, and banking—relegated questions about slavery to the margins of national debate. Neither the Democrats nor the Whigs could win national elections without support from the South, and the price of that support was a solicitous regard for slave owners' special property interests. Each party vied to outshine the other's proslavery credentials within the South without alienating northern voters.[66] Both major parties attracted slave owners, but the Democratic Party ultimately proved to be more

firmly attached to slavery than the Whigs. From its inception as the
Jacksonian party, the Democracy regularly counted on a solid southern
electoral base. Furthermore, Democratic candidates for national office
generally had to win two-thirds of the vote at the Democratic nominating convention, a rule that gave southerners leverage they never enjoyed in the Whig Party.[67] Finally, northern Democrats were generally
more hostile to antislavery on principle than were the northern Whigs.
Not only did northern Democrats reject abolitionism as a species of
overbearing moral reform akin to temperance and Sabbatarianism, but
also they were especially hostile to the lurking prospect of Afro-Amer-
ican citizenship. It was Democrats primarily who carried out the disen-
franchisement of black voters in the North while championing white
male suffrage.[68]

Slave owners took advantage of these networks of power to secure a
prominent place for themselves in the national government. Seven of
the first eleven presidents were slave owners. Fifty-seven percent of all
Supreme Court justices were southerners, as were half of all major
cabinet and diplomatic officials. It can be assumed that most of these
men were also slave owners.[69] This presence had real political consequences. Slave owners successfully prevented the national government
from interfering with slavery when it endangered their interests and involved the national government in slavery when it advanced their interests. The roster of accomplishments is impressive. Slave-owning
politicians got the nation's capital located in the South and firmly protected slavery there. They allowed the national government to prohibit
the importation of slaves into the United States in 1808 but afterwards
blocked any federal prohibition or even meaningful regulation of the
interstate slave trade. They used the country's diplomatic offices to win
compensation for slave owners whose human chattel fled to the British
during the American Revolution and the War of 1812. They dispatched
the army to suppress communities of fugitive slaves in Florida but kept
the navy from supporting British efforts to quash the Atlantic slave
trade until the early 1840s. Proslavery forces also attached slavery to

U.S. territorial expansion. They defused efforts to abolish slavery in the Orleans Territory in 1804 and Missouri in 1819–20, which enabled the expansion of slavery west of the Mississippi. They "removed" the southern Indians, expanding the plantation system in the lands the Indians were forced to leave behind. They brought Texas into the Union as a giant slave state and then made war on Mexico with the evident hope of winning yet more territory for slavery. Many slave-owning politicians were forthright about the need to protect slavery, but often they couched their agenda in the more abstract and transcendent vocabulary of individual and state rights, which had a broader appeal to non–slave owners than the defense of slavery in itself.[70]

Yet the jerry-built edifice of slave owners' hegemony began to crumble in the late 1830s. Tactics used by slave owners alienated many northerners who had previously collaborated with them. The antislavery conversion of two important northern politicians who had previously championed slave owners' interests indicated the changing weather. John Quincy Adams became an avowed enemy of southern slave owners during the fight over the "gag rule" instituted in the House of Representatives from 1836 to 1844 to stifle debate on thousands of petitions calling for the abolition of slavery and the slave trade in the District of Columbia. Martin Van Buren, an original architect of the Democracy, turned against slavery after losing a long and bitter battle with proslavery forces in his party during the mid-1840s. The northern diagnosis of a "slave power" took hold as antislavery activists began to identify maddening constraints that slave owners imposed on the democratic liberties of free northerners.[71] The mirror image of that diagnosis occurred to southern politicians who began to comprehend that neither the existing Constitution nor the two-party system would suffice to protect slavery in the face of a rapidly growing northern free population and an increasingly potent antislavery movement. Confronting what Tocqueville called the tyranny of the majority, they began to articulate an explicitly antidemocratic political theory.

One of the first to think seriously about the slave owners' deteriorating minority position in American politics was the South Carolina planter and statesman John C. Calhoun. Beginning in the battles over the federal tariff in the late 1820s, Calhoun worked out a theoretically sophisticated critique of the tyranny of the majority. He distinguished between the "absolute majority," which was a mere majority of all the people, and the "concurring majority," which was the unanimous assent of each and every major interest in society. He argued that the absolute majority subordinated the weaker interest to the stronger, while the concurring majority allowed for a harmony of interests. Given the constitutional structure of the United States, Calhoun claimed, the country's distinct political interests were organized into states, so each state should have a veto that could be overridden only by a supermajority of the other states in the form of a constitutional amendment. The concurring majority was a recipe for a government in a permanent condition of paralysis, which would have suited those conservatives who, like Calhoun, had come to believe that an overactive national government would someday threaten slavery. The idea of the concurring majority continues to resonate ironically in contemporary thinking about the rights of minority groups in political democracies, but Calhoun's own formulation aimed to protect propertied minorities in the United States from democratic regulation. His theory expressed slave owners' considerable anxiety over enfranchisement of the lower classes, whatever their color.[72]

Between the Mexican War and secession, slave owners tried with increasing urgency to secure a concurring majority in defense of slavery. They denied that the national government had the right to prohibit slavery in its territories, and they tried to extend slavery into western territories where it did not already exist. (Slave owners were supported in these goals by the Supreme Court's 1857 *Dred Scott* decision, which denied that Congress had the power to prohibit slavery in the territories. All five southern Democrats on the Court voted in the 7–2 majority.) They championed the admission of new slave states in order to preserve parity in the Senate. They pressed for a new fugitive slave law to enforce northerners' compliance with the constitutional duty to return runaways. All of these efforts merely exacerbated northern opposition to the "slave power," which in turn reinforced southern slave owners' felt need to protect slavery. Abraham Lincoln's victory in the presidential election in 1860 without any electoral votes from the slave states signaled an end to the de facto concurrent majority in American politics and provoked the rapid secession of seven states from the lower South, beginning with South Carolina. After the clash at Fort Sumter, these were joined by four more slave states, including Virginia. The only slave states not to join the Confederacy were Missouri, Kentucky, Maryland, and Delaware, which happened to be the four slave states with the smallest proportion of enslaved people in their populations.[73]

The "Crittenden compromise" proposed in December 1860 to avert secession reveals the terms of slave owners' continued participation in the Union in the wake of Lincoln's election. The proposal encompassed six constitutional amendments explicitly protecting slavery in various ways and, it might be noted, introducing the word "slavery" into the Constitution for the first time. The amendments would have established federal recognition of and protection for slavery in all territories south of 36° 30′ extending to the Pacific, and a prohibition on interference with slavery in the states where it existed. The sixth Crittenden amendment would have prevented the other five amendments, the three-fifths clause, and the fugitive slave clause from ever being repealed. In short, the Crittenden compromise would have enacted a permanent constitutional guarantee of slave owners' property rights in other human beings. Only such ironclad assurances could have made American democracy safe for slavery, and it is not surprising that Lincoln and his fellow Republicans rejected it. The Republicans' common denominator was opposition to the extension of slavery into new territories and states, which implied at the very least a gradual fading out of slavery over time.[74]

Both fear and hope infused southern slave owners' fateful decision to sunder the Union. Lincoln's repeated assurances that the Republican Party would not emancipate the slaves in the southern states were not a sufficient substitute for the loss of political power that his election signified. Secessionists predicted that the Republican Party would overwhelm the South by the addition of new free states and territories, use its powers of patronage to build up antislavery parties in the slave states, or incite slave insurrection as John Brown had attempted at Harpers Ferry in 1859. To make matters worse for slave owners, some of their slaves appeared to take Lincoln's election as a harbinger of their imminent emancipation. As one slave was alleged to have declared in May 1861, "Lincoln is going to set them all free, and they are everywhere making preparations to aid him when he makes his appearance."[75] The secessionists argued that the Republican ascendancy threatened to expose and enlarge latent social fissures within southern society, and ultimately to overthrow slavery by hook or by crook. The only solution was to place southern society beyond the reach of the abolitionists' political machine. Alongside these fears was a faith that the South could flourish as an independent country. The Charleston poet Henry Timrod captured that spirit in his 1861 poem "Ethnogenesis":

> . . . At last, we are
> A nation among nations; and the world
> Shall soon behold in many a distant port
> Another flag unfurled![76]

Championed most effectively by the southern clergy, Confederate nationalism reflected slave owners' confidence in the economic, political, intellectual, and especially religious foundations of their society. Theirs would be a blessed nation.[77]

Secession was a movement led by slave owners to protect and vindicate slavery. The debates over secession within the South, the various state declarations of the causes of secession, and the speeches and communications delivered by southern secession commissioners reveal beyond any doubt the proslavery bases of secession.[78] But two caveats must be offered to this truism. First, a good number of influential slave owners opposed immediate secession for prudential reasons. It harbored the principle of anarchy and invited terrors far more dangerous than the Republican Party. "Secession is no holiday work," warned Benjamin Hill of Georgia.[79] A second caveat is that many southern non–slave owners also supported secession for their own reasons, although voting returns indicate that districts with fewer slave owners tended to support secession less strongly than those with more slave owners. Southern non–slave owners' tepid support reinforced many slave owners' conviction that independence was necessary to prevent the Republican Party from using its patronage to sow an antislavery party in southern soil.[80] Nevertheless, the Confederate States of America was a true slave owners' republic. In March 1861 the Confederate vice president, Alexander Stephens, declared that the cornerstone of the new government "rests, upon the great truth, that the negro is not equal to the white man; that slavery—subordination to the superior race—is his natural and normal condition."[81] Fulfilling slave owners' long-standing dream of explicit constitutional sanction for slavery, the Confederate Constitution included specific protection for the slave property of citizens, including a guarantee that slave owners could take their slaves into any new territory added to the Confederacy in the future.

While spinning new protections for slavery in the Confederacy, secession swept away the webs of power protecting slavery within the Union. The Republican Party seized the opportunity to enact an antislavery program over the objections of the racist northern rump of the Democratic Party and the remaining slave owners in the border states. Now dominated by the Republicans, the national government admitted Kansas as a free state in 1861. Slaves in the District of Columbia were emancipated in 1862 and their owners compensated. The national government finally recognized Haiti and signed a new treaty with Great

Britain strengthening the U.S. commitment to suppressing the Atlantic slave trade. Slavery deteriorated under the pressure of war in the slave states that remained in the Union, and abolition advanced into the Confederacy with the Union armies, disguised as a "military necessity." Wherever the Union armies went, slave owners lost power over their human property. "There is no barier to prevent the escape of our Slavs who choose to go to the enemy," complained a group of Virginia slave owners in 1864. "They are going constantly."[82] Slaves fled to the Union lines in large numbers and forced the federal government to confront the problem of slavery directly. After the Emancipation Proclamation of January 1, 1863, Union soldiers—including black soldiers—carried the banner of freedom deeper into Confederate territory. Slave owners had gambled that secession would protect slavery, but they lost.[83]

The Civil War and emancipation shattered American slave owners as a class. Contrary to the image of the war as a "poor man's fight," many slave owners and their sons fought and died. "De massa had three boys to go to war, but dere wuzn't one to come home," a former slave recalled. "All the chillum he has wuz killed."[84] Surviving slave owners were defeated and expropriated of their human property. Because of emancipation (and wartime damage to nonhuman property), the average per capita wealth of southern whites declined from almost $4,000 in 1860 to just over $2,000 in 1870.[85] The staggering loss of wealth was only part of their trauma. Former slave owners generally retained their ownership of land but had to find new ways to get former slaves to work for them. Wages, sharecropping, tenancy, debt peonage, and convict leasing were some of the misnamed "free labor" systems that replaced slavery in the South. The Reconstruction Amendments finally eradicated the constitutional basis of slavery and, in an even more radical step, transformed freedpeople into citizens. Not only did black citizenship complicate former slave owners' attempt to reassert class power in the new context of emancipation, but it humiliated them as well with the prospect of racial equality sponsored by the Republican Party. Southern elites eventually rebuilt their power, but not on the basis of slave owning. They relied instead on new combinations of coercion and consent that took another half-century to master.[86]

The destruction of the slave power contributed to the rise of a new economic and political order in the nation as a whole. As *Hunt's Merchant's Magazine* observed in 1870, "The late great civil war broke down certain sections and classes in this country, and transferred wealth and power to new hands."[87] Conflicts between capital and labor supplanted the older struggle between freedom and slavery, yet echoes of that past struggle reverberated in the new era. Bourgeois ideologues argued that individual freedom of contract represented the continuation of the antislavery tradition, while spokesmen for the white working class criticized inequalities of power in the labor market that turned free labor into "wage slavery."[88] All sides affirmed the moral supremacy of free over slave labor yet disagreed as to what free labor meant in the wake of slave emancipation. Over time, a nationwide indeterminacy in the meaning of freedom provided crucial space within which a reborn southern elite eventually disenfranchised, segregated, and impoverished black Americans in the era of Jim Crow. And that achievement, which W. E. B. Du Bois called "a new dictatorship of property in the South through the color line," would shape the history of the United States for another century.[89]

3

Merchants and Manufacturers in the Antebellum North

✥

SVEN BECKERT

During the first half of the nineteenth century, the close-knit and powerful community that had constituted America's northern economic elites unraveled dramatically. New divisions appeared within their ranks that made concerted political action increasingly difficult. And new challengers to their economic, social and political power arose, undermining their once exalted position. Especially after 1830, in the wake of the industrial revolution, everyone from western farmers to northern artisans-turned-manufacturers and urban wage workers confronted the power of merchants and bankers, the oldest segment of the North's economic elite. At the same time, the economic elite in the North became less cohesive and began to fragment into diverse groups with differing political aims and contrasting views of America's economic future. The resulting divisions within their ranks eventually undermined their collective ability to steer the nation and ultimately contributed to the outbreak of the Civil War.

The most important challenge faced by the nation's economic elites was the divergence of their own sentiments and interests. Colonial economic elites, of course, had experienced disagreements and upheavals from time to time, but these were minor compared to the emerging diversity that had surfaced by the 1830s. Southern planters, bolstered by the cotton boom, became ever more forceful in asserting their distinct set of interests, going so far as to find in the South a civilization fundamentally at odds with that of the North. To secure that civilization, as well as their profits, they worked to forge a political environment conducive to slavery and Atlantic trade. Many northern merchants, deeply invested in the plantation economy, sympathized with such an agenda. A small but growing number of them, however, drawing profits from their manufacturing interests and their trade with the West, began to embrace a political economy of domestic industrialization sharply at odds with the interests of the southern planters. Their allies, in turn, were the rapidly growing group of artisans-turned-manufacturers who championed a different vision of economic development, one that focused on domestic industrialization and the expansion of free labor agriculture.

At the same time, economic elites faced challenges from non-elites, particularly the fledgling working class. Though few in numbers, these workers increasingly came to dominate certain urban neighborhoods. Some began to organize in trade unions and engaged in strikes. In a number of cities, urban workers were becoming an important force in local and state politics, threatening the once unassailable power of northern merchants and bankers. How to deal with the economic, social, and political effects of proletarianization thus became an ever more urgent question for the northern economic elites, who were in no way united in their view about how to respond to these social changes.

Just as the industrial revolution turned upside down the way Americans worked and lived, therefore, it also transformed the nation's economic elite. Taken together, the twin challenges of internal differentiation and proletarianization contested the power of economic elites and gave farmers, workers, and slaves new openings to determine the nation's destiny.

✂ Merchants were by far the most important segment of the economic elite in the North before the Civil War. Ever since Europeans began settling North America, merchants had played an important role in the New World. As mercantilist doctrines held that the profits of colonial trade accumulated in the mother country, European powers in North America had focused much of their colonial interest on the extraction of raw materials and agricultural commodities. Alongside explorers, land-hungry farmers, and religiously motivated settlers, merchants were among the first to set foot on the North American continent.[1]

In the years after the Revolution, merchants who had accumulated their wealth in colonial times, along with traders who had taken advantage of the opportunities presented by the upheavals of war, formed the core of the northern economic elite.[2] They organized the sale and distribution of wares largely manufactured in Europe and the financing, collection, and shipping of North American agricultural commodities, especially cotton, but also tobacco, sugar, and rice. In the process, they became deeply involved in the slave economy of the South. Their success rested largely on their access to capital, much of which they drew from wealthier and more powerful traders and bankers in London, Liverpool, Le Havre, Hamburg, and other cities in the Atlantic world.

Because of their central position in the American and Atlantic economy, it was not surprising that within the United States these merchants and merchant bankers stood out in wealth and social status. While our knowledge about the distribution of wealth is imperfect, we know that in 1830, 69 percent of the most affluent Bostonians (those in the top 1 percent of asset holders) were merchants.[3] This top 1 percent owned 16 percent of the city's taxable assets in 1820, 33 percent in 1833, and 37 percent in 1848.[4] By 1860, Philadelphia's wealthiest 1 percent of the population owned 50 percent of the city's assets.[5] In New York, the concentration of wealth was even greater: about nine thousand individuals—1.4 percent of New York's inhabitants, most of them merchants—owned roughly 71 percent of the city's real and personal wealth in the mid-1850s.[6] In contrast, 84 percent of New York's economically active citizens owned no personal or real wealth of consequence.[7]

Given the importance of access to transportation, markets, and information, it is hardly surprising that most prosperous merchants lived in the eastern seaboard's largest cities: Boston, Providence, New York, and Philadelphia. In these cities, merchants brought together the resources of their respective hinterlands, provided plentiful shipping and banking facilities, and created vibrant markets for the sale of goods to be consumed elsewhere. Merchants also resided in smaller ports, such as Portland, Portsmouth, Newburyport, Salem, Marblehead, New Bedford, Newport, New London, New Haven, and Newark. As the century went on, however, these towns would decline in importance as the mercantile elite increasingly concentrated in larger towns and cities—especially in New York, which had the nation's best port, the best connections to a large hinterland, and the most forward-looking merchants. Related to the concentration of trade in a few seaboard cities was the rise of merchant communities in inland towns such as Albany, Buffalo, and Cincinnati, cities in which traders collected regional agricultural resources and shipped them to the East Coast in return for manufactured wares.[8] In a departure from the colonial era, connections to the rich agricultural hinterland mattered as a more fully national economy began to emerge.

Well into the 1820s, however, the world of merchants was still strikingly similar to what it had been in colonial times. No matter their home port, merchants accumulated their capital through simultaneous involvement in a wide assortment of activities. They bought and sold a staggering variety of goods. They organized the shipping of agricultural commodities to the West Indies and Europe. They financed agriculture by advancing credit to capital-hungry farmers. They insured goods in passage. And a small but growing number of merchants even began to invest in manufacturing. Salem trader Joseph Peabody, for example, had started his business career during the early years of the nineteenth century in privateering, before he moved to acquire interests in a large number of ships principally engaged in the Asia trade. Shipping pepper from Sumatra, tea from China, and sugar from the West Indies, he eventually controlled a fleet of eighty-three ships, and invested some of his profits in the Salem Marine Insurance Company, which he directed.[9] Cotton manufacturing also attracted massive investments from a group of wealthy Boston traders.[10] It was, moreover, common among merchants, such as the Astors of New York and the Peppers of Philadelphia, to diversify their capital into the ownership of land, especially urban land, a move that turned out to be a brilliant investment in a rapidly growing and urbanizing nation.[11] Insurance companies, which devoured huge amounts of capital, also proved to be among the favorite investment vehicles of East Coast mercantile elites.[12]

It was about that time, however, that the character of merchant businesses changed significantly from what it had been during the prior two hundred years. The rapidly increasing trade during the European wars, the cotton boom, and the growth of America's domestic markets enabled and encouraged merchants to specialize. By the 1810s, some houses traded exclusively in certain commodities, such as cotton, whereas others provided services such as shipping or financing. Wholesale and retail sales were increasingly handled by separate specialists, and so was the import and export business, while jobbers and auctioneers also contributed to the distribution of goods.[13] While some merchants focused on particular goods, others specialized by function: insurance, shipping, or banking. Bankers in particular now came into their own; some of them, such as the Girards of Philadelphia, the Morgans of Boston, and the Belmonts of New York, assumed powerful positions within their class and the economy more generally. One of the results of such specialization was that merchant interests became more diverse, contributing to some of the political divisions that would emerge prominently during the 1850s.

Even as the character of merchant businesses began to shift, however, their organization remained as it had been throughout history. Usually they were enterprises employing small numbers of people, typically only a few trusted partners—often relatives—and some clerks, who frequently were the sons of friends and business partners. They did not employ many wage workers. To expand the reach and scope of their operations, these merchant houses would create a web of interlocking partnerships, especially with traders in distant ports, which allowed transactions to remain in the hands of those they knew and trusted.[14] The goals of most partnerships were limited—for instance, to invest in a single voyage of one ship.[15] While such small and close-knit businesses allowed for enormous flexibility and rapid adjustments to changing conditions, they also made firms unstable. At any time a partner might die, move away, or look for new business opportunities elsewhere, bringing the partnership arrangements to an end. If a firm was to persist, owners had to allow younger members to join, and the choice of these partners was of crucial importance to the firm's continued prosperity, not least because there was no limit to the active partners' liability. Unlimited liability, in turn, helped to ensure that all partners vigilantly guarded their businesses' operations.[16]

These small and nimble firms began not only to carve out mercantile specialties but also to diversify into manufacturing and to solidify their powerful global position in shipping. They captured the dynamic trade with the newly emerging western states, and they increasingly profited from supplying a rapidly developing domestic market in the North. This ability to accumulate capital rapidly and steadily and to diversify their investments differentiated American merchants from mercantile elites in port cities such as Izmir, Alexandria, and Bombay, whose indigenous merchants were increasingly losing control over domestic and international commerce to British and other European traders.[17] American merchants instead were on their way to freeing themselves from European tutelage.

🐝 The position within the social structure of the young nation that all American merchants shared—characterized, for example, by their ownership of capital and their employment of others for wages—was not enough to make them a community and even less so a ruling class. After all, they competed against one another in the marketplace, had political interests that often put them at odds with one another, and originated from many different places throughout the Atlantic world. Circumstances, however, including wars, political instability, the risky nature of much of their business, and an increasingly diverse population of free farmers and wage workers, forced northern merchants and bankers to forge dense networks with one another. They did so by shoring up their traditional kinship and social connections, by building institutions, and by articulating shared habits, manners, and values. And though they continued to be deeply rooted in particular places— Boston's mercantile elite, for example, was different from that of Philadelphia—the nineteenth century saw them increasingly widen their networks and identities. They married one another across growing distances, invested in ever more remote business ventures, and engaged in collective political mobilization with their counterparts in other cities.[18] Indeed, American merchants were part of a national, Atlantic, and global community of traders that stretched from Boston to Buenos Aires, from Philadelphia to Liverpool, and from New York to Bombay.

It was in the family parlor that the mercantile elite tried hardest to forge a community. The parlor was, indeed, the cockpit of early-nineteenth-century businesses. Because firms were based to a significant degree on families, merchants, together with their wives, devoted extraordinary effort to maintaining and strengthening relationships among relatives and among larger social networks. Kin and friends, after all, helped to mobilize capital, skills, and information and to pass them on to the next generation.[19] Moreover, in a world of underdeveloped communication facilities and weak impersonal institutions, trust was essential to the conduct of business. Merchants and bankers had to allow their distant representatives significant leeway in making decisions. As Boston merchant Patrick Tracy Jackson put it to his factor, who represented him in India, "I depend . . . more upon your judgment when there than upon any directions I can now give for the disposal of any of my concerns."[20] The advance of credit, which was part of most business transactions, similarly was based on the reputation of individuals, at least until the 1850s, when the first credit-reporting agency came into being. Consequently, trustworthy conveyors of information were essential for making investment decisions, and family members were the best and sometimes the only partners in business.[21]

Central to these networks were marriages.[22] Because marriages created new alliances that often brought with them additional capital, information, and expertise, merchants ritualized them in forms strikingly similar to those of market exchanges.[23] They considered good marriage deals so important that even the Dun credit-reporting agency mentioned them in its assessments of the creditworthiness of enterprises.[24] As a Boston lawyer remarked in 1818: "It is an obvious advantage to the young folks to grow up in the midst of a respectable family connection. Weight of character and success are frequently promoted by the *esprit de corps* or *de famille*."[25]

Because business and marriage strategies were so closely linked, merchants were frequently related to one another. In New York, for example, 37 percent of the 163 wealthiest citizens in the 1850s were related, a density of kinship networks that led historian Robert Greenhalgh Albion to speculate that it is "difficult to tell whether the business or marriage ties were the first cause of success."[26] In Salem, in 1810, 42 percent of merchants ran a business alongside a relative. Most impressively, in Boston, a staggering 71 percent of the 79 wealthiest Bostonians had relatives among this small and select group in 1835.[27]

It fell to women to solidify these networks further by writing to relatives, inviting them to family affairs, and visiting them. Women, in effect, spun the threads that held these families together, both emotionally and economically.[28] Even as the public face of this powerful group of capital-owning Americans remained overwhelmingly male, its power was drawn in substantial ways from a much broader intergenerational network of kin and social contacts forged by women.

Family networks were also a prominent source of capital. Inheritance normally followed kinship lines and provided for the accumulation of capital over long periods. Indeed, by the mid-1850s, over two-thirds of all New York households assessed at more than $100,000 had inherited their wealth from the preceding generation. Similarly, 76 percent of wealthy Bostonians fell into this category in 1860.[29]

The institution of family thus countered powerful centrifugal economic forces and the lack of a common history among mercantile families. Kinship networks helped northern gentlemen capitalists—the Belmonts, Peabodys, Astors, Lowells, Whartons, and Steinways—to knit together a cohesive world, and indeed, the imperatives of capital accumulation, the structure of enterprises, and the weak development of banks and capital markets continually moved them to strengthen these nominally domestic networks.[30]

Building on family and kin relationships, merchants and bankers increasingly also created socially exclusive neighborhoods. A family's address imparted status as a member of the "better classes." While, in the early nineteenth century, merchants still lived close to their place of business near the wharves and warehouses, and indeed usually in the very same building, by the 1830s they began to move away from these increasingly crowded and unruly areas into new segregated residential neighborhoods.[31] Boston's mercantile elite had massed itself in the streets in and around Beacon Hill.[32] In New York by mid-century, the city's mercantile elite congregated in and around Union Square and the lower reaches of Fifth Avenue, while in Philadelphia the antebellum mercantile elites made their homes around Washington and Rittenhouse squares.[33] Even in remote Rochester, a historian found that the city's "social geography . . . was class specific" as early as 1834.[34] In their neighborhoods, mercantile families cultivated ways of living that marked them as distinguished and respectable.

As a result, the role of "family" was more than economic. It was the bedrock on which individuals' claims to respectability rested. And central to the maintenance of proper appearance was a system of distinct gender roles.[35] While men bought and sold cotton, negotiated loans, and acquired railroad securities, women fashioned themselves into guardians of the home, a space they and their husbands increasingly defined as being in some fundamental ways different from the public realm. In a world in which most women did manual work, merchant women focused their activities on the reproduction of the family by organizing the household, by maintaining emotional ties between family members, by raising children, and by presenting the family to the public.[36] Merchant women's sphere was only rhetorically private, as it was dominated by and devoted to a high-stakes, ritualized public display of refinement.

In a world of family-centered business based on trust and personal contacts, "character" proved critical. "Integrity of character and truth in the inner man are the prerequisites for success," counseled *Hunt's Merchants' Magazine*.[37] Since there were no formal systems for ranking worth, it was no great surprise that the first systematic efforts at reporting the creditworthiness of individuals focused to a large degree on character. Dun's credit-reporting agency described some traders as "worthy," "honorable," "of good moral character," "a man of family." It referred to others in less favorable terms, as, for example, when it concluded about one businessman that "his habits are free—he is not what might be called strictly temperate."[38] Indeed, "character," according to *Hunt's Merchants' Magazine*, "to a man of business . . . is as dear as life itself."[39]

Further contributing to the sense of "moral collectivity" among gentlemen capitalists was their relationship to work itself. Although most antebellum merchants were not self-made in the sense of having risen from poverty, their money remained largely working capital and provided only a precarious foundation for social status. Risks were often great, and most businesses exhibited a pronounced dependence on their owners' efforts, which made "the American merchant . . . a type of a restless, adventurous, onward-going race of people."[40] Supported by religious beliefs that promised redemption for worldly engagements, and not unlike Benjamin Franklin's and Max Weber's prescriptive theories of capitalism, New York banker Moses Taylor considered "hard work and prudence [to be] governing principles."[41] Unlike southern planters, who forged an identity focused on leisure, Taylor attributed his success to "work[ing] late."[42] As John Lowell of Boston put it, "punctuality . . . is the life and soul of credit."[43] Money demanded constant vigilance, a lesson instilled early on, when many young gentlemen began keeping personal account books that tracked their expenses.[44]

Particular patterns of consumption complemented this intense commitment to work. Women especially participated in public forms of consumption.[45] When Alexander T. Stewart opened his "marble palace"—a department store—in 1846, the *New York Herald* praised him for having "paid the ladies of this city a high compliment in giving them such a beautiful resort in which to while away their leisure hours of the morning."[46] Although notions of modesty and "dignified simplicity" still resonated, they increasingly took a backseat to more elaborate displays of taste and fashion.[47] Travel, another form of consumption, further delineated the boundaries of this society: summers dictated a move to the country; young adulthood meant trips to the American West and to Europe; and sickness required a visit to the spas of Europe. Knowing how to consume and perform, knowing how to deploy one's social capital, became a core element in asserting status and drawing boundaries around the respectable classes.[48]

Merchants also defined their distinct world by the design of the family dwelling. Its layout served to create the illusion of a sphere removed from the harsh realities of the market—a place where "gentlemen" could recover from the world of exchange. Thick carpets, heavy curtains, and ornate wallpaper insulated the abode from the outside world, offering a physical retreat from the noises, odors, and visual blur of the metropolis.[49] Although the home was ostensibly private, its relentless conformity was meant to make public statements. Portraits of living or deceased family members lined its walls, denoting continuity, tradition, and stability. Artfully carved furniture, neo-Grecian sculptures, crystal lights, and memorabilia from trips to exotic places served as testimony to material wealth.[50] By the second quarter of the nineteenth century, public and private spaces within the home were strictly separated; bedrooms and the kitchen remained invisible to visitors.[51] The function of rooms was increasingly specialized. Though modest by later standards, the antebellum merchant home served as an effective stage to display the material wealth and good taste of its inhabitants. It set them apart from fellow northerners who had neither the resources nor the inclination to create such an abode, not least because it was impossible to sustain such a home without the support of servants.

As merchants worked to set themselves apart from the rest of the urban population, they also created and strengthened institutions to sustain their networks. In New York, the most important of these was the Chamber of Commerce, a rapidly growing body of merchants and bankers founded in 1768.[52] It pledged to create a physical and political environment conducive to trade, to safeguard shipping, to construct canals, and to minimize tariffs. In short, it was committed to shoring up the political economy of Atlantic trade. "Its chief function," writes one historian, "seems to have been the facility with which it gave for coordinated expression of the views of the merchants."[53] In Boston, merchants with a very similar agenda had organized a Chamber of Commerce in 1793, while Philadelphia merchants had created that city's Chamber of Commerce in 1801. By 1858, ten Chambers of Commerce were operating in the United States, strengthening solidarities among the mercantile elite.

Augmenting these traditional economic associations was a relatively

new phenomenon: the social club. In Philadelphia, the nation's first so-
cial club, the Philadelphia Club, was founded in 1834. Two years later,
New York "gentlemen of social distinction" formed the Union Club.[54]
By the 1850s, three more social clubs had emerged in New York: the
New York Club, the New York Yacht Club, and the Century Club.[55]
Boston mercantile elites followed suit in 1851 with the founding of the
Somerset Club, an organization of men of social distinction who had
in earlier years congregated at the Temple Club and its successor,
the Tremont Club.[56] Further organizations ranging from the New-
York Historical Society to Harvard University, and from Massachusetts
General Hospital to the New York Bible Society, created powerful,
but largely local, networks.[57] Balls, parties, dinners, New Year's visits,
promenades, and other more informal activities cemented this solidarity among the mercantile elite.

These institutional, family, and kin networks also extended into the
world of politics. Merchant sons aspired to political careers and to fill
offices in local, state, and the national governments. The small scale of
the American state, the absence of elite competitors, and, until the
1820s, the still-restricted franchise allowed the existing association between economic and political power to flourish. Merchants not only
filled positions of political influence themselves but also developed personal relationships with people in elective office.[58] The influence of
northern merchants on political decisions consequently was sometimes
subtle but always powerful, securing infrastructure improvements, corporate charters, and favorable municipal decisions. The domination of
the Massachusetts Federalist Party by Boston merchants, for example,
allowed them to exert considerable influence over local and state politics during the first two decades of the nineteenth century, while their
importance to the Massachusetts Whig Party guaranteed merchants
power into the 1830s and 1840s. U.S. senators, congressmen, judges,
mayors, and state representatives all originated in the Boston mercantile elite.[59] Indeed, as one observer reported, until 1848 "wealthy Bostonians achieved a remarkable degree of political hegemony" in the city

and the state.[60] In New York, large numbers of mayors, governors, and U.S. senators, among others, traced their roots to the city's mercantile elite. Philadelphia merchants and bankers, among them members of the Wharton, Morris, Biddle, and Hopkinson families, were central actors in revolutionary and early national politics.[61] Robert Wharton, for example, began his career as mayor of Philadelphia in 1798 and was re-elected a full fifteen times.[62] This exercise of political power strengthened, in turn, economic, familial, social, and cultural networks.

❧ In the wake of the industrial revolution during the 1830s and beyond, this seemingly stable mercantile community increasingly came under pressure, especially from a newly emerging group of powerful artisans-turned-manufacturers and an ever more mobilized and enfranchised populace. Most significantly, the mercantile elite faced a challenge from "a rising industrialist class."[63] These men had accumulated capital in novel ways, and largely outside the older kinship and social networks of the northern mercantile elite. By the 1840s they were showing up in the higher ranks of the tax rolls at a remarkable rate. The majority of manufacturers were artisans who had expanded their shops and transformed themselves into entrepreneurs.[64] As one historian observed, by mid-century "they were knocking at the doors of political power and social prestige so long guarded by their commercial brethren."[65]

The industrial revolution came late to the United States, compared to England. But once it came, it arrived vigorously. As elsewhere, cotton spinning expanded first as merchants invested some of their capital in spinning mills built along the fast-flowing rivers of New England and the mid-Atlantic states. After 1830, railroads began crisscrossing the United States, devouring fabulous amounts of capital and eventually spurring the growth of coal mining, along with iron and steel production. Simultaneously, in cities such as New York and Philadelphia, Providence and Cincinnati, artisans expanded and reorganized their workshops as domestic markets consumed ever more manufactured goods. Their innovations focused at first not so much on new technologies but on the reorganization of work, as masters hired increasing numbers of unskilled workers to take over ever more subdivided tasks. New York's antebellum garment industry, for example, may have been based on age-old technologies, but it radically reinvented how garments came into being. [66]

Many merchants recognized early on the new industrial opportunities and invested some of their capital in these fledging enterprises. In Providence, for example, early investments in the country's infant cotton and woolen industries came from the town's wealthy overseas merchants, such as Moses Brown, who employed the services of Samuel Slater to erect North America's first cotton spinning mill. [67] In Boston, a group of wealthy merchants, the "Boston Associates," built the country's largest spinning and weaving factories. [68] By 1834, seven out of eight Boston merchants had an interest in the regional textile industry. [69] In various ways, observed historians Glenn Porter and Harold C. Livesay, "capital poured from the mercantile sector of the economy into the manufacturing sector." [70]

While many merchants grasped the new opportunities of the age, a growing group of manufacturers emerged from artisanal trades that did not cross into the world of trade. These manufacturers generally enjoyed few links to merchants, and they were not part of any of the well-established and close-knit merchant communities. Philadelphia textile manufacturer Thomas Dolan, for example, was of "obscure ancestry." [71] Robert Edwin Dietz, a maker of lamps, had first learned carpentry and then experimented in his "leisure hours, striving to burn various hydro-carbons which were at that time introduced for artificial lighting." Once successful, he "purchased with [his] small savings, a lamp and oil business" in 1840. By 1855 he owned a large lamp factory in New York City. [72] And sewing machine manufacturer Isaac Singer had learned the machinist trade in Auburn, New York, and spent more than a decade as a traveling mechanic and inventor before producing the machine that brought his name to households throughout the world.[73] Immigrant manufacturers in particular, according to historian Robert Ernst, often started out "as journeymen or master craftsmen and gradually accumulated enough money to acquire plants and become big employers."[74] Such artisans-turned-manufacturers were concentrated especially in New York and Philadelphia, but a rapidly growing number of them also made their homes in western cities such as Pittsburgh, Cincinnati, and Chicago.[75]

The working-class backgrounds of these manufacturers, their often rough manners and lack of genteel education, their dearth of kinship links to the mercantile elite, and the nature of their work itself marked them as upstarts. As one industrialist observed in 1845, "There is much complaint that mechanics [as many manufacturers called themselves] are not received evenly with merchants and professional men."[76] This divide was especially relevant because the manufacturers began to articulate sets of beliefs and embrace policies frequently at odds with those of the merchants.

The fault line separating the two social worlds is embodied in the life of Peter Cooper. Cooper, one of the major industrialists in mid-century New York, made his fortune in the glue business and later diversified into iron manufacturing.[77] His enormous wealth easily matched that of all but the very richest bankers and merchants. Yet in many ways Cooper and his family lived in a world very different from that of the typical merchant family. Cooper disdained the ostentatious display of riches that wealthy mercantile families had embraced.[78] He dressed simply and allegedly had to be persuaded to purchase a dress suit when he joined the reception committee welcoming the Prince of Wales to New York.[79] The bed in which he slept he had built with his own hands. Although Cooper moved into a respectable New York neighborhood in 1850, he had long lived near his glue factory and right next to the tracks of the New York & Harlem Railroad. Cooper's extraordinary position not only foreshadowed the material possibilities of manufacturing but also showed how the attendant social independence allowed for the emergence of a new kind of worldview.

Despite his extraordinary wealth, Cooper appears to have been typical of most manufacturers of the antebellum years. Manufacturers generally lived in more mixed neighborhoods than the merchants. In New York, for example, instead of congregating around Union Square, they preferred the sixteenth and twentieth wards, which encompassed an area west of Fifth Avenue between Fourteenth and Fortieth streets, where many of their workshops and factories were situated.[80] Characteristically, sugar refiner Alexander Stuart lived next door to his "enormous refinery," just as all three Steinways built brownstones adjacent to their piano factory. Heinrich Steinway's back door even opened directly onto the factory's courtyard.[81]

Mercantile and financial elites looked warily on these manufacturers. George T. Strong, a powerful and wealthy lawyer, derided Cooper as a "self-made millionaire glue boiler."[82] When Cooper received the Prince of Wales, he was chided for "playing the patriarchal Beau Nash [an eighteenth-century British dandy] with an assiduity at least as agonizing to its unaccustomed object as it was amusing to all the world besides."[83] Tellingly, the Dun credit-reporting agency remained quite skeptical about manufacturers long after their fortunes had solidified. In 1860 Dun described machine manufacturer John Roach as a "rough illiterate kind of man," pointing out that he "has made all he is worth."[84] Even Richard Hoe, an extremely successful maker of printing presses, was still just a "machinist" in the eyes of Dun.[85] It was not unusual to see industrialists such as Roach described as "poorly educated, rugged, brusque, and bold."[86] Even in Boston, where ties between merchants and manufacturers were closest, merchants did not always see the manufacturers as social equals.[87]

Contempt ran both ways. Industrialists often scorned the "Wall Street Gentry."[88] Excluded from the social universe of the nation's mercantile and financial elite, industrialists created their own institutions. In Providence, artisans-turned-manufacturers created the Mechanics' Association. In New York, "mechanics and manufacturers . . . found rallying points in the American and Mechanics' Institute."[89] The

New York Mechanics' Institute, for example, offered lectures on "natural and mechanical philosophy," classes in mechanical drawing, and mathematics, and "Meetings, Debates, and Discussions for the benefit of its members."[90] It boasted a library with holdings that included volumes on the natural sciences, engineering, philosophy, and history and ranging from Newton to Voltaire and Adam Smith.[91] In typical fashion, the institute provided a forum for exchanging technical expertise and for opportunities to train apprentices—two central concerns of industrialists.[92] These institutions were the nurseries of a different elite sensibility from that of the merchants, a sensibility that often translated into a distinct set of politics.

Prominent among these sensibilities was temperance. Indeed, temperance movements became vehicles of manufacturers' politics. In Providence during the 1830s, manufacturers spearheaded a movement to limit the consumption of alcohol. Through it, they hoped both to increase the productivity of their growing wage labor force and to improve their own claims to respectability.[93] In Rochester, New York, the city's small manufacturing elite mobilized to assert its authority by embracing evangelical revivals and temperance.[94] Merchants there and elsewhere remained minor participants in these movements.[95]

Living in a world of production, factories, proletarianization, and accelerating technological change also suggested to manufacturers such as Peter Cooper the need to distance themselves from the political economy of their mercantile counterparts. Their relationship to labor was more intimate and more central to their businesses than it had ever been to the nation's merchants. They impatiently asked for the federal government's support in defusing social tensions in America's cities by making land available to free labor agriculture. They also demanded protection for America's fledging industrial enterprises from foreign competition. And they had a virulent distaste for slavery and slaveholders, who they feared would undermine the free labor republic on which their vision of a rapidly industrializing nation rested. Embracing such a political economy of domestic industrialization (which, by the

1850s, would also become central to the program of the Republican Party) divided manufacturers not only from the southern ruling class but also, increasingly, from many of the merchants and bankers of the North.[96] Such rifts within the northern economic elite, in turn, opened the door for other social groups, including workers, to influence the politics of northern cities and states.

✄ As the artisans-turned-manufacturers began to assert themselves, so too did a rapidly growing group of lower-middle-class citizens and wage workers, many of whom had recently arrived from Europe. Boisterous demonstrations, unions, strikes, and non-elite political mobilizations became a common feature of urban life. Consequently, mercantile elites began to lose control over public space and politics, especially in cities and larger towns, where they now faced what they perceived as incomprehensible chaos. As the *New York Herald* complained, the "swearing, drinking, silly boors" of the Bowery had "destroyed all enjoyment" of carriage drives along city streets.[97] The city was noisy, it stank, and it permanently threatened encounters with its most undesirable inhabitants.

In Europe, the bourgeoisie, together with the aristocracy, clearly dominated the public sphere and public space. In the United States, however, the rich were slow to control public space or impose on it their own cultural institutions.[98] Whereas, in the late nineteenth century, economic elites used domination of cultural institutions to construct a class identity and to set themselves apart, in the early nineteenth century their predecessors displayed only modest aspirations for such public cultural influence. Museums, for example, that would later in the century become leading pillars of bourgeois self-definition remained in the first half of the nineteenth century cross-class amusements driven by profit. The Boston Museum, founded in 1841, exhibited stuffed animals and dwarves alongside the works of painters such as Sully and Peale.[99] In New York, Scudder's and Barnum's exhibited bearded ladies, legless wonders, live mud turtles, and bed curtains belonging to Mary, Queen of Scots.[100] These artifacts, along with themed exhibits on topics such as the "missing link" between men and apes, featuring "Mademoiselle Fanny" (an orangutan), attracted an audience ranging from manual workers to the millionaire manufacturer Peter Cooper.[101] "Tasteful" art collections were to be found, if at all, only in private homes. Neither Boston nor New York would see a major public fine arts institution until the late 1870s, nor would the upper class, as Paul DiMaggio has observed, succeed in the "sacralization of art, the definition of high culture . . . and the institutionalization of this classification."[102]

It was at this time, too, that workers, especially skilled workers, began organizing in trade unions and were becoming increasingly experienced in the use of strikes.[103] Throughout the 1830s, 1840s, and 1850s, a variety of workers—coachmen, pianoforte makers, cartmen, firemen and coal passers, house painters, carvers, marble polishers, journeymen ironmolders, box makers, cigar makers, tailors, printers, carpenters, and coopers—demanded higher wages and better working conditions, with mixed but notable success.[104]

Not only at the workplace, on the streets, or at the museums but also—and perhaps more important—in politics did merchants and bankers face an assertive citizenry who made their voices heard. Indeed, it was the dominance of the economic elite in this sphere that drove many working-class people into politics in the first place. In Rochester, whose politics until the mid-1820s had been overwhelmingly dominated by its richest residents, lower-middle-class citizens now captured political offices, and the tone of local deliberations became significantly more receptive to the concerns of working-class voters.[105] In New York, by the 1840s and 1850s, these lower-class citizens enjoyed some success as well. They began to have influence on the city's Democratic Party, finding by the 1850s that the party was responsive to their demands for housing reform and the abolition of the contract system, which had put additional pressure on wages.[106] Trade unions and working-class political organizations also began to have success in positioning their candidates on Democratic Party tickets.[107] And by the 1850s there emerged the figure of the party "boss," who would be receptive to some of the political demands of workers and lower-middle-class citizens.[108] In effect, "the boss, and local parties . . . all bore the imprint of the working classes."[109] Even in Boston, where the city's economic elite was perhaps most successful in securing political offices, their presence in City Hall and in legislatures declined.[110]

The shifting social origins of political officeholders demonstrate this slow but steady erosion of the once towering position of the antebellum mercantile elite. Not that the mercantile elite abandoned all political offices. Indeed, the venerable New York Union Club, testifying to its members' political involvement, counted in the 1850s among its ranks a former secretary of the navy, a U.S. senator, two governors of New York State, four mayors of New York City, and a governor of Rhode Island. Still, the number of upper-class New Yorkers holding political office did decline. Among 103 politically active wealthy New Yorkers, only 12 ran for office in the years between 1850 and 1863, compared to 32 who had been candidates between 1828 and 1840.[111] Of 1,052 Democratic Party activists in 1844, 38 percent were professionals or businessmen, while 33 percent were skilled workers, a substantial number that was probably without comparison in the Western world at large.[112] Increasingly, professional politicians of lower-middle-class or even working-class background moved into positions of political influence.[113]

ⓧ Propertied northerners found it difficult to respond to the challenges posed by an ever more assertive citizenry, not least because merchants and artisans-turned-manufacturers developed distinct understandings of the upheavals generated by industrialization and democratization. Of course, most well-to-do northerners throughout the antebellum years shared a number of common assumptions; they remained committed to progress, markets, and republican government. Emphasizing the fluidity of social divisions and the prevalence of social mobility, they made the denial of any kind of meaningful class divisions the cornerstone of their worldview. In a world dominated by monarchs and feudal traditions, this was a powerful emancipatory vision.

But increasingly, these common views were not enough to enable concerted political action. Merchants, emphasizing the importance of stability and predictability to their business enterprises, shunned disruptions of any kind, and desired a society orderly in its domestic relations and peaceful in its relations to the larger world. To them, order still depended to some extent on social hierarchies, and thus they struggled to maintain their position as stewards of the community. They also embraced an internationalist outlook, seeing themselves as the bearers of a fundamentally cosmopolitan spirit, an outlook undoubtedly strengthened by the memory of the devastating impact that the War of 1812 had had on their business undertakings. "Mercantile pursuits," argued the *American Merchant*, "discourag[e] physical conflicts between nations."[114] Without despotic rulers, enlightened free trade between free nations would create a common interest in preventing war.[115] This desire for peace extended, of course, to their own nation, which would eventually bring merchants into sharp conflict with manufacturers and western farmers.

The merchants' worldview, meanwhile, contrasted sharply with that of manufacturers, which emphasized the ingenuity and inventiveness of America's mechanics as the basis for the United States' rapid economic development. Furthermore, manufacturers were often hostile toward the mercantile elite, whom they saw as non-producers living off the labor of others, agitating for free trade, importing cheap goods from Europe, and providing credit on harsh terms. American industry, they believed, was a "wide-spread elm, with scores of parasites clinging to its trunk," namely, merchants and bankers.[116] Manufacturers asserted that, "unlike commerce," industry consists not merely in the exchange of goods but in "giving them a new form and greatly increased value." Therefore, "as an agent of civilization, all other pursuits fade before it."[117] Manufacturers often saw themselves as part of the "producing classes," or just as "labor," drawing a dividing line between themselves and the commercial or financial bourgeoisie. Indeed, while historian Sean Wilentz correctly noted that "the defense of the 'producing classes' [included] an amalgam of 'honorable' anticapitalist small masters and wage earners," it also allowed more substantial manufacturers to rally under the banner of an ill-defined but deeply rooted producerism.[118] This set manufacturers clearly apart from the mercantile elite and, even more so, its slaveholders.

Central to the manufacturers' worldview was a positive attitude toward labor, which was perhaps not surprising, considering that many of them had risen out of the ranks of the working class themselves. Glorifying the "mechanic arts," they saw "the dignity of labor . . . in its results, and not in the form of employment."[119] For these manufacturers, free labor was the basis of the republic, and in order to secure opportunities for all, the prospects for industry and agriculture had to be promising. Expanding opportunities for farmers, in effect, were to defuse the rising tensions between industrialization and democratization. Horace Greeley, the publisher of the *New York Tribune* and a leading spokesman for this position, wanted for "each man . . . an assured chance to earn, and then an assurance of the just fruits of his labors."[120] To secure the promises of free labor, America's fledging industries needed protection and farmers undisturbed access to the rich lands of the West—a political program that brought manufacturers into sharply drawn conflict with the nation's mercantile elite.

❧ These ideological divisions played themselves out in national politics, resulting in an increasing inability of northern economic elites to defuse the dangerous political tensions that emerged between southern planters and the growing population of free farmers in the expanding West. As early as the 1830s, a mounting debate about slavery and the future shape of the Union had driven a wedge deep between different upper-class groups. The vast majority of northern merchants wanted to accommodate the South, which meant acceding to its political interests. They sought to preserve the Union and were willing to compromise politically as well as ideologically with southern slaveholders on nearly every issue—from the crisis of the mid-1830s and the Compromise of 1850 to the Fugitive Slave Act and Stephen Douglas's Kansas-Nebraska Act.[121] Their ultimate interest in peace and union transcended all other political loyalties, and they exerted their power inside and outside the party system to promote compromise. "The peace . . . of the country," editorialized the *New York Journal of Commerce*, secured merchants' prosperity, and despite many merchants' abhorrence of slavery, called for political compromise with the southern ruling class.[122] They were essentially hoping for the continuation of a political economy focused on facilitating the export of slave-grown agricultural commodities to Europe and the import of manufactured wares in return.

Deeds followed words. In 1851, for example, James Beekman, a New York state senator and real estate speculator, deserted his party, the Whigs, and voted against the nomination of Whig antislavery advocate Hamilton Fish for the U.S. Senate, to the applause of many of New York's merchants.[123] That same year the bipartisan Union Safety Committee nominated a "Union Ticket" for statewide elections, with thousands of merchants signing a pledge that they would vote only for candidates favoring accommodation between North and South.[124] "It is time," they proclaimed, that "the trammels of party subjugation were thrown off, and our intelligent business men . . . stand up for the protection of their true interests."[125] During the 1852 presidential elections, a large number of upper-class New Yorkers again deserted the Whig Party and its candidate, Winfield Scott, and helped elect as president pro-compromise Democrat Franklin Pierce.[126] Bipartisan efforts at compromise with the South remained strong throughout the decade; in 1859, for example, one hundred leading New York merchants organized the "Union Safety Committee" to propagandize pro-Union politics in upstate New York. During the 1860 presidential elections, merchants urged a vote for the candidates endorsed by the Union Committee of Fifteen, which, again, supported northern accommodation to southern political demands.[127]

Most merchants rooted their economic activities in the existing arrangements of the Atlantic economy, especially the export of agricultural commodities and the import of manufactured goods. Trade in cotton was one of their most important businesses, and its sale enabled southerners in turn to purchase manufactured goods from northern merchants. The export of cotton also secured the nation's credit on the European money markets and thus kept the nation's banks afloat.[128] "The whole Commerce of the world turns upon the product of slave labor," argued *Hunt's Merchants' Magazine* quite accurately in 1855.[129] Cotton produced by slave labor, according to the political economist and editor of the *Dry Goods Reporter,* Thomas P. Kettell, "sustain[s] the rates of labor and capital, and secure[s] the prosperity of our country."[130] In an 1860 pamphlet, *On Southern Wealth and Northern Profits,* Kettell succinctly argued that merchants, bankers, and manufacturers, as well as artisans and northern farmers, enjoyed their prosperity only thanks to the south's "peculiar institution."[131] Indeed, the South's riches, he observed, accumulate in the North.[132] "If the South produces this vast wealth, she does little of her own transportation, banking, insuring, brokering, but pays liberally on those accounts to the Northern capital employed in those occupations."[133] Thus, he concluded, "the history of the wealth and power of nations is but a record of slave products."[134]

Such insights and interests motivated many merchants and bankers to struggle hard to maintain the existing structures of the Atlantic economy. The international banker August Belmont, for example, believed that there was no problem justifying the coexistence of slavery in the South and capitalism in the North. Having slave labor harvest the enormous agricultural potential of the United States was a route to prosperity that ultimately would also benefit the working class, he argued.[135] Free trade, territorial expansion through the construction of railroads and the annexation of Cuba, government restraint in religious matters, and a paternalistic attitude toward the white poor, he said, would create a rapidly expanding but socially stable society.[136] Stabilizing the institution of slavery would in effect also soothe the increasingly polarized society of the North. Belmont and his political allies strove for the classic coalition between the North's upper class and the landed gentry of the South, with the peculiar twist of integrating some urban workers into the fold.[137]

Those who, like Belmont, were invested in this order went to great lengths to accommodate the interests of slaveholders. During the 1830s, members of Providence's mercantile elite, for example, mobilized passionately against the growing ranks of abolitionists among the local manufacturers.[138] Boston's textile entrepreneurs, among them the Websters, Winthrops, and Everetts, consistently favored southern appeasement, not least to secure both a continued supply of inexpensive cotton for their factories and access to their crucial southern markets.[139] Indeed, in 1848 they would effectively split the Whig Party in Massachusetts into a "cotton" and a "conscience" faction.[140] Demonstrating a striking inability to imagine a different political economy, the *Journal of Commerce* editorialized in 1850, "We cling to the Compromise [of 1850] as long as there is hope."[141] The South had to be accommodated because "the Union [is] the great source of our dignity, the great spring of our prosperity, and the street-anchor of our safety."[142]

It was not just a defense of southern slaveholders for the sake of maintaining the Union that motivated many northern merchants and bankers. By the 1850s, the political underpinnings of the Atlantic economy itself also seemed threatened by the newly emerging Republican Party's program of tariffs, homesteads, and containment of slavery, endangering the modus vivendi under which the mercantile elite had thrived.[143] Merchants saw very little need for the activist government many Republicans envisioned; they rightly feared that the result would be a political economy fundamentally different from the existing one—a political economy that would undermine their central role.[144] What was at stake for them was nothing less than the future position of the United States in the world economy. Who controlled the federal government mattered a great deal in shaping this future.

Of course, this vision was not shared by all northern merchants.[145] While most took an essentially conservative view of sectional conflict, an important minority were confident that new and profitable arrangements could be forged in opposition to southern planters. At first, they were few in number, composed largely of religiously motivated abolitionists such as the New York merchant brothers Lewis and Arthur Tappan and the Boston merchants James Russell Lowell and Thomas Wentworth Higginson.[146] Yet the increasingly aggressive stance of the southerners, especially in the wake of the introduction of the Kansas-Nebraska Bill in the U.S. Senate, convinced growing numbers that the status quo was impossible to maintain.[147] For them it became necessary to take "united, deliberate, persistent and persevering action" to make sure that "such men no longer possess the Government," as the president of the New York Bank of Commerce, John A. Stevens, proclaimed in May 1856.[148] Such a step was the easier to take because, by the 1850s, an increasing number of merchants drew profits from domestic industrialization, import substitution, and the export of agricultural commodities grown by free farmers, thus rooting them in a different political economy from that of Atlantic trade.

The most important Americans in this group were not the merchants, however, but the manufacturers.[149] For example, among the 102 Providence activists who supported the creation of the Rhode Island Anti-Slavery Society in 1836, the vast majority were artisans and manufacturers, people such as Thomas Davis, who produced jewelry, and went on to become one of the most outspoken anti-slavery Democrats.[150] In New York as well, manufacturers were at the forefront of those calling for a more aggressive position toward the South. Horace Greeley, publisher of the *New York Daily Tribune*, who himself was socially and economically close to manufacturers and was among the first to move into the Republican Party, spoke for many of them when he demanded no "concession to slavery."[151] Greeley, like others, was attracted to the program of the Republican Party not only for its opposition to slavery but also for its broader vision of political economy. The promotion of free and capital-intensive agriculture in the West promised to create growing markets for manufactured goods. Moreover, the expansion of free farming in the West assured urban workers access to property and an escape from permanent proletarian status.

According to these manufacturers, the political power of southern slaveholders over the federal government was a threat to the continued development of the United States and to their own economic well-being. It was not only the spread of slavery as such but also the perception that the expansion of slavery would undermine the republican project, and especially threaten social stability in the North, that made them wary about the aggressive stance of southern slaveholders.[152] The expansionist projects of the South endangered free labor agriculture in the West, and without the "safety valve" of the West, they feared that a permanent working class would emerge in northern cities, further menacing the future of the republic. New Yorker Peter Cooper, iron manufacturer and lifelong Democrat who by 1856 found himself moving closer to the Republican Party, believed passionately that "two or three hundred thousand men" with a material interest in slavery should not be allowed to "continue to control" the government.[153] Their politics were driven by a firm belief in the superiority of the North's economy and system of labor. The New York clothing manufacturer George Opdyke, who ventured into economic and political theorizing with his 1851 *Treatise on Political Economy*, saw slavery as "clearly inconsistent with the principles of justice and political equality" and the root cause of southern economic backwardness. Capital bound in humans, he argued, could not be profitably employed otherwise, and the driving force of economic development—the motivation to work hard—was lacking in slaves, for whom "the hope of gain and the fear of want are both extinguished by the deprivation of freedom." This system, in Opdyke's mind, was in stark contrast to that of the striving and economically successful freemen of the North, including its wage workers.[154] Slave trader and railroad investor Isaac Sherman took a similar stand. As one of the early members of New York's Republican Party and a strong supporter of John C. Fremont's 1856 presidential campaign, he was committed to free labor. "Sooner or later," he wrote in April 1856, "the masses of this country will see that the real issue is the rights of men, the rights of labor . . . Democracy consists in the people ruling through justice, and in harmony with the great principles of equity, and that an attack upon the inalienable right of even a minority, is an aggression on the individual rights of the whole." While Sherman did not advocate interference with slavery in the South, he strongly opposed its extension.[155]

In addition to their opposition to any expansion of slavery westward, manufacturers also differed from most merchants in their view of what policies the government should adopt to promote and protect America's industries. They favored a "fostering hand of government" to shelter manufacturers from overseas competition and to develop the nation's infrastructure. Indeed, industrialists saw the state's support of manufacturing as the key variable in the development of domestic industries.[156] In this alternative vision of a political economy, quite distinct from the interests and inclinations of most merchants, "the products of the manufacturer, mechanic, and artisan, must be exchanged for the products of the cultivator, and these exchanges should form within our Union an internal commerce such as no nation has before exhibited."[157] Higher tariffs in particular would "promote the increased prosperity of American manufacturers." To fulfill this vision and to unlock the potential expansion of their own particular form of capital, industrialists increasingly collided with the political economy of the mercantile elite. It was in this context that the Republican Party provided a political basis for building a very different American society. And indeed, manufacturers were vastly overrepresented among the elite supporters of the young party.[158]

Tentatively, and to varying degrees, a growing number of upper-class Americans saw a future nation without slaveholders. They acknowledged the sharpening contradiction between the forces unleashed by rapid capitalist development and the blossoming of slavery, and they saw the persistence of pre-bourgeois forms of labor as well as the attendant political power of slaveholders over the federal government as damaging their own interests, which they had begun to identify with the national interest. They proposed, in effect, to further the promises of bourgeois revolution. In contrast to the majority of the northern economic elite, they were able to see beyond the sectional and class arrangements of the antebellum years. They were the ideological and political innovators of their class, and, in effect if not in intention, its revolutionary wing.

𝕏 By the late 1850s, American economic elites were sharply divided—socially, culturally, and especially politically. The most significant divide was between the upper classes of the North and the South. Within the North, however, the rise of new manufacturing elites had spotlighted an important rift, one which could be summed up as originating in sharply divergent views on the future of America's political economy. While many northern merchants, in order to continue enjoying privileged access to the levers of national political power, sought the political support of southern planters, most manufacturers, in contrast, found themselves politically aligned with a dynamic and rapidly growing group of free farmers. The conflict between these two groups—merchants and manufacturers—expressed in dramatic political realignments, eventually could not be contained within the nation itself, leading to its disintegration in the winter of 1860–61. In the short term, and especially sharply in the two decades preceding the Civil War, this deep split also hindered the ability of northern economic elites to embrace concerted political action at the local and state levels. This dissension allowed groups of non-elite citizens, who earlier in the century had been largely excluded from political power, to rise to positions of political influence.[159]

Secession and the war that followed struck the greatest political blow to the nation's mercantile elites, since it effectively destroyed the world that had allowed them to thrive economically and politically. Ironically, however, the war resolved many of their conflicts by crushing the political economy of Atlantic trade. The defeat of those who had sought profit from an essentially subordinate role of the United States vis-à-vis European economies allowed the United States and its economic elite, both merchants and manufacturers, to turn themselves into a potent presence on the world scene, united under the banner of continental industrialization. And state-supported industrialization, in turn, allowed these economic elites to gain decisive control over labor. The Civil War, in effect, marked the greatest defeat of northern mercantile elites, but it was also the precondition for the rise of the world's most powerful bourgeoisie during the Gilded Age.[160]

4

Gilded Age Gospels

❧

DAVID NASAW

Mrs. Lightfoot Lee, the wealthy widow who is the heroine of Henry Adams's 1882 novel *Democracy*, moved to Washington because she was "tortured by *ennui*. Since her husband's death, five years before, she had lost her taste for New York society; she had felt no interest in the price of stocks, and very little in the men who dealt in them; she had become serious." She was singularly distressed by New York's millionaires, who, having amassed great wealth, did not know what to do with it. "To let it accumulate was to own one's failure; Mrs. Lee's great grievance was that it did accumulate, without changing or improving the quality of its owners." She decided to relocate to Washington, D.C., so that she might "see with her own eyes the action of primary forces; to touch with her own hand the massive machinery of society; to measure with her own mind the capacity of the motive power. She was bent upon getting to the heart of the great American mystery of democracy and government." Like a passenger on an ocean liner, she wanted to visit "the engine-room and [talk] with the engineer." Mrs. Lee, in short, was abandoning New York City for Washington because "what she wanted, was POWER," and Washington was its seat.[1]

In the closing years of the nineteenth century, the Gilded Age millionaires would make the same journey, at almost the same time, and for the same reason. Whereas they had earlier refused—and rightly—to take Washington and the state capitals seriously as centers of economic decision or policy making, they had, by the late 1880s, begun to understand that democratically elected legislators had the potential to wield enormous power over the economy, and, unless deterred, might begin to do so.

The businessmen did not willingly enter the political realm.[2] Herbert Spencer, their guide in matters social, economic, and political, had, as we shall see, reinforced their self-interested conviction that the state had neither right nor reason to interfere in the workings of the economy. Government might subsidize new railroad construction, support manufacturing with protective tariffs, and pay handsome commissions to financiers who marketed its debt, but beyond that, the political sphere had to be permanently and resolutely walled off from the economic.

The first of the Gilded Age millionaires to be thrust into the political arena were the railroad barons. They entered politics at the state level in the 1870s to defend the railroads' prerogative to set their own rates against agrarian politicians who believed that elected officials had not only the right but also the obligation to intervene in the workings of the economy. By the late 1880s, as politicians at the federal as well as the state level signaled their intention to play an active role in economic matters, other business elites focused their attention—and resources—on Washington, if only to make sure that their particular interests would not suffer from new legislation. In the congressional debates over tariffs, railroad regulation, and antitrust bills, the millionaires divided along sectoral and regional lines. Only toward the end of the century in response to the threat posed by the advocates of "free silver," the monetization of which would have adversely affected all elements, sectors, and regions of the ruling elites,[3] did the businessmen unite—as a ruling class—to safeguard the rights of capital by limiting the power of the people's elected representatives to determine the nation's economic and monetary policies.

If we are to judge from the newspapers, Henry Adams and his fictional heroine, Mrs. Lightfoot Lee, were not the only Americans fascinated—and appalled—by the arrival of the millionaire businessmen. From the mid-1870s onward, the papers were glutted with stories of their comings and goings, their mansions and fêtes, their European excursions and Newport holidays. "This is an age of great fortunes," the *New York Times* exclaimed in one of its many articles on the phenomenon. "Never before in the history of the Republic have there been so many men who are very rich." And "very rich" in 1882, as the *Times* instructed its readers, was quantitatively different from "very rich" in any other era of the nation's history: "One who might have been 'very rich' in 1842 would not be accounted rich at all, with the same fortune, in 1882."[4] The *London Spectator* in a November 1882 article marveled at "the evidence forthcoming from America that fortunes may be accumulated on a scale of which Englishmen have little conception." While the English were pleased to earn 4 percent on their investments, Americans were satisfied with nothing less than "three times to ten times that rate."[5]

The millionaires who drew Mrs. Lightfoot Lee's special ire were those who had accumulated their capital elsewhere—in manufacturing, mining, or railroading—then relocated to New York City and retired from active work. The satanic majesty of late-nineteenth-century capitalism, only hinted at by Mrs. Lee, was its self-propagating nature. Fortunes, once made, continued to grow—and at an alarming rate. While the nouveau riche and their profligate children reclined in the lap of luxury, their money multiplied faster than they could spend it.

Mrs. Lee, like so many other Americans, scorned the millionaires not because they were rich but because they were so often—and, to her mind, so tediously—idle. On this she was in full agreement with legions of political radicals—greenbackers, grangers, agrarians, Alliance-men, free-silver advocates, populists, single-taxers, Marxian and Debsian socialists, anarchists, the Knights of Labor, trade unionists, and the organizers of the workingmen's parties—who stood together in condemnation of unearned fortunes. Labor was, for them, the source of all wealth; capital, a plundering whirlwind which swept away that wealth.[6]

The millionaires, wisely, did not attempt to justify their fortunes by claiming that they had earned them by the sweat of their brow.[7] Although they would not publicly dismiss the work ethic, they paid it little heed. In the new industrial age, they insisted, no individual could create wealth by himself. When, in September 1883, railroad tycoon Jay Gould was asked by a Senate investigating committee how many of the "men who conduct business enterprises and wield the power of capital" were "self-made," he responded that he would not call any of them "*self*-made exactly, for the country has grown and they have grown up with it."[8]

Andrew Carnegie made the same point in an article published in 1906. Wealth, he claimed, was "not chiefly the product of the individual under present conditions, but largely the joint product of the community." To illustrate his point, Carnegie conjured up the stories of four representative Gilded Age millionaires who had made their fortunes, respectively, in railroads in New York, iron and steel in Pittsburgh, meatpacking in Chicago, and mining in Montana.[9]

Not one of these millionaires, Carnegie asserted, had been responsible for creating the wealth of which he and his family partook so disproportionately. The railroad stocks of the first millionaire would have remained worthless had the communities his railroads served not soared in population. Similarly with the iron and steel manufacturer, the meatpacker, and the miner: "Their venture was made profitable by the demand for their products . . . from the expanding population engaged in settling a new continent. Without new populous communities far and near, no millionairedom was possible for them."[10]

Gould's and Carnegie's admission that the individual was not the primary agent in the creation of new wealth posed ideological and political problems for them—and for their generation of Gilded Age millionaires. If the community, for Carnegie, or the country, in Gould's formulation, was the source of all wealth, then why had so much of it accumulated in so few hands? And why should it remain there instead of being distributed more widely—and more equitably—among those who had had a hand in creating it? These were among the many questions posed by the political radicals, questions for which the millionaires had no easy answers.

Carnegie was unique among his contemporaries in that he too was troubled by the seemingly arbitrary and strikingly "unequal distribution of wealth," which, he conceded, "lies at the root of the present Socialistic activity . . . Multi-millionaires, a new genus, have appeared, laden with fortunes of such magnitude as the past knew nothing of. The extremes in the distribution of wealth have never been as great as they are to-day . . . This has naturally attracted the attention of the wage earners and others not deluged by the gold showers." These inequalities had to be addressed, Carnegie warned; they were morally offensive and politically dangerous.[11]

While some of his fellow millionaires, John Davison Rockefeller most conspicuously, would attribute their financial success to God, who, they claimed, had blessed them with riches because they had followed his teachings,[12] Carnegie required a secular version of the Protestant ethic to explain and justify his own oversized fortune. He found it in the works of the British philosopher Herbert Spencer. Spencer became his spiritual and political mentor because Spencer revealed to Carnegie and his generation of millionaires the existence of a providential plan neatly encompassed within the term "evolution," which explained—and, in explaining, justified—the accumulation of so much wealth in so few hands.

The businessmen had accumulated their fortunes, Spencer taught, not because they were more righteous, more pious, more industrious, or more diligent than their employees, but because they possessed what Carnegie called the special "talent for organization and management" required in the new industrial age. "It is a law . . . that men possessed of this peculiar talent for affairs, under the free play of economic forces must, of necessity, soon be in receipt of more revenue that can be judiciously expended upon themselves; and this law is . . . beneficial for the race."[13]

The successful businessman had been entrusted with surplus capital because he was, in the larger evolutionary schema, best suited to spend it wisely on behalf of the community. In the quest for riches, only the fittest had survived—because they were the fittest. Those who had proved their talents in the battle of accumulation, Carnegie argued, were obliged to apply those same talents in spending down their fortunes. It was the duty of the "man of wealth . . . to consider all surplus revenues which come to him simply as trust funds, which he is called upon to administer . . . in the manner which, in his judgment, is best calculated to produce the most beneficial results for the community." By fashioning Spencer's evolutionary philosophy into a high-minded apologia for capital accumulation, Carnegie had rationalized and justified the maldistribution of wealth that so dramatically marked the new Gilded Age. His "Gospel of Wealth" laid out a defense of unrestricted capital accumulation as a "beneficent necessity" for the entire community, rich and poor. The people, he argued, were best served by allowing capitalists to accumulate as much money as they could, because the more wealth that was accumulated in wise hands, the more that could be given away—wisely—by the capitalist-philanthropist acting "as trustee and agent for his poorer brethren, bringing to their service his superior wisdom, experience, and ability to administer, doing for them better than they would or could do for themselves."[14]

Carnegie's solution to the political and social problems generated by the growing maldistribution of wealth—that the rich give away their money before they died—was too radical to be adopted by his fellow millionaires. Nonetheless, in his reliance on Spencer's philosophy to explain the role of the millionaires in the new industrial age, he was well within the mainstream of elite thought. Carnegie's generation of Gilded Age millionaires—and intellectuals—was drawn to Spencer's evolutionary theory because it made sense of historical change by defining it as progress.[15] As Henry Adams, born in February 1838, a little more than two years after Carnegie, recalled in his autobiography, "For the young men whose lives were cast in the generation between 1867 and 1900, Law Should be Evolution from lower to higher."[16]

Carnegie's own discovery of Spencer was a life-altering moment, or at least this was how he described it in his *Autobiography*. "I remember that light came as in a flood and all was clear. Not only had I got rid of theology and the supernatural, but I had found the truth of evolution."[17] Carnegie was not alone in this joyous reception of Spencer's evolutionary philosophy. "In the three decades after the Civil War," Richard Hofstadter has written, "it was impossible to be active in any field of intellectual work without mastering Spencer."[18] Even the fictional Mrs. Lightfoot Lee talks of him "for an entire evening with a very literary transcendental commission-merchant."[19]

In 1882, the year Adams's novel *Democracy* was published, Herbert Spencer embarked on a tour of the United States, though one in which he declined to give any public lectures. The tour culminated in a full-dress banquet with a veritable who's who of American elites in attendance. Carnegie was there, as were journalists E. L. Godkin, Horace White, and Charles Dana; George Roberts, president of the Pennsylvania Railroad; future U.S. senators Carl Schurz, Chauncey Depew, and Elihu Root; congressmen Abram Hewitt and Perry Belmont; Andrew Green, who had been the major force behind the building of Central Park, and Calvert Vaux, one of the park's landscape architects; Albert Bierstadt, the artist; former secretary of state William B. Evarts; businessman Cyrus Field; Charles Francis Adams, Henry's father and former ambassador to Great Britain; William Graham Sumner and

Lester Ward, who would found the American schools of sociology and economics; and two of the country's most influential preachers, Henry Ward Beecher and Lyman Abbott.[20]

Spencer captivated Carnegie's generation not simply because he coined the phrase "survival of the fittest," which became part of their language, but because he constructed a synthetic philosophy that explained everything under the sun and the solar system beyond it. There was, for Spencer, a discernable order to the course of human events and the structure of human societies, study of which would reveal the existence of moral laws that were "like the other laws of the universe—sure, inflexible, ever active, and having no exceptions."[21] Societies that obeyed these laws would prosper; those that disregarded them would not. The social edifice which lacks *"rectitude* in its component parts [and] is not built on *upright* principles . . . will assuredly tumble to pieces. As well might we seek to light a fire with ice, feed cattle on stones, hang our hats on cobwebs, or otherwise disregard the physical laws of the world, as go contrary to its equally imperative ethical laws."[22]

"The enslavement of the negroes," he noted, "serves for a good example." Acting from the precepts of a political economy that did not coincide with moral law, the slave masters had sought for themselves "a mine of wealth" by replacing free with slave labor. "Their golden visions have been far from realized however. Slave countries are comparatively poverty-stricken all over the world . . . West-Indian history has been a history of distress and complainings . . . The southern states of America are far behind their northern neighbors in prosperity."[23]

For Spencer, "beneficent necessity" governed the natural world and human society. "Progress, therefore, is not an accident, but a necessity," as long as the laws of evolution were understood and obeyed, as they had not been by the slaveholders. Spencer banished chance, luck, superstition, and happenstance from the universe, certified that industrial society was governed by "the very laws of life," and asserted that those laws were moral laws. Industrialization had triumphed in England, western Europe, and the United States because it represented a forward step in evolutionary progress. The fact that industrialization also led to the impoverishment of some was regrettable, but it would have been more unfortunate still had those left behind been permitted to derail the forward movement of a new industrial society. "Pervading all nature we may see at work a stern discipline, which is a little cruel that it may be very kind," Spencer had written in *Social Statics*. "It seems hard that an unskilfulness which with all his efforts he cannot overcome, should entail hunger upon the artizan. It seems hard that a labourer incapacitated by sickness from competing with his stronger fellows, should have to bear the resulting privations. It seems hard that widows and orphans should be left to struggle for life or death. Nevertheless, when regarded not separately, but in connection with the interests of universal humanity, these harsh fatalities are seen to be full of the highest beneficence."[24]

Spencer opposed poor laws, state-funded or directed charity, and government interference with the economy not because he wished the poor to live miserably or die faster, but because he believed that such interventions meddled with the natural laws of the economy. "The process *must* be undergone, and the sufferings *must* be endured . . . There is bound up with the change a *normal* amount of suffering, which cannot be lessened without altering the very laws of life."[25]

The political implications of Spencer's argument were clear-cut and easily understood by the American business elites. Nothing and no one, certainly not the state or its politicians, he argued, should be permitted to interfere with the "natural" workings of the industrial economy and the progress of "beneficent necessity." The laws that governed the forward movement of the new industrial age had to be treated as sacrosanct.

It is striking, indeed, how often the multimillionaires justified their business practices by reference to one or another "law" of industrial society, laws which, they asserted, could not be repealed or amended in the political arena. John D. Rockefeller, responding in his *Ran-*

dom Reminiscences to critics who had suggested that there was something unnatural, even criminal, about the extraordinary "increase in the value of [Standard Oil's] possessions," claimed that "it was all done through the natural law of trade development."[26] Jay Gould, asked by the Senate investigating committee if he believed a "general national law" was needed to regulate railroad rates, responded that they were already regulated by "the laws of supply and demand, production, and consumption."[27] Carnegie continually invoked unwritten laws of competition, consolidation, aggregation, supply and demand, and wages and profits to explain why he and his company had succeeded.[28]

With such overt appeals to law, the Gilded Age businessmen were refuting the popular notion that that there was something sinister about their material success. Jay Gould had, after all, been referred to in the newspapers as the Mephistopheles of Wall Street, a backhanded tribute to his otherworldly financial successes. In the wake of the Crédit Mobilier, the "Whisky Ring," and the Erie scandals, Carnegie and Rockefeller took care to distinguish between legitimate businessmen like themselves and those they referred to contemptuously as the "speculators." "The speculator and the business man tread diverging lines," Carnegie explained in a speech to the students of Curry Commercial College in 1885. Speculators were never "citizens of first repute" and would therefore never succeed in the long run. "I have lived to see all of these speculators irreparably ruined men, bankrupt in money and bankrupt in character. Gamesters die poor."[29]

Carnegie was, of course, dead wrong. No matter what Spencer's philosophy might have predicted, the Vanderbilts and Goulds and the politicians who protected them—for a handsome price—did not end up in the poorhouse. On the contrary, they did remarkably well. But that, the business elites would argue, was not the fault of industrial capitalism. As Rockefeller himself acknowledged, "a corporation may be moral or immoral, just as a man may be moral or the reverse; but it is folly to condemn all corporations because some are bad, or even to be unduly suspicious of all, because some are bad."[30]

Spencer's formulations allowed all this malfeasance to be washed away as inconsequential in the long term. The successful businessman, he taught, was successful because he recognized and obeyed the economic laws of the industrial age. The danger to future progress and prosperity came not from those who followed the dictates of evolutionary progress, like the capitalists, but from those who interfered with them.

Jay Gould, when asked by the Senate investigating committee about the danger posed to the people by the newly developing "aristocracy of wealth," responded that there was no "need to be afraid of capital . . . What you have got to fear is large, ignorant masses of population. I don't think the liberties of the people have anything to fear from capital. Capital is conservative and scary [i.e., frightened]; but what you have to fear in a republican government like ours . . . is large masses of uneducated, ignorant people."[31]

Although Gould did not specifically mention the events of July 1877 in his testimony, there could be no doubt that this was what he was referring to. On July 16, 1877, firemen and brakeman working for the Baltimore & Ohio Railroad in Martinsburg, West Virginia, on being informed that their wages were being reduced by 10 percent, walked off their jobs. The West Virginia militia, deployed to keep traffic moving, joined the strikers. The strike quickly spread to Baltimore and on to every major and dozens of minor railroad hubs across the country.

This was the beginning phase in labor's protest against the laws of industrial capitalism that indicated wage cuts as the antidote to depressed profits. In 1883, the year that Gould testified before the Senate committee investigating the relations between labor and capital, the Brotherhood of Telegraphers struck his Western Union Telegraph Company. In 1885 and 1886, Knights of Labor locals led strikes against his railroad lines in the Southwest. Also in 1886, there were walkouts in the Pennsylvania coal mines, at the McCormick reaper works in Chicago, and on New York's streetcars. On May 1, 1886, advocates for the eight-hour day led strikes and protests in several different cities. In

Chicago the demonstrations exploded into violence when a bomb went off in Haymarket Square.

The business elites were universally frightened and appalled at the determination—and the tactics—of striking workers and their unions. There was, however, little agreement on what should be done. While a few of the multimillionaire businessmen, notably John D. Rockefeller and Henry Frick, were opposed to recognizing any labor organizations, most were unsure whether or not to negotiate with them. Were organized trades unions going to make it easier or more difficult to manage large and diverse labor forces? Would there be more or fewer work stoppages if union leaders negotiated written contracts which they might then be obligated to enforce? These questions remained as yet unanswered. When asked by the Senate investigating committee in 1883 whether he thought "the labor unions of the country are an injury or a benefit to the laborers and the country generally," Gould weakly responded, "Well, I cannot say about that." He supported the attempt of workers to organize themselves into mutual aid societies, but opposed the notion that they were entitled to be represented by unions in negotiating wage rates, because, as he reminded the senators, the price of "labor, like everything else, is regulated by the law of supply and demand."[32]

Andrew Carnegie took a different position. In 1886, a year in which over 1,400 work stoppages occurred involving over 400,000 workers, Carnegie delivered two rather strikingly pro-union articles to *Forum*. In the first, published in April just before the eight-hour-day strikes and the Haymarket bombing, he declared himself resolutely in favor of the "right of the working-men to combine and form trades-unions," a right he considered "no less sacred than the right of the manufacturer to enter into associations and conferences with his fellows."[33] Four months later, after the events in Chicago, Carnegie published a follow-up piece in which he not only reaffirmed his position on trades unions but also specifically defended the right to strike of the railway workers on Gould's Wabash system and the streetcar operators on the Third Avenue Railway in New York City.[34]

Responsible unions and their leaders, Carnegie believed, not only provided a check on unscrupulous employers who contravened economic laws by setting wage rates too low, but also, and more important, provided a check on their own members. "Trades-unions must, in their very nature, become more conservative than the mass of the men they represent," he observed. "If they fail to be conservative, they go to pieces." Carnegie had nothing but praise for union leaders who, like Terence Powderly, Master Workman of the Knights of Labor, intervened to avert strikes "against the wishes of the less intelligent members of [the] organization."[35]

Nowhere in Carnegie's 1886 article was there mention of any role the state or federal government might play in resolving labor disputes. For Carnegie, Gould, and their fellow Gilded Age millionaires, disputes between labor and capital were economic issues, pure and simple. The laws of supply and demand which determined wage rates were inviolate. Only when workers attempted to interfere with these laws by striking, and then violently preventing "scabs" from taking their jobs and threatening private property, did the state have the right—and the obligation—to intervene. On this point there was universal agreement among the nation's elites.

In the wake of the 1877 general strike and then again, though to a lesser degree, in 1886, old wealth and new, manufacturers, merchants, and bankers, all called on their elected officials to construct new armories, equip and train militias and "national guards," and rebuild the army that had been decommissioned at the end of the Civil War. Thomas Scott, whose Pennsylvania Railroad had suffered perhaps the greatest property loss in 1877, suggested that troops be garrisoned in those cities which might in the future be the sites of strike activity.[36] In New York City, where there had been no major strikes during 1877, businessmen responded, nonetheless, to what they perceived to be a threat of violence by calling for preemptive military action. When funds were solicited to build a new armory to house an expanded militia, even Junius S. Morgan, Pierpont's father, safely ensconced in his London office, felt obliged to contribute $500.[37]

The businessmen who argued for enhanced police powers to break strikes did not, in doing so, believe that they had trampled on what they still regarded as the inviolable separation between the political and economic realms. They had called on the state to protect private property, not to interfere in the workings of the economy.

Having refortified the state and, though they would have denied it, extended the definition of its rightful police powers, the business elites had effectively defused a major source of opposition. With the assistance of the police, the state militia, and the army, they had maintained order at their workplaces. They would similarly succeed in turning back a threatened workingman's insurgency at the nation's polling places that emerged in the aftermath of the 1886 strikes. In that year alone, workingmen's parties came close to electing mayors in New York City and Chicago and succeeded in doing so in Milwaukee and several smaller cities, from Rutland, Vermont, to Rendville, Ohio.[38] Even in those cities and states where there were the greatest concentrations of organized workers, the workingmen's parties quickly came up against the irrefutable demographic fact that there were simply not enough workers who identified politically as workingmen to control the statehouses or exercise any great influence in national politics. In coalition with other political radicals, labor might have played a larger role in Gilded Age politics, but the cultural, political, ethnic, religious, regional, and social differences that separated the organized workingmen from one another—and from their potential middle-class and agrarian allies—were too great to overcome, especially given the structure of the American political system and the dominance of the two major parties within it.

The elite businessmen of the Gilded Age had far more to fear, as they soon discovered, from the agrarians, who, if initially neither as violent nor as vocal in their opposition to capital as the striking workers, were every bit as dedicated to circumscribing its power. Most of the nation's manufacturing was, in the 1880s and 1890s, contained within a narrow belt that extended from New England south through Pennsylvania and west through Ohio and parts of the upper Midwest. Outside this manufacturing belt a large and increasingly vocal segment of the population in the prairie and southern states was convinced that it was being robbed of its rightful share of the nation's newfound wealth by eastern capitalists who controlled the nation's railroads and set its monetary policy.

It was these "agrarians," organized into what became known as the Grange or the granger movement in the 1870s and 1880s, and thereafter the National Alliances and the People's Party, who posed the greatest challenge to the business elites. Unlike the industrial workers, the agrarians had sufficient votes in the statehouses and in Congress to translate their suspicions of capital into legislation designed to rein in its manifest powers.

The agrarians' chief concerns were with the railroad officials, who, they believed, were overcharging them, and the upholders of the gold standard, who were taking money from their pockets by deflating commodity prices. While the question of the gold standard would, as we shall see, be effectively removed from the political agenda in the late 1870s, the question of railroad rates would dominate the prairie state legislatures throughout the 1870s and into the 1880s.

The issue of railroad regulation was, in fact, the Trojan horse with which the politicians would breach the walls protecting the economy from their interference. As corporations chartered by the states, funded by them and by Congress, and charged with moving the mails in peacetime and the troops in wartime, the railroads were tied to government in a manner quite different from other big businesses. Jay Gould acknowledged as much in his 1883 testimony before the Senate investigating committee. There was a "great difference," he admitted, between businesses, like the railroads, which had sought state incorporation and those that had remained purely "private." "Corporate property," Gould insisted, had "duties to the public" which private property did not.[39]

The granger state legislators, instead of regulating the railroads directly, organized state commissions to oversee them, following the earlier example of the New England legislatures. Unlike the "weak" New England commissions, however, which did little more than collect data and publicize abuses, the "strong" prairie state commissions were explicitly authorized to set maximum rates for passengers and freight.

The railroad directors fought back by unilaterally declaring the new railroad commissions unconstitutional and refusing to obey them until the courts had explicitly directed them to do so. When the state courts ruled in favor of the commissions, the directors took their cases to the Supreme Court, which, in *Munn v. Illinois,* also found in favor of the legislatures' right to organize regulatory commissions.

The courts having failed them, the railroad directors recognized that they had no choice now but to enter the political arena to protect their investments from what they believed was improper interference. They used every weapon in their considerable arsenals to pressure the state legislatures to cease their attempts to regulate railroad rates. They reduced service on roads they claimed were no longer profitable; they hired writers and bribed newspaper editors to publish anti-commission articles and editorials; they recruited and funded candidates favorable to their cause to replace those who opposed them; and they threatened to punish states with strong regulatory commissions by withdrawing investment capital and ceasing any new construction.

In the end, it was their threat to cease investing capital and building new lines, thereby leaving un-served cities, towns, and rural cities forever isolated, that proved decisive. Although the railroads failed to get the prairie state commission laws repealed or the commissions abolished, by 1880 they had succeeded in pressuring the legislators in the four states with "strong" commissions to strip the commissioners of their authority to set rates. "Only hollow oversight commissions were left," observes Gerald Berk, "empowered, like [the New England commissions, to do no more than] collect and disseminate data and publicize the most egregious of rail abuses."[40]

The railroad directors had, in the course of their campaign against the regulatory commissions, learned a valuable lesson. While it might no longer be possible to prevent state legislators from intervening in economic matters, it was possible to minimize the damage they might do. Popular animus against the railroads was too great for the politicians to ignore, but that animus could be contained. "Weak" regulatory commissions were a most effective antidote to democratic rule by elected state officials. Chauncey Depew, who was counsel to William Vanderbilt and the New York Central Railroad from 1875 to 1883, recalled in his memoirs that, while originally an opponent of the commissions, he had become "convinced of their necessity . . . It seemed to me that it was either a commission or government ownership, and that the commission, if strengthened as a judicial body, would be as much of a protection to the bond and stock holders and the investing public as to the general public and the employees." The key word here was "judicial." As long as the commissions were isolated from the pressures heaped on legislators by a railroad-hating public, they might function as effective barriers to political interference.[41]

By the late 1870s, the focus of the political campaign for railroad regulation had begun to move from the state legislatures to Congress. Bills mandating federal railroad regulation were introduced—with considerable support from prairie state congressmen—on several occasions from 1874 to 1886, only to be killed in the Senate or bottled up in conference committees. The final impetus toward passage came in October 1886, when the Supreme Court effectively overturned *Munn v. Illinois* and declared that state commissions could no longer regulate rates on trips that began or ended beyond their borders. With state regulation now rendered unconstitutional, the demand for federal regulation intensified, and the political battleground shifted permanently from the state legislatures to Congress.

In the prairie state legislatures, the railroads' principal opponents had been farmers and local merchants who supported the regulatory commissions. In Congress, the greatest threat would come from other business interests, particularly those in the manufacturing sector. Once the wall between the political and economic spheres had been breached by the establishment of state regulatory commissions—and, by the mid-1880s, the acceptance of the inevitability of some sort of federal regulation—each regional and sectoral business group was compelled to enter the political arena to protect its particular interests.

By the late 1880s, the Senate was already known as the "Millionaires' Club" in recognition of the many businessmen who served there, in large part to protect the interests of their regions and/or sectors. Senator Henry Payne of Ohio, the father of the Standard Oil treasurer, looked after Standard Oil; Senator Leland Stanford, a director of the Union Pacific, protected his railroad's investments on the West Coast; and Senators James Fair and John Jones of Nevada protected the mining interests of their state.

The almost blatant disregard of larger class interests was in sharp contrast to the situation in Europe, where, as Thomas McCraw has written, "political battles during the late nineteenth century pitted a fairly united business community against a powerful labor movement. In America, by contrast, the most conspicuous political warfare of that time matched *one group of businessmen against another:* carriers versus shippers, commodity farmers versus mortgage bankers, small wholesalers and shopkeepers against large firms."[42]

When the gloves came off, these intra-class battles could turn as vitriolic and potentially violent as the disputes between capital and labor. In 1889, in an address to the Pennsylvania state legislature in Harrisburg, with the governor presiding, Andrew Carnegie attacked the Pennsylvania Railroad for extorting money from the people of the state, especially those in the west, by charging Pittsburgh manufacturers twice the rates that Chicago and midwestern industrialists had to pay. In language as provocative as that used by any labor militants,

Carnegie, claiming that he was speaking for "the great army of labor" whose livelihood was imperiled by the Pennsylvania Railroad, recalled that during the Civil War the working people of Pittsburgh had taken to the streets to prevent guns being shipped south. "They did this in the interest of the nation. Are they to be forced into a similar protest against the Pennsylvania Railroad Company carrying supplies past Pittsburgh furnaces to furnaces in other states upon terms they refuse us?" The threat was clear. Unless the railroad reduced the rates it charged to ship coke from southwestern Pennsylvania into Pittsburgh, Carnegie would call on his workers to block shipments through the city to manufactories farther west. "Is it to be expected that, if we are compelled to close our works in consequence of the railway discriminations I have cited, our men will stand calmly looking on and see Ohio and Chicago furnaces fed while ours are idle?"[43] To eliminate the threat of violence, which he had called into being, Carnegie asked the state legislature to establish a "strong" commission to regulate railroad rates.

Not every manufacturer, of course, agreed with Carnegie that the railroads needed regulating. John D. Rockefeller, for example, whose Standard Oil Company profited enormously from rebates, opposed giving an Interstate Commerce Commission the authority to eliminate them. His representative in the Senate, Henry Payne, voted against the final bill because it outlawed rebates.[44] By the time Congress, after extensive debate and lobbying by a wide variety of business groups, passed an Interstate Commerce Act in 1887, that act was so compromised by inconsistencies and ambiguities that it would take the new commissioners several years to figure out precisely what they had been authorized to do.

The business elites, having established their foothold in Congress, fought with one another not only about regulatory policies but also about tariffs. As on railroad regulation, each sector and region pursued its own, very particular interests. Merchants favored low tariffs, the manufacturers high ones, and the farmers tariffs on wheat but free trade for manufactured goods. "The conflict over tariffs," Sven Beckert has written, "pointed . . . to the enormous access of very specific 'interests' to the political decision-making process." The final tariff bills were endlessly complicated with "hundreds of amendments, favoring this or that specific industry or company." The 1894 bill contained more than six hundred amendments.[45]

There was, it appeared, only one issue on which all the business interests could agree, and that was on the necessity of maintaining the gold standard against those who wanted to inflate the currency by coining silver. Those who held large amounts of capital, no matter how or where it had been accumulated, did not want the value of that capital diluted by inflation; those who bought and sold securities in Europe (and that included most major bankers, merchants, manufacturers, and railroad directors) feared that an unstable dollar, not backed by and convertible to gold, would be disastrous for business.

The gold standard proponents evoked Spencerian evolutionary laws by asserting that gold was the only "natural" currency. All other currencies were artificial because they were manmade and their values politically assigned. "Government-made money stood in conflict with nature's creation of true monetary value," notes Gretchen Ritter, summarizing the case made by the "gold bugs." The value of a gold dollar, or a dollar backed by gold, remained steady because its worth was determined by the "bullion within it and not the government stamp affixed to it."[46]

The currency question was so volatile, so regionally inflected, and so destructive to party unity that a majority of Democratic and Republican members of the House voted to affirm, over President Hayes's veto, the 1878 Bland-Allison Act, which, by making silver legal tender but limiting the amount the government could purchase, bought political peace for almost a decade. Removing the currency question from the political arena was in the interest of businessmen of both parties who were agreed that neither the people nor their elected representatives should have any role in setting monetary policy. As James

Garfield had explained in a speech delivered in 1878 and later published in pamphlet form, there was "a higher law above legislation—the law of supply and demand—pervading and covering all," and it alone should determine the shape and value of the nation's currency. "No men are wise enough to do it [regulate currency], and if they were, dare you trust so delicate a thing as that to the partisan votes in Senate and House? If you have so much faith as that in Congress, your faith exceeds mine."[47]

The fact that the major parties were able to take currency questions temporarily off the political agenda with the passage of Bland-Allison in 1878 did not mean that those questions were not discussed elsewhere—in articles, pamphlets, and by the several minor parties that advocated government issuance of greenbacks or free silver as legal currency. While the agitation for the issuance of greenbacks or government-issued "fiat" money had been effectively silenced by the 1880s, the question of silver remained of vital importance, especially in the agrarian West and South, which had suffered from the fall in commodity prices that followed the postwar shrinkage of the money supply and the return to the gold standard.

In 1889–90, as Richard Hofstadter reminds us in *The Age of Reform*, "six new Western states with strong silver movements—Idaho, Montana, North Dakota, South Dakota, Washington, and Wyoming— were admitted to the Union, expanding considerably the silver bloc in the Senate."[48] The result was the passage of a Silver Purchase Act in 1890 which effectively overturned Bland-Allison and mandated that the Treasury buy 4.5 million ounces of silver a month.

Businessmen everywhere were outraged at what they regarded as blatant political interference in economic affairs. The fact that Republicans had voted for the bill was particularly maddening. "The idea of reintroducing silver currency" was, for J. P. Morgan, Jean Strouse has written, "about as welcome as a biblical plague."[49] Andrew Carnegie, the self-appointed voice of the new business elites, took pen in hand to educate the people and their elected representatives on "The ABC of

Money" and the paramount importance of maintaining the gold standard: "In the next presidential campaign, if I have to vote for a man in favour of silver and protection, or for a man in favour of the gold standard and free trade, I shall vote and work for the latter, because my judgment tells me that even the tariff is not half so important for the good of the country as the maintenance of the highest standard for the money of the people."[50]

Carnegie and his fellow millionaire businessmen had, by the early 1890s, become more and more disturbed at the federal government's headlong rush into economic matters they believed it had neither the right nor the wisdom to interfere with. The Silver Purchase Act was a giant step in this direction; so too was the passage that same year, 1890, of an Antitrust Act which was designed, the capitalists feared, to turn back the evolutionary clock and impede progress by interfering with what Carnegie called the "law of aggregation." The combination of smaller firms into larger ones, Carnegie argued, following Herbert Spencer, benefited society by generating efficiencies of production that resulted in cheaper goods: "If there be in human history, one truth clearer and more indisputable than another, it is that the cheapening of articles . . . insures their more general distribution, and is one of the most potent factors in refining and lifting a people, and in adding to its happiness." He continued: "Every enlargement [of the scale of production] is an improvement, step by step, upon what has preceded. It makes for higher civilization, for the enrichment of human life, not for one, but for all classes of men." There was nothing wrong with businesses growing bigger and bigger. On the contrary, "the law of aggregation" dictated that such growth was not just inevitable but a positive good.[51]

The Gilded Age millionaires' rhetorical adherence to the doctrine of the "survival of the fittest," first articulated by Spencer and seized upon by a generation of businessmen, was not, as has been so often and so mistakenly implied, a commitment to competition. It was rather a celebration of the fruits of such competition: bigness, monopoly, and trusts. The fittest firms and businessmen had survived because they had bested, then eliminated, their competition. This was evolutionary progress in its purest form. When the politicians, blinded by an ideological abhorrence of monopoly and bigness, interfered with the law of aggregation to protect the vanquished from defeat and extinction, they interfered with evolutionary progress.

In 1893, less than three years after the passage of the Silver Purchase Act and the Antitrust Act, the nation was plunged into an economic depression which the business elites were quick to blame on legislative meddling. Left alone, without any monetary or antitrust legislation, the economy would have followed the "law of aggregation." Smaller, weaker firms would have been forced out of business or "consolidated" into larger ones. The end product would have been greater efficiencies and economies of production, lower prices, and generalized prosperity. The politicians had, in interfering with the natural workings of the economy, checked the movement toward consolidation (through the Antitrust Act), inflated the currency (with the Silver Purchase Act), and created an environment in which unfit businesses and businessmen were encouraged to compete in the marketplace. This, the capitalists were convinced, had led to overproduction and its inevitable byproduct, depression.[52]

To get the economy back on track, the businessmen had to find some way of reversing what appeared to be a growing sentiment that Congress should determine monetary and economic policy. Although both the Silver Purchase and Antitrust bills had been sponsored by a Republican senator, John Sherman of Ohio, and passed by bipartisan coalitions, they embodied—albeit in compromised form—agrarian demands that the federal government play an active role in the economy. Worse yet, there had appeared on the horizon a new political party, the People's Party or Populists, which had as its raison d'être bringing into the political arena agrarian demands for a decentralized (and therefore inflationary) banking system, tighter antitrust legislation, and the free coinage of silver. The Populists, in their first election, in 1892, had polled over a million votes for their presidential candidate and elected thirteen congressmen, two senators, and three governors. "Business leaders from throughout the nation and from every sphere of enterprise," James Livingston has written, "realized that unless they entered and altered the mainstream of political discourse on economic questions," monetary inflation and free competition "would become government policy."[53]

When the agrarian activists who had already formed their own Populist Party took over the Democratic Party and nominated William Jennings Bryan of Nebraska on a free silver platform, the die was cast. Bryan—and the Democratic platform—made it clear that, if elected, he intended to extend the political realm to encompass economic policy making that had once been excluded from it: "We say in our platform we believe that the right to coin and issue money is a function of government."[54] The platform also made explicit the Bryan Democrats' intention to enlarge "the powers of the Interstate Commerce Commission" and provide for regulation of the "railroads as will protect the people from robbery and oppression." There were also planks denouncing Republican tariff policy for enriching "the few at the expense of the many" and pledging reform.[55]

The nomination of Bryan on such a platform forced the business elites to look past their sectoral and regional differences and unite behind the Republican candidate, William McKinley, who stood for the gold standard and whose campaign was organized by the Ohio industrialist Mark Hanna. The economic elites had, in the past, been more likely to support Republicans than Democrats, but they had managed to get along quite well with Grover Cleveland, who had been instrumental in repealing the Silver Purchase Act in 1893. Regrettably for the businessmen, the Democratic Party of Grover Cleveland was no more.

The mobilization of the business elites—and their available resources—to defeat Bryan and the Democrats in 1896 was unlike anything that had preceded it in American politics. Mark Hanna was able to raise an astonishing amount of money from the business community.

J. P. Morgan was an early contributor to the campaign. Standard Oil gave $250,000 and Rockefeller another $2,500 of his own money. Carnegie not only contributed more than ever before to a presidential campaign but also granted Hanna permission to reprint his primer on hard money as a campaign pamphlet. "It required but a moment for us," Hanna wrote, "to see that the leaflet was admirably calculated to make the money issue of this campaign clear to the simplest mind. We therefore printed and have circulated more than 5,000,000 copies of the leaflet."[56]

The class coalition that formed to protect the economy—and future prosperity—from the ravages of silver continued in place even after the defeat of Bryan in 1896. With the exception of the western silver interests, businessmen from every region and every sector remained united not only against free silver but in opposition as well to a decentralized banking system which, they believed, would be structurally biased toward the overextension of credit.

This is not the place to discuss the movement for banking reform in any detail. Suffice it to say that no mobilization of business elites had ever been as broad or as deep or as persistent as the one assembled in the New York Reform Club's currency committee, the Sound Money Committees attached to city and state Chambers of Commerce, the businessmen's clubs and associations formed to support and fund the McKinley campaign, and the National Sound Money League, which was chartered in 1896 to carry on the campaign "for national honor and sound money" after McKinley's victory.[57]

❧ The class mobilization that occurred around the defense of the gold standard was critically important because it cemented the political strategy that would carry the business elites into the Progressive Era and the twentieth century. The business elites had discovered that the best way to protect the economic realm from political interference was to circumscribe democracy. While they had come to recognize that there was no way to wall off the economic realm completely from the political, they had learned that it was possible to insulate it from electoral politics. The defanged state regulatory commissions had been a first step in this direction—and a critical one. The removal of the silver question from the political agenda, with the defeat of Bryan and the Democrats in 1896 and then again in 1900, was even more important.

The business elites had been able to turn back the Populist threat by outsized funding of their candidates and their messages and, as important, by launching a preemptive ideological attack on the notion, so central to the Populists, that in a democracy, the people, through their elected representatives, had not only the right but the obligation to determine economic and monetary policies. The economic realm, as Herbert Spencer, and before him Adam Smith, had taught the businessmen, and the businessmen now attempted to teach the nation, was self-regulating and self-correcting. It had to be left alone to obey its own evolutionary laws, not those of the politicians. Democracy had its limits, beyond which voters and their elected representatives dared not trespass lest economic calamity befall the nation.

5

The Abortive Rule of Big Money

✤

ALAN DAWLEY

In an oft-quoted exchange, F. Scott Fitzgerald and Ernest Hemingway argued over the place of big money in American society. "Let me tell you something about the very rich," Fitzgerald wrote. "They are different from you and me." "Yes," replied Hemingway, "they have more money."[1] This little debate speaks volumes about class in America. In a proudly democratic society, the very rich have no chance of ever acquiring a lordly mystique. And yet they enjoy powers and privileges that are the envy of kings.

The debate about class was played out in the pageant of events from 1896 to 1932, a period which deserves to be called the Era of Big Money.[2] As if to shake off Hemingway's curse, Gilded Age captains of industry set out to transform themselves from mere money-grubbers into paragons of society enjoying all the dignity and perquisites of an upper class. Not content to rest there, the golden dynasties of the Rockefellers, Morgans, and Aldriches also sought to acquire a monopoly on political power. Although democratic sensibilities would not permit use of the term "ruling class," the new generation of wealthy families linked to industrial and financial corporations sought to bend the destiny of their country to the will of their class.[3]

Needless to say, this project ran counter to established democratic traditions. Struggles against aristocratic privilege at the time of the American Revolution and against slave masters during the Civil War had combined with egalitarian habits in everyday life to produce deep hostility to rule by "the rich, the well-born, and the able," in Alexander Hamilton's famous phrase. By the end of the nineteenth century, there was too much democratic ballast in the American ship of state—democratic ideology, cultural pluralism, popular participation—to allow captains of industry to steer the ship wherever they wanted. Moreover, the fact that both major parties, Republican and Democratic, were loose collections of interests and beliefs that cut across class lines (unlike the typical class-based parties of Europe) meant that political leaders had to hobnob with the hoi polloi.

Partly because of these democratic checks, the attempt at class rule turned out to be a failure. But for anyone seeking an explanation in terms of the impossibility of a ruling class ever taking command in supposedly classless America, there are some surprises in store.[4] On the eve of the Crash of '29, it appeared that democratic traditions were insufficient by themselves to block rule by the rich. In the end, what may have kept big money in check was the workings of American capitalism itself: economic instability, inner conflicts among elites, and an obsession with profit at the expense of social responsibility.

Plutocracy

Changes under way at the end of the nineteenth century pointed toward the consolidation of a national upper class with one foot planted in Wall Street and the other in Washington. In any description of this new class formation, the first thing to note is the central place of big business. Beginning in the Gilded Age with giant combines such as

John D. Rockefeller's Standard Oil and Andrew Carnegie's steel empire, the trend toward concentration of ownership received a big boost
during a wave of business mergers around the turn of the century,
capped by the formation of the United States Steel Corporation in
1901, the world's first billion-dollar enterprise. The new structure of
economic power that contemporaries called "monopoly" and economists later called "oligopoly"[5] offered unprecedented opportunities for
the accumulation of wealth in the everyday profits that poured out of
blast furnaces, oil wells, and machine shops like lava from a volcano.
On top of that were the profits from the stock deals, commissions, insurance charges, and other purely financial transactions that accompanied corporate consolidation. Henceforth, the fate of America's upper
class was tied, for good and for ill, to the fortunes of the corporate
rich.

The rise of corporate and other bureaucratic organizations created
hierarchies of command whose upper layers were occupied by new
managerial and professional elites. One example of the new type was
Raymond Fosdick, a pace-setting social engineer who swam in the
crème de la crème of government and private foundations. The very
model of the cosmopolitan professional, Fosdick first gained prominence as the head of the Commission on Training Camp Activities
during World War I, where he applied scientific methods to the suppression of vice among American troops; he later became director of
the Rockefeller Foundation.[6]

In setting out to tame the wild horses of the competitive marketplace, managers like Fosdick brought some measure of discipline to the
workplace and some top-down control to an unruly society. This, in
turn, led to claims of a "managerial revolution," in which the corporation was said to have brought about the "separation of ownership and
control," a transfer of power from shareholders to managers, and an
all-important shift from profit to productivity as the aim of business
enterprise.[7] Under the banner of "efficiency," the new breed of "scien-

tific managers" were also supposed to have called a halt to the violent labor wars that had disgraced American industrial relations in the Gilded Age.[8]

The facts, however, do not support the managerial claim, and certainly not for a "revolution." The idea that capitalists were overthrown by managers flies in the face of the evidence that in the early twentieth century the topmost layer of the corporate hierarchy consisted of owners who took the lion's share of their compensation in profits and dividends, not salaries. Far from overthrowing the owners of corporate property, the bureaucratization of business opened new channels for the accumulation of wealth. And since they served at the pleasure of the owners, the new cadres of corporate managers, for all their accomplishments, were the servants of power, not the masters.

This points to a distinction between the *upper class* and the *elite* that is important to our analysis.[9] Elites were those who had moved to the top rungs of the ladder of success in law, education, politics, business, or any other field. They were the movers and shakers whose names appeared in *Who's Who*. The upper class, by contrast, was the group of interconnected families that enjoyed social leadership and cultural prestige in society at large. They were the fox-and-hounds set with names in *The Social Register*. It is true that at the topmost echelons the two overlapped.[10] But the requirements for entry were different. For the elites, the key was educational credentials and personal connections, while entry to the upper class required blood, breeding, and money— the more the better.

The turn to "finance capitalism" confirms the impact of big money on upper-class formation. The fact that the world's first billion-dollar corporation was the handiwork of J. P. Morgan, the greatest investment banker of his day, points to the importance of finance in furthering industrial consolidation. Although the extent of financial influence is in dispute,[11] contemporaries had no doubt about its impact. From one end of the political spectrum, Dwight Moody, a Wall Street conservative, hailed the role of finance in *The Truth about the Trusts,* while, from the other, Louis Brandeis advocated trust-busting in *Other People's Money and How the Bankers Use It*.[12]

By all accounts the premier financier was J. Pierpont Morgan. The oversized, cigar-chomping, autocratic Morgan was the perfect target for cartoon caricature, a bloated capitalist able to make or break thousands of livelihoods at the stroke of a pen. In the "Rich Man's Panic" of 1907, for example, newspapers had a field day reporting on Morgan's role as a kind of one-man central bank in restoring order to financial markets after weeks of mounting losses among Wall Street firms. In an effort to stop the hemorrhage, Morgan put together a multimillion-dollar rescue package for two investment trusts teetering on the brink of collapse. The package imposed assessments on the leading trust companies in proportion to their assets. The climax of the drama came when Morgan summoned the principals to his elegant Manhattan mansion for a midnight meeting long remembered by those who were there. Having locked the door, the giant of finance laid a written version of the package on the table and demanded that everyone sign for his share. "There's the place," he said firmly, "and here's the pen." Legend has it that Morgan's bold intervention single-handedly ended the panic, although the timely arrival of a large shipment of gold aboard the *Lusitania* also gave a big boost to business confidence. Another key element of the package involved an offer to have the United States Steel Corporation purchase the Tennessee Coal and Iron Company from a syndicate of investors to prevent the syndicate from going belly-up. It was another demonstration of the close ties between finance and industry.[13]

The centralization of finance in Wall Street had important consequences for the upper class. It reduced once proud centers of money-lending, such as Boston and Philadelphia, to mere provincial locales, and it demoted their notables to second rank. On their way down, local worthies such as the Higginsons, Peabodys, and other Boston Brahmins contributed their share to the bloodlines of the new class, as did other first families—the Whartons and Biddles of Philadelphia and the nabobs of Baltimore and Charleston. Even the old Knickerbocker patricians, whose decline was lovingly chronicled in the novels of Edith Wharton, could not maintain their status against the new corporate rich no matter how blue their blood. As a result of these thickening networks of property and family, what had formerly been a collection of regional family groupings was increasingly knit together in a national upper class.

In the wondrous alchemy of inherited wealth, the base metal of Gilded Age gains was being transformed into golden patrimonies. Sheltered from the storms of the competitive market, the great baronial families—the Rockefellers, Harrimans, and Morgans—consolidated their fortunes in marriage alliances that were the social counterpart of interlocking corporate directorates. From the perspective of High Society, finding the right mate and getting into the right club was exactly what class was all about. According to Dixon Wecter, a leading chronicler of high-end Americans, "a group of families with a common background and racial origin becomes cohesive, and fortifies itself by the joint sharing of sports and social activities, by friendships and intermarriage."[14]

So it was with the marriage of John D. Rockefeller, Jr., and Abby Aldrich. The wedding linked the destinies of the Rockefellers, formerly of Cleveland but now settled in a sumptuous fiefdom north of New York City, to those of the Nelson Aldriches of Rhode Island, whose patriarch sat in the Senate representing New England Brahmins. In what became America's premier dynasty, the children of this privileged couple, including Nelson and David, would carry the family tradition into new arenas of politics and philanthropy. Meanwhile, another marital liaison tied the Rockefellers to the McCormicks of Chicago in a merger of oil money and agricultural machinery that linked the wealth of the nation's first and second cities.

Marriage alliances recruited new talent to the upper class. Take the case of Benjamin Strong, the most powerful banker in the Federal Reserve system. Strong was descended on his mother's side from successful Presbyterian ministers and physicians, and on his father's side from New England Puritans who, as the saying goes, "came to do good and stayed to do well." Blessed with these favorable ethnic and religious networks, Strong got his main chance after settling with his young wife and child in Englewood, New Jersey, where fellow members of the tennis club included Thomas Lamont and other partners in the House of Morgan. Soon Strong was brought in to succeed Lamont as secretary of Bankers Trust, a "bankers' bank" established in 1903 with Edmund Converse as president. After his first wife committed suicide, Strong found the way clear to marry the boss's daughter, Katherine Converse, thus cementing his position in the world of high finance and High Society at the same time.[15]

After two or three generations of heavy lifting, big money could finally begin to relax. According to Wecter, "rough and piratical grandfathers had seized [upper-class] real estate, laid out its railroads, and provided for its trust-funds."[16] To ensure that the progeny of the corporate rich made the best contacts, there were handsome endowments for exclusive social clubs, posh finishing schools, and Ivy League universities. Meanwhile, these same men and women of grand estate were creating new institutions of social control, laying out millions to establish the Russell Sage, Rockefeller, and other philanthropic foundations, just as society dames redirected their charitable efforts away from old-style charity balls toward more professional settlement houses and social work schools.[17]

They could even have a good time. In the never-ending round of tribal display, High Society sailed its yachts, rode to hounds, attended theatrical galas, and came out at debutante balls. Again, Wecter details the goings-on: "The second and third generations, relieved from the counting-house and shop, now begin to travel, buy books and pictures, learn about horses and wine, and cultivate the art of charm." Although no one ever accused J. P. Morgan of being charming, he was a glutton for art treasures and filled his Manhattan mansion with the trappings of European high culture. The setting was described by an awestruck Morgan underling: "In one room were lofty, magnificent tapestries hanging on the walls, rare Bibles and illuminated manuscripts of the Middle Ages filling the cases; in another, that collection of the Early Renaissance masters—Castagno, Ghirlandaio, Perugino, to mention only a few."[18]

High culture had to be defended against the barbarians. With more than a whiff of snobbery, Emily Post laid out precise standards of etiquette, while Henry Dwight Sedgwick, a Philadelphia gentleman, wrote *In Praise of Gentlemen* to celebrate "the law of decorum, the value of form, the abiding pleasure in beauty, the worth of manners, style, dignity, and reticence."[19] Snobbery shaded over into bigotry. To the old-line gatekeepers of polite society, big money was necessary but not sufficient for entry. A proper pedigree was required, too, preferably white, northern European, and Protestant. Despite their wealth, the Guggenheims, Schiffs, and other wealthy Jewish families were not eligible, nor were the Kennedys and other Roman Catholics. According to one insider, bigotry was rampant in the best clubs: "British racialism, Brahmin Bostonian anti-(Irish) Catholicism, any one of a number of possible anti-Semitisms, and the traditional American anti-black racism." In blurring the distinction between "class" and the "race" of white, northern European Protestants, bigotry actually undercut the long-term vitality of the class by keeping out talented recruits from outside the fold.[20]

Building on thickening networks of property and family, the corporate rich moved to reconstruct the state. From the turn of the century to the Great Depression, leading figures set out to create new political institutions and put them under upper-class supervision. Although the term "ruling class" does not slide easily off the American tongue, that is essentially what some aspired to become. They received a head start with the rise of the "money power" in the Gilded Age, culminating in the successful effort of Mark Hanna and his wealthy cronies to make William McKinley president in 1896. Having assembled the largest war chest in American history, Hanna's spare-no-expense campaign thwarted the "free silver" crusade of renegade Democrat William Jennings Bryan, mortal enemy of "gold bugs," and opened an era of Republican dominance lasting until 1932.[21] McKinley's election tied the fate of the country to the will of the corporate rich in ways that would not come undone until the New Deal.

Critics claimed that the ascendancy of "the interests" in Washington represented the advent of "plutocracy." Indeed, the election of senators by state legislatures in debt to big contributors brought so many millionaires to the Senate—as many as a third of the members at the dawn of the twentieth century–that it was dubbed the "Millionaires' Club." Although the Republican Party was a cross-class alliance that included northeastern urban political machines and midwestern farmers, the fact was that the electorate was rigged to reduce the influence of urban workers and immigrants, while representatives of big business gained privileged access to the highest circles of power.

The advent of "plutocracy" was actually a solution to a problem created by the separation of market and state in the nineteenth century. Beginning with the democratic ferment of the Jacksonian era and extending through the liquidation of the southern master class at the end of the Civil War, laissez-faire liberalism decreed that property would no longer ensure automatic access to positions of power the way it had in the earlier era of mercantilism, when men of property were expected to govern. As a result, monied elites were now forced to operate through networks of professional politicians in a state of courts and parties. Under the new arrangements, political favors had a cost, whether it was paid in legal campaign contributions or in bribes. Eventually, those like Hanna with a taste for political rough-and-tumble dispensed with middlemen and bought their way into office themselves.[22]

It is common to regard Theodore Roosevelt as the first president to challenge the power of money. It is true that this proud scion of an old Knickerbocker family fulminated against the "malefactors of great wealth," sought modest regulation of meatpacking and railroads, and initiated one trophy prosecution of the Northern Securities railroad empire which won him the reputation of a "trust-buster." Yet not even this rhetorical champion of the public interest could escape the force of private wealth. Playing second fiddle to Morgan in ending the "Rich Man's Panic" of 1907, Roosevelt authorized a discreet deposit of funds from the U.S. Treasury into New York banks and, more important, gave his promise not to invoke the Sherman Antitrust Act against Morgan's proposed merger of U.S. Steel and Tennessee Coal and Iron. The arm's-length collaboration between the imperious Morgan and the impetuous Roosevelt blessed what many said was a monopolistic takeover and epitomized the emerging confluence of wealth and power between Wall Street and Washington.

The Era of Big Money was a time of American expansion overseas. Having vaulted to the top of the world's industrial powers in the early 1890s, the country launched a series of colonial annexations and military interventions in the Spanish-American War of 1898 which continued under Republican and Democratic administrations alike until the 1930s. Under Presidents Roosevelt and Taft, foreign policy was handed over to men like Elihu Root, corporate lawyer turned business-minded reformer at the Departments of War and State (1899–1909), and Philander Knox, onetime steel industry hireling, who became an indefatigable promoter of American business overseas during his tenure as secretary of state (1909–1913). Gazing out from their photographs in highbrow magazines such as *World's Work*, the likes of Root and Knox exuded pride in having brought about America's growth as a world power.[23]

It is true that the imperial impulse had many sources. Among the most important were strategic interests, social Darwinism, masculine ambition, and the jingoism exemplified in the battle cry "Remember the *Maine!*"[24] The pursuit of empire, in turn, shaped the ideology of the day. For one thing, it bolstered patriarchal values, including the kind of hairy-chested masculinity associated with the pugnacious Theodore Roosevelt, at a time when patriarchy was coming under feminist attack.[25] For another, it reinforced race consciousness, deepening the sense of a presumptive right to rule on the part of white Anglo-Saxon Protestants. According to *World's Work*, the combination of American continental reach and the "earth-girdling spread" of the British Empire had created an Anglo-American imperium that was "the widest domination that has been won by men of the same stock." America's Anglophilic upper classes embraced "the white man's burden," an ideological bond with their British brethren which authors like Rudyard Kipling and W. T. Stead worked hard to strengthen. To these Anglo-American imperialists, the suppression of the Philippine insurrection was justified, in William Howard Taft's words, by the "indubitable fact" that "the Filipinos are at present so constituted as to be utterly unfit for self government." A broader sense of white supremacy was instilled at the series of world's fairs in Chicago (1893), Buffalo (1901), St. Louis (1904), and other cities, where tribal peoples from colonial regions were presented in degrading sideshows. From the hard work of empire building to the leisure-time reflections of empire, diplomats and fair-goers alike took a lesson in social Darwinism, under which Anglo-Saxons, Nordics, or some other north European grouping were supposedly "fit" to ride herd on everybody else.[26]

At the same time, American expansion owed much to class interests. Especially in the Latin American proving ground of U.S. hegemony, the golden dynasties established a network of trade and investment that made much of the region into an economic colony of Yankee capital. Whether this was called "dependency"[27] or "informal empire,"[28] the fact was that leading U.S. firms had large interests in Mexico (Rockefeller, Morgan, Stillman, Dodge), the Caribbean (Morgan, Stillman), and Central America (United Fruit). Cuba offers a case in point. Having become a de facto protectorate in 1902 under the Platt Amendment, Cuba was an inviting opportunity for Yankee corporations, which took over the lion's share of the island's sugar industry— 60 percent by the mid-1920s. Leading the charge was the American Sugar Refining Company, a prime example of the most advanced capitalist methods of the day, including vertical and horizontal integration and the use of modern technology. The company also came under the influence of finance capital when the original stake of the Havemeyer family of New York was augmented by investments from the Boston financiers Kidder, Peabody, & Company. Especially during the boom years of the First World War, Morgan and other Wall Streeters muscled in to reap a lucrative harvest of profits from Cuban sugar, a one-time luxury which was fast becoming a staple in the increasingly sweetened diet of the American consumer.[29]

Beyond the narrow calculus of profit was the upper-class will to power. Believing that they stood at the pinnacle of civilization, empire builders regarded civilized rule over "inferior" peoples as a duty to humanity. As the most prominent of the lot, Teddy Roosevelt had no doubt that his seizure of what would become the Panama Canal Zone furthered the progress of civilization while also advancing toward the destiny of U.S. preeminence in the Western Hemisphere. Despite his disavowal of mercenary motives, Roosevelt's concept of civilization rested on a firm foundation of business principles, as did his moralistic condemnation of "chronic wrongdoing" in the Roosevelt Corollary to the Monroe Doctrine. By making the Caribbean safe for gringo sugar refineries, railroad investors, and bank loans, Roosevelt's actions indisputably served U.S. business interests.

The same was true in the case of the Philippines. U.S. investors looked hungrily on railroad and mining opportunities in the new colony, where Roosevelt's civil governor, William Howard Taft, was busy helping to put down the Philippine insurrection against the U.S. occupation. Taft regarded military conquest as the necessary precondition to the expansion of bourgeois civilization in the tropics. As he wrote home to Root, "The army has brought the Philippines to the point where they offer a ready and attractive field for investment and enterprise, but to make this possible there must be mining laws, homestead and land laws, general transportation laws, banking and currency laws."[30] (A later generation would refer to this as nation building.) When he became president in 1909, the former imperial proconsul presided over "dollar diplomacy" under which the flag followed the dollar overseas. All in all, it is not hard to see why contemporaries believed that they lived in a plutocracy.

The Problems of Plutocracy

Despite their success, the crowned heads of American capitalism felt insecure. Walter Lippmann, one of the most perceptive observers of the American scene, described their predicament: "They have been educated to achieve success; few of them have been educated to exercise power. Nor do they count with any confidence upon retaining their power, nor in handing it on to their sons. They live, therefore, from day to day, and they govern by ear. Their impromptu statements of policy may be obeyed, but nobody seriously regards them as having authority." For that reason, Lippmann, believed, "none of them is *seated on a certain throne,* and all of them are forever concerned as to how they keep from being toppled off."[31]

Lippmann's observation points to a basic problem of plutocracy. In a democratic society, the rich and powerful may be envied, but they are not revered. They may be obeyed, but they are not held in awe. Having "more money," as Hemingway said, does not make them "different from you and me" in the way Fitzgerald meant. Clearly, plutocratic assaults on the citadels of power rubbed democratic nerves raw. Louis Brandeis, the "people's lawyer," won a wide hearing for an attack on finance capitalism which marshaled evidence from the congressional Pujo Committee to warn that rich bankers were using "other people's money" to get even richer. In one biting witticism, Brandeis summed up the whole of banking as "the privilege of taking the golden eggs laid by somebody else's goose."[32] Political corruption also came under attack. Casting a jaundiced eye on the senatorial "Millionaires' Club," Mark Twain quipped, "I think I can say with pride that we have legislators that bring higher prices than anywhere in the world." Populist critics complained about government of, by, and for "the interests," not "the people," and in 1904, muckraking journalist Lincoln Steffens penned the classic indictment of urban corruption, *The Shame of the Cities,* which depicted greedy businessmen carrying off "boodle" from the public treasury.[33]

As this outcry suggests, plutocracy actually undermined the legitimacy of the existing system. In a democratic society, political rulers must win consent of the governed by some combination of power sharing, delivering the goods, social responsibility, and cultural leadership, all of which add up to what was first called "hegemony" by Antonio Gramsci. Even some upper-class conservatives had to admit that corruption sapped confidence in the system, especially after being instructed on the point by English visitor Lord Bryce, who portrayed corruption as the chief flaw in the otherwise splendid American commonwealth. None spoke louder in denouncing the influence peddling of big money than Teddy Roosevelt. With his typical vehemence Roosevelt proclaimed, "Of all the forms of tyranny the least attractive and the most vulgar is the tyranny of mere wealth, the tyranny of a plutocracy."[34]

Partly for these reasons, big money did not have everything its own way. Regional hostility toward Wall Street in the South and West helped put many Bryan Democrats in office, while farmers and skilled workers combined to support insurgent Republicans like Robert La Follette. Urban workers supported machine Democrats and a fair number of socialists who demanded benefits for their constituents, while middle-class reformers sought to curb the power of money in politics. In the first decade of the twentieth century, these forces were gathering in a multifarious movement of progressive reform that would soon place new checks on plutocracy.

Another set of problems arose in foreign affairs. Although there was little they could do to stop U.S. expansion, anti-imperialists warned that foreign conquest undermined the American republic. Drawing the connection between big business and a big navy, they portrayed militarism as a threat to democracy and lambasted "dollar diplomacy" as an oppressive burden on ordinary taxpayers. Many saw imperialism as an outgrowth of big business. Paul Reinsch (later Woodrow Wilson's ambassador to Beijing) asserted in 1900, "It is certain that some of the great trusts are interested in expansion." In a society already afflicted by "corruption in public affairs," and where legislation was "more uniformly favorable to capital and its concentrated interests than to the poorer classes," Reinsch warned that "the central government should not be turned into an instrumentality for advancing powerful centralized interests."[35]

From that day forward, progressive critics warned that imperialism would promote the undemocratic concentration of power at home. During the First World War, Jane Addams and other social reformers in the American Union against Militarism campaigned against U.S. intervention in Mexico and elsewhere on the grounds that foreign military interventions would lead to an oppressive military establishment, a costly imperial administration, and an oligarchy of industrialists. The argument was echoed after the war by the Women's International League for Peace and Freedom.[36]

There were also a few critics of the racist consequences of empire. To a prescient young W. E. B. Du Bois, the problem of the international color line was nothing less than "the problem of the twentieth century." Few contemporaries were as astute as Du Bois in 1903 in setting American segregation and European colonialism in the same global context of "the relation of the darker to the lighter races of men in Asia and Africa, in America and the islands of the sea." Nonetheless, the black and white progressives who joined together to form the National Association for the Advancement of Colored People in 1909 were responding to a central fault in the system that sooner or later would have to be addressed.[37]

Another problem of plutocracy was the treatment of labor. Making sure that the proceeds of labor flowed into the pockets of the owners required constant attention to work disciplines, wage rates, chains of command, injury claims, and a host of other areas where class interests collided. Under a narrow calculus of self-interest, employers pinched and squeezed their employees, often to the point of damaging health and safety, as in such industrial atrocities as the lethal 1911 fire at the Triangle Shirtwaist Company in New York City. In contrast to Europe's *haute bourgeoisie,* steeped in aristocratic values that bonded upper and lower ranks in a common social order, America's newly rich seemed all too eager to play Ebenezer Scrooge to working-class Bob Crachits. That was the kind of image projected by Andrew Mellon, Pittsburgh industrial magnate and future secretary of the treasury, to his estranged wife, the former Nora McMullen, granddaughter of the founder of Ireland's Guinness Brewery. In her divorce proceedings, she railed against the treatment meted out to the "toilers in my husband's vineyard" and objected that none of them were "given the laborer's recognition, toiling and working on the estate and adding to its wealth but not recognized as part of it. The whole community spirit was as cold and hard as the steel it made, and chilled the heart to the core."[38]

As if to confirm their cold-heartedness, industrialists resisted any efforts by their employees to organize unions, often breaking strikes by sending in Pinkertons and the National Guard. For this reason, the Era of Big Money was a time of often violent labor wars, exemplified by the Ludlow Massacre in the Colorado coalfields in 1914, where state militia called in at the behest of the Colorado Fuel and Iron Company, a Rockefeller subsidiary, shot down striking miners and burned their families out of their makeshift homes. Such atrocities tarnished the reputations of the golden dynasties.

The labor question was increasingly a global one. One of the key aspects of the world economy in this period was the growing share of the world's workers coming under the control of American money, whether through large-scale European immigration to the United States or through the export of American capital, especially to Latin America and the Caribbean. As American capital came into contact with tropical labor, class relations were internationalized. In cases such as the building of the Panama Canal, 1906–1914, where West Indian laborers were supervised by Yankee engineers, the relations were direct.[39] But in most cases, local owners hired most of the labor, as in Cuba, where small sugar planters hired cane workers, and national governments, not American gendarmes, took charge of policing them. The fact that these regimes were often repressive—notoriously so in the case of the dictators Porfirio Díaz in Mexico and Juan Vicente Gómez in Venezuela—was a cause of labor discontent. This, too, posed a problem for America's leaders. Unstable conditions in the form of Caribbean coups d'état and social revolution in Mexico roiled the waters of U.S. politics whenever the country intervened overseas. From battles over Philippine annexation to Wilson's Mexican interventions in 1914 and 1916, imperialism was politically divisive.[40]

Finally, plutocracy was destabilized by the very economic dynamism that pushed the corporate rich to the top. What Joseph Schumpeter called "creative destruction"—that is, rapid technological and organizational change—was always sweeping out the old and bringing in whole new industries. On top of that came internal conflicts among diverse sectors of business. Because suppliers, manufacturers, shippers, and wholesalers had different interests, their lobbyists kept bumping into one another while seeking their own "special interest" legislation.

Such divisions undermined upper-class cohesion. Along with new industries, such as automobiles and electronics, came new retinues of corporate rich knocking at the gates of High Society. According to Herbert Pell, there was a constant battle between new-rich "getters" and old-rich "keepers." The fact that most of the "keepers" had themselves been "getters" only a generation or two earlier did not silence the running complaint against the newcomers. In 1913, for example, Henry Cabot Lodge, a Brahmin "keeper," objected that "very modern plutocrats" had ruined society "with their entertainments, their expenditures, their marriages, their divorces, and their scandals." Fifteen years later it was the turn of a Brooklyn matron who had married into Europe's top echelon and had the name to prove it—Mrs. Jerome Napoleon Bonaparte—to lament the fact that "wholesale invasion of the best circles by the *nouveau riche* and the hordes of hangers-on is making places like Palm Beach no more exclusive than Coney Island. Newport, the last stronghold of the elite, has the moneyed intruder at the gates."[41]

A revealing twist on Old Money's complaint against New Money arose in the bitter 1910 divorce that was the talk of the Pittsburgh society pages. In an eloquent diatribe, Nora McMullen Mellon complained that her estranged husband, Andrew Mellon, was obsessed with money at the expense of family: "Always new plans, bigger plans for new dollars, bigger dollars, dollars that robbed him and his family of the time he could have devoted far more profitably to a mere, 'Thank God, we are living.'" Offended at being treated "like his Huns and Slavs," the Irish heiress lamented the cash basis of marriage in the booming steel city, where she was weighed "coldly, dispassionately, on the scales of demand and supply and as a wife ranked merely as a commodity in the great plans of this master financier's lifework. The babies were there: even the male heir was there. Was the wife to be laid off like other hired help when the mills shut down[?]"[42]

The treatment of wives as trophy objects lent itself to the sort of scathing critique found in Charlotte Perkins Gilman's *Women and Economics* (1898). Gilman indicted the Victorian doctrine of "separate spheres" for making women of the leisure class into "over-sexed" ornaments of extravagance in a society where patriarchal rule was, in fact, becoming anachronistic. In a parallel assault on upper-class rituals of ostentatious display, Thorstein Veblen's *Theory of the Leisure Class* (1899) skewered the super-rich for their "pecuniary emulation" of one another's "conspicuous consumption." Far from being defenders of high culture, they were themselves barbarians at the gates.[43]

In a situation where the affairs of state were subject to so much plutocratic influence, there was little to buffer the full fury of the capitalist storm—the whirlwind of "creative destruction," the ups and downs of the business cycle, the exploitation of labor, the relentless pressure for outward expansion. And yet, the reign of big money was by no means absolute. Inequality fueled democratic opposition, while economic dynamism constantly threatened to replace one batch of oligarchs with another. The central irony of the period was that the same system that put the corporate rich on the throne made their reign unstable. New strategies were in order.

Reform, War, and Revolution, 1912–1921

In addressing the problems of plutocracy, the upper class sought to broaden its leadership during the turbulent years of progressive reform and the Great War. While some pursued a managerial strategy of enlightened self-interest, others—often women—joined movements for social justice. Conceding that obsessive pursuit of wealth had torn the social fabric, reformers of both types tried to mend it. No doubt sincere, they also recognized that social responsibility would be repaid in the intangible dividends of greater legitimacy.

Let us look first at the managerial reformers. At a time of muckraking attacks on "special interests," many industrial magnates abandoned the old philosophy of "the public be damned" and embraced enlightened self-interest instead. That meant stabilizing the economy, improving working conditions, and attacking social problems such as prostitution and drunkenness. Better to address such problems through private organizations than to risk government intervention. Through organizations such as the National Civic Federation, for example, they enlisted social workers to draft blueprints for "welfare capitalism" that would harmonize the interests of business, labor, and the public. They also established grand philanthropic organizations, including the Russell Sage, Rockefeller, and Commonwealth foundations, to improve the health and education of the poor. In addition, after outrages such as the Ludlow Massacre, the Rockefellers brought in professional labor mediators to improve industrial relations, and, more important, they turned to advertising men like Ivy Lee and Edward Bernays to improve public relations. These efforts were a great success in co-opting elite professionals who might otherwise have been corporate critics, and they were modestly successful in persuading the general public that big business could be socially responsible. There is less evidence, however, that they actually bettered the conditions of working people.[44]

With labor discontent and other social problems continuing to fester, some in the upper crust broke ranks to participate in movements for social reform. Entering into a cross-class alliance, wealthy socialites became financial angels to middle-class reformers who ran settlement houses, milk stations, and health clinics. Unlike old-fashioned charity, which was merely local, the new organizations, such as the National Child Labor Committee and the National Consumers League, were nationwide networks of benevolence that furthered the restructuring of the upper class.

It was often women who made the break. For example, after the killing of women and children in Ludlow, Abby Aldrich Rockefeller abandoned everything her father, Nelson Aldrich, had stood for to become a principal contributor to the National Women's Trade Union League. When such wealthy "allies" joined protest parades, spectators were treated to the incongruous sight of socialites in mink stoles marching with socialists in shirtwaists. Regarded as eccentrics by hidebound conservatives, the rebel rich knew that their networks of benevolence would have the dual benefit of improving society while winning good will from the public.

It did not take long for these networks to become enmeshed in electoral politics. Indeed, they were a major foundation for the politics of reform that gave the Progressive Era its name. Initially, both managerial and reform camps were attracted to Theodore Roosevelt and his Progressive Party. In a fit of pique over Taft's authorization of an antitrust suit against the U.S. Steel deal he had personally approved in 1907, Roosevelt decided to bolt the Republican Party in 1912. Under the banner of the "New Nationalism," he proposed modest regulation of the trusts through the kind of national bureaucracy later embodied in the Federal Trade Commission. Managerial types saw this as a sensible alternative to radicalism, and he won support from the likes of George Perkins, a Morgan partner. They may have found him unpredictable, but, unlike his cousin Franklin, Teddy was never accused of being a traitor to his class. In addition, proponents of the "New Nationalism" supported moderate social reforms, such as prohibitions on the abuse of women and child laborers. No doubt the upper-class captains in Roosevelt's army of Christian soldiers were sincere in backing these reforms. But they also hoped that moderate reform would stave off more radical solutions of the sort proposed by neo-populist Bryan Democrats who seemed bent on bringing down the money power. They also saw that reform would help legitimate the existing order. As Roosevelt repeatedly argued, "social reform is not the precursor but the preventive of Socialism."[45]

Woodrow Wilson was no less a foe of plutocracy. Indeed, under the banner of the "New Freedom," Wilson called for a breakup of the trusts and a return to competition. "Interest does not bind men together," Wilson said, "interest separates men. There is only one thing that can bind men together, and that is common devotion to right." Despite Wilson's moralistic condemnation of the "interests," the talk in both Wall Street and Washington by the time he took office in 1913 was about how—not whether—to make the state a partner in the management of corporate capitalism. Once in power, Wilson Democrats forgot their campaign rhetoric about breaking up the trusts and pursued government regulation instead.[46]

Even Wall Street had learned a lesson from the Panic of 1907 about the obsolescence of Morgan's trademark response to meddlesome government officials: "Send your man to my man and they can fix it up." What was needed was federal legislation to stabilize money markets, and New York bankers lined up behind the Aldrich Plan for a federally supervised banking system with headquarters in New York. What they got was somewhat different—a regional network of member banks with a chief appointed by the president—although, in practice, the new

Federal Reserve system of 1913 conferred Washington's blessing on Wall Street's preeminence.[47]

In general terms, the new federal bureaucracy was a compromise between plutocracy and democracy. Big business would no longer be able to invoke laissez-faire as a license to run wild, while demands for public control of private enterprise would be set aside. Instead, there would be modest public regulation through new government agencies such as the Federal Reserve, the Federal Trade Commission, and the Food and Drug Administration. At a time when more radical demands were in the air, the new machinery incorporated limited public regulation in order to preserve the underlying principle of private control. The effect was to reduce the role of "plutocracy" in politics, both as an actual force and as a galvanizing issue.[48] Insofar as it reduced the contradiction between capitalism and democracy, bureaucracy maintained the continuity of the capitalist system by changing it.

A second consequence of federal bureaucracy was to reinforce the remaking of the upper class along national lines. That is, the new federal agencies were incubators of truly *national* elites whose outlook transcended regional and sectoral interests and who became, as we have seen, prime candidates for entry into the upper class.

The Great War hastened both of these developments. To be sure, there was populist grumbling and antiwar worry about the fact that J. P. Morgan & Co. was the official U.S. purchasing agent for the British government. Morgan skimmed off $30 million in commissions on the $3 billion worth of direct purchases made by the Allies, and he took additional millions in interest on a $500 million Anglo-French loan, the biggest single foreign loan in U.S. history (on the way to a grand total of $1.5 billion in war loans). Yet as soon as the United States joined the Allies, Morgan's millions were portrayed as the just rewards for patriotism. The same patriotic aura hung over the scores of corporate executives and Wall Street financiers, such as Bernard Baruch, who trooped to Washington to become "dollar a year men."

Meanwhile, John D. Rockefeller burnished his reputation as a public

benefactor by donating some $70 million to Belgian relief and other
good causes. In the same way, the war was also a golden opportunity
for society dames to show their benevolence after the fashion of Abby
Rockefeller, who supervised Red Cross volunteers, by performing public service on the plethora of women's councils set up to conserve food,
improve public health, and take care of the injured. No doubt the patriotism was genuine, but it was also good public relations.[49] All in all, by
turning plutocrats into patriots, the war temporarily furthered the upper-class quest for legitimacy.

With respect to the labor question, however, the war taught contra-
dictory lessons. On the one hand, the urgent need for labor peace convinced even conservatives of the virtue of power sharing between capital and labor. Former President Taft, for example, signed on as co-
chair of the War Labor Board, which stood briefly as a prime example
of a bureaucratic mediation between capitalism and democracy. On the
other hand, fear entered the hearts of the propertied as they witnessed
the mounting number of major strikes in the United States set against
the backdrop of the Bolshevik Revolution in Russia and disorder in
Europe. Facing off against a mass of disorderly workers, otherwise
conflicting "interests" drew together in solid opposition to sharing
power with labor and mounted a largely successful Open Shop drive in
industry. In the same vein, the postwar Red Scare all but eliminated the
call for social justice from the higher circles by painting even moderate
reforms such as setting minimum wages and maximum hours as dangerous experiments in communism.[50]

The gulf between the classes was deepened by patricians who tight-
ened their embrace of eugenic and racist arguments against immigrants
from southern and eastern Europe. Against the wishes of large employers of cheap immigrant labor, Congress accepted racial arguments
and shut the doors against Slavs, Italians, and Jews in the restrictive
quotas of 1921 and 1924. The victory of restrictionists has puzzled historians: if business was in the saddle and labor was weak, why did the
American Federation of Labor win out over the National Association

of Manufacturers? Approaching this puzzle through a broader class perspective brings us closer to a solution. Whatever the narrow interests of employers, the broader goals of the upper classes included preserving their cultural leadership and social status against the boatloads of newcomers crowding America's shores. Patrician followers of Madison Grant and Lothrop Stoddard sought to keep the national patrimony in the hands of Anglo-Saxon bluebloods by enacting a racial form of nationalism into law.[51]

In expressing class aims in ethnic ("racial") form, the upper crust was very much in the American grain. Working-class neighborhoods, after all, were steeped in their own varieties of Polish, Italian, or other ethnic customs.[52] The result of casting upper-class identity in WASP terms, however, was to deepen the division separating the classes by driving an ethnic wedge between them. In addition to violating the hallowed American creed of equality, racism in all its forms was a formidable obstacle to winning consent from the urban masses. Whereas Polish immigrants working in Pittsburgh might seek to follow in the footsteps of fellow immigrant Andrew Carnegie, they could not walk with the nativist snobs of the Immigration Restriction League, any more than African Americans could admire the bigots of the Eugenics Record Office. In the short run, the tribalism of the 1920s may have given temporary comfort to the descendants of the *Mayflower*, but in the long run, in a society as diverse and dynamic as the United States, a merely WASP establishment could not last.[53]

Corporate Feudalism, 1922–1932

Big money reached for new forms of power in the 1920s. Through public-spirited corporations and institutions of public benevolence, a new generation of the corporate rich attempted to throw off the old "robber baron" reputation, don the mantle of enlightened self-interest, and take command of foreign and domestic policy. What critics saw as corporate domination, admirers saw as the foundation of a benevolent establishment, what the sociologist E. Digby Baltzell (following Tocqueville) dubbed a "business aristocracy." From fawning admirers like Fitzgerald to sophisticated observers like Baltzell, observers asked America's corporate rich to turn themselves into something more substantial than Hemingway's money-grubbers. Although many never got beyond Jay Gatsby, Fitzgerald's reckless and destructive fictional hero, a significant segment tried to move from the old plutocracy toward more public-spirited leadership.

In their landmark study *The Modern Corporation and Private Property* (1932), Adolf Berle and Gardiner Means described the "corporate system" evolving in the 1920s as the latter-day equivalent of the feudal system, in which the corporation seemed to be superseding the state as "the dominant form of political organization." For this transition to take place, public-spirited executives would have to override both the narrow pecuniary interests of their stockholders and the technocratic power of the managerial elite and "set forth a program comprising fair wages, security to employees, reasonable service to their public, and stabilization of business." In other words, they would have to be willing to make the supreme sacrifice and "divert a portion of the profits from the owners of passive property."[54]

In fact, there was movement toward some of these goals. Though hopelessly inadequate from the perspective of the 1930s, the effort to smooth out the ups and downs of the business cycle was significant in comparison to the old dog-eat-dog competition. The effort was embodied in corporate planning, trade associations, and the kind of top-level collaboration exemplified by the 1919 formation of the Special Conference Committee, a consortium of giant firms that included Standard Oil, DuPont, and General Electric.[55] These new forays into economic planning took place alongside the continuing work of the National Industrial Conference Board and the National Bureau of Economic Research in reporting on market conditions. In a similar vein, corporations expanded "welfare capitalism" by offering retirement plans, profit sharing, and paid vacations to a somewhat wider circle of employees, and they launched publicity campaigns intended to show that business had such a strong social conscience that government-sponsored social welfare was unnecessary. Meanwhile, corporate apologists insisted that corporations were public benefactors because the likes of General Electric and General Motors delivered a seemingly endless flow of consumer goods.

To be sure, plutocratic self-interest did not disappear. Special interests feasted on public resources, as revealed in the Teapot Dome scandal and in Treasury Secretary Andrew Mellon's notorious tax rebates to the rich, including millions to Mellon's own companies. These raids on the public treasury show the continued potency of pecuniary values in all their corrosive influence. In fact, the distribution of wealth reached something of a Mount Everest of inequality in 1929, when the gap between rich and poor was wider than at any other time in the twentieth century. The resulting vulgarity and profligacy of the Jazz Age showed how much remained of Veblen's "conspicuous consumption."

Nonetheless, new attitudes were in the air. There was a new sophistication in upper-class taste for modern art and architecture. For example, Abby Rockefeller contributed great sums to launch the Museum of Modern Art, and John J. Raskob teamed up with Al Smith to spend money from DuPont and Metropolitan Life Insurance in building the glorious art deco cathedral known as the Empire State Building.

In Washington, the new attitude was evident in Herbert Hoover's Commerce Department. Drawing on his wartime experience as head of the Food Administration, Hoover argued the case for "associationalism," the idea that trade associations and corporate management should work cooperatively with government to serve the public. Following Hoover's lead, the Federal Trade Commission, for example, assisted business with research on market conditions and sponsored conferences aimed at promoting business cooperation rather than competition. Such intertwining networks of corporate and state bureaucracy moved beyond narrow self-interest toward what was promoted as a new kind of benevolent partnership between business and government.

Overseas, the corporate rich took U.S. foreign policy beyond "dollar diplomacy." Although "special interests" continued to play a strong hand, especially in Congress, the internationalist wing of corporate America pursued a broader strategy of world power. Under outward-looking Charles Evans Hughes, the State Department brokered a major international arms agreement at the Washington Naval Conference of 1921–22. The same business leaders conducted what was called "bankers' diplomacy." Led by Benjamin Strong, the preeminent figure at the Federal Reserve, key American bankers such as Thomas Lamont worked closely with their European counterparts Hjalmar Schacht and Montague Norman, the heads of the German and British central banks, respectively. The Federal Reserve under Strong functioned as the U.S. counterpart to the European central banks, a fact underscored by the close personal relationship between Strong and Norman, who liked to vacation together in the south of France. Strong was not timid about criticizing the narrow nationalism of "America First" Republicans such as Henry Cabot Lodge, who pushed through historically high tariffs after the war. "If we put a prohibitive tariff upon imports," Strong objected, "we by so much restrict our exports, and further, make it impossible for those who owe us money to pay it."[56]

Corporate internationalists took the lead in stabilizing the world economy in the financial agreements embodied in the Dawes Plan (1924) and the Young Plan (1929) for rescheduling German reparations payments. The internationalist outlook gained ground during the brief golden years between 1924 and 1929 when international bankers seemed to have succeeded in restoring a measure of stability to world affairs. Under these unusually favorable conditions, there was a brief prefiguring of the kind of "Atlanticism" that came on strong after the Second World War, in which new processes of class formation operated on a transatlantic scale.[57]

High finance was not the only internationalist influence on the upper class. There were strong social ties across the Atlantic as well. For over a generation, American money had been marrying into European nobility and appropriating aristocratic styles—witness Morgan's medieval tapestries—with the aim of staking out a claim to be the youthful successor of Europe's faded aristocracy. That claim was fortified by wealthy tourists who followed in British and French footsteps on the paths of empire. Like Europeans who had appropriated knowledge of the Oriental peoples they conquered, American cosmopolitans were getting to know the peoples of Latin America, Asia, and Africa and appropriating knowledge of their cultures as a way of increasing their own cultural capital. For decades, world's fairs and museums had brought exotic places to America's shores, but now, as the United States acquired an empire in the tropics, it was the turn of the wealthy tourist to board train, plane, and cruise ship and go to visit them. Through ads in high-end magazines like *Vanity Fair,* travel agencies beckoned the leisure class "to glide easily over ruined Maya temples and pyramids into the heart of mysterious Haiti through the Indies, Mexico, Central and South America." For those who preferred Africa, there was "the immensely picturesque native side of South Africa," with its "wild war dances, weird age-old tribal customs, the dignified Zulu chief and his retinue of dusky wives."[58]

The Crash of '29 and the ensuing depression of the 1930s put a crimp in these travel plans. Nonetheless, like passengers aboard the *Titanic* in the first moments after hitting the iceberg, High Society continued to behave in the first months of the depression as if nothing had happened. During the week in late October when the *New York Times* headlined "Worst Stock Crash," the society page calmly reported on the transatlantic migration of plumed socialites from their summer abodes to their winter quarters. Spotting a family on the move with their aristocrat-by-marriage daughter in tow, the society page reported, "Mr. and Mrs. Samuel Norris and the latter's daughter, Countess Alexandrine von Beroldingen, who have been at the St. Regis, are sailing tonight on the Augusta for Rome."[59]

In Washington, too, political leaders tried to pretend that disaster could be avoided. Cooperation with big business remained the order of the day. Within weeks of the great stock market crash of October 1929, Hoover invited corporate leaders to a series of White House conferences to help coordinate a response. In reviewing the results of a gathering of some four hundred "key men" in December, Hoover drew a historical contrast with the lost world of ruthless competition: "The very fact that you gentlemen come together for these broad purposes represents an advance in the whole conception of the relationship of business to public welfare . . . This is a far cry from the arbitrary and dog-eat-dog attitude of the business world of some thirty or forty years ago."[60]

In many respects, Hoover was right. Neither President Grant nor Cleveland would have thought to summon the cream of the business world to coordinate a joint public-private response to the depressions of their day. Indeed, it is doubtful that at any time prior to the Great War businessmen would have been willing to do what leading executives did in 1929–30 in joining with their rivals in a well-publicized pledge to maintain wage rates at the expense of profits, or to issue solemn promises to "share the work." When banks continued to fail in record numbers, no previous president—not even Wilson—would have thought to call bankers to Washington to participate in a rescue operation to back up the Federal Reserve's easing of credit to member banks. Yet in early October 1931, Hoover gathered leading bankers together at the ornate Washington home of Secretary Mellon and won their agreement to create a $500 million credit pool to assist weaker institutions.[61] Finally, when that private effort fizzled out, none of Hoover's predecessors would have considered creating something like the Reconstruction Finance Corporation (RFC) to provide public loans to private enterprise in peacetime.

Corporate leaders themselves had come a long way since the plutocratic days of the Panic of 1907. In the earlier episode, President Roosevelt had played second fiddle to the leading banker in the land, and the market had taken precedence in a multimillion-dollar rescue package. In the crisis of the 1930s, however, the roles were reversed, Hoover took the lead, and the state entered directly into the process of capital accumulation to the tune of $2 billion in the first year of the RFC alone. The shift from Morgan's Manhattan library to Mellon's Washington home symbolized the growing importance of the federal government, while the fact that the loans went to railroads, banks, and other large firms points to the remaining power of the corporate oligarchy. It is possible to imagine this new power structure consolidating a permanent ruling class.

As it was, that possibility was ruled out by the instability and insecurity built into the capitalist system. As the economic downturn of 1929–30 became the "Great Depression," the pull of economic self-interest in the higher circles became glaringly apparent. Internationalism had attracted only a minority within the national upper class to begin with, and now the nationalism of the majority was evident in economic policy as Congress raised high tariff rates even higher in the 1931 Hawley-Smoot Tariff. In a similar vein, the continued decline in the level of economic activity in the early 1930s exposed the submerged rock of self-interest built into "welfare capitalism." Never amounting to more than 2 percent of payrolls, corporate "welfare" was most extensive in health and safety measures, where it repaid dividends in the form of higher productivity. For the same reason, it was least extensive in cash benefits for accidents, retirement, and unemployment, the very areas where workers needed it the most. With ever-lengthening bread lines making a mockery of welfare capitalism, upper-class charity was also falling short as the coffers of benevolence were rapidly being drained dry. All in all, the corporate rich failed miserably to meet their responsibilities toward the poor.[62]

Under these conditions, criticism of plutocracy returned in full force. Sharpening the knives for an attack on the overweening power of "America's Sixty Families," one critic echoed Veblen in lambasting "the politics of pecuniary aggrandizement" and "the press of the plutocracy." The worse things got, the more voters abandoned pro-business Republicans to support an increasing number of Democrats, notably Franklin Roosevelt in 1932, along with a growing number of third-party progressives. Lippmann's swipe at the corporate rich—"nobody seriously regards them as having authority"—was coming true with a vengeance. So thorough was the loss of the corporate mystique that big banks and munitions makers came under attack in the Senate's Nye Committee for manipulating the United States into what was now seen as the disaster of the Great War.[63]

Progressives like Charles Beard won a wide hearing for the view that reducing the power of big business was a necessary step toward a non-interventionist foreign policy. Reviewing the history of the American republic between the Spanish American War and the Great Depression, Beard concluded that "foreign policy and domestic policy are aspects of the same thing." At every critical juncture, he argued, "control over international relations" came down to a struggle for "control over domestic policies and forces." Worried that American leaders might be tempted to respond to the depression of the 1930s with the same kind of imperial expansion as in 1898, Beard held out the vision of a more egalitarian "commonweal" at home as the way to keep expansionists in check. Events gave this idea some support in the early 1930s with the simultaneous arrival of the New Deal and the Good Neighbor Policy. Franklin Roosevelt repudiated the (Teddy) Roosevelt Corollary to the Monroe Doctrine, abrogated the Platt Amendment, and otherwise turned his back on the habit of sending the marines into Latin America to collect debts owned to U.S. banks. All in all, popular resistance to concentrated power was finally gaining traction.[64]

With the corporate rich falling off the throne, professional elites were heading to Washington to take their place. Roosevelt's New Deal flung open the door to men (and a handful of women) who had been waiting in the wings during the ascendancy of corporate grandees. As talented lawyers, social workers, professors, and engineers set to work, it soon became clear that Roosevelt had tapped a rich source of creative energy. With the New Deal paving the way, a new political economy emerged by the late 1940s in which market and state were reunited in a regulatory regime that bears comparison to the old mercantilism of the eighteenth century. In what became known as the Establishment, rejuvenated corporate capitalists shared power with the bureaucratic and professional progeny of the New Deal and with the military-industrial complex that grew out of the Second World War.

In the meantime, the supreme irony of the period from the depression of the 1890s to the depression of the 1930s was that the corporate rich were unable to monopolize political power because they were too closely tied to moneymaking for their own good. To be sure, democratic traditions and popular protest exercised important checks on upper-class power. But what finally did them in was their inability to go beyond the bottom line when the system could no longer deliver the goods. It turned out Hemingway was right after all.

The lesson for the future of democracy in America, however, is not very comforting. If the corporate rich in the Era of Big Money failed to become a ruling class, it was not for lack of trying. Whether the super-rich of the twenty-first century, emboldened by the profits of globalization, deregulation, and privatization, will succeed in a similar bid for unchecked power remains to be seen. But the possibility cannot be ruled out.

6

The Managerial Revitalization of the Rich

※

JACKSON LEARS

By the 1890s, the American ruling class had grown corpulent and corrupt. Its members were the target of increasing moral outrage from reformers and the butt of ridicule from satirists like Thorstein Veblen, who viewed their lavish ways as merely the outmoded excrescence of a plutocracy on the way out. But Veblen, it turned out, was egregiously mistaken. During the first several decades of the twentieth century, the American ruling class remade itself, not only by collaborating with public policymakers but also by creating new cultural values and institutions. This revitalized culture provided an unprecedented sense of élan and solidarity that flourished until the economic collapse of the early 1930s, and survived in various forms well into the post–World War II era.

According to Veblen's influential scenario, flabby plutocrats had devolved into a "leisure class" and would eventually lack sufficient know-how to run the vast corporations that had enriched them. A "new class" of salaried technicians and professionals would become the vanguard of a managerial revolution. The separation of ownership and

control in the corporation would open the door to a genuine meritocracy. So Veblen, James Burnham, and others in this technocratic tradition hoped, but events developed differently. Some sort of managerial
revolution occurred, but it never substituted managers of corporations
for the owners of capital as the new men of power. On the contrary:
the established ruling class used the managerial ethos to revitalize and
transform its cultural hegemony at a critical historical moment.[1]

At the turn of the last century, the ruling class was roiled by internal
conflict—between local and cosmopolitan, patrician and parvenu, paternalist duty and irresponsible extravagance. The managerial ideal of
merit seemed to dissolve these tensions, to create a common criterion
for elite status. To sustain legitimacy, the meritocratic model had to
possess at least some empirical validity. Old-monied leaders like Theodore Roosevelt and Charles William Eliot (president of Harvard for
four decades) recognized this, and sought to broaden the WASP mainstream by opening elite institutions to ambitious outsiders, even if they
were Jews or Catholics. At the same time, old and new universities
alike began revamping their curricula to provide the technical training
necessary to manage the emerging corporate economy; the founding
of Harvard Business School in 1907 was a case in point.

The standard of merit also meant that established elites had to demonstrate their leadership in business and public life. There were various
ways to do this. As Charles Ponce de Leon has shown, corporate leaders used the new "profession" of public relations to transform themselves from "robber barons" into "industrial statesmen" and "progressive philanthropists." Yet the rhetoric of duty was more than just
smoke and mirrors, at least for some prominent men. Roosevelt's
strenuous quest for personal revitalization, for all its manic silliness, led
him from provincial snobbery into a life of lasting public service.
Endicott Peabody's mission was equally successful. Under Peabody's
stern leadership, the Groton School aimed to indoctrinate the sons of
the rich in a severe creed of paternalistic responsibility for the larger
good. More than a few took this creed seriously.[2]

The remade ruling class became more meritocratic (albeit largely within its own ranks) than the old ruling class had been, more able to meet managerial demands for expertise and moral demands for public service. Much of this revitalization involved a retailoring of Victorian manliness to meet the demands of modernity, but upper-class women also played a critical role through the selective assimilation of feminism, avant-garde art, and other novel forms of cultural experiment. Judicious attention to merit (in actuality as well as appearance) provided fresh legitimacy for existing economic privilege.

Yet alongside the meritocratic impulse toward openness there was an equally powerful tendency toward ethnocentrism and attachment to invented Anglophile traditions. Indeed, this exclusivity was a crucial part of the new ruling-class consciousness. Despite the emphasis on public service at Groton and a few similar institutions, prep schools joined country clubs and metropolitan men's clubs in creating sites of self-recognition for wealthy boys and men. Doctrines of Anglo-Saxon supremacy were codified in admissions policies at clubs and schools, culminating in the Jewish quotas established at Ivy League universities in the 1920s. Through the first three decades of the twentieth century, snobbery slowly gained the upper hand over public-spirited principle.[3]

This was part of a subtle shift in the revitalization of the ruling class, a gradual tilt from moral to physical and psychological standards for success. Although Roosevelt came close to celebrating action for its own sake, to him character remained crucial. But by the 1920s, morality played an increasingly marginal role in the managerial worldview. The "Big Men," the men of moment, were expected to radiate a constant supply of energy, or "vim." They were also expected to conform to youthful and uniform standards of physical attractiveness on the Anglo-Saxon model. The new institutions of national advertising and mass-marketed entertainment created a sleeker, more streamlined symbolic universe for the rich to cavort in; in the ads and the movies, established wealth was exceptionally deft at accommodating itself to the new world of flappers and fast cars. The 1920s marked the apogee of streamlined ruling-class style: rich men (at least in the advertisements) were leaner, fitter, and more energetic by far than their Gilded Age predecessors. And rich women were more seductive. They (and their consorts) had become Beautiful People.[4]

Yet a leitmotif of loss remained. For decades, established elites had sustained their power by declaring that it was in decline, or had already disappeared. Novelists collaborated in this fiction, throwing a veil of melancholy over inherited wealth: the golden age of probity was in the past, the vulgar parvenu repeatedly displaced the discriminating but ineffectual patrician. F. Scott Fitzgerald complicated those categories, dissecting status rivalries with a gimlet eye but in the end reinforcing the romantic narrative of the vulnerable rich, done in by their own privilege. Fitzgerald understood how quickly new money could be legitimated through association with the "best" schools and clubs; he also knew how implacably those institutions could maintain their exclusivity. But mainly he endowed the rich with psychological depth. The Beautiful People, for Fitzgerald, were often Beautiful Losers, lonely and misunderstood and self-destructive. They inhabited a glamorous, apolitical realm, light years away from the morally charged arena of the Progressive Era. And they were far more interesting than bloated plutocrats.

In 1929 the Beautiful Losers became losers in fact as well as fiction. The cultural apparatus they had created was shaken by the Great Depression, but it was not destroyed. Advertising icons temporarily donned overalls to show their solidarity with the working class; Hollywood skewered the pomp of wealth and celebrated the plain folk. But the leading investment banks and Wall Street law firms and advertising agencies, the Ivy League universities and exclusive prep schools, even the country clubs and restricted summer resorts—all these institutions survived and eventually even flourished again. Nor were they dedicated solely to the protection of narrow class interests. The ethos of public service resurfaced in the administration of Franklin Roosevelt, godson of Theodore and a Groton alumnus. Recovering a sense of paternalistic responsibility while preserving its exclusivity, the ruling class remained a vital force, despite the widespread assumption that it was dying or already dead. We still live with its heirs, many of whom continue to exercise significant economic and political power. Reports of its death, like those of Mark Twain's, have been greatly exaggerated.

Turn of a Century: Crisis and Revitalization

Historians have become wary of invoking "crisis" as an explanation for American cultural change, and with good reason. From earliest colonial times, American public life has been pervaded by Protestant aspirations and anxieties—dreams of creating a righteous community, fears that the community is falling into moral degeneracy. An emotionally charged political discourse has produced extravagant expectation and bitter disappointment. Such a hyperventilated atmosphere produces constant talk of crisis. So it should come as no surprise that historians have found crises at every turn in American history.

Nevertheless, one can plausibly claim that the late nineteenth century was a moment of genuine crisis in American ruling-class culture. Rarely have elites expressed their insecurities so openly, for such a wide variety of reasons, as they did in the decade or so leading up to 1900. The plutocracy that had commandeered the ship of state seemed unable to keep the craft on course. Skillful monopolists like John D. Rockefeller, Sr., had rationalized the chaos of entrepreneurial capitalism to suit their interests, but their enterprises lacked legitimacy. They faced mounting challenges from an angry working class, which felt dispossessed of skills and security, as well as from middle- and upper-class reformers who were appalled at the spectacle of small businessmen squeezed to bankruptcy and legislatures purchased wholesale.[5]

Yet the social tensions were only the most obvious part of the crisis. What really set elite spokesmen to worrying was the sense that their own "leadership class" was not up to the challenges it faced. Men of wealth seemed increasingly oblivious to any sense of public responsibility. Old republican fears about the corrupting power of luxury seemed confirmed by the antics of the rich at opulent resorts like Saratoga Springs, where extravagant spending and display became the norm. Consider the dubious achievement of the dapper Berry Wall, who kept a room at the United States Hotel in Saratoga Springs, and who became known as "king of the dudes" after appearing in forty complete changes of costume one August day in 1888. This was the sort of silliness that drove Veblen and other republican moralists crazy. For them, escapades like Wall's provided conclusive evidence that the rich were becoming effete and ineffectual.[6]

The problem of elite decline went beyond mere frivolity. Degeneration encompassed body, mind, and spirit. Flabby bodies were a sign of decaying character; revitalization required a toughening of muscular as well as moral fiber. The agenda of revitalization was in place by the 1890s, but it had been in the making for some time. During the decades after the Civil War, affluent and educated Americans, especially in cities, felt increasingly cut off from direct, unmediated experience and yearned to reconnect with "real life" through passionate action.

One source of that yearning—especially among men—was the war itself. Memories and fantasies of military heroism helped create more secular and more insistently physical models of male development. The ideal of manliness emerging after the war, as Kim Townsend writes, was "still an honorable man, but now a stronger, a tougher, a less thoughtful man" than his mid-century predecessors had been. The old ideal, observed a Harvard Phi Beta Kappa speaker in 1894, was an introspective spiritual seeker with a "towering forehead, from which the hair was carefully brushed backwards and upwards to give the full effect to his remarkable phrenological development." That wan figure had given way to the new athletic man of "mass" and "power," but there was no reason why this fellow could not be a good Christian too. On the contrary, the spread of "Muscular Christianity" on college campuses and other playgrounds of well-to-do youth gave men a chance to reclaim religion from "feminizing" influences.[7] The retooling of the male ideal was not simply an attempt to recover wartime heroism. It was also an effort to encourage adjustment to a more urban, more sedentary, and more highly organized society. To many moralists, the depletion of rural population was at least as disturbing as the closing of the frontier. Urban occupations "do almost nothing to make one sturdy and enduring," observed the novelist Robert Herrick in 1895, striking a common chord of complaint. Nor was the danger simply physical: city-dwelling parents deprived their offspring of the chance to develop the superior "farm bred mind," warned Myron Scudder, an advocate of "Muscular Christianity" and a leader in the Men and Religion Forward movement, in 1910. At the same time, the economy was becoming more bureaucratically "rational" as well as more urban and industrial. The emerging corporate system posed fundamental challenges to familiar ideas of personal identity. Salaried employees (even if they were at the executive level) no longer possessed "the economic and moral independence of former days," as *The Independent* observed in 1903. Interdependence loomed, and with it (implicitly) weakness.[8]

The specter of debility haunted white-collar men at all social levels, from the executive to his shipping clerk, but it was peculiarly disturbing to those at the top. Fortunately for the fate of their class, though, elite men had been implementing an agenda of revitalization in schools and colleges for several decades. By 1900 it had begun to bear fruit.

The best-known embodiment of revitalization was Theodore Roosevelt, a nearsighted, asthmatic boy who turned his own struggle to overcome weakness into a lesson for an entire "leadership class." The struggle began early. When he was twelve, a doctor told young "Teedie" that he must "make his body" or his mind would languish. The boy vowed, "I'll make my body." He began to devote himself to exercise, inaugurating a regime of frenetic activism that he never abandoned. His classmates at Harvard remembered him racing about the Yard, all noise and bustle—a combination of aggressive physicality and unremarkable intellect. Devoted to bodily purity, he never smoked or swore, avoided excessive drinking (or tried to), and abstained from premarital sex. He won admission to all the right Harvard clubs, including the Porcellian, the holy of holies. Combining class prejudice, Victorian morality, and physical vigor, Roosevelt was the ideal man to rally a ruling class beset by fears of decay.[9]

Roosevelt's political ascent epitomized the restoration of character and public responsibility in elite men. For him at least, the project involved shedding some of his inherited snobbery and ethnocentrism. As a New York State assemblyman in the 1880s, he discovered that he enjoyed the company of lower Manhattan characters like Jake Hess, a German Jew, and Joe Murray, an Irish Catholic. They helped corral ethnic votes for Roosevelt, and he, in turn, began to pay some attention to working-class needs—as in his sponsorship of a state law restricting the manufacture of cigars in tenements. As New York City police commissioner during the 1890s, he joined Jacob Riis's effort to discover "how the other half lives." His sympathy for the impoverished grew alongside his distaste for racial and religious bigotry. He defined "True Americanism" in 1894 as the creation of "a community of interest among our people" that transcended ethnic divisions and promoted "fair treatment" for all. And in his presidential administration he included not only muscular (Protestant) Christians like Gifford Pinchot, William Phillips, and Henry Stimson but also Charles Bonaparte, a patrician Catholic from Maryland, as secretary of the navy and Oscar Straus, the first Jewish member of a presidential cabinet, as secretary of commerce and labor. And—to the outrage of southern senators—he dined with Booker T. Washington in the White House. Indeed, his commitment to meritocracy and noblesse oblige intensified as his career advanced, leading him from the Square Deal policies of his presidency to the Progressive Party platform of 1912, which anticipated most of the welfare state created by the New Deal.[10]

Roosevelt epitomized the coming of the managerial revolution to the White House. More than any president before him, he aimed to put technical expertise at the service of the commonweal—professionalizing, in effect, the old republican tradition. This was apparent in his pioneering advocacy of wilderness conservation through efficient management. The conservation movement sought to professionalize the Forest Service in the name of protecting certain sacred spaces, many of which resonated with frontier mythology (as represented in Roosevelt's own *Winning of the West*). Conservation was both a move toward more efficient management and an instrument of ruling-class solidarity. Meritocratic ideals of efficiency melded with ethnocentric myths of masculinity to ratify elite rule. This doubleness typified the managerial revolution in the United States, as it did Roosevelt himself.

For all his egalitarianism and tolerance, there was another side to Theodore Roosevelt—the side that celebrated the Darwinian struggle between nations and believed in regeneration through empire. After his own struggle to overcome weakness, Roosevelt was simply unable to separate moral courage from physical courage. For him the formation of character would always be firmly rooted in flesh and bone. This obsession with bodily manliness made him susceptible to militarist and racialist fantasies. War was the ultimate test of men and nations, and preparation for it began in the womb. The opponent of bigotry still worried that old-stock Americans were committing "race suicide," and made regeneration a project in recovering WASP manhood. During his presidency, Roosevelt's speaking engagements became a magnet for large families, some holding signs that read "No Race Suicide Here!" In Redlands, California, in 1903, Roosevelt remarked: "The sight of these children convinces me of the truth of a statement made by Gov. Pardee, when he said that in California there is no danger of race suicide. You have done well in raising oranges, and I believe you have done better raising children."[11]

The connection between California and fecundity was not fortuitous. By the early twentieth century the West was a well-known site of regeneration for eastern dudes. Roosevelt himself had popularized the idea with his foray into the Black Hills in the 1880s, which provided him abundant opportunities for virile self-assertion. When a foulmouthed bully taunted him repeatedly as "four-eyes," the well-bred easterner could take it no longer: "As I rose, I struck quick and hard with my right just to one side of the point of his jaw, hitting with my left as I straightened out, and then again with my right . . . When he went down he struck the corner of the bar with his head . . . he was senseless." Sometimes a man had to do what a man had to do—even, perhaps especially, if he was a gentleman. For Roosevelt as for many of his contemporaries, body and mind were twinned through unquestioning adherence to a few unchanging, bedrock principles: fair play, personal honor, moral and physical courage.[12]

Strong virtue existed apart from privilege. The "entirely original American gentleman" could be found on the Dakota prairies as well as the playing fields of Harvard, according to Roosevelt's friend and admirer Owen Wister, who also played a crucial role in creating the West as a venue for upper-class revitalization. The protagonist of Wister's novel *The Virginian* (1902) embodied the emerging ideal of the toughened-up gentleman. A figure of few words, slow to anger but implacable in his quiet sense of personal honor, he is at home on the range but also in the company of books (provided they have plenty of action) and refined women. Wister made it plain: a touch of western spontaneity could save gilded youth from the eastern diseases of morbid self-consciousness, perpetual indecision, and paralysis of the will.[13]

William James agreed. In 1903 he fretted openly that "the Ph.D. Octopus" would ensnare thoughtful graduate students, transforming them into drones who lacked "individuality and bare manhood." Three years later, reflecting on "the social value of the college bred" to an audience at Stanford University, James warned against the "sterilized conceit" and "priggishness" of upper-class social and intellectual coteries. "If democracy is to survive, it must catch the higher, healthier tone," James warned, and no one was more crucial to setting that tone than college-bred men (and, less explicitly, women). He returned to the theme of revitalization in "The Moral Equivalent of War" (1910), envisioning a nationwide civilian boot camp for the "luxurious classes": "To coal and iron mines, to freight trains, to fishing fleets in December, to dish-washing, clothes-washing, and window-washing, to road-building and tunnel-making, to foundries and stoke-holes, and to the frames of skyscrapers, would our gilded youths be drafted off, according to their choice, to get the childishness knocked out of them, and to come back into society with healthier sympathies and soberer ideas."[14]

James, in short, shared a lot of concerns with Theodore Roosevelt, and for a couple of years James even thought that Roosevelt would be a good candidate to succeed Charles William Eliot as president of Harvard. But ultimately Roosevelt was too relentlessly anti-intellectual for James. "You college men," the former Rough Rider bellowed out to an audience of Harvard students in 1907, "be doers rather than critics of the deeds that others do." James was disgusted by this mindless activism. His idea of revitalization was the reconnection of the "luxurious classes" to the difficulties routinely experienced by the rest of the world's population; this might make them better democrats, more humane and public-spirited leaders, James thought. James was also an intellectual, an anti-imperialist, and a pacifist in search of a "moral equivalent of war." For Roosevelt, there was no such equivalent. Nothing could measure up to the bracing challenge of the battlefield.[15]

Roosevelt and his circle developed a crucial counterargument against antimodern militarists like Brooks Adams, who claimed that the martial virtues had withered with the rise of bourgeois society. On the contrary, Roosevelt and other imperialists insisted, a war in the service of American commercial expansion could be as morally regenerative as any fought for religious or patriotic ends. Indeed, all these motives could be combined with the restoration of manliness: this was the core of the imperialists' civilizing mission. The alternative, Alfred Thayer Mahan warned in 1897, was a slide into degeneracy comparable to ancient Rome's. There was a disturbing parallel, Mahan thought, between the contemporary United States and imperial Rome after it had abandoned its "strong masculine impulse" and "degenerated into that worship of comfort, wealth, and general softness which is the ideal of the peace prophets of to-day." The reassertion of masculine vigor led directly to war for empire.[16]

Leading educators stressed the connection between the playing field and the battlefield, between "manly sports" at college and imperial adventures abroad. "The time given to athletic contests . . . and the injuries incurred on the playing field are part of the price the English-speaking world has paid for being world-conquerors," said Senator Henry Cabot Lodge in 1896. Six years later, after the vanquishing of Spain and the conquest of the Philippines, President Eliot of Harvard announced that he and his faculty were engaged in the creation of an American aristocracy: "The aristocracy which excels in many sports, carries off the honors and prizes in the learned professions and bears itself with distinction in all fields of intellectual labor and combat; the aristocracy which in peace stands firmest for the public honor and renown, and in war rides first into the murderous thickets." The American aristocrat's path led from "manly sports" through meritorious achievements that ended in "murderous thickets." Athletic prowess and imperial leadership were twinned, for Eliot (despite his distrust of football) as for Cecil Rhodes. In his will, which created the Rhodes scholarship, the British imperialist listed "fondness of and success in manly outdoor sports" as one of the chief criteria for the award. Sport was ensconced in the scholarship award that revivified the Anglo-American elite.[17]

Still the challenge of empire could provide only sporadic regeneration; not even the bellicose Roosevelt was an advocate of permanent war. Creating and sustaining a vital "leadership class"—what later became known as an "Establishment"—was a constant task, new with each new generation. The goal was not trivial. To lead in a democracy, elites had to take the idea of public duty seriously, even if they defined it according to their class-blinkered vision of society. This was a subtle paternalism, tempered by ideals of social responsibility, and superior in many ways to the "devil take the hindmost" creed of laissez-faire. Yet, like most ruling-class creeds, it conflated the interests of a narrow elite with those of society and indeed humanity at large. This outlook blended sincere belief and disingenuous strategy. To maintain legitimacy in a democratic culture that distrusted inherited wealth and even denied its existence, elites had to disguise their inherited privilege and embrace a meritocratic standard—or at least appear to embrace it. They had to come to terms, in short, with the managerial ethos of expertise, even as they preserved connections to an actual and imagined past. And they managed to pull off this complicated task for much of the twentieth century.

Reclaiming Authority in a Managerial Age

One key to the remaking of the ruling class was the socialization of its young. Even while William James was worrying about "gilded youths," educators younger than he were revamping prep schools and colleges to inculcate a sense of public responsibility—class-bound but genuine—in their students. A few elite academies had existed since the eighteenth century (Andover and Phillips Exeter, for two), but it was not until the 1880s and 1890s that the modern prep school emerged as an instrument of ruling-class socialization. Like other custodians of the (allegedly static) genteel tradition in the late nineteenth century, educators were caught up in a "strenuous mood." In 1884 the founders of the Groton School chose Endicott Peabody as the school's first head, with the express mission of restoring physical and moral fiber to the sons of the rich. Peabody pursued that goal by creating what the sociologist Erving Goffmann would call a "total institution" where boys were constantly supervised and subject to Spartan discipline. This regime was in place for decades; Averell Harriman and Dean Acheson remembered it with bitterness from their time there in the twenties.

Yet Harriman and Acheson were just the sort of public figures that Groton's system was designed to produce.[18]

Of course, the system was not foolproof. A Groton alumnus named George Martin remembered that Peabody constantly advised the boys "to go into the professions and keep away from Wall Street," but Martin thought this advice fell on deaf ears. Although Peabody "urged the boys to be true to themselves and drop out of their parents' income class, they did not hear him. They were going to make enough money to send their sons to Groton." The rhetoric of duty grew tiresome to students like Ellery Sedgwick, later editor of the *Atlantic Monthly*. "In season and out," Sedgwick recalled, "public service was held up to every boy as a shining goal. It is God's mercy that all of us didn't go into it!"[19]

Still, many of them did. The historian James McLachlan reports:

In 1933, shortly before its fiftieth anniversary, this tiny school with fewer than a thousand alumni out of college could number among its graduates one man serving as president of the United States; two men who had served as Secretary of State; three senators; a congressman; ministers or ambassadors to Japan, Turkey, Canada, Denmark, Greece, Switzerland, the Dominican Republic, El Salvador, and Cuba; a governor-general; two state governors; two assistant secretaries of the navy; one of the Treasury; one of the Army; two lieutenant-governors; a police commissioner of New York City; a civil service commissioner of New York, and a governor of the Federal Reserve Bank.[20]

Nor was Groton alone. Through the early decades of the twentieth century, Choate, Phillips Exeter, and other prominent prep schools compiled comparable records of placing alumni in public life. They were engaged in a common enterprise—the melding of patrician and parvenu into a coherent ruling class. Their curricula emerged only gradually from the rigid classicism of the traditional academy, with

mathematics and science lagging behind literature, but academic expertise was less important than educating the whole man. In the accents of
muscular Christianity, educators presented a vision of life at the top as
a difficult moral struggle. Being rich and influential was no picnic;
power and pain were twinned. Enveloped in ascetic ideals of duty, the
privileged young were exhorted to "be somebody" (not the contemporary "be yourself.") This was partly old-fashioned Protestant moral-
ism, but the pedagogical brew was flavored with other ingredients as
well. After 1900, success increasingly required conformity to newly
standardized ideals of physical vitality and attractiveness. To be somebody, you had to look like somebody—vigorous, young, and preferably Anglo-Saxon. In the Anglophile atmosphere of the prep school,
standards were especially rigid and ethnocentric: the right "look" was
essential to status ascent, and even status survival.[21]

The prep school prepared the privileged young for rule. A dozen or
so private secondary schools constituted the chief sluiceway into Ivy
League colleges and from there into key economic, political, and cultural institutions—the "best" law firms and investment banks and universities, the blue chip corporations. While this was the world that was
supposedly being transformed into a meritocracy, admission to it remained largely governed by class, ethnic, and gender restrictions. During the early twentieth century, elite apologists did little to deny those
restrictions, but they did begin the refrain that later became a mantra:
these boys are here because they're the "best."[22]

A handful of educators tried to make that claim real. Peabody was
one; Charles Eliot was another. Like Roosevelt, he sought an infusion
of new blood from non-WASP sources. The contemporary rhetoric of
"diversity" has many antecedents, but part of its lineage can be traced
to Eliot's "American Democracy," a speech he gave in 1902. While
"the democracy preserves and uses sound old families," he said, "it
also utilizes strong blood from foreign sources." Accordingly Harvard
admissions began to cast a wider net, seeking more students from ethnic minorities. By the time Eliot retired in 1909, out of about 2,100 stu-

dents there were five African Americans, eight Italian Americans, fifty Irish Americans, and fifty-six Jewish Americans; among the foreign students there were thirty-three Russian Jews and nineteen Chinese. This ethnic diversity, however limited, provided access for the occasional brilliant outsider (such as Walter Lippmann, class of 1910); it also provided legitimacy for the new meritocratic creed. So did the elective system, which Eliot substituted for the creaking classical curriculum. The young men who had the self-discipline to choose their own courses, Eliot believed, were America's rightful elect.[23]

Yet both Eliot and his successor, Abbott Lawrence Lowell, assumed that the meritocracy they were designing would continue to be stocked by "the descendants of old, well-to-do American families." Indeed, Lowell did his best to ensure this by instituting the infamous quota system for Jews. Class divisions persisted at Ivy League schools even as they were modernizing their curricula and claiming to embrace a new meritocratic model. Similar patterns developed at public universities outside the Northeast. Fraternities, eating clubs, sports teams, secret societies, and other status-marking organizations proliferated on college campuses from Harvard, Yale, and Princeton to Berkeley and Virginia. Extracurricular "college life" enhanced elite solidarity and self-awareness. Despite college presidents' rhetoric, this was not a golden age of merit. It was around the turn of the century, after all, that the "gentleman's C" appeared.[24]

Women remained a key part of this picture, and not merely as replenishers of Anglo-Saxon stock. They also oversaw the realm of leisure, which was growing more important to the maintenance of ruling-class hegemony. More cultural institutions appeared to provide venues for elites to mingle, celebrate themselves, and recognize one another—as well as re-create their energies for the competitive fray. Some were stag settings like the metropolitan men's clubs, but many were presided over by women.

Among them were the rituals of elite society, the coming out parties and weddings that were increasingly staged in public venues and bathed in the glare of newspaper publicity. Barriers between private and public became more porous, in everything from interior design (which stressed the need for flow between inside and outside) to society page reporting. The rich were joining the dramatis personae of the emerging celebrity culture. Ruling-class leisure was becoming more informal and more public, and women acquired fame simply for the parties they threw. The only "democratic" feature of these rituals was their availability in the emerging mass media, where they could provide vicarious entertainment to an audience hungry for titillation.[25]

Yet after 1900, ruling-class women had more serious ambitions as well. They played an increasingly visible and important role in cultural institutions that had previously been controlled by men—museums, art galleries, orchestras. In the imposing new institutions funded by women like Isabella Stewart Gardner and Gertrude Whitney, art became sacred and professional at about the same time. Once again the allegedly anemic "genteel tradition" proved adaptable to the challenges of managerial modernity. If only by virtue of their wealth and taste, rich women were able to legitimate the avant-garde forms of art that had scandalized the previous generation—Gertrude Whitney in the Museum of American Art (opened 1931) that bears her name, and Abby Rockefeller, even more emphatically, in the Museum of Modern Art (opened 1929). Ruling-class women made sure that their culture was flexible enough to accommodate and eventually canonize modernism. Like their male counterparts, they refused to rest content with Victorian gentility, recognizing that openness to merit required openness to artistic experiment as well.[26]

Wealthy women also spread class legitimacy through philanthropic giving, not only by encouraging their husbands' stewardship (as rich men's wives from Abby Rockefeller to Melinda Gates have done) but also by contributing their own. The American version of the Tory radical (or at least the Tory progressive) was born in the years after 1900, often enough among old-money WASPs. Jane Addams, fundraising for Hull House, used to say that she could raise almost as much money in a summer on Mount Desert Island (a Maine coast retreat for old Yankee money) as she could the rest of the whole year. The leisurely pace of resort life proved conducive to generosity.[27]

Rich people had been congregating at seaside and mountain retreats since the antebellum era, but during the early twentieth century these settings became more socially significant. They were, among other things, status testing grounds, opportunities for old money and new, eastern and western elites, to cultivate the finer points of snobbery. At Newport one sultry day in August 1906, Edward Wharton (Edith's husband) thumbed his way home from town in a butcher's cart. According to local lore, a nouveau riche "westerner" (which could have meant he was from Chicago or Pittsburgh) saw Wharton and said, "I wouldn't do that if I were you." To which Wharton replied, "No, if I were you, I wouldn't do that either." But the West could turn the tables, too. "One simply doesn't wear diamonds in the daytime," clucked an elderly Palm Beach matron to a younger woman from Denver. "I thought not too," said the latter, "until I had them!"[28]

But ultimately the resorts were more important for bringing the rich together than for demarcating differences among them. Dozens of local settings served regional elites, but the national ruling class came together at watering places dominated by the Anglophile northeastern set—Newport, Bar Harbor, Tuxedo Park (New Jersey), and Palm Beach, along with dozens of lesser-known spots such as Jekyll Island, Georgia. The nearly universal policy of accepting membership cards from comparable-status clubs in other regions reinforced the cohesion of the members, reminding them of their common participation in a national elite. Another centripetal force was the exclusion of Jews (along with African Americans and other people of color). This prohibition, enforced by most private clubs throughout the early twentieth century, sometimes caught up the occasional Jewish meritocrat. Once the Palm Beach Bath and Tennis Club sent a letter to its members requesting that they refrain from bringing Jewish guests to the club. This provoked Bernard Baruch, a prominent Jewish member, to resign. But as a pillar of the Establishment, he did so quietly.[29]

Like prep schools and colleges, clubs created a collective identity for movers and shakers. In August 1930, when the journalist James Gerard identified "64 Men Who Run America," fifty of them were "men about clubs." "They themselves," Gerard wrote, "are too busy to hold political office, but they determine who shall hold such offices." This was a self-important exaggeration (particularly for that historical moment, when the power of established elites was wavering in the aftermath of the market crash), but it accurately captured a persistent point of view. Along with a healthy dose of arrogance, the outlook of the "men about clubs" contained a strong trace of paternalism, an assumption that rich men had a duty as well as a right to intervene in public affairs. This was the attitude that led the aged and ailing J. P. Morgan to ask his friend George Harvey, the editor of *Harper's*, to convey a message to the newly elected President Woodrow Wilson. Morgan, no Democrat, had opposed Wilson, but now he asked Harvey to tell the president that "if there should ever come a time when he thinks any influence or resources that I have can be used for the country, they are wholly at his disposal." Morgan embodied the combination of old money, managerial acumen, and paternalist magnanimity that characterized the remade ruling class of the pre–World War I era.[30]

With respect to leisure, Morgan was a transitional figure. Part aesthete and connoisseur, he acquired objets d'art for the sensuous enjoyment they provided him—a pleasure hardly reducible to "conspicuous consumption." But his collecting trips took place in a whirl of manic energy. On the rare occasions when he did slow down, he had therapeutic ends in view. For him as for other driven Victorian men, play was re-creation of mind and body; its aim was to ready them for the rigors of the workplace. Whenever Morgan or his contemporaries felt a debilitating bout of neurasthenia coming on, they dropped everything and took off on a long sea voyage. This was the characteristic manic-depressive pattern of the old ruling class: intense work punctuated by periodic and sometimes extended breakdowns. The remade ruling class, in contrast, embraced a managerial ethos of continuous "peak performance." Nervous breakdowns had to fit into a tighter schedule. Long sea voyages were not on the agenda, and even temporary stillness was a sign of defeat.

The new and more demanding performance ethic was epitomized by Frederick Winslow Taylor, the "father" of scientific management. His career revealed how the appearance of technical expertise could revitalize the cultural hegemony of inherited privilege. A pampered son of Main Line Philadelphia, Taylor grew impatient with the indolent ways of inherited wealth. Like Theodore Roosevelt (his near contemporary), Taylor sought pastimes more demanding than organizing polo matches or lounging at Alpine spas. At Phillips Exeter Academy, he drove himself to long hours of study and eventually had to withdraw owing to "eyestrain" in the middle of his junior year. It was the characteristic nervous breakdown of the upper bourgeoisie, though it occurred a little earlier than most. Taylor's self-treatment, in contrast, was strikingly at odds with cultural conventions and family expectations, though it anticipated the fin-de-siècle longings to connect with "real life."[31]

After eighteen months of depression and indecision, Taylor took a job as an apprentice pattern maker at a family friend's factory, the Ferrell & Jones pump works, making wooden patterns for iron molds. It was a difficult and demanding task, but for Taylor the work was satisfying. What he learned of materials and techniques seemed to him a secret knowledge, unavailable to his foppish friends back on the Main Line. Unlike Teddy Roosevelt, who never pretended he was anything but an eastern gentleman out West, Taylor wanted to be one of the boys. He took up cursing, though so ineptly that the results were often comic.[32]

Taylor's awkward swearing captured the anomalies of his situation. His rebellion against gentility was constrained by his privilege. He was not looking at a life's work as a pattern maker, and everyone knew it. After a few months he was off to another apprenticeship as a machinist (also at Ferrell & Jones). He took six months off to work at the Philadelphia Centennial, where he represented a group of New England machine tool manufacturers to potential foreign buyers—another job that came through a family connection. Finally in 1878 he completed his apprenticeship at Ferrell & Jones and took a machinist's job at Midvale Steel Company. Members of the Midvale hierarchy were frequent guests at the Taylors' dinner table. Another friend of a friend was the president of the Stevens Institute of Technology in Hoboken, where Taylor managed to obtain a degree in mechanical engineering without ever attending a class. Everywhere he turned, Fred found family friends in key positions. His efforts at solidarity with the workers were always compromised by his class connections.[33]

This became plain when Taylor was promoted to foreman of a machine shop at Midvale. Obsessed with increasing productivity in a resistant workforce, he devised a differential piece rate, which paid more to workers who produced more. To fix the higher rate, Taylor broke each job into segments, timed the swiftest possible performance of each, and reassembled them to demonstrate "the one best way" to machine a locomotive wheel or overhaul a boiler. As productivity at Midvale increased, Taylor's reputation spread, and in 1890 he left the plant to take up freelance work as the first "management consultant."[34]

Taylor spent much of his career, until his death in 1915, searching for scientific law in the workplace, but it is an open question how much he found there and how much he put there. The more closely one examines his "science," the more spurious it seems. Calculations were based on arbitrarily chosen figures. The appearance of precision counted for more than the actuality. (One of Taylor's assistants routinely recorded three seconds as ".00083 hours.") From the outset the results were mixed. Few workers were willing to endure the oppressive toil required to become a "high-priced man." After several days of Taylor's experiments in increasing productivity at Bethlehem Steel, for example, only the cloddish "Schmidt" (described at length in *Principles of Scientific Management*) was left from the original group of ten workers Taylor had picked for their speed, strength, and commitment. When Taylor recalled his stint at Bethlehem in *Principles*, he put a triumphant façade on what was actually a disaster. Scientific management did not last at Bethlehem; its "science" was bogus, it threw the plant into turmoil, and its failure got Taylor fired. Yet Taylor turned the Bethlehem experience into a parable of progress, a key moment in the inexorable movement toward utopian harmony between workers and managers. Submission to science, the impartial arbiter, would render old class hatreds obsolete. Meritocratic standards would cancel the conflict between labor and capital.[35]

In conflating his own narrow class interest with the interests of the entire society, Taylor adopted a universalizing rhetorical strategy familiar to apologists for wealth and power. But his scientific idiom resonated with particular force in the early twentieth century. Faith in the neutrality of technical expertise was the core of the managerial ethos, and scientific management appealed to a broad swath of the American population. But it did not appeal to the workers at the Watertown Arsenal in Massachusetts and the Rock Island Arsenal in Illinois. When the House Labor Committee held hearings to investigate workers' grievances, Taylor was called to testify. As he squirmed on the stand, the committee chair, William Wilson, skewered his system's claims to science, pointing out that employers could use time and motion study to serve their own ends, to create their own self-interested definitions of unproductive work. "It ceases to be scientific management the moment it is used for bad," Taylor responded lamely. After this weak performance, Taylor asked for a transcript of his sworn testimony, which he was (amazingly) allowed to rewrite completely, putting his statements in a stronger light. Privilege continued to confer power. The final committee report rebuked Taylor, but only mildly, and it did nothing to stop the spread of Taylorism throughout American industry. During the 1920s, unions weakened and gradually ceded control over the labor process in exchange for higher wages. In the literature of management theory, Taylor's work acquired canonical status: *Principles* became the *ur*-text of an academic discipline. As business schools multiplied, the neutral language of social science would provide legitimacy for what remained a largely class-bound intellectual project.[36]

But academic prestige alone was insufficient to underwrite the new, managerial version of ruling-class cultural hegemony. Even if one accepted its claims to "science," Taylorism was still a bloodless parody of economic rationality, the more egregiously so as more complex visions of human nature became popularized among the professional elite. As early as the 1920s, even management theorists began to formulate more psychologically sophisticated approaches to workers' motivation. Psychology became a key component of the developing managerial ethos—not just as a tool for manipulating workers but as a key to understanding the human self. A vague and largely unarticulated "depth psychology" lay behind many of the strategies for ruling-class revitalization, in particular the assumption that savage needs survived beneath the veneer of bourgeois civilization (especially among boys and men). This vitalist impulse joined Theodore Roosevelt and William James with psychologists such as G. Stanley Hall; it crossed class and ethnic barriers, energizing a broad quest for regeneration among middle- as well as upper-class men; it helped account for the vogue of bodybuilding at the turn of the century and the popularity of *Tarzan* in the 1910s.

In the making of a managerial self, vitality played a crucial counterpoint to productivity. It kept the thrum of Taylorism from becoming a death rattle. Amid obsessive efficiency (or the simulation of it), there had to be room for spontaneity; indeed, the two tendencies reinforced each other. In everyday life, men shackled to managerial routine craved instinctual release off the job; in the organized fantasy purveyed by the emerging mass media, the successful man or woman was full of boundless energy, as avid in play as in work. Advertising, film, and fiction made the remade rich seem effervescent and full of fun. By the

1920s, vitality and productivity combined to define a new managerial self, for both men and women alike. Public duty merged with personal efficiency, morality with physicality. The new model of success was slimmer, more energetic, and more glamorous than its straitlaced predecessor had been. Whether it was any more humane or satisfying depended on one's point of view.[37]

Energy, Meritocracy, Melancholy: The Revitalized Rich

The merger of mental and physical excellence appeared to validate the managerial fiction of meritocracy. Only the "best" would rise to the top of the developing corporate hierarchy. To maintain its superiority, the new ruling class would need to avoid anemic gentility; resilience required a dash of primitive vitality. Projecting superhuman vitality onto dark-skinned bodies, middle- and upper-class white men strained to capture and deploy that strength in modern business life. As African Americans and Native Americans reached a social nadir, they achieved a new status as icons of primal force. The vitalist worship of force provided a common pool of aspiration for executives and stockroom boys. It sanctified the hegemony of top managers by assuming they had scaled the corporate heights through superior personal power.

Celebrity bodybuilders embodied this pointedly sanitized primitivism. The important thing about the Prussian-born Eugene Sandow, whose muscles dazzled American audiences at the turn of the century, was not just that he was "the perfect man" (as the promoter Florenz Ziegfeld presented him) but that he was the perfect *European* man. The whiteness of his skin offered crucial reassurance that ordinary desk-bound blokes could reconnect with their arboreal origins. This was not simply an antimodern escape. As John Kasson perceptively observes, Sandow "raised a new, potentially more punishing 'scientific' standard against which to measure one's inadequacy. The concept of a perfect body, ostensibly devised in opposition to modern industrial society, in fact capitulated to the presumption that perfection lay in materially defined, standardized, and repeatable processes and product." National advertising drove the point home, in ad campaigns for everything from Quaker Oats to Gillette blades: the perfect body was a scientifically managed body, systematically maintaining levels of peak performance at all times.[38]

The increasing physicality of criteria for success revealed the diffusion of popularized Darwinism in managerial thought. The magazine *System*, whose title succinctly defined the managerial impulse, devoted itself to puzzling out the process of natural selection among businessmen. Here was another meritocratic standard, this one overtly rooted in biology. *System* increasingly identified top executives as "big men" who stood out from their smaller colleagues. Clean-cut appearance and standardized attractiveness mattered, but so did qualities such as size, strength, and quickness.[39]

Preoccupation with bodily energy reinforced primitivist longings. Edgar Rice Burroughs, the author of *Tarzan of the Apes* (1914) and many sequels, was also a writer for *System*. Tarzan demonstrated that the strength and agility of a gorilla could flourish within the body of an English aristocrat (his real name was Lord Greystoke). The popularity of the *Tarzan* books revealed that primitivist yearnings for revitalization reached well into the middle class. But it was the "big men" who managed to transform those yearnings into an agenda for class revitalization.[40]

The rise of advertising and public relations ensured that the new vitality of the rich would be expressed in standardized, sanitized form. From the 1910s through the early 1930s, advertising universalized the experience of the very wealthy. Razor blades, cold cream, and other mass-produced commodities were typically associated with elegant ladies and gents in evening clothes. In advertising, the rich inhabited a luxurious utopia that was—implicitly and potentially—available to all ambitious consumers. At the same time, beginning with Rockefeller's hiring of Ivy Lee in 1914, corporate chieftains increasingly employed public relations counselors to reshape their representation in the mass media. As muckraking lost its vogue, businessmen joined their wives in the star system of celebrity journalism. Whether they owned their firms (George Westinghouse, Henry Ford, P. D. Armour) or managed them (Gerald Swope of General Electric, Walter Teagle of Standard Oil), their magazine profiles made clear that their authority derived from technical knowledge as well as unceasing labor and charismatic leadership. Even their philanthropies were more efficiently administered than the old scattershot charities had been. They epitomized the new meritocratic standards of managerial capitalism.[41]

The society pages collaborated in producing a comprehensive account of "the wholesome rich," as Charles Ponce de Leon has shown—men and women who combined physical radiance with civic responsibility. To be sure, a privileged few could still be scorned as idle or dissipated; Walter Winchell and other tabloid journalists made a specialty of this. But drunkenness and marital infidelity were the failures of weak individuals, "poor little rich girls" like Barbara Hutton and Doris Duke; they were hardly characteristic of the rich as a class, whose leisure pursuits were mostly down-to-earth and family oriented—and even at their most extravagant merely a sign of charming eccentricity. By the 1920s, in the discourse of mass-circulation journalism, the bloated plutocracy had been galvanized into an energetic, magnanimous, and magnetic elite.[42]

Similar imagery surfaced in the imaginative literature of the time. During the 1920s, the fiction of Edith Wharton, Theodore Dreiser, and F. Scott Fitzgerald indirectly reaffirmed the rehabilitation of the rich—though no one would claim that this was the authors' intention. Wharton surveyed the transformation of a staid, provincial New York elite into a dynamic, cosmopolitan ruling class with the knowingness of a born insider. Dreiser described the playgrounds of the privileged with the plaintive whine of an outsider craving admission. And Fitzgerald deployed his double status as outsider and insider to explore the myriad ways in which the rich were "different from you and me." Fitzgerald created a compelling symbolic universe that paralleled the one produced by advertising. His wealthy characters were as beautiful as the people in the Cadillac ads, but complex and vulnerable, too—and even, sometimes, suffused with tragic grandeur. Covering the revitalized rich with a mantle of melancholy, he reinforced the fiction of elite decline.

Wharton's *Age of Innocence* (1920) dissects the power of bourgeois conventions in the New York of the 1870s—especially their power to thwart any outward breach of Victorian sexual propriety. The protagonist, Newland Archer, yields reluctantly to the implacable force of that code: he finally gives up the woman he adores, the Countess Olenska, to return to the path of conjugal duty. The novel concludes with a scene set in the early twentieth century; in it, Wharton provides a capsule summary of the revitalization of the ruling class. Thirty years have passed since Archer renounced the countess; he is now a widower with three grown children. He ponders "the new state of things" that has developed for men like himself since the 1870s. Inspired by Theodore Roosevelt among others, they had explored a range of civic life beyond "the narrow groove of moneymaking, sport, and society." Archer had served in the state assembly, contributed articles to reform journals, helped to found the Grolier Club and the first hospital for crippled children—"had been, in short, what people were beginning to call 'a good citizen.'"[43]

As good citizenship became more fashionable among the elite, criteria for admission loosened. The scrutinizing of social origins became less intense. After all, as Archer muses, "of what account was anybody's past, in the huge kaleidoscope where all the social atoms spun around on the same plane?" New money could become respectable virtually overnight, once it acquired associations with the right cultural institutions. Archer's children typify the insouciance of the rising generation. They lack his obsessive scruples—especially his son Dallas, who is almost a parody of the brash young professionals who began revitalizing elite culture along managerial lines after the turn of the century. Fresh out of architecture school and about to join a firm in Chicago, he is a fount of mindless energy; "tumultuous enthusiasm and cocksure criticism tripped each other up on his lips." He lacks his father's sense of public responsibility, but the older man is tolerant. "The boy was not insensitive, he knew, but he had the facility and self-confidence that came of looking at fate not as a master but as an equal. 'That's it; they feel equal to things—they know their way about,' he mused, thinking of his son as the spokesman of the new generation which had swept away all the old landmarks, and with them the signposts and the danger signal." This was the way each "new generation" liked to think of itself, especially after 1900—energetic, assertive, undaunted. This new élan was at the core of the remade ruling class. Wharton sensed it, even as she maintained her distance.[44]

Dreiser, in contrast, longed to inhale the atmosphere of vitality that he associated with the very rich. For him, especially by the 1920s, the wealthy inhabit a realm of intoxicating sweetness. This is the perspective of Clyde Griffiths, the feckless but ambitious protagonist of *An American Tragedy* (1925), who starts out as a bellman in the haunts of the well-to-do. For him (as for Dreiser), glimpsing the fashionable younger set of Kansas Citians from the corridors of the Green-Davison Hotel is like looking through "the gates of paradise"; and the Union League Club in Chicago, Clyde's second job, seems "an Eveless paradise" where men of affairs quietly confer and take their ease. One of them is his uncle Samuel Griffiths, a prosperous collar manufacturer in Lycurgus, New York, who first takes a shine to Clyde because he looks so much like his own son Gilbert. Dreiser insistently links physical appearance with social status, contrasting Samuel Griffiths and Clyde's father, Asa. The successful Samuel is a "swell-looking guy," clean-cut, trim, "quick, alert, incisive"; the pathetic Asa is overweight, "oleaginous and a bit murky." In Dreiser's updated version of Victorian taxonomy, physiognomy is destiny.[45]

The ruling class rules through its command of appearances. To Clyde, the youthful rich in Lycurgus are all at least conventionally attractive, and some stunningly so. In their dinner jackets, cummerbunds,

and taffeta party dresses, they float through a dream landscape of midnight balls and moonlit boat rides. Clyde is allowed admission because
he is a Griffiths and he is "good-looking." Yet ultimately the power of
personal attractiveness reveals its limits. When a plain-speaking debutante named Gertrude Trumbull refers to his good looks, Clyde beams
nervously and denies it. She insists he's even better-looking than his
cousin Gilbert, but good looks won't do him much good without
money. "People like money even more than they do looks," she observes. Clyde lacks money, and eventually his handsome face proves
inadequate to save him from his apparent complicity in the drowning
of his pregnant working-class girlfriend. Throughout Clyde's trial,
Dreiser continues to characterize class conflict in terms of physical appearance. The district attorney is a man with a broken nose, which
makes him unattractive to women and resentful of men with more
erotic appeal. He seethes at "the wretched rich! The idle rich!" It is as
much their good looks as their idleness that appalls him. Populist resentment, Dreiser implies, could be reduced to personal envy. The author, like his protagonist, has been seduced by the glamorous rich.[46]

Fitzgerald, too, was enraptured, but he always held part of himself in reserve, nurturing an analytic detachment that Dreiser could
never master. Fitzgerald craved acceptance into the inner circles of the
wealthy, but he knew he would never be at home there. His distance
both sharpened and softened his focus. He anatomized the social rituals
of the rich, but situated them in the recent past of his own youth, sur-
rounding them with a haze of melancholy and loss. He always made it
clear that he was writing from the perspective of a young upper-middle-class man, straining for social ascent but never quite pulling it off.
"Let me tell you about the very rich," he wrote in "The Rich Boy"
(1926). "They are different from you and me. They possess and enjoy
early, and it makes them soft where we are hard, and cynical where we
are trustful, in a way that, unless you were born rich, it is very difficult
to understand. They think, deep in their hearts, that they are better

than we are . . . Even when they enter deep into our world or sink below us, they still think that they are better than we are. They are different."[47]

"The Rich Boy" in that story is Anson Hunter. Born in New York in 1893, the eldest of six heirs to a fortune of $15 million, he grows up accepting the deference paid him as part of the natural order of things. After Yale and a stint as a naval aviator at Pensacola, he enters the social world of postwar New York—also Southampton, Tuxedo Park, and Hot Springs. But he is never a mere playboy. He divides his life between "intelligent hedonism" by night and hard work in a prominent brokerage firm by day. The static, closed elite of the 1890s had opened its doors to new money, earned through technical expertise and shrewd investment in airplanes or automobiles. To a certain extent Anson resents the loss of the old exclusivity, "yet he himself was a part of this change, and his strong instinct for life had turned him in his twenties from the hollow obsequies of that abortive leisure class." Anson's wealth has made him cynical, a man without illusions. In matters of the heart, this proves a problem. Swept away by Paula Legendre, a dark and serious beauty from California whose parents keep a winter residence in Pensacola, Anson can never quite bring himself to commit to her. He lets her get away, and finds himself alone at twenty-nine, with a thickening waist and nothing to do on Saturday afternoon but have drinks at the Yale Club with a new generation who no longer recognize him.[48]

Loneliness and vain regret afflict the newly rich as well as those with inherited wealth—"all the sad young men," as Fitzgerald called them, whose soaring aspirations for romance are fated for frustration even if they realize their material ambitions. In "Winter Dreams" (1922), young Dexter Green of Black Bear, Minnesota, is beset by vaulting ambitions that lead him to pass up a business course at the state university "for the precarious advantage of attending an older and more famous university in the East, where he was bothered by his scanty funds." He was not "merely snobbish . . . He wanted not association with glittering things and glittering people—he wanted the things themselves. Often he reached out for the best without really knowing why he wanted it—and sometimes he ran up against the mysterious denials and prohibitions in which life indulges." After graduating from that "famous university," Dexter makes big money fast, establishing a chain of laundries that cater to the rich who gather at Big Bear Lake and other resort communities in the upper Midwest. One summer evening a few years after graduation, he meets Judy Jones, motorboating on one of those lakes. A piano is playing in the distance, the plaintive tune emanating from a "dark peninsula" across the way. It is a song popular five years before, when Dexter was a sophomore, standing outside the college gym, longing to be inside at a prom he couldn't afford. Although Dexter can now afford proms, can even afford the likes of Judy Jones, he still feels uncomfortable when he enters her house for the first time. He imagines it "peopled by the men who had already loved Judy Jones. He knew the sort of men they were—the men who when he first went to college had entered from the great prep schools with graceful clothes and the deep tan of healthy summers." But now Dexter can compete with those gods on their own terms. He has money.[49]

Like Dreiser, Fitzgerald understood the connections between money and sex. When Dexter tells Judy, "I'm probably making more money than any man my age in the Northwest," he immediately creates an erotic charge between them: "An almost imperceptible sway brought her close to him . . . [S]he communicated her excitement to him lavishly, deeply, with kisses that were not a promise but a fulfillment . . . kisses that were like charity, creating want by holding back nothing at all." Yet in the end Judy Jones proves unattainable, a mercurial flirt whose desire for Dexter flares up unpredictably but then dies away, igniting again on a chance encounter at the University Club in Minneapolis (after Dexter has become engaged to another woman), only to cool within a month. Years later, after the war, Dexter hears that she's married a cad and faded fast.[50]

Whether their money is old or new, Fitzgerald's rich are Beautiful People, "with graceful clothes and the deep tan of healthy summers"—but they are enveloped in an aura of lost illusions and missed opportunities. *The Great Gatsby* (1925) is the definitive formulation of this type. Gatsby himself seems just to have stepped out of an advertisement for Arrow Collars or Hart, Schaffner & Marx. "Ah," says Daisy Buchanan languorously to him one stifling hot Long Island afternoon, "you look so cool."

> "You always look so cool," she repeated.
> She had told him that she loved him, and [her husband] Tom Buchanan saw. He was astounded. His mouth opened a little, and he looked at Gatsby, and then back at Daisy as if he had just recognized her as some one he knew a long time ago.
> "You resemble the advertisement of the man," she went on innocently. "You know the advertisement of the man—"
> "All right," broke in Tom quickly. "I'm perfectly willing to go to town. Come on—we're all going to town."[51]

By the 1920s, comparing someone to an advertising icon was a way of expressing admiration, even love, for him (or her). Yet Gatsby's apparent perfection is flawed by his doomed desire for the unattainable—his determination that Daisy tell the crude but powerful Tom she never loved him. Like Fitzgerald himself, Gatsby yearns to recapture the fresh bloom of youthful romance. His crippling nostalgia cracks the surface of his smooth self-presentation. The rich can be deluded too.

Fitzgerald's Beautiful Losers were often sympathetic characters. They were also the subtlest representation of what the revitalization of the ruling class had accomplished as a cultural movement. By the 1920s the revitalized rich were secure in their sense of superiority; the new mass media had made them the stars of celebrity culture and created a shimmering surface of elegance to represent their way of life. Fitzgerald, by focusing on their private frustrations, supplied shadow and depth to this portrait. At the acme of elite power and prestige, he created a complex fiction of elite decline—more psychologically dense than the simple notion of patrician yielding to parvenu. Even if the Beautiful Losers clung successfully to their wealth, their unfulfilled longings made money seem irrelevant, and their vulnerability reinforced the vague sense that elites were somehow too fragile for democracy—that, despite all evidence to the contrary, they were somehow being hustled toward the exit. The fictions of loss obscured the persistence of privilege.

The protracted aftermath of the 1929 stock market crash left the revitalized ruling class shaken and divided but still hanging on to a large measure of legitimacy. Confronted by the crisis of capitalism and the coming of the New Deal, many rich people retreated into their lairs, lamenting their exclusion from public life. For decades, the Pot and Kettle Club of Bar Harbor had toasted the president of the United States on the Fourth of July; but after Franklin Roosevelt came to power, the members toasted the Constitution of the United States— which they believed had been abandoned.[52] The stance of principled powerlessness concealed the survival of power (even, one suspects, from the club members themselves). Declarations of decline obscured the resilience of old money, its eventual accommodation with Roosevelt's regulatory regime, and the possibilities for reasserting its influence as "Dr. New Deal" gave way to "Dr. Win-the-War."

Meanwhile, the New Deal itself offered different opportunities for the deployment of privilege—a chance to reassert the paternalist ideal of public responsibility. Even old-stock Republicans like Endicott Peabody eventually recognized this. He had voted for Hoover in 1932, remembering Franklin Roosevelt as "a quiet, satisfactory boy of more than ordinary intelligence, taking a good position in his form but not brilliant." But by 1936 Peabody was convinced that the polices of this Groton alumnus epitomized the school's ideals. "I am in hearty agreement with you," he wrote Roosevelt, "in what seems to me the two great purposes of your life: first, making it possible for all the people of the nation who are willing to work being given an opportunity to do so and to carry on work under worthy conditions; secondly, to join with others who are like-minded in endeavoring to bring peace to the nations."[53] It would be hard to find more fitting testimony to the revitalization of the rich, which at its best involved both the maintenance of power and the magnanimity to use it wisely.

7

The Foreign Policy Establishment

✣

GODFREY HODGSON

In January 1902 a successful New York lawyer named Henry L. Stimson went down to Washington to attend the annual dinner of the Boone and Crockett Club, an association of well-bred big game hunters.[1] He and his wife, Mabel, went to stay with their friend Gifford Pinchot, chief forester of the United States and intimate friend of President Theodore Roosevelt. The afternoon before the dinner, Stimson and a friend borrowed two of Pinchot's horses and went for a ride in Rock Creek Park. It had been raining, and the creek was high.

Suddenly Stimson was hailed by name by four men walking through the woods on the far side of the creek. At first he was astonished, because he did not know many people in Washington. Then he recognized the high-pitched voice of President Roosevelt, jokingly asking him to swim the creek and join them. Then another voice, much better known to him, that of his former law partner, Elihu Root, now Roosevelt's secretary of war,[2] called out, "The President of the United States directs Sergeant Stimson of Squadron A to cross the creek and come to his assistance by order of the Secretary of War."

"That's an order, sure enough," Stimson cried out to his companion and shouted back, "Very good, sir!" and put Gifford Pinchot's old horse Jimmie at the creek. The horse, like its rider, obeyed orders, but it lost its footing in the spate and "began to roll and plunge downstream," as Stimson recalled later, "a good deal of the time both of us being completely under water." Eventually Stimson, up to his chest in the swift, icy water, was able to lead the horse downstream to a break in the masonry wall that revetted the bank, get him up the bank, and ride him down to where the president of the United States and the secretary of war stood, looking "like two small boys who had been caught stealing apples."

Roosevelt muttered something about how he had not thought the order would be obeyed because it was impossible. "Mr. President," said Stimson, "when a soldier hears an order like that, it isn't his business to see that it is impossible." Roosevelt laughed and said, "Well it was very nice of you to do it; now hurry home and drink all the whisky you can." And that night at the dinner he hailed Stimson as "young Lochinvar," after the romantic hero of the old Scots ballad.

Sixty years later, at the height of the 1962 Cuban missile crisis, President Kennedy secretly summoned elder statesmen to advise him. One of them was Dean Acheson, President Truman's secretary of state in the most dangerous hours of the Cold War. Another was Robert Abercrombie Lovett. A pioneer of aviation in World War I, he had been assistant secretary of war in World War II, had served as undersecretary of state and secretary of defense in the Truman administration, and had been offered his pick of the three top jobs in President Kennedy's cabinet: State, Defense, or Treasury. Lovett was the son of Judge Robert Scott Lovett, legal adviser and close friend of the railroad magnate E. H. Harriman, father of the diplomat and Democratic governor of New York, Averell Harriman, who in turn had been the close friend of the younger Lovett at Groton and Yale.[3]

When he arrived at the White House, Lovett went straight to the national security adviser's crowded office in the basement of the West

Wing. The office belonged to McGeorge Bundy, whose father, Harvey Bundy, had been Lovett's colleague as assistant secretary to Henry Stimson when Stimson was secretary of war during World War II. There on a side table he spotted a small photograph of Bundy's mentor, Colonel Stimson. "All during the conversation," Lovett recalled later, "the old Colonel seemed to be staring me straight in the face." Finally Lovett said to Bundy, "Mac, I think the best service we can perform for the President is to try to approach this as Colonel Stimson would."[4]

⚘ It is not true, whatever you might be tempted to think, that American foreign policy was governed and directed for sixty years exclusively by the friends and relations of Henry Lewis Stimson. Still, that proposition is closer to being true than one would ever expect in a nation notoriously suspicious of aristocracy and elitism.

The fact is that for three-quarters of the twentieth century, from the Spanish-American War to the end of the Vietnam War, the foreign policy of the United States was decisively influenced by a comparatively small group of men who belonged to what has been loosely but usefully called the American foreign policy Establishment.

The concept of "the Establishment" was invented by the British Tory journalist Henry Fairlie to describe the informal network of men who wielded power and influence at the apex of political and business life in Britain in the 1950s. Fairlie's Establishment was not defined by wealth or even by hereditary connections. Although he assumed that many of the men he was talking about had been formed by elite institutions such as Eton and Winchester, Oxford and Cambridge (approximate British equivalents of Andover and Groton, Harvard and Yale), he was talking about men who were powerful by virtue of their careers and office, not because of hereditary wealth; he specifically mentioned the head of the Anglican Church, for example, the leader of the Institute of Chartered Accountants, the director-general of the BBC, and top civil servants.

Fairlie's idea was imported into the United States, more or less as a joke, by the political editor of the *New Yorker*, Richard Rovere, in a spoof in the *American Scholar* in 1961. Gradually the idea, and the word, came into common parlance, and in the process became changed. The Establishment came to mean something as vague as "the rich," or "the privileged." But there was an Establishment. It was a specific group, with definable characteristics. It acquired prestige and influence by being seen to be right about the need for American involvement in the two world wars. It led opinion in the Cold War, but overreached, first with more or less disreputable covert actions, mostly in the Third World, such as the disaster at the Bay of Pigs, and then, with terminal effect for its own influence, in Vietnam.

There were in fact five major acts in the history of the foreign policy Establishment. Its origins in the First World War introduced its cast of characters, its institutions, and its ethos. (Its prehistory, indeed, lay in the Theodore Roosevelt circle, and particularly in the character and ideas of Elihu Root, who combined a successful corporate law practice in New York with devotion to the honor and greatness of the United States as well as to the ideals of arbitration and cooperation in international affairs.) The second was its success in the so-called Great Debate over American involvement in World War II—successful at least in the sense that Pearl Harbor made the U.S. belligerency that the Establishment advocated inevitable. The third, and perhaps most identified with the core of the Establishment, was leadership in the organization of the nation at war with the Axis, and especially in the development of and the decision to use the atomic bomb. Fourth was the Establishment's advocacy of a middle course of containment in the Cold War. And the fifth act was the fatal extension of Cold War containment and counterinsurgency force to the developing world and especially to Vietnam.

At the end of the Gilded Age, an American upper class had emerged, headquartered in the Northeast, especially in New York and Boston, but national in influence. Its base was in industrial wealth and in the financial sector, but its members took pains to distinguish themselves from mere business spokesmen. They were usually products of elite boarding schools, colleges, and professional schools, especially law schools, and in practice of a very small number of schools, colleges, and graduate schools. Over and over again in the biographies of the men (and they were almost all men) who directed American foreign policy from the 1900s to the 1960s the same few names recur.

Among the boarding schools, it was Phillips Andover (Stimson's school); Groton (Acheson's and Harriman's, and indeed Franklin Roosevelt's); St. Paul's in Concord, New Hampshire, where the diplomat and Soviet expert Charles E. Bohlen was educated and so was the CIA official Cord Meyer; and the Hill School, near Philadelphia, alma mater of Robert Lovett and (much later) of George H. W. Bush's secretary of state, James Baker.

Among universities it was not even the whole of the Ivy League but preeminently Harvard, Yale, and Princeton;[5] among graduate schools it was Harvard Law, Yale Law, sometimes Columbia, and only occasionally great middle western universities like Michigan and Wisconsin.

Indeed, it is startling to discover how many of the key figures in managing America's foreign relations were not just undergraduates at Yale but members of a single secret senior society there, Skull and Bones. This bizarre institution still maintains a gloomy "tomb" on the Yale campus where the great and the good come to mingle with ambitious undergraduates in an atmosphere of moral uplift and Victorian jocularity amid mementos of a sinister nineteenth-century cult of Native American skulls. Stimson, Lovett, Harriman, Acheson, Harvey Bundy and his two sons, McGeorge and William, for example, were all "Bonesmen," not to mention George Herbert Walker Bush and his father, Senator Prescott Bush.[6] So were several of the key figures in the early years of the CIA.[7]

Such evidences of the concentration of influence over American foreign policy in the hands of a tiny elite have not surprisingly engendered a good deal of conspiracy theory.[8] The truth rather was that, except in time of war, not many Americans between 1917 and 1968 were interested in foreign affairs, and fewer still were expert in that highly specialized field. The United States had succeeded in negotiating the nineteenth century with remarkably few of the entanglements in world politics against which George Washington had warned in his farewell address. There were occasional scuffles in the Caribbean. There was the triumphant aggression of the Mexican War, in which a border dispute was used as a pretext for the annexation of Texas, the Southwest, and California. But in the main the United States relied on the Monroe Doctrine, the breadth of two oceans, and Britain's Royal Navy to keep the quarrels of "the Powers" at a distance. In the early twentieth century, foreign trade was a tiny proportion of the American economy, less than 5 percent of the gross national product in 1900.

Because many of them worked as international bankers and lawyers, the Establishment products of elite eastern education were an exception. They shared political assumptions, among them a history, a policy, an aspiration, an instinct, a technique, and a dogma.[9] They were also defined by a class, a culture, a dynasty, and a style. But more important is what they did. For better or for worse, their contribution to the creation of the American superpower was immense.

Vietnam divided them and stripped them of their aura of invincibility. Since then, other elites with different agendas, especially neoconservatives more interested in the Middle East than in western Europe, have replaced them. But the Establishment's influence lives on. Its members made it possible for America to win two world wars and the Cold War. In the process they transformed the United States from a largely pacifist state into a national security state, from a bulky herbivore to a man-eating tiger.

The prevailing culture in the foreign policy Establishment was that of New England boarding schools and Ivy League universities, of the older established Protestant denominations (especially Episcopalian and Presbyterian), of Wall Street and Boston's State Street law firms, and of the clubs their partners frequented. It was capitalist but liberal, patriotic but internationalist, Anglophile though critical of England, masculine but not macho, cultivated but not usually intellectual, loyal to schools, colleges, clubs, family, and nation, deeply committed to an ideal of public service and to an ethos of individual stoicism. The culture of the twentieth-century American gentleman, you might say, was what had become of the Puritan who no longer believed in the Puritan God. The fierce Puritan creed, the metaphysical and militant passion of Oliver Cromwell and Jonathan Edwards, of John Winthrop and Roger Williams, might have gone. The stern voice of duty, and the conviction of righteousness, remained.

The dynasty began with Henry Lewis Stimson and even further back with Stimson's law partner and mentor, Elihu Root. Its direct line ran through Stimson's aide and protégé, Harvey Bundy, to the latter's sons, William Putnam Bundy, son-in-law of Dean Acheson, and his younger brother McGeorge. But the American foreign policy Establishment was broader than a single family. It welcomed all, or almost all, who shared its ideals, its purposes, and its style. They had in common a particular ethos, powerfully shaped, even for those of them who were Catholics or Jews or agnostics, by a Protestant ethic. The New England boarding schools had borrowed from British "public schools" an explicit value system typified by the Reverend Endicott Peabody, the rector of Groton, and by the Reverend Samuel Drury of St. Paul's, an ethic of service, self-discipline, stoicism. The style was an American variant of that of the Victorian British empire builder: modest in demeanor but unmistakably conscious of superiority. Like the Victorians, they could say, "They didn't want to fight, but by Jingo, if they did . . . !"

The Establishment was not a cultural circle or another name for the old ruling class. It was a foreign policy Establishment, and its agenda was from first to last concerned with the place of the United States in the world. The history goes back to the Republican nationalists Elihu Root and Colonel Stimson, but also to Woodrow Wilson's Democratic friend Colonel Edward House and the businessmen, lawyers, and scholars he gathered round him, first in New York, then in Paris in 1919 in the "Inquiry" to advise the American mission at the peace conference.

The Establishment's policy, from start to finish, was to oppose isolationism and to work, within the limits of its own sense of morality, to maximize American power and influence in the world. That did not mean simply that the United States should be involved in the world, should be—as the phrase went—"interventionist." It also meant that the United States should remain primarily oriented toward Europe, as opposed to Latin America or Asia, the natural fields of action for the elites of the South and the West. For all the occasional recruits from the Middle West and Texas (George Kennan[10] or Will Clayton[11]) this was essentially an eastern Establishment; its worldview was that of New York and Washington, Boston and New Haven.

Its aspiration was not modest: it was to the moral and political leadership of the world, no less. Specifically, it aspired to supersede the British Empire in its double role of protecting a certain Western liberal, capitalist world order, and at the same time of preaching Western values to what Rudyard Kipling called "lesser breeds without the law." It was true of many figures in the Establishment mold, as was said of the CIA's Desmond FitzGerald, that "his inspiration was the British Empire."[12] It was not true, as the Establishment's enemies, like Senator Joseph McCarthy, alleged, that they wanted to preserve the British Empire. They wanted to replace it.

Its instinct was for the political and ideological center. It was repelled by raw business self-interest, and uninterested in radical agendas of social change. To take an obvious example, the typical Establishment figure found racism distasteful, but placed the need for action toward racial equality low on his list of priorities. The Establishment stood for a liberal capitalism. Establishment members had no objection in the world to capitalism; many of them, after all, had inherited more or less substantial capital, and most of them worked, as bankers or lawyers, at the heart of the capitalist system, often literally on Wall Street.

At the same time, capitalism, its members believed, ought to protect "the widow and the fatherless." As Theodore Roosevelt put it in 1912, "This country will not be a permanently good place for any of us to live in unless we make it a reasonably good place for all of us to live in."[13] Not a revolutionary or a radical creed, to be sure, but one that separated the typical Establishment member from more ruthless capitalists in the robber baron tradition.

Key members of the Establishment—Root, Stimson, the elder Bundy, and later John J. McCloy, John Foster and Allen Dulles, and McGeorge Bundy, for example—were all Republicans, and an internationalist Republican was necessarily a man of the center, defined in opposition to the isolationist right as well as to Democratic liberals. Only after the New Deal did substantial numbers of the Establishment become Democrats. Even then, the center was the place where consensus could be sought and maintained.

The Establishment's technique involved working not through electoral politics but out of the public eye, chiefly through the executive branch. There were exceptions, like the two Roosevelts, Averell Harriman, and Nelson Rockefeller. But more characteristic were those like Henry Stimson, who ran for governor of New York but lost. In an age of ethnic machines, all but the most ambitious of privately educated WASPs were not drawn to electoral politics, and if they were, they were not often successful. Their great opportunity resulted from the relative weakness of the permanent federal civil service, and in particular from the hidebound stuffiness of the old foreign service. When the scope and size of government did expand during the New Deal and even more in World War II, President Roosevelt "needed help."[14] He turned to look for it wherever it could be found. Two of the most valuable sources of appropriate talent were "dollar a year men" from Wall Street (they didn't need government salaries) and academics from the great Ivy League graduate schools. The Establishment's first opportunity came during and immediately after World War I, when few others were interested in foreign affairs; the second came during and immediately after World War II, when not enough others had the relevant expertise.

The Establishment's dogma, finally, shaped by the threat of Soviet communism and the Cold War, was containment: not war, but the threat of war. It was George Kennan, certainly an Establishment figure, if untypically self-doubting and unclubbable, who launched that strategy, first inside government with his celebrated "long telegram" of February 22, 1946, and then to the world, or at least to a world of rarefied power and expertise, in his June 1947 article, signed "X," in the Establishment's house journal, *Foreign Affairs*.[15]

There was a consensus that American power should be used to contain Soviet power and to prevent it and its ideology of communism from spreading. But consensus did not equal conformity. Even on the specific theory of containment itself there were fierce disagreements. Did Kennan, for example, mean that the Soviet Union should be contained militarily, as his writings seemed to imply, or only politically, as he insisted he had intended?

Indeed, members of the foreign policy Establishment differed so profoundly from one another on important questions that some have doubted whether the term means anything at all. How could one speak, for example, as if both Dean Acheson and John Foster Dulles were members of the Establishment when they opposed each other so bitterly on so many issues? How can one trace its origins back to both Elihu Root, Theodore Roosevelt's secretary of state, and Colonel House, Woodrow Wilson's trusted adviser, when everyone knows that Roosevelt (and Root) despised Wilson and all his works, while Wilson could not stand Roosevelt?

These objections have often been made by leaders of the Establishment itself. When in 1973 I went to interview McGeorge Bundy, he impatiently brushed aside the very idea that there was any such thing as a foreign policy Establishment.[16] It was all explained, he insisted airily, by Vilfredo Pareto and his theory of the circulation of elites. Certainly Dean Acheson and John Foster Dulles, for example, or George Kennan

and Paul Nitze, did profoundly disagree. The dangers of oversimplification are to be avoided. They do not, however, demolish the usefulness of the idea that there was a foreign policy Establishment, still less
the case for trying to understand it.

❦ In the spring of 1917, the German government gambled on unrestricted submarine warfare to knock Britain out of the war. At the
same time the head of the German foreign office, Arthur Zimmerman,
offered to help Mexico recover Texas, California, and the other territories lost in the Mexican War. In the ensuing outrage, Woodrow Wilson
could no longer keep the United States out of the war. He remained,
however, profoundly suspicious of the motives of the Entente powers
(Britain, France, Russia, and Italy) and of the secret treaties by which
they had bound themselves to help one another to the territories of
Germany, Austria-Hungary and the Ottoman Empire after the war.
(Even after an American army of 2 million men was fighting alongside
the French and the British on the western front, Wilson refused to refer
to them as allies, insisting instead on the term "associated powers.")
On September 2, 1917, Wilson therefore asked his close friend and foreign policy adviser Colonel House to get together a group of men to
find out what the different allies would insist on at the peace conference
and "prepare our case with a full knowledge of the position of all the
litigants."[17] The motive was as much to prepare to resist the Allies'
claims as to promote a common strategy for the peace.

In London and Paris, professional diplomats were already hard at
work on preparing for the postwar settlement. But House did not recruit the members of what came to be called "the Inquiry" from the
State Department or the foreign service. For one thing, there simply
was no adequate body of brains and knowledge there to recruit. For
another, as a Texas Democrat and progressive, he did not trust the old
school of American diplomats, almost all Republicans, to share his and
Wilson's zeal for a "new diplomacy."[18] Instead, he turned to academics
at Harvard, Columbia, and other great eastern graduate schools, some

of them young patricians who knew Europe from prewar tours or from studying there; others were European emigrants and exiles with special knowledge of the ethnic politics and irredentist claims of one European people or another.

If things had developed a little differently, House might have been unequivocally a co-founder, with Stimson, of the Establishment tradition. But during the Paris peace conference, Wilson and House fell out. Then Wilson's treaty and the League of Nations were defeated by the Republicans, led by Henry Cabot Lodge. House was left on the outside of political life. But his instincts—nationalist, internationalist, interventionist, critically Anglophile, elitist—qualified him to be at least an honorary founding member of the foreign policy Establishment.

The young professors, mostly from Ivy League colleges, recruited to the Inquiry included several of the most brilliant young scholars of their generation, many of them historians, among them Samuel Eliot Morison and Charles Homer Haskins from Harvard; Charles Seymour, later president of Yale; and E. S. Corwin, the great constitutional scholar from Princeton. Altogether 65 percent of the more important contributors had taken their final degree at just four universities: Harvard, Yale, Columbia, and Chicago.[19]

Arguably, the Inquiry's most important work was done before it had fully gotten off the ground, for President Wilson's Fourteen Points, made public in a speech on January 8, 1918, followed closely drafts put together by House and some of the first recruits to the Inquiry, especially Walter Lippmann. The voluminous studies produced later by the Inquiry, some two thousand of them altogether, had relatively little direct impact on the peace conference. But after the conference was over, key members of the Inquiry, led by the first professor at Harvard to teach anything other than American or British history, Archibald Cary Coolidge, helped to create two of the Establishment's key institutions, the Council on Foreign Relations and its hugely influential journal, *Foreign Affairs*.[20]

When the American peacemakers reached home, they found the atmosphere deeply unsympathetic to their aspirations for a League of Nations to guarantee world peace. The Senate's rejection of the Versailles treaty had given an impetus to isolationism. Warren G. Harding was elected president. The general climate was highly unfavourable to idealistic commitment to internationalism, let alone to close ties with Britain. In June 1918, however, none other than Colonel Stimson's role model, Elihu Root, had convened a group mostly drawn from the financial sector and the New York bar to form what was soon called the Council on Foreign Relations.

The original idea was that Archibald Cary Coolidge should edit the council's journal, *Foreign Affairs*. But Coolidge had been appointed librarian of the Harvard University library and was reluctant to leave Cambridge. So the editorship was split in two. Coolidge stayed at Harvard, and Hamilton Fish Armstrong, a young journalist and Princeton graduate, was hired to do the work that could be done only in New York. During the 1920s the council and its journal established their reputation. Coolidge and Armstrong went out of their way to commission articles from isolationists such as Senator William E. Borah of Idaho, as well as by many of the best-known statesmen of Europe at the time. They even published articles by the great African American leader W. E. B. Du Bois, and also by Soviet writers.

Foreign Affairs kept alive interest in international affairs, especially in the New York business community. It gradually encouraged the development of sister organizations in more than a dozen other cities, and poured forth research on many subjects, especially China. Its evening meetings in New York attracted many of those who would become leading scholars in international relations as well as many who would hold high office in the State Department, the Treasury Department, and later in the Department of Defense and the CIA.

The council was always clearly opposed to isolationism. Until the late 1930s, the isolationists had things mostly their own way. In Congress, isolationist sentiment was strong enough to pass four restrictive neutrality acts in the late 1930s. It was not until after Hitler's rise to power, and specifically his reintegration of the Rhineland into Germany in 1936, Japan's increasingly aggressive conduct in China, and the semi-covert intervention of Germany and Italy on one side and the Soviet Union on the other in the Spanish civil war that the great debate between interventionists and isolationists was joined.

The issue was between "interventionists," who believed it was more important, in the interests of the United States, to ensure a British victory over the Axis than for the United States to keep out of the war, and isolationists, who believed that it was more important to keep out of the war than to prevent a British defeat by Germany and its allies. Committees were formed to rally public opinion on either side of the argument. Moderate interventionists supported the Committee to Defend America by Aiding the Allies, chaired by William Allen White, the newspaper publisher from Emporia, Kansas.[21] White and his executive director, Clark Eichelberger, lobbied for repeal of the neutrality laws and supported President Roosevelt's policy of giving all aid to the democracies short of war. From early 1941 on, a more strongly interventionist group, the Fight for Freedom Committee, came into existence, calling for America's participation in the war as a full belligerent.

The isolationists were an extraordinarily diverse cross-section of American life.[22] In the Senate, for example, they included arch-conservative Robert Taft; the progressive Hiram Johnson of California, who had been Theodore Roosevelt's running mate in 1912; the prairie radical Gerald Nye of North Dakota; and the progressive Robert La Follette, Jr., of Wisconsin. Both former President Herbert Hoover and former Republican candidate Alf Landon were non-interventionists, but so too were the New Dealer and critic of capitalism Adolf Berle, General Hugh Johnson (the former head of the New Deal's National Recovery Administration), and the best-known labor leader in the country, the mineworkers' John L. Lewis. William Randolph Hearst, head of the nation's most powerful newspaper chain, was strongly anti-interventionist, as were the scourge of Wall Street, John T. Flynn, and the anti-Semitic radio priest Father Charles Coughlin. After the signing of the Nazi-Soviet pact in the late summer of 1939, the Communist Party reversed its policy and came out for isolation, as did many Roman Catholics, most Trotskyists, the German-American Bund, many Irish Americans, and plenty of liberals who thought the United States should concentrate on solving its own problems before getting involved in those of Europe.

These political opposites had no national coordinating body until the formation, in September 1940, of the America First Committee.[23] It was started in the heart of Establishment territory, at the Yale Law School, by a young graduate student, R. Douglas Stuart, Jr., who had studied international relations at Princeton. He was helped by none other than Kingman Brewster, Jr., scion of one of the oldest Yankee clans and destined to be president of Yale, ambassador to the Court of Saint James, and a partner in the Stimson law firm.

As time went on, however, America First became more clearly identified with various elements of the American right. Stuart prevailed on General Robert E. Wood, chairman of the board of Sears Roebuck, to be the chairman of America First, though he later stepped down. Another committee member was William Regnery of Chicago, later the key publisher of conservative books.[24] Most controversial of America First's supporters was Colonel Charles Lindbergh, who had been living in Germany for several years and inflicted severe damage on the anti-interventionist cause by his notorious anti-Semitic speech at Des Moines in September 1941.[25]

The Council on Foreign Relations came out clearly on the interventionist side. Allen W. Dulles was the younger brother of John Foster Dulles. (The brothers were the grandsons of John Watson Foster of Watertown, New York, a Civil War general turned international lawyer who had been secretary of state in the administration of President Benjamin Harrison, and their "Uncle Bert," Robert Lansing, was secretary of state under Woodrow Wilson.)[26] During World War I, Allen Dulles had served as a secret agent in the Swiss capital, Bern, a listening post where one could learn what was happening in Germany. (He was to return to the same post in World War II.) After the war he practiced law at his brother's firm, Sullivan and Cromwell, in which capacity he interviewed Hitler shortly after he became chancellor in 1933. Dulles came back from that meeting and the ineffectual Geneva disarmament conference and plunged into the activity of the Council on Foreign Relations. He persuaded the council to start a high-level study group, ostensibly to discover how the United States might keep its neutrality in the event of a European war, but actually to combat isolationism. In 1935 he and the editor of *Foreign Affairs*, Hamilton Fish Armstrong, worked up the records of this discussion group into a book, *Can We Be Neutral?* Its conclusion—sharply different from that taken at the time by his brother, the future secretary of state—was trenchantly interventionist: "No nation can reach the position of a world power as we have done without becoming entangled in almost every quarter of the globe in one way or another. We are inextricably and inevitably tied to world affairs."[27]

Three months after the Munich agreement of 1938, in which British prime minister Neville Chamberlain sought to appease Hitler, Armstrong wrote a ninety-four-page article reminding Americans that they too might soon face a similar choice to the one Chamberlain had failed to confront.[28] In October 1938 Dulles and Armstrong co-authored another challenge to non-intervention. Neutrality laws, they argued, were entirely inadequate as a guarantee that the United States could keep out of war. International troublemakers "believe they can count on a passivity which . . . is quite alien to the American temper. The question is, how can we make them aware of this and do it effectively and in time?"[29]

Was Franklin Delano Roosevelt a member of the Establishment? He was certainly a hereditary member of one of the oldest rootstocks of the American upper class, descended from Dutch patroons, Hudson Valley squires, and millionaire New York merchants. He was educated at Groton and Harvard, even if he was turned down by the most socially august of the Harvard clubs, the Porcellian. (Cousin Theodore, in announcing his daughter Alice's marriage to the future Speaker of the House, Nicholas Longworth, proudly told Kaiser Wilhelm II of Germany, "Nick and I are both in the Porc, you know.")[30] Roosevelt the Happy Warrior did not share the Establishment's distaste for electoral politics. But he did have centrist instincts. He also had a steadily internationalist attitude, even if he had to conceal his preference for intervention. He admired Colonel House, whose advice he frequently sought,[31] and Colonel Stimson.

In May 1940 Stimson had lunch with Roosevelt at the White House and was alarmed by what he heard about the war and the isolationist Congress. He decided to state his case clearly. Characteristically, he did so in two speeches, one at Andover and one at Yale. He told the boys at Andover that they were lucky to have been offered a clear choice between good and evil. (One of those who heard him, George Herbert Walker Bush, went straight out and volunteered for the U.S. Navy.) From Andover, Stimson went to New Haven, where he gave a radio talk on the theme that the United States could not, in its own interest, allow Britain to be defeated by Nazi Germany.

The next day the president of the United States phoned, offering Stimson the job of secretary of war. Roosevelt had decided to replace the two most isolationist members of his cabinet with two Republican interventionists, Frank Knox, a newspaper publisher from Chicago who had been Alf Landon's vice presidential running mate in 1936, and Stimson himself. From that moment on, Colonel Stimson filled the War Department with those he regarded as the finest flower of the eastern foreign policy Establishment. He brought in John J. McCloy and Robert Lovett as assistant secretaries and Harvey Bundy as his personal assistant.

Stimson put George Harrison, head of the Federal Reserve under Hoover, in charge of S-1, the code name for the Manhattan Project to build an atomic bomb. In many respects the atomic bomb was the special achievement and the special responsibility of the foreign policy Establishment, and it is worth asking to what extent the bomb, and the decision to use it, were shaped by the Establishment's values and attitudes.

Formally, the decision was taken by the Interim Committee at a meeting on May 30 and 31, 1945, and communicated to President Truman by Stimson and Assistant Secretary McCloy the following day. There was discussion of the possibility of warning Japan. That was rejected because of the loss of face if the weapon did not work. (For all anybody knew, since it had not been tested as a bomb dropped from an airplane, it might not.) There was discussion of a demonstration. That was rejected because of fears that the Japanese might move American prisoners of war into the designated target area. Many later historians have suggested that the use of the weapon was motivated in whole or in part by the wish to keep the Soviet Union out of the war in the Pacific so as to deprive Stalin of a say in the postwar settlement in East Asia.[32] Stimson's first biographer states that he found no evidence of this.[33] Kai Bird, in his biography of the Bundy brothers, concludes from a memorandum written by their father, Harvey Bundy, and only declassified in 1973 (well after Morison's book was published in 1960), that Bundy and Stimson were indeed aware that the bomb would be dropped before the Soviet Union declared war on Japan.[34] Moreover, Harvey Bundy was well aware that Stimson believed as early as the Potsdam conference in July that the war could be ended without the use of the atomic bomb, if the Japanese were told that the United States would allow the monarchy to continue in a constitutional form. In any case, it is clear that, within the small group of men who knew of the bomb's appalling capabilities, the decision had long been taken to drop it.[35]

Most of the key members of the foreign policy Establishment (as opposed to the elected politicians and the scientists) involved in the decision to drop the atomic bomb were lawyers, and they displayed a lawyerlike propensity to make the case they thought their clients, two successive presidents of the United States, wanted to hear. It was not that they were unaware of the consequences of their actions or of the gravity of the responsibility they were taking on themselves. "War was death," wrote Harvey Bundy, "and the question now was to get it over with."[36] McCloy said that both he and Stimson had "long and painful thoughts about the atomic triumph." Stimson appears to have had a minor heart attack when he heard that the bomb had been dropped. He retreated to the St. Hubert's Club at Ausable, New York, an upperclass Episcopalian summer resort camp in the Adirondacks, where he gave a solemn talk about the need to control the atomic weapon. Then he returned to Washington and attempted at his last cabinet meeting to persuade the Truman cabinet that the United States should offer to ban the bomb.[37] These promptings of morality, however, did not prevail against the core values of the Establishment: stoicism, patriotism, a respect for the military virtues, and perhaps also a determination not to be softer than less privileged mortals. These were the values that were needed to confront the Axis between European fascists and Japanese militarists. The war effort, led at the top of the civilian government by a group of men who were the epitome of the Establishment, was spectacularly successful.

If after victory in 1945, though, the Establishment ever cherished the hope of going back to making money on Wall Street during the week and playing tennis and sailing on the weekends, that hope was to be disappointed. It was not long before America seemed to face an even greater danger, from the Soviet Union.

This was—to its members' eyes, at least—the Establishment's finest hour. It played a leading part in creating the institutions and ethos of the postwar world and of the national security state with which America confronted the Cold War. The United Nations and the Bretton Woods institutions, the International Monetary Fund and the World Bank, were conceived before Franklin Roosevelt's death, and if the Establishment was strongly represented in the Roosevelt administration, it was only one of a kaleidoscope of competing traditions and interests, from southern conservatives in Congress to industrial labor. During the Truman administration, Stimson's contemporaries retired. Their place was taken by the Acheson generation: Averell Harriman, Charles Bohlen, George Kennan, Robert Lovett, John J. McCloy, the ill-fated James Forrestal, and Acheson himself.

Their monuments were the Marshall Plan to revive the economy and so preserve the democracy of western Europe, and NATO, the defensive alliance to save Europe from Stalinist aggression and incidentally to guarantee American hegemony in Europe for two generations. (The Establishment was less interested in Japan and China.) The National Security Act of 1947, which merged the War and Navy departments in a new Department of Defense, and created the National Security Council in the White House and the Central Intelligence Agency, were institutions infused with the ethos and staffed with the personnel of the Establishment.

The paladins of the Truman administration were joined in the forming and execution of American foreign policy in the late 1940s and the 1950s by men young enough to have served, often with great distinction, as junior officers or intelligence operatives in World War II. David Bruce (a scion of the Mellon family from Pittsburgh), and a whole swarm of idealistic but privileged young men who had served (as Bruce did) in the Office of Strategic Services (OSS) during the war, would now serve under Allen Dulles in the new CIA that came into existence in July 1947: Frank Wisner, Richard Bissell, Tracy Barnes, Desmond FitzGerald, Richard Helms, William Colby, John Bross, Cord Meyer.[38]

The agency in those years, it was said, had the atmosphere of a Yale class reunion. OSS was so full of the well connected that it was known as "Oh-so-social." The CIA included rough-hewn types as well. But the preponderance of Ivy League graduates in general, and especially graduates of Yale, Harvard, and Princeton, and above all of Yale in the early years of the agency, is still astonishing. Robin Winks cites some compelling calculations. As late as the Nixon administration, 26 percent of CIA employees with college degrees had received those degrees from Ivy League institutions, and of those, 86 percent were from Harvard, Princeton, and Yale. When advanced study is taken into consideration, and with Columbia added to the list, Winks notes, the dominance is even greater.[39]

❧ The foreign policy Establishment and the postwar intelligence community have so far usually been studied as entirely separate phenomena. In reality, they were the same kind of people, and often (in the persons, for example, of Allen Dulles or William Bundy) the same people. Between the end of World War II and the Kennedy administration, American interactions with the outside world, especially the higher echelons of foreign policy, diplomacy, and intelligence, were dominated by men from three or four eastern universities. As Winks says of that period, "The Ivy League institutions were havens of the well connected."[40]

This was the period of what, in another context, I have called "the liberal consensus."[41] The essence of that consensus was a vast deal, whereby conservatives more or less grudgingly accepted the outlines of a social democratic New Deal, while all but the most radical liberals embraced a sternly anticommunist foreign policy. This was the position of the foreign policy Establishment. The Great Debate about isolationism was over.

In the belief that the United States had to save the world from a new, Soviet totalitarian tyranny, Dean Acheson stood at Armageddon and persuaded Senator Arthur Vandenberg and the Republicans he represented that the United States must be responsible for containing communist expansion.[42] In that same belief, younger Yale graduates (and others) organized, and sometimes took part in, covert action from the Baltic to Indonesia and the Philippines.[43]

The Establishment's triumph in rising to the challenge of the Cold War with the Soviet Union in Europe was inextricably connected with the roots of its coming tragic failure in Southeast Asia. For if the Establishment's instinct was centrist and restrained, its policy depended nonetheless on mobilizing American resources for a conflict that was ultimately military.

John F. Kennedy's inaugural address, concerned almost exclusively with the "long twilight struggle" against communism, was written by Theodore Sorensen, a graduate of the University of Nebraska. But it expressed with perfect pitch the beliefs of the Harvard, Yale, and Princeton graduates who had been junior officers in the war against Axis domination, and stood ready to fight a second round against the tyrannous empires of Stalin and Mao.

It was not long, however, before that consensus, and the foreign policy Establishment which had reached the apogee of its power under it, began to dissolve. Multiple causes were at work, within and outside the American upper class. The first unmistakably visible crack was the Bay of Pigs. The fiasco utterly discredited Richard Bissell, Yale graduate and economics professor.[44] He and Allen Dulles took the blame. But it also led to soul-searching and finger-pointing inside the intelligence and foreign policy community.

In the next few years the civil rights movement and the Kennedy assassination shook the national morale. As the 1960s went on, there was a general questioning of authority of every kind, from the bosom of the family to the White House. Fathers, teachers, professors, priests, officers, executives, and politicians were all asked, often rudely, to justify themselves and their authority. That was one Sixties, the Left Sixties, so to speak; at the same time the Sixties of the Right, taking off from the campaign to choose Barry Goldwater for the Republican presidential nomination in 1964, now began to challenge the liberal consensus from the opposite direction. Both inevitably shook the disproportionate power of the Establishment over foreign policy. Both were offered an opportunity by the strategic blunder and tactical incompetence of Vietnam.

By the time Richard Nixon was inaugurated in 1969, a liberal era was ending and a conservative hegemony was approaching. The war in

Vietnam raised questions that the foreign policy Establishment was not successfully able to answer. Was the United States to be the world's policeman? What would be the geographical limits to American responsibility? In what circumstances would the use of force be justified to defend strategic interests? If the lesson of Munich had been that appeasement of dictatorships did not work, what would be the lessons of Vietnam?

The background to the tragedy of Vietnam was a decision taken as early as the postwar 1940s in Moscow. Once it was clear that the United States was organizing an alliance to defend western Europe from direct military attack, an alliance backed by the threat of nuclear weapons, the Soviet leadership decided, instead of bludgeoning the West, to strangle it. The Red Army remained in eastern Europe in massive force. But Soviet policy increasingly switched to encouraging anti-colonial and other national movements in what was now called the Third World: in the Caribbean and Latin America, in Africa, in the Middle East, Indonesia, and Southeast Asia. It was a great mistake (one often made in Washington) to see all such movements as essentially brought into being by Moscow. Everywhere in the 1950s, authentic movements for freedom, or at least for national self-determination, were boiling up, their causes specific to the experience of each country. Yet everywhere Moscow, and often Beijing, too, were involved, encouraging, fomenting, arming, and funding such rebellions. So the United States found itself committed to maintaining the status quo (sometimes represented by undemocratic and colonial regimes) almost anywhere subversion could be represented as likely to lead to the local success of communism.

From combating communism in Europe, the U.S. government, with the CIA as point man, found itself committed to trying to understand and to influence the politics of literally dozens of faraway countries of which it knew little, to paraphrase the hapless Neville Chamberlain's description of Czechoslovakia in 1938: Angola, Guatemala, Indonesia, Zaire.[45]

In the process, Washington, and the Establishment, had enough successes to believe it had learned how to counter subversion. From its origins as the successor of General William "Wild Bill" Donovan's OSS, the CIA was only partly an intelligence agency. The more glamorous part of its work was that of the Deputy Directorship of Plans (DDP). That was the cover name for "covert action," which could mean "counter-insurgency"—fighting up-country against rebellions of the kind described—or political coups backed by more or less overt small-scale warfare. The Soviet Union had upped the ante by encouraging wars of national independence to deny the West markets and raw materials. The United States, by responding almost everywhere, globalized the Cold War.

Both the grand North Atlantic alliance and the small wars in Asian, African, and Latin American jungles were largely led by Establishment types. In 1953 the CIA, in the person of Kermit "Kim" Roosevelt, another Groton boy[46] and a grandson of President Theodore Roosevelt, with an assist from the British Secret Intelligence Service, overthrew the radical government of Mohammed Mossadeq in Iran and reinstalled the Shah on the Peacock Throne. The next year the CIA, led by Tracy Barnes (Groton, Yale, and Harvard Law), a cousin of the Whitneys, led an operation to remove Jacobo Arbenz, a leftist though noncommunist president, from office in Guatemala. In the same years Colonel Edward Lansdale, legendary as the model for the antihero of Graham Greene's novel *The Quiet American*, and backed by another quintessentially Establishment figure, Desmond FitzGerald,[47] broke the Hukbalahap rebellion in the Philippines. The consequence of these and other undercover operations, which lost nothing in the telling back in Washington, was a deepening faith in the idea that communism in the developing world could be defeated by small operations in which propaganda and political intrigue would be backed by force on a small but lethal scale.

This faith in "little wars" and covert action had rubbed off on the

Establishment CIA men from their contacts, during and after World War II, with the British, who had learned in imperial adventures to use cunning, surprise, and secrecy to make up for a shortage of resources. The official British obsession with secret warfare was not only aggressive but also defensive, inflamed by an exaggerated estimate of German "fifth column" operations. American intelligence officers from "Wild Bill" Donovan on acquired from the British an exaggerated obsession with infiltration.[48] "By the end of the war," one historian writes, "sabotage, guerrilla attack, secret intelligence, and other forms of irregular warfare spread everywhere . . . [American intelligence officers'] faith in shadow warfare was further nurtured by a . . . gross overestimate of the effectiveness of British covert operations."[49] By the Kennedy administration, Mao Zedong's thoughts on guerrilla warfare were required reading for the ambitious national security official, and enthusiasts for counterinsurgency warfare, like the State Department's Roger Hilsman, were influential.[50]

✎ The proliferation of "shadow warfare" in the 1950s culminated in the disastrous Bay of Pigs invasion of Cuba in 1961. This brutally exposed false assumptions of every kind. It was also unmistakably an Establishment operation. Backed by Allen Dulles, who had led the Establishment's charge against isolationism in the Great Debate of 1939–1941, it was run by Richard Bissell and Tracy Barnes. The invasion was in some measure inspired by the success of Barnes's operation in Guatemala. It proved a disaster mainly because its planners, in characteristic Establishment fashion, ignored the political implications, domestic and international. John F. Kennedy, who never ignored the political implications of anything, insisted that the American involvement must be deniable. Dulles and Barnes simply assumed that Kennedy would have to bail the operation out.[51]

By the fall of 1962, the perceived threat from Cuba seemed to have been neutralized by Kennedy's firm, if devious, handling of the missile crisis.[52] Washington's attention switched to the far more remote threat from communist movements in the former French colonies of Indochina.

The commitment to Vietnam grew out of the secret war in Laos, where—while Averell Harriman strove to achieve a negotiated settlement—the CIA paid nine thousand Meo tribesmen in the hope that they could defeat a communist army. (This, like other CIA projects for using Indochinese ethnic minorities against the Vietnamese majority, came under the responsibility of Desmond FitzGerald, who was chief of the DDP's Far East division unit in 1963, then head of DDP from 1965 to his death in 1967.)[53]

In Vietnam, as in Laos, Washington was initially of two minds whether American involvement was necessary.[54] The question there at first appeared in a different guise: Should the United States support the corrupt and undemocratic regime of President Ngo Dinh Diem (not to mention his brother and his fearsome sister-in-law, Madame Nhu, whose response to unrest among the Buddhist clergy was to call for a "monk barbecue")? Less than three weeks before President Kennedy was assassinated, the Diem brothers were murdered in a coup openly approved of by Kennedy's ambassador in Saigon, Henry Cabot Lodge. By the time Lyndon Johnson focused on Vietnam, he was listening to advisers—including such central Establishment figures as McGeorge Bundy and Averell Harriman—who were for the most part telling him that the United States could not allow a communist revolution to occur in South Vietnam.

Neither the knife-in-mouth counter-insurgency warriors nor their Establishment masters were quick to realize the implications of the raw violence that underlay a strategy in Southeast Asia that purported to be about exporting American ideals to the developing world. The muscular Christianity of the Reverend Endicott Peabody could not survive exposure to a world in which Americans fought communist subversion with the systematic massacres of the Phoenix program, in which tens of thousands of Vietnamese were murdered in cold blood by Asians working under American orders.[55]

✎ It was the prolonged agony of Vietnam that divided and discredited the foreign policy Establishment and, by robbing it of its reputation for wisdom, destroyed its influence. Neither the division nor the discrediting, however, happened overnight. Several of President Johnson's key advisers—notably his national security assistant, McGeorge Bundy, and Bundy's elder brother, the assistant secretary of state for the Far East, William Bundy—were classic Establishment members. Neither of the Bundys was without severe doubts over the wisdom of the commitment in Southeast Asia. In 1964, however, both brothers were responsible for the decision to ask Congress for a Tonkin Gulf Resolution. This took advantage of a murky naval encounter, in which North Vietnamese vessels may or may not have attacked U.S. ships, to get congressional authority for war. In the spring of 1965, Mac Bundy, who had just visited South Vietnam, played a leading role in the decisions to send U.S. troops to South Vietnam and to bomb North Vietnam. Both Bundy brothers, and others from an Establishment background,[56] played a vocal part in selling the Vietnam policy, not least at a series of meetings at the Council on Foreign Relations.

One reason for the Establishment's disarray over Vietnam was that its members had always thought western Europe and the Middle East were much more important to the United States than Asia. John J. McCloy, in particular, who by this time was often half jocularly referred to as the chairman of the Establishment, was asked by Johnson to go to Saigon as ambassador, but refused.[57] He was not initially against an American presence in Vietnam; he simply thought it was a diversion of resources and of Washington's political priorities from western Europe, where the solidarity of NATO was being challenged by General de Gaulle and others and by pressures for troops cuts by the British and German governments. Indeed, he resented the way Vietnam was knocking what he regarded as more important issues in Europe off the front pages. And, as the lawyer who represented several major oil companies, he also thought that the Middle East was a higher priority than Southeast Asia.

Throughout the period from 1960 to 1968, the Council on Foreign Relations (CFR) organized no study group on Southeast Asia. Early in 1965, however, it did poll its members. A rough quarter of them favored expansion of the American war effort, another quarter favored disengagement, and half were for muddling through. Again, at first McCloy agreed with George Kennan, George Ball, and Averell Harriman that the United States should not be drawn into a land war in Asia. In early June 1965, in a commencement address at Haverford College in his native Philadelphia, McCloy said, "I do not yet see clearly . . . light through the tunnel." (At about that time Philip Hamburger wrote in the *New Yorker* that the advocates of the war, who often said they saw light at the end of the tunnel, were "right about the tunnel, wrong about the light.") Then he was talked into a more favorable view by the administration spokesmen who visited the CFR, who included Henry Cabot Lodge, General Maxwell Taylor, and Bill Bundy.

The narrative that most clearly charts the part played by Vietnam in the growing division and eventual discrediting of the Establishment is that of the "Wise Men," the group of elder statesmen outside government to whom Lyndon Johnson turned for advice. As the sheer size and difficulty of the task that would be involved in defeating the Viet Cong rebels and their supporters in North Vietnam became plain, the Establishment mind gradually changed. Patriots the Establishment men certainly were, and disinclined to shrink from conflict. Certainly most of them felt instinctively, as McCloy did, that once the honor of the United States was at stake, it must be maintained. Defeat was unthinkable. But they were also practical men, many of them lawyers. They would not shrink from a day in court if there were any chance of winning. But if the case was hopeless, they knew that they might have to settle out of court.

Lyndon Johnson was aware of his relative inexperience in foreign affairs. He was impressed, perhaps overimpressed, by the Establishment's reputation for expertise and wisdom. He wanted to recruit its prestige. In July 1965 a group of about twenty distinguished elder statesmen that included Dean Acheson, Robert Lovett, and John J. McCloy was invited for briefings on Vietnam at the State Department. The next day a smaller group of them met the president and enthusiastically endorsed plans for escalation in Southeast Asia. Acheson told the president he had "no choice but to press on."[58] This was the policy Acheson had counseled in the early days of the Cold War: stand up to the communists. With approval he recorded that "my colleagues came thundering in like the charge of the Scots Greys at Waterloo." (Not for nothing had Acheson's grandfather been an officer in the British army: he knew of its glories.) The next day McGeorge Bundy told his staff, "The mustache was voluble."[59]

On July 22, 1965, McCloy and Arthur Dean, the senior partner in the leading Wall Street law firm of Sullivan and Cromwell, who had been the head of the disarmament agency in the Kennedy administration, were invited back for a second meeting. McCloy asked why Hanoi couldn't be bombed. And, later in the year, after President Johnson ordered a bombing halt in the hope of persuading Hanoi to negotiate peace, both McCloy and Lovett told Bundy that they were in favor of starting bombing again. So far, no break in the Establishment's Cold War stance.

On January 27, 1966, there was a second full Wise Men group meeting. McCloy, Harriman, the Bundy brothers, George Ball, Arthur Dean, and Clark Clifford were present. Whatever private misgivings there might have been, there was still no open breach over the president's war.

Yet already there were signs of division. When the administration wanted to set up a citizens' group to lobby for the war, Hamilton Fish Armstrong, the editor of *Foreign Affairs*, thought it would be bad idea: it would look like "control of government policy by reactionaries, Wall Street, the East, the Establishment."[60] In the end McCloy, David Rockefeller, and Acheson did join a "Committee for an Effective and Durable Peace in Asia." Its less than gung-ho manifesto reflected the Establishment's instinct for the center ground.

In 1967 the president's friend Jim Rowe and a keen-as-mustard White House aide, John Roche, started a "Citizens Committee for Peace with Freedom in Vietnam," with former Senator Paul Douglas as its head. Former President Eisenhower and Acheson joined. But Bob Lovett and Mac Bundy dragged their feet. McCloy refused to join, while George Ball, as a "Europeanist," consistent in his skepticism about the Vietnam enterprise, compared them, savagely, to "buzzards, sending the young men off to be killed."[61]

Things did not go well in Vietnam. In May 1967 one of Defense Secretary Robert McNamara's aides, former Harvard law professor John McNaughton, told his boss that the war had caused "the worst split in more than a century."[62] Privately, McNaughton said, "This war is shit." On November 1 and 2 of that year the Wise Men came to town again, among them Johnson's adviser Clark Clifford, who had worked in the White House with President Truman, as well as the president's friend Abe Fortas,[63] Mac Bundy, Averell Harriman, Douglas Dillon, Arthur Goldberg, and Arthur Dean. They were briefed in an optimistic vein by the chairman of the Joint Chiefs, General Earle Wheeler. "This is a matter," said Acheson, "we can and will win." "Getting out of Vietnam," said Bundy, "is as impossible as it is undesirable."[64]

The Establishment leadership was still on board. But it was troubled. Many distinguished figures were being angrily questioned by their children and wives about how they could support a policy that seemed both futile and morally bankrupt.

On January 30, 1968, came the Tet offensive.[65] The Viet Cong rose all over the country, even penetrating the perimeter of the American embassy in Saigon. Later historians, especially those of a conservative tendency, interpreted it as a defeat for the Viet Cong and Hanoi. At the time, it was certainly a political defeat for the Johnson administration. On February 27 at a meeting on Vietnam at the State Department, McNamara, once the partisan of perseverance, lost control. "They've dropped more bombs than in all of Europe in World War II and it hasn't done a fucking thing," he shouted, and then broke down sobbing.[66]

The same day the usually cool Dean Acheson also lost his temper with the president of the United States. He felt he was being given the runaround. He stalked out of the White House, and when Mac Bundy's successor, Walt Rostow, called to ask him to come back, the old gentleman answered, "Tell the President he can take Vietnam and stick it up his ass."[67]

On March 25 came the climactic meeting with the Wise Men. Bundy summarized their view for the president: "We can no longer do the job we set out to do in the time we have left, and we must begin to take steps to disengage." General Wheeler explained that the Pentagon was not intent on a "classic military victory." "Then what in the name of God are five hundred thousand men out there doing," Acheson burst out, "chasing girls?"[68]

Less than a week later, Lyndon Johnson tacked on to a televised speech in which he announced a halt to the bombing of North Vietnam a statement that he would not seek reelection.

The Wise Men of the foreign policy Establishment had changed their position. They had won again, but it was a Pyrrhic victory. Walt Rostow died in the last political ditch. "I thought to myself," he reflected, "that what began in the spring of 1940 when Henry Stimson came to Washington ended tonight. The American Establishment is dead."[69]

✗ That fall, Richard Nixon captured the White House. For the next decade, American foreign policy was dominated by Henry Kissinger.

He, too, came from Harvard. He had been the director of a study
group at the Council on Foreign Relations and advised Nelson Rockefeller.[70] He had even worked briefly and unhappily as a consultant with
McGeorge Bundy in the early years of the Kennedy White House. But
a member of the foreign policy Establishment he was not. In the 1970s,
in foreign policy as in other fields, there appeared what the journalist
and White House aide under Bill Clinton, Sidney Blumenthal, called a
"counter-establishment" of the right.[71] In foreign policy terms, new
groups, based in new institutions, such as the American Enterprise Institute in Washington, D.C., and the Hoover Institution at Stanford
University in Palo Alto, California, drawing their personnel and their
economic support from different parts of the country and subscribing
to different orthodoxies and a different ideology from those of the old
Establishment, were coming to the fore. A crucial moment was the formation in 1975 of the Committee on the Present Danger, and the campaign of Senator Henry "Scoop" Jackson for president in 1976. These
incidents saw the beginning of a new, neoconservative orthodoxy to
replace the centrist instincts of the Establishment.

In the 1980s and 1990s a new generation took over from the high-
minded amateurs of the Establishment. No longer was foreign policy
necessarily the business of the only elite that was interested. Foundations, think tanks, and graduate schools trained a new class of foreign
policy professionals. In many respects they were far better prepared to
handle America's growing international responsibilities than the men
from Groton and Yale, Harvard Law and Wall Street. It remains to be
seen whether they will do a better job. Certainly their focus was different. Many were disillusioned with Europe. After the collapse of the Soviet Union, there was less interest in the recondite arguments of strategic studies, more in what was called a "neo-Wilsonian" approach,
dedicated to spreading what the new neoconservative elite saw as the
best of American values.

As early as the Kennedy administration, there had been signs that the American right was reviving. The liberal consensus was ending. The year 1962, for example, brought no fewer than three book-length denunciations of the Council on Foreign Relations.[72] After the Nixon victory in the 1968 election, attacks on the foreign policy Establishment in general and the Council on Foreign Relations and the Trilateral Commission in particular multiplied.[73] But now they were joined by attacks, some equally fierce, but most of them ambivalent, from the liberal and radical left. In general, while the attacks from the right came from small, provincial publishers in the South and West, attacks from the left (as right-wing conspiracy theorists might expect) came from big, established New York publishers.[74] Several of these writers, moreover, were less than severe in their judgments of the Establishment: they came to mock, and stayed, if not to cheer, at least to be grudgingly impressed. On the right, in contrast, something akin to paranoia reigned. A study by James Perloff accused the Council on Foreign Relations of being behind almost every event in American history in the previous seventy-five years that could be seen, from a conservative point of view, as deleterious.[75] Perloff moved from saying that "Wall Street and the Council on Foreign Relations enjoyed an early love affair with the Bolsheviks"[76] by way of blaming the council or its members for Yalta, Cold War spy scandals, and the Chinese Revolution, to Vietnam. President Carter's administration was riddled with council members, Perloff pointed out, and even Ronald Reagan was not guiltless of this contamination.[77]

🖎 It is plain that any account of the foreign policy Establishment encounters serious difficulties of definition. Was Edward House a member? Was Franklin Roosevelt? If Allen Dulles falls within the definition, what of his elder brother, Foster? The foreign policy Establishment, it seems to me, was neither a conspiracy nor a fantasy. If, as McGeorge Bundy said, it was merely an example of "the circulation of elites,"[78] it was a significant one. It was certainly a sustained episode in

the history of the American upper class. It was also a crucial phase in
the history of American foreign policy. What had the Establishment
achieved, and where had it failed?

A comparatively tiny but extremely effective and public-spirited
fragment of American society played a crucial part in helping the
United States to confront the reality and the challenges of world
power. In its first great trial, during the Wilson administration, many
of whose personnel could be described as proto-Establishment, America succeeded in destroying the militarism of imperial Germany and its
allies, but failed at the Paris peace conference to bring about a peace
that conformed to its ideals or even to its interests. That very failure
called the foreign policy Establishment into being.

In the Great Debate of the late 1930s and early 1940s, the Establishment's instincts were healthier and its judgment wiser than that of the
isolationists, even if it was the reckless folly of imperial Japan and Nazi
Germany in attacking the United States, rather than the arguments of
Henry Stimson and his friends, that finally abolished isolationism. Total war hardened the younger generation of the Establishment. Victory
validated its credentials. But war gave way not to peace but to Cold
War. Confronted by the threat the Soviet Union seemed to pose to the
freedom of Europe and to American hegemony, the Establishment presided over the militarization of American policy and to some degree of
American society in the creation of a "national security state."

It is natural now to question the Establishment's commitment to
containment in Europe and counter-insurgency almost everywhere
else. Yet in the 1950s it would have required superhuman political courage to have made serious attempts to reach accommodation with the
Soviet Union. The choice of policy in the Third World, however, was
less inevitable. The stubborn folly of Vietnam, of which it can be said,
as was said of Napoleon's judicial murder of a Bourbon prince, that
it was "worse than a crime, it was a mistake,"[79] resulted from the hubris of believing that there was nothing the United States could not
achieve, no battle that could not be won. That miscalculation re-

bounded on the Establishment that was largely responsible for the war and in the end was marginalized by it. The Establishment's greatest failure, however, resulted from its indifference to and its lack of understanding of the spirit of a leveling age. In Reagan's America, a new ruling class, its power rooted in new money and justified by new ideas, was ready to push aside the Reverend Peabody's patrician Puritans.

8

Conservative Elites and the Counterrevolution against the New Deal

✖

MICHAEL LIND

Between the 1960s and 2000, New Deal liberalism in the United States was overthrown by the conservative movement. Having captured the Republican Party, conservatives created first a Republican presidential majority and then a Republican majority in Congress. The toppling of Rooseveltian liberalism by Reaganite conservatism resulted from more than a clash of ideas about society. The process involved the displacement of one set of elites by another, with a different group of economic, ethnic, and regional constituencies.

The New Deal coalition included many industrial state mayors and political machine bosses, along with a number of southern and western politicians. Notwithstanding this, the mid-century liberal establishment, which included liberal Republicans as well as Democrats, overlapped to a large degree with the patrician northeastern establishment and the public service mandarinate of the Ivy League and the major nonprofit foundations—the same elites which had been influential in the earlier Progressive Era. Consequently, appeals to white working-class resentment of the East Coast elite, pioneered in national politics by George Wallace, became the stock-in-trade of Republican conservatives, who combined an anti-intellectual "culture war" with the agenda of corporations and wealthy individuals who wanted to roll back the regulatory and social welfare achievements of the New Deal. Although the Bush family was an estranged northeastern elite dynasty, most of the leaders of the Republican right were from the South and the West, some of them former segregationist Democrats who became Republicans during the civil rights era. As the states of the former Confederacy became the base of Republican conservatism, southern conservatives used their successful political synthesis of folksy populism, laissez-faire economics, militarism, and religious fundamentalism to appeal to working-class whites in other parts of the country, such as Catholic "white ethnics" in the Midwest, who resented the old northeastern elite, intellectuals, and racial and sexual minorities. At the elite level, the southern conservatives found allies among some Wall Street financiers and corporate CEOs as well as among the "neoconservatives," who were ex-liberal and ex-radical intellectuals and policy experts.

By the twenty-first century, a coalition of southern whites and northern white Catholics dominated by southern and western politicians controlled American politics. The pattern was familiar to students of American history; it represented a reprise of the pattern of American politics from 1800 to 1860, when a Jeffersonian elite leading a coalition of southerners and Catholic immigrants in the North controlled Washington, D.C., most of the time. As the new millennium began, the northeastern establishment and the Ivy League had lost power in the United States to a right-wing southern and western counter-establishment allied at the grass-roots level with Protestant evangelicals and fundamentalists and at the elite level with a small but influential faction of neoconservative intellectuals and political operatives.

Politics Moves Upward and Southward

In the last third of the twentieth century, American society was transformed by a number of long-term trends. Internal migration shifted the geographic center of gravity from the Northeast and Midwest to the South and West, while international migration, concentrated in a small number of states, increased the percentage of foreign-born and nonwhite Americans. The Republican Party, based increasingly in the South and West, benefited from the geographic shift in America's population. The Democrats, increasingly a party of the Northeast, Midwest, and West Coast, lost a secure presidential majority in 1968 and a secure congressional majority in 1994. As a result of productivity increases and the expatriation of industry, manufacturing declined to the point where three-quarters of Americans were employed in the service sector by the end of the century. Union membership plummeted outside of the public sector, and political party institutions declined along with traditional partisanship. In politics, the churches of white and black evangelical Protestants eclipsed unions and party machines as the most important grassroots political organizations in the Republican and Democratic parties, respectively. At the elite level, politics was increasingly structured by lobbies and single-issue advocacy groups rather than by broad-based political parties with coherent ideologies. The electronic mass media replaced the print media as the chief means of political communication.

Among these complex changes, two particularly important trends stand out: an upward shift and a southward shift in American politics.

The period from the 1960s until the early twenty-first century in the United States witnessed what Christopher Lasch once called a "revolt of the elites." The political influence of the American working class declined along with its major institutional expressions, the labor union and the party machine. The social center of gravity in American politics shifted upward. This was evidenced in the rightward shift of the government in economics and the leftward shift with respect to social issues—shifts which reflected the interests and values of the college-educated overclass that now dominates both national parties.

While the social center of gravity in American politics moved upward, the geographic center of gravity moved southward. The major beneficiary of the changes in American life after the 1960s was the southern right. "The South, for good or ill, has been bidding the nation to follow its lead," writes the historian Bruce J. Schulman. "The South has passed on much to other regions—a fondness for high technology, a craving for defense industry, a suspicion of unions, a divided economy, an antipathy to welfare, an uneasy accommodation between black urban leaders and white business conservatives."[1]

The rise of the southern right came as a surprise. During the civil rights revolution of the 1950s and 1960s, it appeared that the South would be integrated into the American mainstream. Instead, in the final third of the twentieth century, America was integrated into the southern mainstream. The rise to primacy in the federal government of politicians from the states of the former Confederacy was only one manifestation of a long-term trend: the southernization of the United States. The southernization of American society was visible in many realms, from civil rights, where political polarization along racial lines came to define national politics, to economics, where the age-old southern formula of tax cuts, deregulation, free trade, and commodity exports came to define the national mainstream.

Between the mid-twentieth century and the early twenty-first, the United States experienced progress in many areas, ranging from the elimination of formal racial and gender discrimination and the diffusion of liberal attitudes toward sex and censorship to public support for environmental conservation. But the southernization of American life warped, when it did not retard, the general progress toward higher living standards and greater personal liberties that the United States shared with the other advanced industrial democracies. If the southern border of the United States had run along the Mason-Dixon line rather than the Rio Grande, then American history in the last decades of the old millennium would have been quite different.

At the elite level, the result of all of these trends was a shift in political power from the remnants of the northeastern Republican Establishment as well as from post–New Deal liberal elites based in organized labor, the civil rights movement, and the academy to an ascendant southern–Sun Belt elite and its allies in the financial sector and parts of the media. With an economic outlook shaped by the commodity-exporting capitalism and the low-wage, small-government tradition of the South and West, and a view of the world influenced by southern Jacksonian militarism and Protestant fundamentalism, the latest in a series of American elites began to remake the nation.

The Third Republic: Conservatives Take Control

The present American regime, it can be argued, represents a Third Republic of the United States.[2] The First Republic endured from the Founding and collapsed in the Civil War. The Lincoln administration and its successors laid the groundwork for the Second Republic, which lasted until the Great Depression. The Third Republic, the product of the New Deal and the civil rights revolution, was assembled by the presidents from Franklin D. Roosevelt to Lyndon B. Johnson.

In 1932 an unlikely coalition of southern conservatives, western populists, urban industrial workers, and reformist northern Protestants, united by hostility to the northern industrial capitalist elite, elected Franklin Roosevelt and put an end to the Second Republic. The New Deal had two agendas—one for the northeastern-midwestern core and one for the agrarian periphery. In the Northeast and Midwest, the New Deal was identified with the redistribution of bargaining power and income toward the working class. In the southern and western periphery, by means of state capitalist projects like the civilian Tennessee Valley Authority and military bases, the New Dealers in the federal government built a modern infrastructure in the hope of decentralizing industry throughout the United States.[3]

The geographic decentralization of industry and wealth was a goal shared both by the progressive New Dealers in all regions and by elite southern conservatives, whose support in Congress was indispensable for the New Deal coalition. Conservative southern Democrats used their political power to block federal programs that threatened to destabilize the class and racial hierarchies of southern society. Menial and agricultural workers—categories including the majority of black southerners—were exempted from most federal labor and social insurance reforms, and large southern landowners reaped the greatest benefit from New Deal farm aid policies. And southern conservatives in the United States Senate managed to delay major congressional civil rights reforms, which would otherwise have taken place in the late 1940s, until the mid-1960s.

Despite the success of southern Democrats in limiting the scope and radicalism of the New Deal, the United States was dominated by New Deal liberalism from the 1930s to the 1970s. Republican presidents like Eisenhower and Nixon had to accommodate themselves to the prevailing liberal consensus. Under President Lyndon Johnson, New Deal ideals received their final expression with the enactment of Medicare and Medicaid, the last major social insurance programs established in the United States.

The New Deal era ended, however, in the 1960s, and a new era of conservative political dominance began, producing a Republican majority in the presidency and Congress by the turn of the twenty-first century. Although some conservative rejectionists wanted to repeal the New Deal and the civil rights revolution, the majority of conservatives sought to promote their agenda within the established framework of the Third Republic. This strategy led mainstream conservatives to promote partial privatization of Social Security and Medicare rather than their abolition. And mainstream conservatives, rather than inviting accusations of racism by calling for the repeal of civil rights legislation, claimed that affirmative action on the basis of race betrayed the color-blind vision of the Civil Rights Act of 1964. Finding it difficult to muster congressional support for the repeal of popular federal programs, the administrations of both Ronald Reagan and George W. Bush instead pursued a strategy of "starving the beast" by cutting taxes and preventing the growth of spending or the creation of new government programs—at the expense, in both presidencies, of ballooning federal deficits.

The period from the 1970s until the early twenty-first century, then, can best be understood not in terms of the establishment of a new American "republic" but in terms of the capture and modification of the Third Republic of the United States by conservatives hostile to the political values of its New Deal liberal founders. Rather than abolish the foundations of Franklin Roosevelt's America, the resurgent right in the late twentieth and early twenty-first centuries adopted a strategy of working within the system that mid-century liberals had established while gradually undermining programs and institutions of which they disapproved.

Race and the Rise of the Right

The New Deal coalition of the 1930s to the 1960s had united segregationists and civil rights reformers in a single alliance based on the use of federal power to redistribute income among classes and regions. The civil rights revolution of the 1950s and 1960s destroyed the New Deal coalition and replaced it with a new political realignment based on race.

Almost as soon as it had coalesced, the New Deal coalition began to fall apart over issues of race. The southern "Dixiecrats" split away from the Democratic Party in 1948 and voted for the segregationist Strom Thurmond, in protest against President Harry Truman's support for civil rights reform. Between the 1940s and the 1970s, southern Democrats and northern Republicans frequently voted together in Congress as part of what was called "the conservative coalition." Beginning with Barry Goldwater and Richard Nixon, architect of the "southern strategy," Republican tacticians sought to win over white southern Democrats alienated from their party because of its stand on black civil rights and its cultural liberalism.

Conservatives were also able to take advantage of anti-black sentiments among working-class whites in the North because of demographic change. The mechanization of southern agriculture—a process accelerated by New Deal farm subsidies—had displaced much of the South's black rural proletariat to the cities of the industrial North and West at a time when industry was being relocated to low-wage areas in the American South or West or to Third World countries. In 1900, nine out of ten black Americans lived in the rural South. By 1990, blacks made up a third of the combined population of the ten largest cities in the United States and, combined with nonwhite immigrants, formed the majority in New York and Los Angeles.[4]

The high rates of poverty and crime among southern migrants in the North produced "white flight" to the suburbs and universalized a kind of anti-black politics that previously had been confined to the South. Following the civil rights revolution, Republican conservatives avoided endorsing racism directly and distanced themselves from those who did. When, in 2002, Senator Trent Lott of Mississippi praised the 1948 presidential campaign of the segregationist Strom Thurmond, the public outcry forced him to resign as Senate majority leader. Nevertheless, many of the issues chosen by Republican politicians, such as welfare reform in the 1990s, were surrogates for appeals to the racial anxieties of white Americans. By the 1990s, the "southern strategy" had succeeded in making whites in the former Confederacy the most important constituency of what had once been the party of Lincoln and the North. In the meantime, the Democratic Party had absorbed many former progressive and centrist Republicans, and its new heartland was found in the regions that had supported the GOP between Lincoln and Hoover: New England, the upper Midwest, and the West Coast. Working-class Catholics in the industrial Midwest, wavering between the mostly northern Democrats and the predominantly southern and western Republicans, became the most important swing voters in presidential elections by 2000.

Identity Politics and the Democrats

Racial demagogy was not limited to the right. Instead of trying to win back the white working class, the Democratic Party after the 1970s put its hopes in a "rainbow coalition" strategy that sought to build a new Democratic majority on the basis of blacks, Latinos, and the liberal minority within the white population. Mainstream liberal supporters of the civil rights revolution, such as President Lyndon Johnson and Vice President Hubert Humphrey, for reasons of politics as well as principle, had favored race-neutral law and opposed "benign" racial discrimination on behalf of racial minorities. Bayard Rustin, a leading black liberal, argued that racial preference policies would destroy the liberal coalition between the white working class and black Americans. (Large-scale Latino and Asian immigration had only begun in the 1960s.) The fears of the color-blind liberals came true when the Democratic Party as a whole, in pursuing the "rainbow coalition" strategy, rejected race-neutral reform in favor of racial discrimination against white Americans.

By the mid-1970s, the Democrats added Latinos to blacks as a group eligible for racial preferences. The "compensatory justice" argument for affirmative action for black Americans would not work for Latinos, most of whom came to the United States following the liberalization of U.S. immigration laws in the 1960s. The rationale for racial quotas was changed from compensation for past injustice to the promotion of "diversity." Corporations and universities, fearful of protests by black and Latino activists, adopted quotas in the private as well as the public sector, and under their influence the Supreme Court, albeit by narrow majorities, has upheld a number of racial quota schemes.[5]

Democratic politicians and activists tended to respond to criticisms of racial preferences by denouncing critics as racists. Although he challenged the left wing of the Democrats on economics and foreign policy as president, Bill Clinton avoided challenging the racial preference policies which had become Democratic orthodoxy. During the 1992 presidential campaign, he had denounced a black pop star named Sister Souljah for her comment that blacks ought to kill white people rather than one another. As president, however, he avoided any challenge to left-wing orthodoxy about racial preferences and multiculturalism. He said that racial preferences should be "mended, not ended," and engaged in televised debates about race in America.

Racial preferences were not the only example of identity politics on the left. The left wing of American liberalism also favored multiculturalism, bilingualism, and amnesties for illegal aliens. Diatribes by leftist scholars and activists against white Americans and Western civilization played into the hands of demagogic conservative Republicans seeking to appeal to disaffected white Democrats. Bilingual policies also alarmed white citizens, particularly in states like California, Texas, and Florida in which the Spanish-speaking population was growing rapidly. And the support by Democratic politicians of mass amnesties for immigrants who had broken U.S. immigration laws was widely interpreted as a desperate attempt to compensate for the party's unpopularity by seeking to naturalize foreigners who had broken American laws in order to bring them to the polls.

Race and Realignment

The result of the race-based realignment in the 1960s was a pattern of racially polarized politics that changed little in the three subsequent decades. No Democratic presidential candidate has won a majority of the white vote since Lyndon Johnson in 1964. The only white ethnic group that remains consistently Democratic is the Jewish American minority, who voted for Al Gore over George W. Bush by 80 percent to 17 percent. The Republican Party capitalized on the disaffection of many former white Democrats to create a presidential majority, broken only by the one term of Jimmy Carter and the two terms of Bill Clinton, and, beginning in 1994, a majority in both houses of the U.S. Congress.

In 1996 Clinton was reelected, winning overwhelming majorities of
the black and Latino vote and losing the white vote to Republican rival
Bob Dole by only 3 percentage points. In 2000, however, substantial
movement of white voters toward the Republicans gave the Republican
Party control of the presidency and of both houses of Congress, which
the Republicans held in the mid-term election of 2002. In the 2000
presidential race, the Democratic deficit in the white vote grew from
the 3 percent of 1996 to 12 percent. White men alone preferred Bush to
Gore by a remarkable 24 percentage points. Only 10 percent of black
voters in 2000 voted for Bush.

A poll taken by the Joint Center for Political and Economic Studies in September and October 2002, prior to the mid-term congressional elections, revealed stark ideological divisions between whites
and blacks.[6] In 2002 the Republican Party won the two-party vote by 53
percent to 47 percent. According to the Gallup Poll's analysts following
the election, "By far the largest divide among American voters continues to be racial." In the words of the noted American political analyst
Ruy Texeira, "Last November [2002] was all about the white vote."[7] In
that year's U.S. Senate elections, non-Hispanic whites preferred Republicans to Democrats by a factor of 55.1 to 44.9 percent. Latinos preferred Democrats by a factor of 67.1 to 32.9 percent, while blacks gave
the Democrats an overwhelming 93.8 percent of their vote, compared
to only 6.2 for Republicans. In races for state governor, the preference
of white voters for Republicans over Democrats was even higher, 62.8
percent to 37.2 percent.

Many Democrats continued to believe that the growth of nonwhite
immigrant numbers (chiefly Latinos) would inevitably give their party
a majority. This seemed plausible, given that the percentage of foreign-
born Americans, most of them Latin Americans, had risen to 9.5 percent by 1999, from a low of 4.7 percent in 1970.[8] And by the early
twenty-first century, California and Texas had nonwhite majorities.

The nonwhite population, however, was concentrated in a few large
states, which were underrepresented, compared to white-majority

states, in the electoral college and the U.S. Senate. And immigrant voters were far less likely to register and to vote than native-born Americans. For example, if citizenship and turnout rates of Latinos and Asians were to remain at their levels of 2000, in 2040 whites—by then roughly one-third of the population of California—would still account for 53 percent of California's voters.[9] In 2002, only 17 percent of the votes in Texas were cast by Latinos. The rainbow coalition strategy, even if it were successful in California, Texas, or New York, was unlikely to succeed on the scale of the nation, which might have a white majority well into the twenty-first century, if not into the twenty-second.[10]

To make matters worse for Democratic strategists favoring a "rainbow coalition" strategy for winning a national majority without winning more white votes, internal migration within the United States may help the Republicans. As nonwhite immigrants have poured into California, New York, and other entry states, millions of white Americans have moved into the less crowded and more culturally homogeneous American hinterland. The malapportionment of the electoral college and the U.S. Senate gives voters in the Rocky Mountains and plains states grossly disproportionate power in the federal government. This explains why, even though a majority of Americans cast their ballots for Al Gore in 2000, George W. Bush was "selected" by the electoral college, thanks to western votes. And as noted earlier, the small-population states of the West, in alliance with the more populous southern states, are also responsible for the Republican majority in the U.S. Senate.

The Overclass and the Transformation of Liberalism

The shift from the class-based politics of the New Deal era to the race-based politics of the post–civil rights era was accompanied by the diminution of working-class influence. The decline of organized labor, combined with the expansion in numbers and affluence of the managerial-professional overclass, transformed the definitions of "liberalism" and "progressivism" in the last decades of the twentieth century. During the New Deal, the base of the left was organized labor, and economic egalitarianism defined the politics of the left. Beginning with the civil rights era, the social base of the left in the white population shifted to affluent college-educated professionals more concerned with issues such as feminism, environmentalism, and foreign policy than with the "bread and butter" issues of old-fashioned "lunch-bucket liberalism."

As industrial jobs were expatriated to low-wage states or countries, the American workforce became polarized between low-wage service sector workers and a well-paid managerial-professional elite—the "overclass."[11] Members of the overclass, based in politically powerful professions like the law and medicine and the professoriat, were protected by licensing laws from competition by foreigners or immigrants. Unlike factory workers or janitors, American lawyers could not be replaced by lawyers in India or by unlicensed immigrants from Latin America. It is the artificial monopolies created by professional licensing, rather than a transition to a "knowledge economy," that explains why American professionals tended to flourish at a time when workers exposed to foreign and immigrant competition suffered. (In the early years of the twenty-first century, as U.S. corporations began to outsource jobs to foreign managers, professionals, scientists, and engineers, the elite consensus in favor of free-market globalism began to fray.)

Beginning in the 1960s, political liberalism was transformed from a movement concerned chiefly with working-class standard-of-living issues to a quality-of-life movement reflecting the values and interests of the college-educated elite. The political scientist Jeffrey M. Berry points out that in 1963, two-thirds of bills before Congress dealt with economic growth or redistribution, while only one-third involved quality-of-life issues like environmentalism or consumerism. By 1991, however, "seventy-one percent of all congressional hearings that year took

up legislation that had quality-of-life concerns at the center of the polices being debated, while just 29 percent of the domestic legislation involved exclusively economic issues. Analysis of each bill revealed that
groups such as the Wilderness Society, the Sierra Club, the Consumer Federation of America, and the Ralph Nader organizations often pushed the legislation forward."[12] Liberal interest groups, because
of the elite nature of their donors, are far better funded than most conservative interest groups, many of which rely on small donations raised
by direct mail campaigns.[13] According to Berry, "as liberal citizens
groups mobilized their followers in the 1960s and '70s, Ralph Nader
liberalism began to eclipse Hubert Humphrey liberalism . . . At the
same time, the success of those groups has pushed traditional liberal
concerns for the poor and disadvantaged further to the margins of
American society."[14]

The political divisions within the national overclass tended to occur
over social issues rather than economic issues. Within the overclass,
there was a consensus in favor of investor-friendly globalization and
high levels of immigration. Globalization benefited professionals and
executives in the United States who hoped to achieve higher returns
from investments abroad than from investments in American capital
and labor. The members of the managerial-professional overclass also
tended to be employers of menial labor—nannies, gardeners, maids—
whose wages were kept low by the high levels of unskilled immigration
that began in the 1960s. While the overclass enjoyed a buyer's market
in labor and services, the median real wage in both manufacturing and
services dropped between 1979 and 1996.[15]

The Decline of the Parties

Another major transformation in American politics in the last part of
the twentieth century was the weakening of the major parties as organizations.

Until the 1970s, party leaders chose party nominees at state and national conventions, and party machines connected leaders and rank-and-file members at the grass-roots level. By 1972, however, upper-middle-class reformers, critical of secretive decision making by party leaders in "smoke-filled rooms," prevailed on both parties to turn over the nomination of their candidates to caucuses or primaries. The primary/caucus system and campaign finance reform, which were intended to democratize the American political system, backfired. The McCain-Feingold campaign finance reforms, enacted by Congress in 2002 and upheld by the Supreme Court in 2003, by limiting the amounts of "soft money" that could be spent on candidates by the parties promised to reduce the role of the national parties even further.

By weakening the parties, the reformers created a political vacuum that was filled by millionaires and billionaires who "self-financed" their own political campaigns. The increase in the number of rich politicians was a result of the 1976 decision in *Buckley v. Valeo,* which upheld campaign finance limits on contributions to candidates but struck down limits on how much of their own resources candidates could spend on their campaigns. The most prominent self-financed political candidate was the billionaire H. Ross Perot, who in his 1992 campaign for the presidency drew more votes than any third-party candidate since Theodore Roosevelt had run as the Progressive Party nominee in 1912. But Perot was merely the most visible of a number of politicians who spent their own fortunes to obtain office, often with little or no support from the political parties to which they nominally belonged. In 1984 Senator Daniel Patrick Moynihan complained: "At least half of the members of the Senate today are millionaires . . . We've become a plutocracy . . . The Senate was meant to represent the states; instead it represents the interests of a class."[16]

The replacement of conventions by primaries and caucuses led to the domination of the nominating process in both parties by single-issue groups like the religious right in the Republican Party and members of the environmentalist and feminist movements and black and Latino ethnic activists in the Democratic Party. All of these groups represented significant constituencies in American society. In a traditional strong-party system, these constituencies would have compromised with others in the party. But in the era of weak parties that began in the 1970s, the primary loyalty of many political activists was to a single-issue group rather than to the party as a whole.

The incentives to compromise and to moderate extremist rhetoric were further weakened by the imperatives of fund-raising by single-issue groups. Activists on the left depended heavily on subsidies from a few major liberal foundations. The need to renew their grants gave them an incentive to argue that the situation was always bad and perpetually getting worse in the areas of their concern, ranging from the environment to race relations.

The single-issue groups of the right, such as the National Rifle Association (NRA), the Moral Majority, and the Christian Coalition, by contrast, depended heavily on small donations solicited by direct-mail campaigns. Alarmist and apocalyptic rhetoric helped them to raise money and dominate political primaries. The same rhetoric, however, tended to force them to define political compromise as betrayal.

The definition of politics as moral crusading was most pronounced among the religious leaders who emerged as political kingmakers in the last third of the twentieth century. American society as a whole became more secular and tolerant with each decade. The rise of political clerics was the result not of a "great awakening" in American society in general, but rather of the weakening of the political parties. As old-fashioned party machines dissolved, the largest organizations with grassroots membership that could be mobilized in political campaigns were the churches. The Catholic Church played only a minor role in politics. But evangelical Protestant churches in the southern tradition—both black and white—moved to fill the void left by the declining party organizations. Black Protestant preachers like Jesse Jackson and Al Sharpton became more influential in Democratic politics. But their influence was dwarfed by that of white southern Protestant preachers like Jerry Falwell and Pat Robertson, who became kingmakers in the

Republican Party. Preachers who could deliver busloads of the faithful
to the polls on Election Day replaced old-fashioned political bosses.
The capture of the nominating process in both parties by Protestant
churches explains why fervent Christian religiosity seeped into American politics during the rise of southern political hegemony in the latter
part of the twentieth century. Not only conservative Republicans like
George W. Bush but also southern Democrats like Jimmy Carter and
Bill Clinton spoke of their personal relationship with Jesus in a language familiar in the South—and among the descendants of southern
black immigrants in the cities of the North.

By the end of the twentieth century, American politics was dominated by individualistic billionaires and true believers belonging to
various religions and secular ideologies. People who were neither rich
nor highly ideological found themselves marginalized. Their disaffection expressed itself as growing alienation from both national parties
and declining levels of voter turnout. In December 2000, following the
bitter partisan debate over the installation of George W. Bush as president by the electoral college, 42 percent of Americans identified themselves to Gallup pollsters as independents—a greater number than either self-identified Republicans or Democrats.[17]

Conservative Victories in the War of Ideas

In the new era of weak party loyalties, conservatives owed their success in changing the national debate about domestic and foreign policy in large part to their organizational superiority over their political rivals. The so-called neoconservatives were particularly successful
in dominating national debate. Ironically, neoconservative tactics and
strategy were modeled on those of the communist left. During the
1930s the Trotskyist movement, which produced a number of leading
neoconservative figures, set up its own network of little magazines and
institutions to combat those of the Stalinist left in the United States and
Europe. Following World War II, anti-Stalinist socialists collaborated

with anticommunist liberals in founding the Congress for Cultural Freedom, which opposed Soviet-sponsored cultural front groups. The influence of the cultural front model can be seen on the neoconservative movement, which, beginning in the 1970s, created a political-intellectual network linking elite journals like *The Public Interest* and *The National Interest*, political monthlies or weeklies like *Commentary* and *The Weekly Standard*, think tanks like the American Enterprise Institute (AEI), and projects agitating for particular policies, like the Committee on the Present Danger in the 1970s and the Project for a New American Century in the 1990s and early 2000s. Irving Kristol, who had co-edited the anticommunist liberal magazine *Encounter* in the 1950s when it was subsidized by the CIA, and his son William and their associates were at the center of this network.

Their allies in the Protestant fundamentalist subculture had a network of their own. Between the 1920s and the 1960s, the mostly southern fundamentalists, alienated from modern society, had built their own counterculture of Christian bookstores, Christian radio and television stations, and even pseudoscientific "creation science" institutes that sought to refute modern biology and geology. In response to the sexual revolution and cultural liberalism of the 1960s, fundamentalists under the leadership of the television preachers Jerry Falwell, founder of the Moral Majority, and Pat Robertson, founder of the Christian Coalition, had a preexisting base from which they were able to capture the Republican Party and influence state and federal governments. Like the secular neoconservatives, the Protestant fundamentalists combined sectarianism with innovative use of up-to-date media strategies.

The American left handicapped itself in its response to the neoconservative-fundamentalist alliance by its media and political strategies. Instead of fighting the populist right to influence public opinion, the left focused on persuading the college-educated elite, through media like National Public Radio (NPR), the Public Broadcasting Service (PBS), and prestigious journals. After the 1960s, the left dominated the academic subculture at the price of losing its influence beyond the campus. Meanwhile, from the 1960s to the early twenty-first century, the political energy of idealists on the left was dissipated in the promotion of divisive ethnic and gender identity politics, leaving the realm of political economy largely uncontested.

Both conservative and liberal intellectuals depended to a large degree on foundation funding. Liberal foundations like the Ford and Rockefeller foundations had far greater resources than those of the right, like the Bradley and Olin and Smith-Richardson foundations. Neoconservatives, however, used their limited resources to better effect by subsidizing cadres of young public intellectuals accustomed to print and TV and radio debate, and by subsidizing books intended to promote conservative ideas, such as the racist anti-welfare tract *The Bell Curve* by Charles Murray and Richard Herrnstein. By contrast, the foundations of the left supported projects rather than thinkers and publicists. And much of the money from the liberal foundations went to projects in relatively noncontroversial areas like children's welfare and environmentalism. The frequent choice of noncontroversial topics reflected compromises between the progressive program officers at left foundations and their more conservative boards of directors. All of these self-defeating strategies by the center-left produced conservative victories by default in the war of ideas.

The Decline of the Northeast and Midwest

In the second half of the twentieth century, the success of New Deal programs of rural electrification and industrial decentralization in the South and West made possible a massive internal migration to air-conditioned homes and prosperous cities in those former backwaters. Between 1950 and 2000, the regional population as a percentage of the total U.S. population declined in the Northeast (29 to 23 percent) and Midwest (26 to 19 percent), while it grew in the South (31 to 36 percent) and the West (14 to 22 percent).[18] On the list of the ten largest cities by population size in 1950 and 1990, Baltimore (number 6) was replaced by San Diego, St. Louis (number 8) by Dallas, and Boston (number 10) by San Antonio.[19]

Between 1868 and 1950, in all of the presidential elections except for one, at least one of the two national party presidential candidates came from one of five states: Ohio, New York, Illinois, Indiana, and New Jersey.[20] The post-1945 shift in population created two new presidential dynasties: a California dynasty (Nixon, Reagan) and a Texas dynasty (Johnson and the two Bushes—who constituted a literal dynasty). The power of the South in national politics was exaggerated by its alliance with the states of the interior West, whose small populations have always been enormously overrepresented in the electoral college and the U.S. Senate. In the late nineteenth and early twentieth centuries, the northern Republicans gained a political bonus thanks to the rapid admission of then-Republican western states, with small populations predominantly of New Englanders and midwesterners of Yankee Protestant ancestry, reinforced in the Midwest and Great Plains by culturally similar Germans and Scandinavians: Nebraska (1887), Colorado (1876), North Dakota (1889), South Dakota (1889), Montana (1889), Washington (1889), Idaho (1890), Wyoming (1890), Utah (1896), Oklahoma (1907), New Mexico (1912), and Arizona (1912). As a result of agrarian discontent, Franklin Roosevelt was able to detach these states from the Republican Party during the New Deal. The formerly Democratic southern conservatives who captured the Republican Party, in turn, used the cultural alienation of white hinterlanders from the post–civil rights era Democratic Party to build a Republican majority in all three branches of the federal government by the early twenty-first century.

According to the U.S. Census Bureau's data on domestic net migration from 1995 to 2000, core Democratic states like California, New York, and Massachusetts lost population, while almost all of the gains came in states that have contributed to the Republican presidential and Senate majorities, including Arizona, Colorado, and Nevada.[21] Southern dominance of American politics was so great after 1960 that the only Democrats elected president in the last third of the twentieth century were southerners—Lyndon Johnson, Jimmy Carter, and Bill Clinton.

Dixie Demagogy Goes National

The increased influence of southern politicians was not simply a result of the shift in the U.S. population to the South and West and the racial polarization of American politics. Southern politicians were preadapted by their tradition of reactionary populism to exploit the opportunities created by the transformation of American society and politics in the latter part of the twentieth century.

The South's tradition was one of single-party dominance by the Democrats. But "no-party politics" may be a better description. The major questions of southern social life—the racial order, the class system, the economy, and religion—could not safely be discussed in public between the end of Reconstruction and the civil rights era. The result was a divorce between governance and politics. Governance was the monopoly of the allied elites of the private and public sector. Politics was theater, dominated by demagogues like "Cotton Ed" Smith, Huey "The Kingfish" Long, and W. Lee "Pass the Biscuits, Pappy" O'Daniel. Only rarely, as in the case of Long, did demagogues incite class war. Most of the time they specialized in appeals to religion, waving the flag (either the Stars and Stripes or the Stars and Bars would do), and xenophobic hostility toward those outside the southern white Protestant community—blacks, Yankees, Jews, Catholics, liberals, and "communists" (a catchall term of abuse).

In the first two-thirds of the twentieth century, southern demagogy seemed primitive and repugnant to the rest of the country. Instead of being a relic of the rural past, however, southern political demagogy proved to be the wave of the future. The weakening of the parties by post-1960s reforms resulted in a political culture based on factions and individuals of a kind long familiar in the southern states. In an era in which "attack ads" on television and radio became the major form of communication from candidates to citizens, southern-style demagogy proved to be highly successful. It is no coincidence that the Republican political strategist Lee Atwater and one of his most successful Democratic counterparts, James Carville, were southerners schooled in the politics of their region.

Anti-intellectual populism was a characteristic of southern politicians—left, right, and center. What became known as "culture war politics" or "identity politics" in the late twentieth century had always been the staple of southern demagogues, who specialized in inflammatory appeals to racial identity, sexual morality, religious belief, and jingoistic patriotism. Ironically, liberal activists in the federal judiciary accidentally unleashed this kind of politics by nationalizing issues of sex and censorship as well as race which had previously been fought out in state legislatures and city councils. The nationalization of issues like abortion, homosexual rights, and censorship occurred in the 1960s and the 1970s at the very moment when print journalism, with its restricted, elite audience, was giving way to television and talk radio, with their mass audiences and low standards. The major beneficiaries of these trends were the southern right and its national allies, who took advantage of the traditional values of the working-class majority.

Perhaps the purest example of demagogy in politics involved the issue of public funding for the arts. During the 1930s, New Deal liberals had sought public funding in order to wrest control of art away from Eurocentric tastemakers and tiny cliques of the fashionable rich in New York, Boston, and other eastern cities. The Works Progress Administration and other federal arts programs were gutted by conservatives in Congress in the late 1930s, upset by the radicalism of some of the artists. After the National Endowment for the Arts and National Endowment for the Humanities were created during the Johnson presidency, they were quickly captured by the "art world" of the northeastern seaboard. Instead of taxing the rich to subsidize aesthetic populism, federal arts programs taxed working-class Americans to subsidize avant-garde artists and the wealthy patrons who were their chief audience. By the 1990s, before conservative populists in Congress imposed regional quotas, almost half of federal arts subsidies flowed to Manhattan. Targeted at working-class audiences, denunciations of taxpayer funding for obscene or incomprehensible art became a staple of conservative rhetoric. Liberals found themselves defending works of art whose shock value often exceeded their aesthetic merit. All of this was very far from the original New Deal idea of post office murals and outdoor pageants depicting local history.

Controversies like these provided conservatives with highly emotional "wedge issues" which they used to pry apart the new alliance of elite progressives and working-class populists. The defection of George Wallace from the Democratic Party in 1968 marked the beginning of the divorce between white working-class populism and Democratic liberalism. The disaffection of the white working class from elite progressivism gave conservatives an opportunity to destroy the New Deal coalition and replace it with a Republican majority. In the time-tested tradition of southern conservative-populist alliances, this new Republican alliance focuses on appeals to religion, patriotism, and "traditional values," along with thinly disguised race-baiting, in order to weld elite economic conservatives, who are often social liberals, with working-class white social conservatives, who are frequently left of center in their attitudes toward big business and the economy.

The Counterrevolution of Business against Labor

The alliance of conservatism with populism made possible a sustained onslaught by the right against organized labor in the United States. The Golden Age of American unionism began in 1935, when the National Labor Relations Act legalized collective bargaining. Until the 1970s, the AFL-CIO's political action committee was the largest and most important PAC in national politics.

The 1970s marked a counterrevolution against labor by the business community, aided by conservative politicians. Increasingly, business viewed labor not as part of a three-way compact including government but as the enemy. The journalist Thomas B. Edsall described the shift: "During the 1970s, business refined its ability to act as a class, submerging competitive instincts in favor of joint, cooperative action in the legislative arena. Rather than individual companies seeking only special favor in the reward of a contract, in the dropping of an antitrust case, or in State Department assistance in gaining exclusive franchising rights in a foreign country, the dominant theme in the political strategy of business became a shared interest in the defeat of bills such as consumer protection and labor law reform."[22]

Business PACs outspent labor PACs for the first time in the 1978 elections.[23] The shifting balance of power was evident in the same year in the successful attempt by the business community to persuade Congress to reject the Labor Reform Bill, which would have made the organization of the workplace easier. This was a major victory for the Business Roundtable, founded by corporate executives in 1972. When President Reagan fired striking air traffic controllers in 1982, his administration signaled a new alliance between government and business against labor.

The hostility of corporate America and its political allies was not the only reason for labor's decline. Even in the absence of corporate decisions to expatriate factory jobs, employment in the industrial sector would have declined as a result of mechanization and automation. As the manufacturing sector shrank, the unions failed to organize expanding sectors. Beginning in the 1970s, most of the growth in employment took part in the sectors of the workforce hardest to organize, such as service workers and white-collar workers. The increase of immigrants, both legal and illegal, in the workforce also made unionization difficult. Until the 1980s, organized labor favored immigration restriction in order to raise wages and make unionization easier. The reversal of course by the AFL-CIO, which now officially favors attempts to unionize not only legal but illegal immigrants as well, was a sign of desperation

rather than of confidence. The only growth in union membership occurred among public sector employees, such as schoolteachers. As a
proportion of the civilian labor force, unionized labor plummeted to 12
percent by 2000.[24] And a majority of union members worked for federal, state, or local governments.

In the decline of organized labor, the conservative South played a
key role. Even in the mid-twentieth century, at the height of labor's
growth and influence in the industrial states, southern politicians and
employers had used laws and intimidation to thwart attempts at unionization of the southern workforce. The ability of businesses to move
jobs to the anti-union South gave anti-labor executives enormous leverage, as did their alliance with anti-union southern politicians in
Washington, D.C.

From Raising Wages to Subsidizing Poverty

One faction of the Democratic Party adapted to the new conservative hegemony in American politics by competing with the Republican Party for the loyalty of the business elite and professionals. Bill
Clinton, more than any other American politician, represented the
"neoliberal" combination of free-market conservatism and social liberalism characteristic of the American overclass. He supported feminism
and gay rights—and also policies favored by economic conservatives
and libertarians, including the NAFTA free-trade agreement between
the United States and Mexico and large-scale unskilled immigration.

Clinton's major antipoverty initiative was the earned income tax
credit (EITC), a wage subsidy for poor workers. Increasing the EITC
was supported by Clinton's allies in the centrist Democratic Leadership
Council as an alternative to raising the minimum wage. Between 1978
and 1989 Congress had permitted the real value of the minimum wage
to erode. As a result, the minimum wage lost 31 percent of its value.
According to the Economic Policy Institute, the shrinking minimum
wage accounted for 22 percent of the increase in inequality among

men—and 42 percent of the growth in inequality among women—between the top and bottom tenths of the American wage scale. Four increases in the 1990s, culminating in the 1997 legislation that established the rate at $5.15 an hour, failed to restore the minimum wage to the standard of the 1960s, and an attempt to raise it to $6.15 was rejected by Congress in 2000. To permit workers to escape the federal definition of poverty, the minimum wage would have had to be raised to more than $8.00 an hour.

Neoliberals preferred the EITC to the minimum wage as a strategy for combating poverty among working Americans because it is a subsidy for business and affluent employers. Enacted in 1975, the EITC program was sponsored by Senator Russell Long of Louisiana, and its greatest champion in the Clinton administration was Treasury Secretary Lloyd Bentsen of Texas. It was no accident that the EITC should appeal to relatively conservative southern Democrats like Long, Bentsen, and Clinton. The weakness of organized labor in the South means that southern Democratic politicians have often been as dependent as Republicans on the support of business lobbies and investors. The EITC permitted centrist and conservative Democrats to do something for low-wage workers without threatening their friends and donors in industries that rely on cheap labor. In subsidizing the worker who toils for low wages, the EITC simultaneously subsidizes the employer, who can continue to pay workers less than they need to subsist at or above the federal poverty line.

In addition to being a benefit paid by American taxpayers as a whole to low-wage businesses and the consumers who buy their products and services, the EITC is probably an interregional corporate welfare program for the South. The South, which has the lowest wages, the lowest levels of employment benefits, and the lowest rate of unionization in the United States, inevitably receives a disproportionate share of federal EITC money. First, in the early and mid-twentieth century, the southern elite, having used legislation and violence to smash organized labor, built low-wage textile factories and car factories to force those in high-wage regions like New England and the Midwest out of business. Then, in the late twentieth century, southern Democratic politicians in Washington, like Long, Bentsen, and Clinton, arranged for taxpayers in the former mill towns of New England, as well as in the Midwest, the prairie states, the mountain states, and the West Coast, to supplement the inadequate paychecks of exploited southern workers. The EITC succeeded in lifting many Americans out of poverty—but it did so in a way that did not threaten the economic interests of southern business and the national overclass.

From Progressive to Regressive Taxation

In the area of taxation, too, the influence of southern-style conservatism on American politics was evident. The southern states traditionally have combined low public spending with low and regressive taxation. From the 1970s to the early twenty-first century, during the period of Republican presidential hegemony interrupted only by Clinton's two terms, the amount of taxation at the federal level was reduced—and its burden was shifted from the rich to the working class and the poor.

Under Ronald Reagan and George W. Bush, Congress enacted massive tax cuts, which in the absence of commensurate spending cuts created enormous federal deficits. By 2001 the United States ranked twenty-seventh among thirty OECD (Organization for Economic Cooperation and Development) countries in the percentage of total taxation (federal, state, and local) as a percentage of GDP. While taxes on the rich were slashed, the highly regressive Social Security tax rose from 3.3 percent of GDP in 1965 to 6.9 percent.[25]

The regressive nature of overall national taxation was further increased by the devolution of federal responsibilities to the states in areas like welfare. State taxes tend to be more regressive than federal taxes because it is easier for individuals and corporations to move within the country to avoid taxes than to leave the country. States therefore tend to rely on sales and excise and property taxes. Many states do not have an income tax.

The state tax systems of southern states are generally among the most regressive in the nation. With no state income tax, Texas, the political base of both Presidents Bush and Republican House Majority Leader Tom DeLay, had one of the ten most regressive tax systems in the United States. In 1995 the top 1 percent of non-elderly Texan married couples, with incomes of $395,000 or more, paid only 4.4 percent of their income in state taxes, compared to those making less than $19,000, who paid 13.8 percent of their income in sales and excise taxes and property taxes.[26] By means of tax cuts for the rich and the shifting of government from Washington to state capitals, conservative politicians sought to nationalize the southern model of taxation.

The Decline of the Northeastern Foreign Policy Establishment

The counterrevolution of the southern right was not limited to domestic policy. Accompanying the general decline of the Northeast has been the decline of influence of the northeastern Establishment on U.S. foreign policy. Throughout the twentieth century, old-stock northeastern Protestants like Averell Harriman, Dean Acheson, and McGeorge Bundy, with backgrounds in Ivy League universities, New York investment banks, and leading foundations, had been the dominant elite in foreign policy in both Republican and Democratic presidential administrations. Their outlook was usually Anglophile, Atlanticist, and internationalist.

Some elite southerners, like Woodrow Wilson's adviser Colonel Edward M. House, and James Baker, the secretary of state under President George Herbert Walker Bush, were assimilated into the ethos of the northeastern foreign policy Establishment. Southerners, however, had always been underrepresented in the foreign service and the U.S. intelligence agencies and overrepresented in the U.S. military. The martial ethic shared by elite and non-elite southerners—drawing on the aristocratic tradition of the southern planter oligarchy and the bellicosity of the Scots-Irish hill country South—was often correlated with contempt for diplomacy and fervent support for the use of military force.

As the power of southern and western politicians grew in the last third of the twentieth century, they frequently looked for expertise outside the distrusted and resented northeastern elite. WASP patricians increasingly were displaced by military officers, often of southern origin, and by civilian foreign policy intellectuals from non-WASP backgrounds, some of them foreign-born, such as Henry Kissinger and Zbigniew Brzezinski.

The decline in influence of northeastern Atlanticists accompanied the end of the post-1945 foreign policy consensus during the Vietnam War. Cold War internationalism was attacked by the left wing of the Democratic Party and the right wing of the Republican Party. The 1970s and 1980s saw a series of attempts by individual presidents to devise an alternate formula for American grand strategy: European-style *Realpolitik* by Richard Nixon, human rights universalism by Jimmy Carter, and the revival of containment by Ronald Reagan. The end of the Cold War produced no new consensus. The Clinton administration, which emphasized global integration by means of commerce, was succeeded by the George W. Bush administration, which saw the world in black and white military terms even before the Al Qaeda terrorist attacks of September 11, 2001.

In the kaleidoscopic confusion of post–Cold War American foreign policy, the most powerful faction was that of the neoconservatives, many of whom were former Cold War liberals or anticommunist socialists who had broken with the left wing of the Democratic Party during the Vietnam era. Like the old northeastern Establishment, the neoconservatives were a small, well-educated elite, mostly northeastern and metropolitan and largely Jewish. In the 1980s and 1990s the support of neoconservatives for hard-liners in Israel led them to cement an alliance with the Protestant fundamentalists of the religious right, whose ardent "Christian Zionism" resulted from their own interpretation of Christian theology. Neoconservative ideology—incubated in think tanks like the American Enterprise Institute in Washington, D.C.—was disseminated to the right-wing populists of the South and West via Rupert Murdoch's Fox TV network and his American political magazine, the *Weekly Standard*, as well as by conservative talk radio hosts like the popular Rush Limbaugh.

In the administration of George W. Bush, neoconservatives like Deputy Secretary of Defense Paul Wolfowitz, Undersecretary of Defense for Policy Douglas J. Feith, and Vice President Dick Cheney battled with Secretary of State Colin Powell, a self-described "Rockefeller Republican" who represented the older internationalism of northeastern Republicans. In the aftermath of the terrorist attacks on New York and Washington, D.C., of September 11, 2001, President Bush tilted decisively toward the neoconservatives. The policy of the U.S. government became the policy advocated by the neoconservatives during their years out of power during the Clinton administration: a massive military buildup; rejection of treaties and international organizations and the adoption of aggressive American unilateralism; almost uncritical support for the policies of Ariel Sharon's Likud regime toward the occupied Palestinian people; and the invasion and occupation of Iraq, which had been advocated by Cheney and Wolfowitz during the first Persian Gulf war but rejected by then-President George Herbert Walker Bush and then-Chairman of the Joint Chiefs of Staff Colin Powell. Neoconservative experts and journalists like the military analyst Elliot Cohen, Norman Podhoretz, the editor of *Commentary*, and Clinton's former director of central intelligence, James Woolsey, blurred the distinctions between Israel's war with the occupied Palestinians and the struggle against the Al Qaeda terrorist network by speaking of a "World War IV" between the West and "Islamism"—a category so elastic that it could include not only Sunni and Shia Muslims but also secular Ba'ath Party members in Iraq and Syria and secular Palestinian nationalists.

Under George W. Bush, as a result of the alliance between the neoconservatives and southern and western politicians, U.S. foreign policy was transformed. The United States was alienated from all of its major European allies except for Tony Blair's Britain. The Americans had joined Israel as occupiers of an Arab nation, and, like Israel, confronted a determined insurgency. Unlike the war in Afghanistan, which was a rational response to the Taliban regime's support for the Al Qaeda terror network, the Bush administration's foreign policy was not a logical reaction to events. Its unilateralism and militarism reflected the traditional distrust of diplomacy and pro-military attitudes of southerners and their allies in the interior West. And the shift in focus from Europe and Eurasia to the Middle East reflected in part the eclipse of the Eurocentric northeastern Protestant Establishment by a new and aggressive counter-establishment of southern Christian Zionists and predominantly Jewish neoconservatives who, for different reasons, considered Israel the most important foreign country.

Globalization and the American Economy

The southern influence on the Third American Republic was strikingly evident in the realm of the economy. During the Second Republic, between the Civil War and the New Deal, the United States had protected its domestic industries with high tariffs. Thanks to the influence of southerners like FDR's secretary of state Cordell Hull, after World War II the United States sought to universalize free trade—a goal traditionally supported by the commodity-exporting elites of the South and West. From 1945 until the 1970s, increasing access to foreign markets benefited owners and workers in the U.S. industrial sector, because the nation emerged from World War II with a near-monopoly in manufacturing. In the 1970s, however, as Europe and Japan and the "Little

Tigers" of East Asia caught up, industrial workers began to support protectionism. Unlike in the past, northern manufacturing elites did not support a return to protectionism. In order to cut labor costs, they moved their factories to the low-wage, low-tax states of the South and West, where local political elites had successfully prevented the unionization of the workforce, or to low-wage workforces in poor nations such as Mexico and Malaysia.

The rise of the southern–Sun Belt elite has been accompanied by the disintegration and disappearance of the old northeastern elite based in manufacturing. The historic struggle between the commodity producers of the South, who favored free trade, and the manufacturers of the North, who favored protection of domestic industry, lost its relevance with the growth of transnational manufacturing in the final third of the twentieth century. Instead of seeking to sell finished American products to foreign consumers, more and more U.S. corporations sought to employ inexpensive foreign labor to manufacture goods to be sold to the American market. Globalization finally ended the long civil war between the two wings of American capitalism. Northern manufacturing elites seeking foreign labor for transnational production operations abandoned their traditional protectionism and united with the capitalists of the southern and western commodity sector to promote investor-driven globalization. As a result, both manufacturing capitalists and commodity capitalists, under the misleading name of "free trade," seek a liberal regime in foreign investment permitting them access to foreign labor (the manufacturers) or foreign natural resources (the commodity capitalists, such as oil producers).

United in its commitment to globalization on American terms, the U.S. business community financed the revival of laissez-faire capitalist economics by endowing university chairs of economics and subsidizing the business press and pro-business think tanks. By 2000, only a few marginal organizations, like the U.S. Business and Industrial Council, still lobbied for the policies promoting domestic manufacturing that had been the core of the economic agenda of the Federalist and Whig parties and of the Republicans from Abraham Lincoln to Herbert Hoover.[27]

Globalization : Market versus Empire

The decline of the older midwestern protectionism and isolationism did not mean the triumph of a single version of globalism in American foreign policy. On the contrary, both the Democratic Party and the Republican Party defined globalization in different ways, a fact influenced by the changing nature of their domestic industrial constituencies.

While corporate influence on American politics had grown at the expense of that of organized labor after the 1960s, the private sector elite was divided in its loyalties along sectoral lines. In the 2000 presidential campaign, venture capital favored the Democrats by a margin of 3 to 2. The entertainment industry was also a strong supporter of the Democratic Party. At the same time, the Republicans received two-thirds of the contributions from the defense industry and 80 percent of those from the oil, gas, and agribusiness industries.[28]

The Clinton administration's approach to globalization, under the leadership of Treasury Secretary Robert Rubin, reflected the interests of the Democratic Party's financial contributors. Its support for international enforcement of intellectual property rights was important to Hollywood, which was concerned about the pirating of American movies, and also to Silicon Valley, concerned about the pirating of American software. The emphasis on liberalizing global finance—a policy that made possible the Asian economic crisis of the mid-1990s—served the interests of the Wall Street investors who made big contributions to the Democratic Party. In its zeal for the "enlargement" of "market democracies" as a panacea for international conflict, the Clinton administration sometimes seemed to promote a version of Marxist economic determinism, in which capitalism automatically produced democracy and world peace as by-products.

While the Clinton Democrats sought to make the world safe for

Hollywood and investment capital, the Republicans had different priorities. Despite their reputation as the party of big business, Republicans were more likely than Democrats to think of globalization in military rather than economic terms. But there was no contradiction. Increasingly, the Republican Party had become the party of military-linked state capitalism. By the end of the twentieth century, what Republican President Dwight Eisenhower had described (and dreaded) as "the military-industrial complex" had become an active constituency of the Republican Party. The members of the U.S. military are disproportionately conservative and Republican, and many retired officers go to work for aerospace companies and other defense contractors, including Lockheed Martin, Raytheon, General Dynamics, and Martin Marietta, whose major if not sole clients are the U.S. government and its allies and client states like Israel. The fact that these companies are private in form, even if they function as de facto extensions of the government, permits these firms to finance politicians with campaign contributions and to lobby policymakers.

Closely linked with the defense contractor industry is the U.S. oil industry. Because of the importance of Middle Eastern oil concessions to U.S. oil companies, the American energy industry has a unique stake in American military and diplomatic policies in the region. The link between the U.S. military-industrial complex and the oil industry is provided by firms which specialize in large-scale military and civilian construction overseas. The most important has long been Bechtel, the world's largest construction company, a family-held corporation that has been a player in U.S. politics since the New Deal era. Among the American officials who have worked for Bechtel have been Ronald Reagan's secretary of defense, Caspar Weinberger, and his secretary of state, George Shultz.[29]

The intertwining of the defense, energy, and overseas construction industries was evident in the second Bush administration. Both President George W. Bush and Vice President Dick Cheney had been executives in the oil industry in Texas. Bush's political career had been financed in part by Enron, the energy giant whose bankruptcy created a political scandal as well as economic shock waves. Cheney's firm, Halliburton, included among its enterprises Dresser Industries, the firm for which George Herbert Walker Bush had worked when he moved to Texas after World War II. Following the invasion of Iraq, Halliburton was awarded a substantial contract for Iraq's reconstruction, to be paid for out of American tax revenues. The Bush administration's first proconsul for occupied Iraq, General Jay Garner, was a retired military officer who had gone to work for a defense contractor. The Pentagon, in charge of accepting bids for the reconstruction of Iraq, announced that companies from countries that had opposed the war, including Germany, France, and Russia, would not be eligible for contracts.

This kind of aggressive mercantilism, while it may have contradicted the libertarian principles of traditional free-market Republicans, was typical of the approach of conservatives from the state-capitalist defense-energy-construction sector, for whom the military and military-linked firms were scarcely distinguishable. The temporary imposition of protectionist steel tariffs by Bush exhibited the same kind of economic nationalist thinking. Like the military-industrial complex and the energy sector, the "old industries" that supported the Republican Party, like agribusiness, were heavily dependent on government subsidies or protection, and were often sympathetic to a belligerent unilateral nationalism in the realm of trade as well as in the military and diplomatic arenas.

The Counterrevolution of the Right in Perspective

At the beginning of the twenty-first century, the United States was ruled by an elite unlike that of the mid-twentieth century. In 1950 the dominant liberal political elite included civic-minded northeastern patricians, national union leaders, and leading academics along with big-city mayors from the Northeast and Midwest. In 2000 the makeup of the newly dominant conservative political elite was quite different: southern and western politicians had replaced the formerly dominant northeasterners and midwesterners, corporate executives and financiers who celebrated unfettered capitalism and rejected notions of noblesse oblige had shouldered aside the old East Coast Establishment, and television preachers like Pat Robertson had replaced urban mayors as kingmakers in electoral politics.

It is now clear that in the Third Republic of the United States that took shape between the 1930s and the 1960s, there have been two eras: the New Deal era from Roosevelt to Johnson, and the conservative era that followed.[30] The continuity between the two has been provided by the South. Following the civil rights revolution, southern conservatives, earlier the partners and sometimes the opponents of New Deal reforms, moved into the Republican Party, which they transformed into the vehicle of a distinctively southern right quite different from the conservative traditions of the Northeast and Midwest.

The tragedy of the New Deal, in retrospect, was that Franklin Roosevelt and his successors industrialized the South without liberalizing it. The issue at stake was whether the New Deal's programs of federal regional development in the South and West would remodel those societies along northeastern-midwestern lines or merely modernize and empower traditional regional elites. The answer is now clear. By enriching without revolutionizing the South, the New Deal empowered the most reactionary conservatives in the United States. And in the last third of the twentieth century and the beginning of the twenty-first, southern conservatives and their allies in other regions went from triumph to triumph in an America which increasingly resembled the traditional South: a low-wage society with weak parties, weak unions, and a political culture based on demagogic appeals to racial and ethnic anxieties, religious conservatism, and militaristic patriotism. Whether and when demographic, cultural, and economic changes would undermine this conservative elite, and inaugurate a new era in American politics under a different elite, only the future would reveal.[31]

Coda : Democracy in America

❧

STEVE FRASER AND GARY GERSTLE

Ruling America tells a story about the relationship between wealth and power over the course of the nation's history. Its contributors examine the way distinctive economic and social elites have exercised their predominance and justified their preeminence (or have failed to do so). But of course all these elites have had to operate within a democratic political system and an informal but no less rich tradition of democratic belief and custom. Democracy is an invisible presence in this book, like dark matter: we can sense its ubiquity, its hovering existence, without measuring it directly. Every elite examined here, even the "slave power," has had to reckon with democracy as its limiting case, its horizon of possibility. Democracy echoes in each chapter, but from afar, reminding us of its weighty absence.

Yet democracy is vital to this history of ruling elites in America. It has again and again haunted the imaginations and political calculations of the propertied and privileged. The logic of democracy is inherently dangerous to their presumptions and sense of security. In theory, people can vote against property by electing to regulate it, level it, redistribute it, confiscate it, or even to abolish it. The more drastic of these options are rarely if ever on the agenda (although in the case of slavery the threat of abolition was real). But how better can we describe the landmarks of American political history—the Bill of Rights, Jacksonian democracy and its war on the "Monster Bank," the Emancipation Proclamation, populism's refusal to be crucified on a "cross of gold," the trust-busting furor of the Progressive Era, the New Deal's purging of the "money changers from the temple"—than as barricades against the overweening pretensions of the propertied?

In America, democratic resistance to the domination of great wealth has been salutary. Aroused farmers and industrial workers, aspiring entrepreneurs and vigilant middle-class consumers, deserve most of the credit for those laws and institutions that established the prerogatives of the public to restrain the appetite of property. Rarely have elites pioneered on the frontiers of democratic reform. And when they have, one can always hear in the background the rumbling of popular discontent. Would there have been grass-roots political parties and the humbling of aristocratic pretension without the egalitarian passions that overran Jacksonian America? Would there have been a war against slavery without the plebeian demand that the slaveocracy not be allowed to close off the main avenue of economic opportunity—land for "free labor" in the West? Would the railroad barons, the great industrial tycoons, the corporate trust makers, and the financial overlords of Wall Street have been subjected to government regulation without the dogged resistance of the Grange, the Greenback-Labor parties, the Populists, the antitrust movement, and the Socialist Party of Eugene Debs? Without the 1877 railroad strike, bloody Haymarket and Homestead, the Knights of Labor and the AFL, the Wobblies and the CIO, would there ever have been laws to guarantee the rights of workers to organize, to abolish child labor, to put a limit on the hours one might be coerced into working, to protect the health and safety of coal miners and oil riggers and garment cutters, to pry open the lockbox of the workplace and make it obey something other than the relentlessly impersonal laws of the free market? Without these and numberless other instances of mass mobilization, the history of American elites—and indeed of all of America—would look quite different, far less civilized. Democracy has restrained the aspirations of the wealthy to rule America.

It has also, ironically, convinced many ordinary people that in America everyone could become wealthy. All the instances of collective democratic insurgency we have mentioned, and many others besides, have occurred within a culture simultaneously committed to individualism and to the private pursuit of happiness. Long ago Alexis de Tocqueville wrote about the tension between liberty and equality in the New World's first democracy. A man of conservative instincts and breeding, he worried a great deal about the dangers of the "tyranny of the majority" and how it might cripple the achievement of individual excellence and liberty, leaving in its wake a society of numbing mediocrity and conformity. A society seeking to invigorate its democracy paid little heed to Tocqueville's anxieties, and he was all but forgotten for more than a century.[1] However much the French aristocrat may have shortchanged the civilizing influence of the egalitarian instinct, he perceived something indubitably true: namely, that while the new democracy was called upon to brake the elevation of the few, it carried out that mission so that the many might engage in the race for individual self-aggrandizement. American democracy thus has limited the power of the wealthy while encouraging the many to pursue the main chance. The conviction that American democracy promised every man an opportunity to become rich inhibited just how far assaults on entrenched elites, in Toqueville's day and since, have been apt to go. But it also made ordinary Americans furious at attempts by the high and the mighty to close off access to wealth and power.

There is a third way in which democracy figures as a ghostly presence in this book. While elites have naturally enough resisted popular incursions that would limit their economic freedom and their political supremacy, they have themselves grown up in a culture suffused by democratic and egalitarian traditions. Increasingly they have adopted a democratic demeanor and portrayed their motivations, purposes, and policy as grounded in the principle of popular sovereignty. This has been true, though to varying degrees, since the Revolution. Moreover, this has been more than and something other than mere cynical calculation on the part of empowered elites. Even the social Darwinism of the Gilded Age, after all, grounded its defense of hierarchy in the implacable working out of supposedly natural laws that presumably applied to Everyman. Part of the patrician sophistication that marked Jefferson and the two Roosevelts was their openness to cultural currents and political opinions originating beyond and beneath the borders of their own social class. Teddy Roosevelt was by no means a committed democrat—he would be the first to boast of that—but he was both savvy and sincere in his belief that the government had to protect the general welfare against the predations of the irresponsible rich. To be sure, political shrewdness and moral hypocrisy made their weight felt in the ways elites maneuvered to maintain their privileged positions. The manner in which the great railroads and Wall Street banks captured turn-of-the-century public institutions such as the Interstate Commerce Commission and the Federal Reserve and made them serve narrower, self-interested purposes are two cases among many. But to reduce everything to the level of disingenuous political performance is to undervalue the way democracy has functioned silently as a form of self-discipline, subtly informing the internal life of the powerful, establishing limits to their sense of entitlement. On rarer occasions, usually at moments of profound crisis, elites have fractured internally over their attitude toward social upheaval, with a fragment even allying itself with democratic forces.

The New Deal is for good reason the most enduring case. The elite fragmentation of that time extended far beyond Franklin Delano Roosevelt's becoming a "traitor to his class" and breaking with his gentrified world in order to expose its selfishness, condemn its social callousness, and subject it to a chastening public shaming and supervision. The New Deal was much more than one man's apostasy. It represented an active collaboration between disaffected circles of the business and financial community with social insurgents from the country's industrial workshops, urban barrios, and zones of rural devastation, and from the ranks of ghettoized ethnic Catholics and Jews and marginalized cosmopolitan intellectuals. That Roosevelt and the New Deal he championed never had any intention of uprooting the capitalist foundations of American society is hardly a secret: FDR himself went to great lengths to make that plain at the time. Nor would the New Deal have managed to achieve what it did without the energy, militance, and intelligence of its popular allies, especially in the labor movement. It is also true that the New Deal regime itself was in a perpetual state of indecision, advancing and then retreating across the broad front of reform, finally abandoning further inroads into the redoubts of corporate power with the return of recession in the late 1930s, and then of course with the outbreak of war. Nevertheless, the Roosevelt years left behind a set of laws and institutions that for a half-century established a democratic presence inside the heart of the country's political economy. Moreover, the New Deal structures and commitments compelled the wealthy and powerful to operate within constraints, and to pay elementary attention to the imperatives of social welfare and social justice.

Today we live among the ruins of the New Deal. The counterrevolution against it, first gaining power under Ronald Reagan, is still hard at work trying to dismantle what remains. The counterrevolution's agenda explicitly and prominently favors the interests of great corporations and the wealthy. That is hardly a secret. But the latest irony of American democracy is that this re-ascendancy of wealth and power presents itself as a popular rising, a freedom movement of the oddest, not to say most perverse, sort. Its champions rail against overbearing government, enslaving regulation, and the dead hand of bureaucratic hierarchy. In this incongruous liberation struggle, the meaning of freedom is encompassed by, is virtually exhausted by, the logic of the free market. Liberty prevails where property is at liberty to do what it will. The New Deal's democratic reckoning with "economic royalists" and the "Tories of industry" is now castigated as the latest incarnation of Tocqueville's "tyranny of the majority." Talk of emancipation takes place alongside the most meticulous care and feeding of the nation's chief business and financial institutions; yet the talk is so fiery, so full of zealous idealism, that it reaches beyond cynicism and captures the imagination of millions of ordinary people who believe that their future, too, will be paved with gold.

Ironic indeed! But what does this strange inversion imply about the present and future relationship between wealth and power on the one hand and democracy on the other? The contributors to this book presume an antipathy, sometimes latent, sometimes overt, between elite domination and popular resistance to that domination. Can we make that same presumption now? It would seem not. No social opposition today, nor for the last quarter-century, approaches in organizational scale, in emotional depth, or in programmatic coherence the great counterweights of the past: no Jacksonian leveling, no Populist prairie fire, no Progressive trust busting, no socialist visionary alternative, no massed choruses of "Solidarity Forever." The democratic urge to rein in the dangerous ambitions of privileged elites has grown frail.

Yet it would be premature to pronounce that democracy is dead. Its very weakness may embolden elites to overreach, to transgress some line of egalitarian and democratic faith too precious to be ignored. And at that point a democratic movement may stir, grounded, perhaps, in a reinvigorated labor movement, or in an anti-globalization alliance, or in protests against the high-handed unilateralism of U.S. foreign policy. And if that happens, a portion of the American elite, worried about economic decline at home or America's plummeting reputation abroad, may well align itself with that movement, thereby strengthening its political and economic muscle. But that story belongs to future historians, who, with the historical record before them, will know whether democracy made a comeback in early-twenty-first-century America. Here we can only stress how important democracy has been to the disciplining of past elites and how important its revival will be to the regulation of those who today hold great wealth and exercise disproportionate power in America.

Notes

Acknowledgments

Contributors

Index

Notes

❦

Introduction

1. Charles A. Beard, *An Economic Interpretation of the Constitution of the United States* (1913; New York: Macmillan, 1952).

2. See, by Arthur M. Schlesinger, Jr., *The Age of Jackson* (Boston: Little, Brown and Company, 1945); *The Age of Roosevelt* (Boston: Houghton Mifflin, 1957–1960): *The Crisis of the Old Order, 1919–1933* (Boston: Houghton Mifflin, 1956); *The Coming of the New Deal* (Boston: Houghton Mifflin, 1958); and *The Politics of Upheaval* (Boston: Houghton Mifflin, 1960).

3. Vernon Louis Parrington, *Main Currents in American Thought: An Interpretation of American Literature from the Beginnings to 1920*, 3 vols. (New York: Harcourt, Brace and Company, 1927–1930).

4. Louis Hartz, *The Liberal Tradition in America* (New York: Harcourt, Brace, 1955); Richard Hofstadter, *The Age of Reform: From Bryan to FDR* (New York: Knopf, 1955); Richard Hofstadter, *The Paranoid Style in America Politics and Other Essays* (New York: Knopf, 1965).

5. David M. Potter, *The Impending Crisis, 1848–1861* (New York: Harper and Row, 1976); David M. Potter, *People of Plenty: Economic Abundance and the American Character* (Chicago: University of Chicago Press, 1954).

6. W. E. B. Du Bois, *Black Reconstruction in America, 1860–1880* (New York: Harcourt, Brace and Company, 1935).

7. John Adams, *Discourses on Davila: A Series of Papers on Political History* (1790; Boston: Russell and Cutler, 1805), 91–92.

8. James Madison, *Writings*, ed. Jack N. Rakove (New York: Library of America, 1999), 531.

9. Charles Francis Adams and Henry Adams, *Chapters of Erie and Other Es-*

says (Boston: J. R. Osgood and Company, 1871); Brooks Adams, *Law of Civiliza-tion and Decay* (New York: Macmillan, 1896). See also Daniel Aaron, *Men of Good Hope: A Story of American Progressives* (New York: Oxford University Press, 1951), 254, 260, 276.

  10. Richard Hofstadter, *Social Darwinism in American Thought*, with an intro-duction by Eric Foner (Boston: Beacon Press, 1992).

  11. Thorstein Veblen, *The Theory of the Leisure Class: An Economic Study of Institutions* (New York: Macmillan, 1912); Thorstein Veblen, *Absentee Ownership and Business Enterprise in Recent Times: The Case of America* (New York: B. W. Huebsch, 1938).

  12. Henry George, *Progress and Poverty* (San Francisco: W. M. Hinton & Company, 1879); Henry Demarest Lloyd, *Wealth against Commonwealth* (New York: Harper & Brothers, 1894); Edward Bellamy, *Looking Backward, 2000–1887* (Boston: Ticknor and Company, 1888); Ignatius Donnelly, *Caesar's Column: A Story of the Twentieth Century* (1894; Cambridge, Mass.: Belknap Press of Harvard University Press, 1960).

  13. Louis D. Brandeis, *Other People's Money and How the Bankers Use It* (New York: F. A. Stokes, 1914); Charles Edward Russell, *Lawless Wealth: The Origins of Some Great American Fortunes* (New York: B. W. Dodge and Company, 1908); Upton Sinclair, *The Moneychangers* (New York: B. W. Dodge & Company, 1908); Theodore Dreiser, *The Financier* (New York: A. L. Burt, 1912); Theodore Dreiser, *The Titan* (New York: John Lane Company, 1914); Jack London, *The Iron Heel* (1907; Westport, Conn.: Lawrence Hill, 1980); John Dos Passos, *USA* (a trilogy): *The 42nd Parallel* (1930; Boston: Houghton Mifflin, 1946); *1919* (1932; Boston: Houghton Mifflin, 1946); *The Big Money* (1936; Boston: Houghton Mifflin, 1946).

  14. Ferdinand Lundberg, *America's Sixty Families* (New York: Vanguard Press, 1937).

  15. Matthew Josephson, *The Robber Barons* (New York: Harcourt, Brace and Company, 1934).

  16. Adolf A. Berle and Gardiner C. Means, *The Modern Corporation and Pri-vate Property* (1932; New York: Macmillan, 1948).

  17. C. Wright Mills, *The Power Elite* (New York: Oxford University Press, 1956).

  18. Richard Rovere, *The American Establishment and Other Reports, Opinions, and Speculations* (New York: Harcourt, Brace & World, 1962); Daniel Bell, *The End of Ideology* (Glencoe, Ill.: Free Press, 1960); Daniel Bell, ed., *The Radical Right* (Garden City, N.Y.: Doubleday, 1963); E. Digby Baltzell, *The Protestant Es-tablishment: Aristocracy and Caste in America* (New York: Random House, 1964);

David Reisman (with Nathan Glazer and Reuel Denney), *The Lonely Crowd: A Study of the Changing American Character* (New Haven: Yale University Press, 1950); Mills, *Power Elite*, 243; Robert Dahl, *Who Governs? Democracy and Power in an American City* (New Haven: Yale University Press, 1961).

19. Eugene D. Genovese, *The Political Economy of Slavery: Studies in the Economy and Society of the Slave South* (New York: Pantheon Books, 1965); Eugene D. Genovese, *The World the Slaveholders Made: Two Essays in Interpretation* (New York: Pantheon Books, 1969); Eugene D. Genovese, *Roll, Jordan, Roll: The World the Slaves Made* (New York: Pantheon Books, 1974); Eric Foner, *Free Soil, Free Labor, Free Men: The Ideology of the Republican Party before the Civil War* (New York: Oxford University Press, 1970); Eric Foner, *Reconstruction: America's Unfinished Revolution* (New York: Harper & Row, 1988). Other authors and more books might easily be added to this list, which is only meant to be suggestive: Kevin Phillips, *Wealth and Democracy: A Political History of the American Rich* (New York: Broadway Books, 2002); G. William Domhoff, *Who Rules America?* (Englewood Cliffs, N.J.: Prentice-Hall, 1967); Eric Foner, *The Story of American Freedom* (New York: W. W. Norton, 1998); Noam Chomsky, *Hegemony or Survival: America's Quest for Global Domination* (New York: Metropolitan Books, 2003); Barbara Ehrenreich, *Nickel and Dimed: On (Not) Getting By in America* (New York: Metropolitan Books, 2001); Michael Harrington, *The Other America* (New York: Macmillan, 1962); Herbert G. Gutman, *Power and Culture: Essays on the American Working Class* (New York: Pantheon Books, 1987); David Montgomery, *The Fall of the House of Labor: The Workplace, the State, and American Labor Activism, 1865–1925* (New York: Cambridge University Press, 1987).

20. The more notable books include Ron Chernow, *The House of Morgan: An American Banking Dynasty and the Rise of Big Business* (New York: Atlantic Monthly Press, 1990); Ron Chernow, *Titan: The Life of John D. Rockefeller, Sr.* (New York: Random House, 1998); Jean Strouse, *Morgan: An American Financier* (New York: Random House, 1999); Maury Klein, *The Life and Legend of Jay Gould* (Baltimore: Johns Hopkins University Press, 1986); Maury Klein, *The Life and Legend of E. H. Harriman* (Chapel Hill: University of North Carolina Press, 2000).

21. We have written elsewhere about the emergence in the 1930s of this politico-economic formation and the shakeup in elites that it entailed. See Steve Fraser and Gary Gerstle, eds., *The Rise and Fall of the New Deal Order, 1930–1980* (Princeton, N.J.: Princeton University Press, 1989); and Steven Fraser, *Labor Will Rule: Sidney Hillman and the Rise of American Labor* (New York: Free Press, 1991).

1. The Dilemma of Ruling Elites in Revolutionary America

1. Still extremely valuable is Robert R. Palmer, *The Age of the Democratic Revolution: A Political History of Europe and America, 1760–1800*, 2 vols. (Princeton: Princeton University Press, 1959–1964). For Palmer, both the aristocratic reaction and egalitarianism were gathering momentum before the French Revolution broke out in 1789.

2. For an earlier attempt to address many of the issues in this chapter, see Gary J. Kornblith and John M. Murrin, "The Making and Unmaking of an American Ruling Class," in *Beyond the American Revolution: Explorations in the History of American Radicalism*, ed. Alfred F. Young (DeKalb: Northern Illinois University Press, 1993), 27–79.

3. Jonathan I. Israel, ed., *The Anglo-Dutch Moment: Essays on the Glorious Revolution and Its World Impact* (New York: Cambridge University Press, 1991); and John Brewer, *The Sinews of Power: War, Money, and the English State, 1688–1783* (New York: Alfred A. Knopf, 1989).

4. For the colonial population, see U.S. Bureau of the Census, *Historical Statistics of the United States, Colonial Times to 1970*, vol. 2 (Washington, D.C.: Government Printing Office, 1975), 1168. See also John Brewer, *The Pleasures of the Imagination: English Culture in the Eighteenth Century* (New York: Farrar Strauss Giroux, 1997); Richard L. Bushman, *The Refinement of America: Persons, Houses, Cities* (New York: Alfred A. Knopf, 1992); David S. Shields, *Civil Tongues and Polite Letters in British America* (Chapel Hill: University of North Carolina Press, 1997); Ned Landsman, *From Colonials to Provincials: American Thought and Culture, 1680–1760* (New York: Twayne Publishers, 1997); and Jack P. Greene, "Legislative Turnover in British America, 1696 to 1775: A Quantitative Analysis," *William and Mary Quarterly*, 3d ser., 38 (1981), 442–463 (hereafter cited as *WMQ* and assumed to be 3d ser.). For levels of wealth concentration, compare John A. James, "Personal Wealth Distribution in Eighteenth-Century Britain," *Economic History Review*, 2d ser., 41 (1988), 559, table 6, with Alice Hanson Jones, *Wealth of a Nation to Be: The American Colonies on the Eve of the Revolution* (New York: Columbia University Press, 1980), 164, table 6.2.

5. Compare Joyce E. Chaplin, *An Anxious Pursuit: Agricultural Innovation and Modernity in the Lower South, 1730–1815* (Chapel Hill: University of North Carolina Press, 1993), with Allan Kulikoff, *Tobacco and Slaves: The Development of Southern Cultures in the Chesapeake, 1680–1800* (Chapel Hill: University of North Carolina Press, 1986); Mary M. Schweitzer, *Custom and Contract: House-*

hold, Government, and the Economy in Colonial Pennsylvania (New York: Columbia University Press, 1987); and Daniel J. Vickers, *Farmers and Fishermen: Two Centuries of Work in Essex County, Massachusetts, 1630–1850* (Chapel Hill: University of North Carolina Press, 1994). For comparative wealth levels in the colonies, see Jones, *Wealth of a Nation to Be*, 96, table 4.2.

6. T. H. Breen, "'Baubles of Britain': The American and Consumer Revolutions of the Eighteenth Century," *Past & Present*, 119 (May 1988), 73–104; and John M. Murrin, "The Legal Transformation: The Bench and Bar in Eighteenth-Century Massachusetts," in *Colonial America: Essays in Politics and Social Development*, ed. Stanley N. Katz and John M. Murrin, 3d ed. (New York: Alfred A. Knopf, 1983), 540–572.

7. Bernard Bailyn, *The Ideological Origins of the American Revolution* (Cambridge, MA: Belknap Press of Harvard University Press, 1967); Bernard Bailyn, *The Origins of American Politics* (New York: Alfred A. Knopf, 1969); John M. Murrin, "Political Development," in *Colonial British America: Essays in the New History of the Early Modern Era*, ed. Jack P. Greene and J. R. Pole (Baltimore: Johns Hopkins University Press, 1984), 408–456; James H. Hutson, "The Emergence of the Modern Concept of a Right in America: The Contribution of Michel Villey," *American Journal of Jurisprudence*, 39 (1994), 185–224; Daniel T. Rodgers, *Contested Truths: Keywords in American Politics since Independence* (New York: Basic Books, 1987), 45–79; and T. H. Breen, *The Lockean Moment: The Language of Rights on the Eve of the American Revolution: An Inaugural Lecture Delivered before the University of Oxford on 15 May 2001* (New York: Oxford University Press, 2001).

8. Incisive discussions of class in the early modern Anglo-American world include Keith Wrightson, "Class," in *The British Atlantic World, 1500–1800*, ed. David Armitage and Michael J. Braddick (New York: Palgrave Macmillan, 2002), 133–153; Ronald Schultz, "A Class Society? The Nature of Inequality in Early America," in *Inequality in Early America*, ed. Carla Gardina Pestana and Sharon V. Salinger (Hanover, NH: University Press of New England, 1999), 203–221; and Greg Nobles, "Class," in *A Companion to Colonial America*, ed. Daniel Vickers (Malden, MA: Blackwell Publishers, 2003), 259–287.

9. Bernard Bailyn, *The New England Merchants in the Seventeenth Century* (Cambridge, MA: Harvard University Press, 1955); Robert E. Wall, "The Decline of the Massachusetts Franchise, 1647–1666," *Journal of American History*, 59 (1972–73), 303–310; John M. Murrin, "The Menacing Shadow of Louis XIV and the Rage of Jacob Leisler: The Constitutional Ordeal of Seventeenth-Century New York," in *New York and the Union: Contributions to the American Constitutional*

Experience, ed. Stephen L. Schechter and Richard B. Bernstein (Albany: New York State Commission on the Bicentennial of the United States Constitution, 1990), 29–71; Frederick M. Tolles, *Meeting House and Counting House: The Quaker Merchants of Colonial Philadelphia, 1682–1763* (Chapel Hill: University of North Carolina Press, 1948); Stephen Brobeck, "Revolutionary Change in Colonial Philadelphia: The Brief Life of the Proprietary Gentry," *WMQ*, 33 (1976), 410–434.

10. David A. Williams, *Political Alignments in Colonial Virginia Politics, 1698–1750* (New York: Garland Publishing, 1989); David A. Williams, "The Small Farmer in Eighteenth-Century Virginia Politics," *Agricultural History*, 43 (1969), 410–421; Charles S. Sydnor, *Gentlemen Freeholders: Political Practices in Washington's Virginia* (Chapel Hill: University of North Carolina Press, 1952); John Gilman Kolp, *Gentlemen and Freeholders: Electoral Politics in Colonial Virginia* (Baltimore: Johns Hopkins University Press, 1998); Rhys Isaac, *The Transformation of Virginia, 1740–1790* (Chapel Hill: University of North Carolina Press, 1982).

11. Peter H. Wood, *Black Majority: Negroes in Colonial South Carolina from 1670 through the Stono Rebellion* (New York: Alfred A. Knopf, 1974); Philip D. Morgan, "Work and Culture: The Task System and the World of Lowcountry Blacks, 1700 to 1880," *WMQ*, 39 (1982), 563–599; Philip D. Morgan, *Slave Counterpoint: Black Culture in the Eighteenth-Century Chesapeake and Lowcountry* (Chapel Hill: University of North Carolina Press, 1998); and for the cultural tone of South Carolina politics beginning in the 1730s, see Robert M. Weir, "'The Harmony We Were Famous For': An Interpretation of Pre-Revolutionary South Carolina Politics," *WMQ*, 26 (1969), 473–501.

12. Brendan McConville, *Those Daring Disturbers of the Public Peace: The Struggle for Property and Power in Early New Jersey* (Ithaca: Cornell University Press, 1999); Thomas L. Purvis, "Origins and Patterns of Agrarian Unrest in New Jersey, 1735 to 1754," *WMQ*, 39 (1982), 600–627; Irving Mark, *Agrarian Conflicts in Colonial New York, 1711–1775*, 2d ed. (Port Washington, N.Y.: Ira J. Friedman, 1965); Sung Bok Kim, *Landlord and Tenant in Colonial New York: Manorial Society, 1664–1775* (Chapel Hill: University of North Carolina Press, 1978); and Gary B. Nash, *The Urban Crucible: Social Change, Political Consciousness, and the Origins of the American Revolution* (Cambridge, Mass.: Harvard University Press, 1979).

13. We have taken these honorific titles from the legislative and judicial records of provincial Massachusetts. The major exception to the pattern was the Pennsylvania assembly, which was dominated by the Quaker Party for most of the century. Quakers did not use titles. For the pattern of patriot versus loyalist

among high officeholders, see James Kirby Martin, *Men in Rebellion: Higher Government Leaders and the Coming of the American Revolution* (New Brunswick, N.J.: Rutgers University Press, 1973).

14. The standard study remains Edmund S. Morgan and Helen M. Morgan, *The Stamp Act Crisis: Prologue to Revolution,* 3d ed. (Chapel Hill: University of North Carolina Press, 1995).

15. On types of mobs and how the public reacted to them, see Pauline Maier, *From Resistance to Revolution: Colonial Radicals and the Development of American Opposition to Britain, 1765–1776* (New York: Alfred A. Knopf, 1972).

16. Morgan and Morgan, *Stamp Act Crisis,* 150–158, 199–202.

17. Ibid., 202–204, 206–207; Mark, *Agrarian Conflicts in Colonial New York,* chap. 5.

18. Sylvia R. Frey, *Water from the Rock: Black Resistance in a Revolutionary Age* (Princeton: Princeton University Press, 1991), 51; *The Papers of Henry Laurens,* ed. George C. Rogers, Jr., et al., vol. 5 (Columbia: University of South Carolina Press, 1976), 53–54; Arthur Zilversmit, *The First Emancipation: The Abolition of Slavery in the North* (Chicago: University of Chicago Press, 1967).

19. Rachel N. Klein, *Unification of a Slave State: The Rise of the Planter Class in the South Carolina Back Country, 1760–1808* (Chapel Hill: University of North Carolina Press, 1990); Richard M. Brown, *The South Carolina Regulators* (Cambridge, MA: Harvard University Press, 1963); A. Roger Ekirch, *"Poor Carolina": Politics and Society in Colonial North Carolina, 1729–1776* (Chapel Hill: University of North Carolina Press, 1981); James P. Whittenburg, "Planters, Merchants, and Lawyers: Social Change and the Origins of the North Carolina Regulation," *WMQ,* 34 (1977), 214–238; Paul H. Smith, "The American Loyalists: Notes on Their Organization and Numerical Strength," *WMQ,* 25 (1968), 259–277; Benjamin Quarles, *The Negro in the American Revolution,* with a new introduction by Gary Nash and a new foreword by Thad W. Tate (1961; Chapel Hill: University of North Carolina Press, 1996).

20. The most careful study of the American response to the collapse of British authority is David Ammerman, *In the Common Cause: American Response to the Coercive Acts of 1774* (Charlottesville: University Press of Virginia, 1974). See also Jackson Turner Main, "Government by the People: The American Revolution and the Democratization of the Legislatures," *WMQ,* 23 (1966), 391–407; Edward Countryman, *A People in Revolution: The American Revolution and Political Society in New York, 1760–1790* (Baltimore: Johns Hopkins University Press, 1981); and Ronald Hoffman, *A Spirit of Dissension: Economics, Politics, and the Revolution in Maryland* (Baltimore: Johns Hopkins University Press, 1973).

21. Judith L. Van Buskirk, *Generous Enemies: Patriots and Loyalists in Revolutionary New York* (Philadelphia: University of Pennsylvania Press, 2002), 92–105, esp. 102–103 (quotations and reproduction of the self-portrait).

22. For political alignments in the 1780s, see Jackson Turner Main, *Political Parties before the Constitution* (Chapel Hill: University of North Carolina Press, 1973).

23. David P. Szatmary, *Shays' Rebellion: The Making of an Agrarian Insurrection* (Amherst: University of Massachusetts Press, 1980); John L. Brooke, "To the Quiet of the People: Revolutionary Settlements and Civil Unrest in Western Massachusetts, 1774–1789," *WMQ*, 46 (1989), 425–462; Leonard L. Richards, *Shays's Rebellion: The American Revolution's Final Battle* (Philadelphia: University of Pennsylvania Press, 2002).

24. Richard B. Morris, *The Forging of the Union, 1781–1789* (New York: Harper & Row, 1987), 232–244.

25. On the background of the delegates, see Forrest McDonald, *We the People: The Economic Origins of the Constitution* (Chicago: University of Chicago Press, 1958); and Morris, *Forging of the Union*, 268–275.

26. Max Farrand, ed., *The Records of the Federal Convention of 1787*, rev. ed., 4 vols. (New Haven: Yale University Press, 1937), 1:48 (Sherman and Gerry), 49 (Wilson). The words in brackets were inserted by Madison many years after the convention, probably after 1819.

27. Ibid., 1:18–23 (Virginia Plan), 242–245 (New Jersey Plan, quotation at 245). For North's Conciliatory Proposition, see Bernard Donoughue, *British Politics and the American Revolution: The Path to War, 1773–75* (London: Macmillan and Company, 1964), 223–224, 248–251.

28. Farrand, *Records of the Federal Convention*, 1:282–293, quotations at 288.

29. Staughton Lynd, "The Compromise of 1787," *Political Science Quarterly*, 81 (1966), 225–250.

30. Farrand, *Records of the Federal Convention*, 1:486; 2:371.

31. Recent histories of the Philadelphia convention include Jack N. Rakove, *Original Meanings: Politics and Ideas in the Making of the Constitution* (New York: Alfred A. Knopf, 1996); and Carol Berkin, *A Brilliant Solution: Inventing the American Constitution* (New York: Harcourt, 2002). For Madison's statement, see Jacob E. Cooke, ed., *The Federalist* (Middletown, Conn.: Wesleyan University Press, 1961), 63. In the census of 1790, Baltimore and Boston had a combined population of 31,541. David T. Gilchrist, ed., *The Growth of the Seaport Cities, 1790–1825* (Charlottesville: University Press of Virginia, 1967), 28, table II.

32. Jonathan Elliot, ed., *The Debates in the Several State Conventions on the*

Adoption of the Federal Constitution, as Recommended by the General Convention at Philadelphia in 1787, 2d ed., 5 vols. (Philadelphia: J. B. Lippincott & Co., 1861), 2:247–248.

33. For the Articles of Confederation, see Merrill Jensen et al., eds., *The Documentary History of the Ratification of the Constitution*, 27 vols. (Madison: State Historical Society of Wisconsin, 1976–), 1:86–94, esp. 93 (Art. 13). For defeat of the impost amendments of 1781 and 1783, see ibid., 19:xxviii–xxxi, xxxvii–xl.

34. Farrand, *Records of the Federal Convention*, 1:123.

35. McDonald, *We the People*, provides a state-by-state analysis of support for and opposition to ratification.

36. For the ratification struggle, see Robert Allen Rutland, *The Ordeal of the Constitution: The Antifederalists and the Ratification Struggle of 1787–1788* (Norman: University of Oklahoma Press, 1966). A succinct but compelling discussion of the emergence of popular sovereignty in the struggle over state constitutions is in Palmer, *Age of the Democratic Revolution*, 1:213–238.

37. Gerald Stourzh, *Alexander Hamilton and the Idea of Republican Government* (Stanford: Stanford University Press, 1970); Drew R. McCoy, *The Elusive Republic: Political Economy in Jeffersonian America* (New York: W. W. Norton & Co., 1980), 146–152; Stanley Elkins and Eric McKitrick, *The Age of Federalism: The Early American Republic, 1788–1800* (New York: Oxford University Press, 1993), 92–131.

38. Alexander Hamilton, "Report on Public Credit," in *Writings*, ed. Joanne B. Freeman, Library of America (New York: Literary Classics of the United States, 1999), 535.

39. Ibid., 544.

40. McCoy, *Elusive Republic*, 136–145; Elkins and McKitrick, *Age of Federalism*, 136–145; Lance Banning, *The Sacred Fire of Liberty: James Madison and the Founding of the Federal Republic* (Ithaca: Cornell University Press, 1995), 298–316.

41. Elkins and McKitrick, *Age of Federalism*, 146–153; Banning, *Sacred Fire of Liberty*, 316–321.

42. Alexander Hamilton, "Report on a National Bank," in *Writings*, 575–612; Elkins and McKitrick, *Age of Federalism*, 226–228, 258–261.

43. Alexander Hamilton, "Report on the Subject of Manufactures," in *Writings*, 647–734, quotations at 665, 666; John E. Crowley, *The Privileges of Independence: Neomercantilism and the American Revolution* (Baltimore: Johns Hopkins University Press, 1993), 146–155.

44. Lance Banning, *The Jeffersonian Persuasion: Evolution of a Party Ideology*

(Ithaca: Cornell University Press, 1978); McCoy, *Elusive Republic*, esp. 152–161; Joyce Appleby, *Capitalism and a New Social Order: The Republican Vision of the 1790s* (New York: New York University Press, 1984); John R. Nelson, Jr., *Liberty and Property: Political Economy and Policymaking in the New Nation, 1789–1812* (Baltimore: Johns Hopkins University Press, 1987); Elkins and McKitrick, *Age of Federalism*, 79–92, 195–208; Herbert E. Sloan, *Principle and Interest: Thomas Jeffersonan and the Problem of Debt* (New York: Oxford University Press, 1995), esp. chap. 3.

45. Thomas Jefferson, "Notes on the State of Virginia," in *Writings*, ed. Merrill D. Peterson, Library of America (New York: Literary Classics of the United States, 1984), 290; James Madison, "Republican Distribution of Citizens," in *Writings*, ed. Jack N. Rakove, Library of America (New York: Literary Classics of the United States, 1999), 512.

46. Banning, *Sacred Fire of Liberty*, 58–75; McCoy, *Elusive Republic*, 137–145; Nelson, *Liberty and Property*, 66–79.

47. Thomas Jefferson to the President of the United States [George Washington], May 23, 1792, in *Writings*, 986. On the anticapitalist dimensions of Jeffersonian thought, see Robert F. Shalhope, *John Taylor of Caroline: Pastoral Republican* (Columbia: University of South Carolina Press, 1980); Michael Merrill, "The Anticapitalist Origins of the United States," *Review*, Fernand Braudel Center for the Study of Economies, Historical Systems, and Civilizations, 13 (Fall 1990), 465–497.

48. Robert E. Wright, *Hamilton Unbound: Finance and the Creation of the American Republic* (Westport, Conn.: Greenwood Press, 2002), chap. 3; Robert E. Wright, *The Wealth of Nations Rediscovered: Integration and Expansion in American Financial Markets, 1780–1850* (New York: Cambridge University Press, 2002), chaps. 1–4, 8.

49. James Roger Sharp, *American Politics in the Early Republic: The New Nation in Crisis* (New Haven: Yale University Press, 1993), 31–112; John Taylor, *Disunion Sentiment in Congress in 1794: A Confidential Memorandum Hitherto Unpublished*, ed. Gaillard Hunt (Washington, D.C.: W. H. Lowdermilk and Co., 1905), quotation at 21.

50. James Madison, "Speech in Congress Opposing the National Bank," February 2, 1791, in *Writings*, 482, 486.

51. Noble E. Cunningham, *The Jeffersonian Republicans: The Formation of Party Organization, 1789–1801* (Chapel Hill: University of North Carolina Press, 1957), chaps 1–2; James Madison, "A Candid State of Parties," in *Writings*, 531.

52. Madison, "A Candid State of Parties," 532; Roland M. Baumann, "Phila-

delphia's Manufacturers and the Excise Taxes of 1794: The Forging of the Jeffersonian Coalition," *Pennsylvania Magazine of History and Biography*, 106 (1982), 3–39; Alfred F. Young, *The Democratic Republicans of New York: The Origins, 1763–1797* (Chapel Hill: University of North Carolina Press, 1967), chaps. 13–18; Elkins and McKitrick, *Age of Federalism*, 303–593; Sharp, *American Politics in the Early Republic*, 69–184.

53. Thomas Jefferson, "Draft of the Kentucky Resolutions," in *Writings*, 449, 453; James Madison, "Virginia Resolutions against the Alien and Sedition Acts," in *Writings*, 589.

54. Jeffrey L. Pasley, *"The Tyranny of Printers": Newspaper Politics in the Early American Republic* (Charlottesville: University Press of Virginia, 2001), 105–131.

55. Thomas Jefferson to Judge Spencer Roane, September 6, 1819, in *Writings*, 1425. For contrasting interpretations of the historical significance of the election of 1800, see, for example, Richard Hofstadter, *The Idea of a Party System: The Rise of Legitimate Opposition in the United States, 1780–1840* (Berkeley: University of California Press, 1972), 128–150; and Sharp, *American Politics in the Early Republic*, 226–227, 267–275.

56. Gordon S. Wood, *The Radicalism of the American Revolution* (New York: Alfred A. Knopf, 1992), chap. 19; Chilton Williamson, *American Suffrage from Property to Democracy* (Princeton: Princeton University Press, 1960), chaps. 8–11; Alexander Keyssar, *The Right to Vote: The Contested History of Democracy in the United States* (New York: Basic Books, 2000), chap. 2 and appendix; Alan Taylor, "From Fathers to Friends of the People: Political Personas in the Early Republic," *Journal of the Early Republic*, 11 (Winter 1987), 465–491; Jeffrey L. Pasley, "1800 as a Revolution in Political Culture: Newspapers, Celebrations, Voting, and Democratization in the Early Republic," in *The Revolution of 1800: Democracy, Race, and the New Republic*, ed. James Horn, Jan Ellen Lewis, and Peter S. Onuf (Charlottesville: University of Virginia Press, 2002), 121–152; Peter Dobkin Hall, *The Organization of American Culture, 1700–1900: Private Institutions, Elites, and the Origins of American Nationality* (New York: New York University Press, 1984), esp. chaps. 5–6; Robert F. Dalzell, Jr., *Enterprising Elite: The Boston Associates and the World They Made* (Cambridge, Mass.: Harvard University Press, 1987), chaps. 2–3; Robert William Fogel, *Without Consent or Contract: The Rise and Fall of American Slavery* (New York: W. W. Norton & Co., 1989), esp. chap. 3.

57. Sharp, *American Politics in the Early Republic*, 243–249; Leonard L. Richards, *The Slave Power: The Free North and Southern Domination, 1780–1860* (Baton Rouge: Louisiana State University Press, 2000), 42.

58. Thomas Jefferson, "First Inaugural Address," in *Writings*, 492–494.

59. Catherine Allgor, *Parlor Politics: In Which the Ladies of Washington Help Build a City and a Government* (Charlottesville: University Press of Virginia, 2000), 32–33.

60. Marshall Smelser, *The Democratic Republic, 1801–1815* (New York: Harper & Row, 1968), 45–57.

61. Augustus John Foster, *Jeffersonian America: Notes on the United States Collected in the Years 1805–6–7 and 11–12 by Sir Augustus John Foster, Bart.*, ed. Richard B. Davis (1954; Westport, Conn.: Greenwood Press, 1980), 163. On the democratization of politics in the North, see Paul Goodman, *The Democratic-Republicans of Massachusetts: Politics in a Young Republic* (1964; Westport, Conn.: Greenwood Press, 1986), 73–85; David Hackett Fischer, *The Revolution of American Conservatism: The Federalist Party in the Era of Jeffersonian Democracy* (New York: Harper & Row, 1965), 187–192, 203–211; Taylor, "From Fathers to Friends of the People"; Pasley, "1800 as a Revolution in Political Culture." On the connection between racial slavery, democratic ideology, and the Jeffersonian coalition in the South, see Edmund S. Morgan, *American Slavery, American Freedom: The Ordeal of Colonial Virginia* (New York: W. W. Norton & Co., 1975), chap. 18; John Ashworth, "The Jeffersonians: Classical Republicans or Liberal Capitalists?" *Journal of American Studies*, 18 (December 1984), 425–435.

62. Roger G. Kennedy, *Mr. Jefferson's Lost Cause: Land, Farmers, Slavery, and the Louisiana Purchase* (New York: Oxford University Press, 2003).

63. *Annals of Congress*, 15th Cong., 2d Sess. (1818–1819), vol. 1, quotations at 1204–5, 1211; Richards, *Slave Power*, 52–82; Joshua Michael Zeitz, "The Missouri Compromise Reconsidered: Rhetoric and the Emergence of the Free Labor Synthesis," *Journal of the Early Republic*, 20 (Fall 2000), 447–485; Sean Wilentz, "The Missouri Crisis Revisited: Slavery, Democracy, and the Constitution in the Early Republic," Gaspar G. Bacon Lecture on the Constitution of the United States, May 2, 2002, Boston University (unpublished paper in possession of the authors).

64. Thomas Jefferson to John Holmes, April 22, 1820, in *Writings*, 1434.

65. Shalhope, *John Taylor of Caroline*, 197–199; Noble E. Cunningham, Jr., *The Presidency of James Monroe* (Lawrence: University Press of Kansas, 1996), 93–104; Wilentz, "Missouri Crisis Revisited," 15; Glover Moore, *The Missouri Controversy, 1819–1821* ([Lexington]: University of Kentucky Press, 1953), 170–217.

66. David Donald, "An Excess of Democracy: The American Civil War and the Social Process," in *Lincoln Reconsidered: Essays on the Civil War Era*, 2d ed. (New York: Vintage Books, [1960]), 209–235; John William Ward, *Andrew Jack-*

son: Symbol for an Age (New York: Oxford University Press, 1955), 46–78; Richard H. Brown, "The Missouri Crisis, Slavery, and the Politics of Jacksonianism," *South Atlantic Quarterly*, 65 (Winter 1966), 55–72; Charles Sellers, *The Market Revolution: Jacksonian America, 1815–1846* (New York: Oxford University Press, 1991), 301–331; Eric Foner, *Free Soil, Free Labor, Free Men: The Ideology of the Republican Party before the Civil War* (New York: Oxford University Press, 1970), 90–98.

67. Robert Gray Gunderson, *Old Gentlemen's Convention: The Washington Peace Conference of 1861* (Madison: University of Wisconsin Press, 1961), 10–12, 28–32; Sven Beckert, *The Monied Metropolis: New York City and the Consolidation of the American Bourgeoisie, 1850–1896* (New York: Cambridge University Press, 2001), 94–96; Foner, *Free Soil, Free Labor, Free Men*, esp. chap. 1; Ralph A. Wooster, *The Secession Conventions of the South* (Princeton: Princeton University Press, 1962), 19–20, 32–33, 54–55, 71–72, 87–88, 106–107, 128–129, 144–145, 160–161, 176–178, 198–199; James M. McPherson, *For Cause and Comrades: Why Men Fought in the Civil War* (New York: Oxford University Press, 1997), esp. chap. 1; Abraham Lincoln, "Message to Congress in Special Session," in *Speeches and Writings*, ed. Don E. Fehrenbacher, 2 vols., Library of America (New York: Literary Classics of the United States, 1989), 2:259.

2. The "Slave Power" in the United States, 1783–1865

1. For the history of the "slave power" concept, see Leonard Richards, *The Slave Power: The Free North and Southern Domination, 1780–1860* (Baton Rouge: Louisiana State University Press, 2000), chap. 1; David Brion Davis, *The Slave Power Conspiracy and the Paranoid Style* (Baton Rouge: Louisiana State University Press, 1969).

2. John Gorham Palfrey, *Papers on the Slave Power* (Boston: Merrill, Cobb & Co., 1846), 12–13.

3. Population statistics drawn from Inter-University Consortium for Political and Social Research, *Historical, Demographic, Economic, and Social Data: The United States, 1790–1970*, computer file (Ann Arbor: Inter-University Consortium for Political and Social Research [producer and distributor], 197?).

4. *American State Papers: Commerce and Navigation*, 2 vols. (Washington, D.C.: Gales and Seaton, 1832), 1:24–33, 322.

5. Kenneth Morgan, "George Washington and the Problem of Slavery," *Journal of American Studies* 34, no. 2 (2000): 279–301. Washington's property holdings

placed him high on the list of Virginia's wealthiest one hundred planters. See Jackson T. Main, "The One Hundred," *William and Mary Quarterly*, 3d ser., 11 (July 1954): 354–384.

6. Thomas Jefferson, *Writings*, ed. Merrill Peterson (New York: Library of America, 1984), 289. On the South in the 1780s, see John Richard Alden, *The South in the Revolution, 1763–1789* (Baton Rouge: Louisiana State University Press, 1957), chaps. 20–21.

7. For southern politicians' contribution to territorial expansion, see Joseph A. Fry, *Dixie Looks Abroad: The South and U.S. Foreign Relations, 1789–1973* (Baton Rouge: Louisiana State University Press, 2002), chaps. 1–2.

8. Richards, *The Slave Power*, 43–45.

9. For the decline of slavery in the early national North, see Ira Berlin, *Many Thousands Gone: The First Two Centuries of Slavery in North America* (Cambridge, Mass.: Harvard University Press, 1998), chap. 9.

10. Quotation from Ulrich B. Phillips, *Plantation and Frontier Documents: 1649–1863*, vol. 1 (Cleveland: Arthur H. Clark Co., 1909), 289. Statistics from Stuart Bruchey, *Cotton and the Growth of the American Economy, 1790–1860: Sources and Readings* (New York: Harcourt, Brace, & World, 1967), tables 1A, 3C.

11. Bruchey, *Cotton and the Growth of the American Economy*, tables 2B, 3A, 3J, 3L.

12. *Congressional Globe*, Senate, 35th Cong., 1st Sess., appendix (1858), 70.

13. Based on Robert Fogel's estimate that tobacco, rice, and sugar accounted for 21 percent of the slave population in 1850. Robert Fogel, *Without Consent or Contract: The Rise and Fall of American Slavery* (New York: W. W. Norton, 1989), 30

14. James Oakes, *The Ruling Race: A History of American Slaveholders* (New York: Vintage Books, 1982), 50.

15. Robert Starobin, *Industrial Slavery in the Old South* (New York: Oxford University Press, 1970), chap. 1.

16. Fogel, *Without Consent or Contract*, 102–107; Richard Graham, "Economics or Culture? The Development of the U.S. South and Brazil in the Days of Slavery," in *What Made the South Different?*, ed. Kees Gispen (Jackson: University Press of Mississippi, 1990), 97–124.

17. Starobin, *Industrial Slavery in the Old South*, chap. 6.

18. William Kauffman Scarborough, *The Overseer: Plantation Management in the Old South* (1966; Athens: University of Georgia Press, 1984), 69. On slave owners' interest in slave reproduction, see Marie Jenkins Schwartz, *Born in Bond-*

age: Growing Up Enslaved in the Antebellum South (Cambridge, Mass.: Harvard University Press, 2000), chap. 1.

19. Michael Tadman, *Speculators and Slaves: Masters, Traders, and Slaves in the Old South* (Madison: University of Wisconsin Press, 1996), 12.

20. John W. Blassingame, ed., *Slave Testimony: Two Centuries of Letters, Speeches, Interviews, and Autobiographies* (Baton Rouge: Louisiana State University Press, 1977), 118. For slaves' experiences in the slave trade, see Walter Johnson, *Soul by Soul: Life inside the Antebellum Slave Market* (Cambridge, Mass.: Harvard University Press, 1999).

21. Drew Gilpin Faust, ed., *The Ideology of Slavery: Proslavery Thought in the Antebellum South, 1830–1860* (Baton Rouge: Louisiana State University Press, 1981), 39.

22. On slave owners' capital gains from rising slave prices, see Gavin Wright, *The Political Economy of the Cotton South: Households, Markets, and Wealth in the Nineteenth Century* (New York: W. W. Norton, 1978), 139–144. Nine hundred dollars in 1860 was roughly equivalent to $18,350 in 2003. This estimate is derived from *Handbook of Labor Statistics*, published by the Bureau of Labor Statistics, which suggests a multiplier of 20.39 to convert 1860 values into 2003 values (*www.minneapolisfed.org/research/data/us/calc/hist1800.cfm*, accessed December 14, 2003).

23. Lee Soltow, *Men and Wealth in the United States, 1850–1870* (New Haven: Yale University Press, 1975), 101, 103, 166–167, 195n6. Soltow reports a Gini Coefficient of .813 for wealth among free men in the North in 1860, and .845 for free men in the South.

24. William Kauffman Scarborough, *Masters of the Big House: Elite Slaveholders of the Mid-Nineteenth-Century South* (Baton Rouge: Louisiana State University Press, 2003), 13, 241. Aggregate statistics on slave owning and residence compiled from Appendix D.

25. Peter Kolchin, *Unfree Labor: American Slavery and Russian Serfdom* (Cambridge, Mass.: Harvard University Press, 1987), 54.

26. The debate is examined in Mark M. Smith, *Debating Slavery: Economy and Society in the Antebellum American South* (New York: Cambridge University Press, 1998).

27. On the southern household, see Elizabeth Fox-Genovese, *Within the Plantation Household: Black and White Women of the Old South* (Chapel Hill: University of North Carolina Press, 1988), chap. 1.

28. James Henry Hammond, "Letter to an English Abolitionist," in *The Ideol-*

ogy of Slavery: Proslavery Thought in the Antebellum South, 1830–1860, ed. Drew Gilpin Faust (Baton Rouge: Louisiana State University Press, 1981), 190.

29. Scarborough, *The Overseer,* 68.

30. Kenneth M. Stampp, *The Peculiar Institution: Slavery in the Ante-Bellum South* (New York: Vintage Books, 1989), chap. 4.

31. Eugene Genovese, *Roll, Jordan, Roll: The World the Slaves Made* (New York: Pantheon Books, 1974).

32. Sally Hadden, *Slave Patrols: Law and Violence in Virginia and the Carolinas* (Cambridge, Mass.: Harvard University Press, 2001), 71.

33. Thomas Morris, *Southern Slavery and the Law, 1619–1860* (Chapel Hill: University of North Carolina Press, 1996), 218.

34. Peter P. Hinks, *To Awaken My Afflicted Brethren: David Walker and the Problem of Antebellum Slave Resistance* (University Park: Pennsylvania State University Press, 1997), 217–219.

35. Ronald Edward Bridwell, "The South's Wealthiest Planter: Wade Hampton I of South Carolina, 1754–1835" (Ph.D. diss., University of South Carolina, 1980).

36. Soltow, *Men and Wealth,* 143–144.

37. Frederick Law Olmsted, *The Cotton Kingdom: A Traveller's Observations on Cotton and Slavery in the American Slave States, 1853–1861,* ed. Arthur M. Schlesinger (1953; New York: Da Capo Press, 1996), 574.

38. On the relationship between slave owners and non–slave owners in the antebellum South, see especially Eugene D. Genovese, "Yeoman Farmers in a Slaveholders' Democracy," *Agricultural History* 49, no. 2 (1975): 331–342.

39. J. William Harris, *Plain Folk and Gentry in a Slave Society: White Liberty and Black Slavery in Augusta's Hinterlands* (Baton Rouge: Louisiana State University Press, 1985), 83–90.

40. Steven Hahn, *The Roots of Southern Populism: Yeoman Farmers and the Transformation of the Georgia Upcountry, 1850–1890* (New York: Oxford University Press, 1983), chap. 3.

41. Manisha Sinha, *The Counterrvolution of Slavery: Politics and Ideology in Antebellum South Carolina* (Chapel Hill: University of North Carolina Press, 2000), 80.

42. Susan Wyly-Jones, "The 1835 Anti-abolition Meetings in the South: A New Look at the Controversy over the Abolition Postal Campaign," *Civil War History* 47, no. 4 (2001): 289–309.

43. Clement Eaton, *The Freedom-of-Thought Struggle in the Old South* (New York: Harper & Row, 1964), 187.

44. Harris, *Plain Folk and Gentry in a Slave Society*, 121.

45. Statistics on emigration from Virginia compiled from David Hackett Fischer and James C. Kelly, *Bound Away: Virginia and the Westward Movement* (Charlottesville: University Press of Virginia, 2000), 325.

46. Don E. Fehrenbacher, *Constitutions and Constitutionalism in the Slaveholding South* (Athens: University of Georgia Press, 1989), chap. 1.

47. William J. Cooper, Jr., *The South and the Politics of Slavery, 1828–1856* (Baton Rouge: Louisiana State University Press, 1978), chap. 2.

48. Harry L. Watson, "Conflict and Collaboration: Yeomen, Slaveholders, and Politics in the Antebellum South," *Social History* 10 (1985): 273–298; Hahn, *Roots of Southern Populism*, chap. 3.

49. Edward E. Baptist, "The Migration of Planters to Antebellum Florida: Kinship and Power," *Journal of Southern History* 57, no. 3 (August 1996): 527–554.

50. Richard Lowe and Randolph Campbell, "Wealthholding and Political Power in Antebellum Texas," *Southwestern Historical Quarterly* 79, no. 1 (1975): 25.

51. Donald Wooster, *Politicians, Planters, and Plain Folk* (Knoxville: University of Tennessee Press, 1975), 41, and idem, *The People in Power* (Knoxville: University of Tennessee Press, 1979), 125, 128, 133, 138, 143, 148, 153. Wooster's data do not include Delaware.

52. Daniel P. Jordan, "Mississippi's Antebellum Congressmen: A Collective Biography," *Journal of Mississippi History* 38 (May 1976): 170.

53. Richard C. Lounsbury, ed., *Louisa S. McCord: Political and Social Essays* (Charlottesville: University Press of Virginia, 1995), 245. Two histories that trace the development and dissemination of proslavery ideas over time are Larry E. Tise, *Proslavery: A History of the Defense of Slavery in America, 1701–1840* (Athens: University of Georgia Press, 1987), and Jeffrey Robert Young, *Domesticating Slavery: The Master Class in Georgia and South Carolina, 1670–1837* (Chapel Hill: University of North Carolina Press, 1999).

54. Tise, *Proslavery*, esp. chap. 5. A classic expression of the proslavery contrast between free and slave society is George Fitzhugh, *Cannibals All! or, Slaves without Masters* (Cambridge, Mass.: Belknap Press of Harvard University Press, 1960). Fitzhugh's thought is analyzed in Eugene D. Genovese, *The World the Slaveholders Made: Two Essays in Interpretation* (New York: Pantheon Books, 1969), pt. 2.

55. Stephanie McCurry, "The Two Faces of Republicanism: Gender and Proslavery Politics in Antebellum South Carolina," *Journal of American History* 78 (March 1992): 1245–64.

56. My analysis of the proslavery argument is indebted to the "elementary

structure of signification" explained in Agirdas Julien Greimas, *On Meaning: Selected Writing in Semiotic Theory,* trans. Paul J. Perron and Frank H. Collins (London: Frances Pinter, 1987), chap. 3. For other applications of this approach, see Fredric Jameson, *The Political Unconscious: Narrative as a Socially Symbolic Act* (Ithaca, N.Y.: Cornell University Press, 1981); and Anders Stephanson, *Kennan and the Art of Foreign Policy* (Cambridge, Mass.: Harvard University Press, 1989), chap. 8.

57. Lynda Lasswell Crist and Mary Seaton Dix, eds., *The Papers of Jefferson Davis,* vol. 6, (Baton Rouge: Louisiana State University Press, 1989), 147–148.

58. Eric Foner, *Free Soil, Free Labor, Free Men: The Ideology of the Republican Party before the Civil War* (New York: Oxford University Press, 1970), 308–313.

59. On the difference between intensive and extensive networks of power, see Michael Mann, *The Sources of Social Power,* vol. 1, *A History of Power from the Beginning to A.D. 1760* (New York: Cambridge University Press, 1986), 7–10.

60. For a fascinating defense of the three-fifths clause, see Federalist no. 54, written by James Madison, in *The Debate on the Constitution,* ed. Bernard Bailyn, vol. 2 (New York: Library of America, 1993), 196–201.

61. Richards, *The Slave Power,* chap. 2.

62. Kenneth C. Martis and Gregory A. Elmes, *The Historical Atlas of State Power in Congress, 1790–1990* (Washington, D.C.: Congressional Quarterly, 1993), 136, 150. The southern proportion of the country's free white population decreased from 40 percent in 1800 to 30 percent in 1860.

63. Don E. Fehrenbacher, *The Slaveholding Republic: An Account of the United States Government's Relations to Slavery,* ed. Ward McAfee (New York: Oxford University Press, 2003), 268.

64. Kinley J. Brauer, *Cotton Versus Conscience: Massachusetts Whig Politics and Southwestern Expansion, 1843–1848* (Lexington: University of Kentucky Press, 1967); Thomas H. O'Connor, *Lords of the Loom: The Cotton Whigs and the Coming of the Civil War* (New York: Charles Scribner's Sons, 1968), emerson quoted at 67.

65. Sven Beckert, *The Monied Metropolis: New York City and the Consolidation of the American Bourgeoisie, 1850–1896* (New York: Cambridge University Press, 2001), 20–23, 85–89.

66. Cooper, *The South and the Politics of Slavery.*

67. Richards, *The Slave Power,* 113–116.

68. For a provocative analysis of the different relationship of Democrats and Whigs to slavery, see John Ashworth, *Slavery, Capitalism, and Politics in the Antebellum Republic,* vol. 1, *Commerce and Compromise, 1820–1860* (New York: Cambridge University Press, 1995), chap. 5. On slavery and the Democratic Party, see

Richards, *The Slave Power*, chap. 5; Joel H. Silbey, "'There are other questions beside that of slavery merely': The Democratic Party and Antislavery Politics," in *Crusaders and Compromisers: Essays on the Relationship of the Antislavery Struggle to the Antebellum Party System*, ed. Alan M. Kraut (Westport, Conn.: Greenwood Press, 1983), 143–175; Sean Wilentz, "Slavery, Antislavery, and Jacksonian Democracy," in *The Market Revolution in America: Social, Political, and Religious Expressions, 1800–1880*, ed. Melvyn Stokes and Stephen Conway (Charlottesville: University Press of Virginia, 1996), 202–223.

69. Philip H. Burch, Jr., *Elites in American History* (New York: Holmes & Meier Publishers, 1981), 236–237. For a comparison of southern slave owners with other landed elites, see Steven Hahn, "Class and State in Postemancipation Societies: Southern Planters in Comparative Perspective," *American Historical Review* 95 (February 1990): 78–83.

70. Fehrenbacher, *Slaveholding Republic*. See also William Dusinberre, "President Polk and the Politics of Slavery," *American Nineteenth-Century History* 3, no. 1 (Spring 2002): 1–16.

71. William Lee Miller, *Arguing about Slavery: The Great Battle in the United States Congress* (New York: Knopf, 1996).

72. *The Papers of John C. Calhoun*, ed. Clyde N. Wilson, vol. 11 (Columbia: University of South Carolina Press, 1978), 640. An especially forceful argument concerning the antidemocratic outlook of South Carolina's planter-politicians can be found in Manisha Sinha, "Revolution or Counterrevolution?: The Political Ideology of Secession in Antebellum South Carolina," *Civil War History* 46 (2000): 205–226.

73. The outstanding study of the road to secession remains David M. Potter, *The Impending Crisis, 1848–1861*, completed and edited by Don E. Fehrenbacher (New York: Harper & Row, 1976).

74. Ibid., chap. 19. Secession allowed slave owners to codify these basic constitutional protections for slavery in the Confederate Constitution. See the comparison of the U.S. and C.S.A. constitutions in James M. McPherson, *Ordeal by Fire: The Civil War and Reconstruction*, 3d ed. (Boston: McGraw Hill, 2001), Appendix A–3.

75. Quoted in Armstead L. Robinson, "In the Shadow of Old John Brown: Insurrection Anxiety and Confederate Mobilization, 1861–1863," *Journal of Negro History* 65 (Autumn 1980): 288. Enslaved people's interpretation of Lincoln's election is also addressed in Steven Hahn, *A Nation under Our Feet: Black Political Struggles in the Rural South from Slavery to the Great Migration* (Cambridge, Mass.: Harvard University Press, 2003), 65–68.

76. *The Poems of Henry Timrod* (New York: E. J. Hale & Sons, 1872), 100.

77. For the religious basis of Confederate nationalism, see Drew Gilpin Faust, *The Creation of Confederate Nationalism: Ideology and Identity in the Civil War South* (Baton Rouge: Louisiana State University Press, 1988); Mitchell Snay, *Gospel of Disunion: Religion and Separatism in the Antebellum South* (Chapel Hill: University of North Carolina Press, 1993), chaps. 5–6.

78. A recent study showing the proslavery origins of secession is Charles B. Dew, *Apostles of Disunion: Southern Secession Commissioners and the Causes of the Civil War* (Charlottesville: University Press of Virginia, 2001).

79. William W. Freehling and Craig M. Simpson, eds., *Secession Debated: Georgia's Showdown in 1860* (New York: Oxford University Press, 1992), 102.

80. Studies of secession are numerous. Some of the best are William L. Barney, *The Secessionist Impulse: Alabama and Mississippi in 1860* (Princeton: Princeton University Press, 1974); Daniel W. Crofts, *Reluctant Confederates: Upper South Unionists in the Secession Crisis* (Chapel Hill: University of North Carolina Press, 1989); Michael P. Johnson, *Toward a Patriarchal Republic: The Secession of Georgia* (Baton Rouge: Louisiana State University Press, 1977); Peyton McCrary, Clark Miller, and Dale Baum, "Class and Party in the Secession Crisis: Voting Behavior in the Deep South, 1856–1861," *Journal of Interdisciplinary History* 8 (Winter 1978): 429–457.

81. Johnson, *Toward a Patriarchal Republic*, 135.

82. Ira Berlin, Barbara J. Fields, Steven F. Miller, Joseph P. Reidy, and Leslie S. Rowland, *Free at Last: A Documentary History of Slavery, Freedom, and the Civil War* (New York: New Press, 1992), 153.

83. Ira Berlin, Barbara J. Fields, Steven F. Miller, Joseph P. Reidy, and Leslie S. Rowland, *Slaves No More: Three Essays on Emancipation and the Civil War* (New York: Cambridge University Press, 1992).

84. Leon F. Litwack, *Been in the Storm So Long: The Aftermath of Slavery* (New York: Vintage Books, 1980), 165. For statistics on casualties from the superelite slave-owning families, see Scarborough, *Masters of the Big House*, 329.

85. Soltow, *Men and Wealth*, 181.

86. Eric Foner, *Reconstruction: America's Unfinished Revolution, 1863–1877* (New York: Harper & Row, 1988); Hahn, "Class and State in Postemancipation Societies." The classic study of the slow restoration of southern power is C. Vann Woodward, *Origins of the New South, 1877–1913* (Baton Rouge: Louisiana State University Press, 1951).

87. Quoted in Richard Bensel, *Yankee Leviathan: The Origins of Central State Authority in America, 1859–1877* (New York: Cambridge University Press, 1990), 349.

88. Amy Dru Stanley, *From Bondage to Contract: Wage Labor, Marriage, and the Market in the Age of Slave Emancipation* (New York: Cambridge University Press, 1998), chap. 2.

89. W. E. B. Du Bois, *Black Reconstruction in America, 1860–1880* (New York: Atheneum, 1962), 707.

3. Merchants and Manufacturers in the Antebellum North

I am grateful to Charles Forcey, Deborah Gesensway, Erin Sprague, and the editors of this volume for their help in writing this chapter. Parts of this chapter are based on earlier versions of the material in Sven Beckert, *The Monied Metropolis: New York City and the Consolidation of the American Bourgeoisie* (New York: Cambridge University Press, 2001).

1. Bernard Bailyn, *The New England Merchants in the Seventeenth Century* (Cambridge, Mass.: Harvard University Press, 1955).

2. See also Frederic Cople Jaher, *The Urban Establishment: Upper Strata in Boston, New York, Charleston, Chicago, and Los Angeles* (Urbana: University of Illinois Press, 1982), 21.

3. Ibid., 22.

4. Edward Pessen, *Riches, Classes, and Power before the Civil War* (Lexington, Mass.: D.C. Heath, 1973), 39; see also Ronald Story, *The Forging of an Aristocracy: Harvard and the Boston Upper Class, 1800–1870* (Middletown, Conn.: Wesleyan University Press, 1980), 3.

5. Pessen, *Riches, Classes, and Power,* 40.

6. Sven Beckert, *The Monied Metropolis: New York City and the Consolidation of the American Bourgeoisie* (New York: Cambridge University Press, 2001), 19.

7. Ibid., 19.

8. See also Paul E. Johnson, *A Shopkeeper's Millennium: Society and Revivals in Rochester, New York, 1815–1837* (New York: Hill and Wang, 1978), 16.

9. Walter Muir Whitehill, *Captain Joseph Peabody: East India Merchant of Salem, 1775–1844* (Salem: Peabody Museum, 1962), 15, 23, 24, 55.

10. Robert F. Dalzell, *Enterprising Elite: The Boston Associates and the World They Made* (Cambridge, Mass.: Harvard University Press, 1987), 29.

11. E. Digby Baltzell, *Philadelphia Gentlemen: The Making of a National Upper Class* (Glencoe, Ill.: Free Press, 1958), 93; Pessen, *Riches, Classes, and Power,* 66.

12. Pessen, *Riches, Classes, and Power,* 67.

13. Glenn Porter and Harold C. Livesay, *Merchants and Manufacturers: Stud-*

ies in the Changing Structure of Nineteenth-Century Marketing (Baltimore: Johns Hopkins University Press, 1971), 7, 20, 30.

14. Robert Greenhalgh Albion, *The Rise of New York Port, 1815–1860* (New York: Charles Scribner's Sons, 1939), 264.

15. Ibid., 267.

16. For related information, see Barry E. Supple, "A Business Elite: German-Jewish Financiers in Nineteenth-Century New York," *Business History Review* 31 (Summer 1957), esp. 509.

17. Marika Vicziany, "Bombay Merchants and Structural Changes in the Export Community, 1850 to 1880," in *Economy and Society: Essays in Indian Economic and Social History* (Delhi: Oxford University Press, 1979), 163–196; Marika Vicziany, *The Cotton Trade and the Commercial Development of Bombay, 1855–75* (London: University of London Press, 1975); Elena Frangakis-Syrett, "Commerce in the Eastern Mediterranean from the Eighteenth to the Early Twentieth Centuries: The City-Port of Izmir and Its Hinterland," *International Journal of Maritime History* 10, no. 2 (1998), 125–154; E. R. J. Owen, *Cotton and the Egyptian Economy* (Oxford: Oxford University Press, 1969).

18. For evidence, see Jaher, *Urban Establishment*, 42, and Pessen, *Riches, Classes, and Power*, 216–218.

19. This is also emphasized by Johnson, *A Shopkeeper's Millennium*, 22.

20. Quoted in Jaher, *Urban Establishment*, 23.

21. John Crosby Brown, *A Hundred Years of Merchant Banking: A History of Brown Brothers and Company, Brown Shipley & Company, and the Allied Firms* (New York: privately printed, 1909), 24.

22. See also Pessen, *Riches, Classes and Power*, 213.

23. Elizabeth Blackmar, *Manhattan for Rent, 1785–1850* (Ithaca: Cornell University Press, 1989), 141–142.

24. See, for example, "Anson G. Phelps Dodge," entry of October 15, 1859, Dun Papers, Baker Library, Harvard Business School, 345:600 (N); Robert S. Buchanan, entry of April 1, 1851, ibid., 340:56.

25. Quoted in Story, *The Forging of an Aristocracy*, 5. See also Charles Haynes Haswell, *Reminiscences of an Octogenarian of the City of New York* (New York: Harper & Brothers, 1896), 514.

26. Jaher, *Urban Establishment*, 206; Albion, *The Rise of New York Port*, 254.

27. Jaher, *Urban Establishment*, 73; Johnson, *A Shopkeeper's Millennium*, 26.

28. See Pierre Bourdieu, *Distinction: A Social Critique of the Judgment of Taste* (Cambridge, Mass.: Harvard University Press, 1984).

29. Jaher, *Urban Establishment*, 72, 203.

30. The importance of kinship networks is also emphasized by Betty G. Farrell, *Elite Families: Class and Power in Nineteenth-Century Boston* (Albany: State University of New York Press, 1993), 59.

31. Albion, *The Rise of New York Port*, 254; Pessen, *Riches, Classes, and Power*, 169.

32. Farrell, *Elite Families*, 25.

33. Beckert, *Monied Metropolis*, 56; Baltzell, *Philadelphia Gentlemen*, 175.

34. Johnson, *A Shopkeeper's Millennium*, 53.

35. See especially Nancy Cott, *The Bonds of Womanhood: "Woman's Sphere" in New England, 1780–1835* (New Haven: Yale University Press, 1977), 64, 72.

36. Farrell, *Elite Families*, 78.

37. See *Hunt's Merchants' Magazine and Commercial Review* 35 (1856), 388; 31 (1854), 263; 34 (1856), 60; 31 (1854), 59; 41 (1859), 644; 34 (1856), 59.

38. See, for example, Dun Papers, 374:35, 41, 61, 63, 71, 75, 117.

39. *Hunt's Merchants' Magazine and Commercial Review* 33 (1855), 390.

40. Ibid., 41 (1859), 644; 39 (1859), 140.

41. Daniel Hodas, *The Business Career of Moses Taylor: Merchant, Finance Capitalist, and Industrialist* (New York: New York University Press, 1976), 10.

42. Ibid., 37. See also *Hunt's Merchants' Magazine and Commercial Review* 32 (1855), 522.

43. Quoted in Jaher, *Urban Establishment*, 38.

44. Anna Robeson Burr, *The Portrait of a Banker: James Stilman, 1850–1918* (New York: Duffield, 1927), 42; John Ward, Diary, April 1–20, 1864, New-York Historical Society; *The Autobiography of Benjamin Franklin*, reprinted as *Benjamin Franklin's Autobiography*, ed. J. A. Leo Lemay and P. M. Zall (New York: Norton, 1986), 54.

45. Lisa Tiersten, "Redefining Consumer Culture: Recent Literature on Consumption and the Bourgeoisie in Western Europe," *Radical History Review* 57 (Fall 1993), 116–159; William Leach, *True Love and Perfect Union: The Feminist Reform of Sex and Society* (New York: Basic Books, 1980), 222–226.

46. *New York Herald*, September 18, 1846, 2; see also Christine M. Boyer, *Manhattan Manners: Architecture and Style, 1850–1900* (New York: Rizzoli, 1985), 90.

47. *Hunt's Merchants' Magazine and Commercial Review* 31 (1854), 61; 33 (1855), 558; 30 (1854), 649. Calls against "extravagances" can also be found in the *United States Economist* 13 (June 18, 1853), 18.

48. Bourdieu, *Distinction*, 114.

49. John A. Kouwenhoven, *Partners in Banking: An Historical Portrait of a Great Private Bank, Brown Brothers Harriman & Co., 1818–1968* (New York: Doubleday & Company, 1968), 85.

50. See, for example, "A Parlor View in a New York Dwelling House," 1854, reprinted in Allen Churchill, *The Upper Crust: An Informal History of New York's Highest Society* (Englewood Cliffs, N.J.: Prentice-Hall, 1970), 46. For illustrations of typical bourgeois furniture, see Eileen Dubrow and Richard Dubrow, *American Furniture of the Nineteenth Century* (Exton, Pa.: Schiffer Publishing, 1983); Elan Zingman-Leith and Susan Zingman-Leith, *The Secret Life of Victorian Houses* (Washington, D.C.: Elliott & Clark Publishing, 1993).

51. See Katherine C. Grier, "The Decline of the Memory Palace: The Parlor after 1880," in *American Home Life, 1880–1930: A Social History of Spaces and Services*, ed. Jessica H. Foy and Thomas J. Schlereth (Knoxville: University of Tennessee Press, 1992), 51.

52. *Annual Report of the Chamber of Commerce of the State of New York, for the Year 1858* (New York: Wheeler and Williams, 1859), 340–350.

53. Albion, *The Rise of New York Port*, 265.

54. Francis Gerry Fairfield, *The Clubs of New York* (New York: H. L. Hinton, 1873), 59. See also Reginald Townsend, *Mother of Clubs: Being the History of the First Hundred Years of the Union Club of the City of New York, 1836–1936* (New York: William Edwin Rudge, 1936); David Black, *The King of Fifth Avenue: The Fortunes of August Belmont* (New York: Dial Press, 1981), 60.

55. Townsend, *Mother of Clubs*, 2, 84–87. See also Thomas Bender, *New York Intellect: A History of Intellectual Life in New York City, from 1750 to the Beginnings of Our Own Time* (Baltimore: Johns Hopkins University Press, 1987), 135.

56. Baltzell, *Philadelphia Gentlemen*, 337; Pessen, *Riches, Classes, and Power*, 224.

57. Farrell, *Elite Families*, 31.

58. On Boston, see Jaher, *Urban Establishment*, 26; on New York, see Beckert, *Monied Metropolis*, 81–82.

59. Farrell, *Elite Families*, 32; Jaher, *Urban Establishment*, 26, 54.

60. Farrell, *Elite Families*, 32.

61. Baltzell, *Philadelphia Gentlemen*, 81.

62. Ibid., 87. For more examples, see Johnson, *A Shopkeeper's Millennium*, 71; Pessen, *Riches, Classes, and Power*, 284, 285, 287.

63. Robert Ernst, *Immigrant Life in New York City, 1825–1863* (Syracuse: Syracuse University Press, 1994), 17.

64. See Sean Wilentz, *Chants Democratic: New York City and the Rise of the American Working Class, 1788–1850* (New York: Oxford University Press, 1984), 107–142; Lisa B. Lubow, "From Carpenter to Capitalist: The Business of Building in Postrevolutionary Boston," in *Entrepreneurs: The Boston Business Community, 1700–1850*, ed. Conrad Edick Wright and Katheryn P. Viens (Boston: Northeastern University Press, 1997), 181–210.

65. Ernst, *Immigrant Life in New York City*, 17.

66. Michael Zakim, *Ready-Made Democracy: A History of Men's Dress in the American Republic, 1760–1860* (Chicago: University of Chicago Press, 2003), 37.

67. John S. Gilkeson, *Middle-Class Providence* (Princeton: Princeton University Press, 1986), 18.

68. United States, Secretary of the Interior, *Census of the United States in 1860*, 379, 380, 382, 384; Carl M. Degler, "Labor in the Economy and Politics of New York City, 1850–1860" (Ph.D. diss., Columbia University, 1952), 49. See, for example, the reports on Cornelius Delamater in Dun Papers, "Cornelius Delamater," entry of September 14, 1857, 316a:185, entry of October 9, 1869, 411:100L, and "Novelty Iron Works," 368:400, 431, 440, 441; Dalzell, *Enterprising Elite*.

69. Jaher, *Urban Establishment*, 49.

70. Glenn Porter and Harold Livesay, *Merchants and Manufacturers: Studies in the Changing Structure of Nineteenth-Century Marketing* (Baltimore: John Hopkins Press, 1971), 78.

71. Quoted in Baltzell, *Philadelphia Gentlemen*, 96.

72. Fred Dietz, *A Leaf from the Past: Dietz Then and Now* (New York: R. E. Dietz Company, 1914), 60, 74, 77, 94.

73. *The National Cyclopedia of American Biography, Being the History of the United States*, vol. 30 (New York: James T. White, 1943), 544.

74. Ernst, *Immigrant Life in New York City*, 93.

75. Catherine Elizabeth Reiser, *Pittsburgh's Commercial Development, 1800–1850* (Harrisburg: Pennsylvania Historical and Museum Commission, 1951); Henry A. Ford et al., *History of Cincinnati, Ohio* (Cleveland: W. W. Williams, 1881).

76. James J. Mapes, *Inaugural Address Delivered Tuesday Evening, January 7, 1845, before the Mechanics' Institute of the City of New York* (New York: Institute Rooms, 1845), 11.

77. Allan Nevins, *Abram S. Hewitt, with some Account of Peter Cooper* (New York: Harper, 1935), 55, 59, 61; Edward C. Mack, *Peter Cooper: Citizen of New York* (New York: Duell, Sloan and Pearce, 1949), 35, 40, 44, 69, 204, 205.

78. *Scientific American*, March 29, 1879, 193.

79. Nevins, *Hewitt*, 144.

80. Beckert, *Monied Metropolis*, 62.

81. *Scientific American*, January 10, 1880, 17; Richard K. Lieberman, *Steinway & Sons* (New Haven: Yale University Press, 1995), 21.

82. Entry for October 22, 1860, in *The Diary of George Templeton Strong*, ed. Allan Nevins and Milton Halsey Thomas, vol. 3 (New York: Macmillan, 1952), 52.

83. *New York Times*, 17 October 1860, 3.

84. "John Roach," entry of June 4, 1860, Dun Papers, 317:229.

85. "Richard Hoe," entry of May 1851, ibid., 360:51.

86. Leonard Alexander Swann, *John Roach, Maritime Entrepreneur: The Years as Naval Contractor, 1862–1886* (Annapolis: U.S. Naval Institute, 1965), 23.

87. Jaher, *Urban Establishment*, 48.

88. Peter S. Hoe to Robert Hoe, New York, October 20, 1857, Hoe Papers, Library of Congress, Washington, D.C.

89. Alexander D. Bache, *Anniversary Address before the American Institute, of the City of New-York, at the Tabernacle, October 28th, 1856, during the Twenty-eighth Annual Fair* (New York: Pudney & Russell, 1857), 32.

90. *Catalogue of the Library of the Mechanics' Institute of the City of New York* (New York: A. Baptist, Jr., 1844), 63. For the composition of the leadership of the Mechanics' Institute, see Mapes, *Inaugural Address*, 2.

91. See *Catalogue of the Library of the Mechanics' Institute of the City of New York;* Mapes, *Inaugural Address*, 9.

92. Mapes, *Inaugural Address*, 9.

93. See Gilkeson, *Middle-Class Providence*, esp. 23–36.

94. See Johnson, *A Shopkeeper's Millennium*.

95. See ibid., 137.

96. Beckert, *The Monied Metropolis*, 78.

97. *New York Herald*, July 15, 1850, quoted in Roy Rosenzweig and Elizabeth Blackmar, *The Park and the People: A History of Central Park* (Ithaca: Cornell University Press, 1992), 28.

98. Alexis de Tocqueville, *Democracy in America*, ed. Phillips Bradley, 2 vols. (New York: Vintage Books, 1945), 1:198; 2:114. For a discussion that focuses on New York City, see Mary P. Ryan, *Civic Wars: Democracy and Public Life in the American City during the Nineteenth Century* (Berkeley: University of California Press, 1997), 37, 74–75.

99. Paul DiMaggio, "Cultural Entrepreneurship in Nineteenth-Century Boston," in *Nonprofit Enterprise in the Arts: Studies in Mission and Constraint* (New York: Oxford University Press, 1986), 43.

100. Andrew Stulman Dennett, *Weird & Wonderful: The Dime Museum in America* (New York: New York University Press, 1997), 18, 26.

101. Ibid., 30; Rossiter Raymond, *Peter Cooper* (Boston: Houghton Mifflin, 1901), 69. For the general point, see also Ryan, *Civic Wars*, 38.

102. DiMaggio, "Cultural Entrepreneurship in Nineteenth-Century Boston," 43, 50.

103. Wilentz, *Chants Democratic*, 373, 377.

104. Degler, "Labor in the Economy," 14, 15, 16, 18.

105. Johnson, *A Shopkeeper's Millennium*, 74.

106. Amy Bridges, *A City in the Republic: Antebellum New York and the Origins of Machine Politics* (New York: Cambridge University Press, 1984), 115. See also Ryan, *Civic Wars*, 308.

107. Bridges, *A City in the Republic*, 116.

108. Ibid., 123.

109. Ibid.

110. Jaher, *Urban Establishment*, 54.

111. Amy Bridges, "Another Look at Plutocracy in Antebellum New York City," *Political Science Quarterly* 97 (1982), 62; Gabriel A. Almond, *Plutocracy and Politics in New York City* (Boulder: Westview Press, 1998), 59–70.

112. Anthony Boleslaw Gronowicz, "Revising the Concept of Jacksonian Democracy" (Ph.D. diss., University of Pennsylvania, 1981), 49.

113. Townsend, *Mother of Clubs*, 136.

114. *American Merchant* 2 (November 1858), 35.

115. See, for example, Charles F. Hoffman, *The Pioneers of New-York: An Anniversary Discourse Delivered before the St. Nicholas Society of Manhattan, December 6, 1847* (New York: Stanford and Swors, 1848), 14.

116. Abraham Oakey Hall, *Anniversary Address before the American Institute, at Palace Garden, October 29, 1859* (New York, 1859), 24.

117. *Transactions of the American Institute of the City of New-York for the Year 1857* (Albany: C. Van Benthuysen, 1858), 44; Hall, *Anniversary Address before the American Institute*, 24–27.

118. Wilentz, *Chants Democratic*, 17.

119. *Transactions of the American Institute of the City of New-York for the Year 1856* (Albany: C. Van Benthuysen, 1857), 29, 37.

120. *New York Weekly Tribune,* May 2, 1846, 3.

121. On the Compromise of 1850, see *New York Commercial Advertiser,* June 13, 1850, 1f; October 24, 1850, 2.

122. *Journal of Commerce (JoC),* November 1, 1860, 2.

123. Among many others, see letters by A. A. Belknap, Hiram Ketchum, Robert Wetmore, and J. DePeyster Ogden to Beekman, all February 1851, Political Correspondence, Misc. Mss. Beekman, Box 25, James Beekman Papers, New-York Historical Society.

124. See *JoC,* October 24, 1850, 2.

125. Ibid.

126. Philip Sheldon Foner, *Business and Slavery: The New York Merchants and the Irrepressible Conflict* (Chapel Hill: University of North Carolina Press, 1941), 74–78, 84–86.

127. *JoC,* November 6, 1860.

128. See, for example, "August Belmont," in *Encyclopedia of American Business History and Biography: Banking and Finance to 1913,* ed. Larry Schweikart (New York: Facts on File, 1990), 40.

129. *Hunt's Merchants' Magazine and Commercial Review* 32 (1855), 264, quoting the *Richmond (Virginia) Dispatch.* See also *Hunt's Merchants' Magazine and Commercial Review* 28 (1853), 326–327; 39 (1858), 523; 41 (1859), 129–130. See also Thomas P. Kettell, *Eighty Years' Progress of the United States* (New York: L. Stebbins, 1864), 119–121.

130. Kettell, *Eighty Years' Progress of the United States,* 122.

131. Thomas P. Kettell, *On Southern Wealth and Northern Profits, as Exhibited in Statistical Facts and Officials Figures: Showing the Necessity of Union to the Future Prosperity and Welfare of the Republic* (New York: George W. & John A. Wood, 1860), 3, 19, 34, 60, 172, 173.

132. Ibid., 98.

133. Ibid., 30.

134. Ibid., 10.

135. Iver Bernstein, *The New York City Draft Riots: Their Significance for American Society and Politics in the Age of the Civil War* (New York: Oxford University Press, 1990), 133–134.

136. Ibid., 133.

137. *JoC,* November 5, 1860.

138. Gilkeson, *Middle-Class Providence,* 39.

139. Jaher, *Urban Establishment,* 55.

140. Ibid.; Farrell, *Elite Families,* 32.

141. *JoC*, July 2, 1850, 2.

142. Chamber of Commerce, *Proceedings of the Chamber of Commerce of the State of New York at the Opening of Their New Rooms, June 10, 1858* (New York: John A. Douglas, 1858), 11.

143. See, for example, *JoC*, June 18, 1860, 3; July 4, 1850, 2.

144. *Hunt's Merchants' Magazine and Commercial Review* 40 (1859), 519; 41 (1859), 129–130.

145. For Boston, see Richard Abbott, *Cotton & Capital: Boston Businessmen and Antislavery Reform, 1854–1868* (Amherst: University of Massachusetts Press, 1991), 4.

146. Jaher, *Urban Establishment*, 56.

147. See *JoC*, July 4, 1850, 2; John Ashworth, *Slavery, Capitalism, and Politics in the Antebellum Republic*, vol. 1, *Commerce and Compromise*, 1820–1860 (New York: Cambridge University Press, 1995), 125–191.

148. *New-York Daily Tribune*, May 31, 1856, 8; June 11, 1850, 4.

149. Gilkeson, *Middle-Class Providence*, 40.

150. Ibid., 44.

151. Horace Greeley, *Recollections of a Busy Life, Including Reminiscences of American Politics and Politicians, from the Opening of the Missouri Contest to the Downfall of Slavery* (New York: J. Ford and Company, 1868), 31, 354, 397; James Livingston, *Pragmatism and the Political Economy of Cultural Revolution, 1850–1940* (Chapel Hill: University of North Carolina Press, 1994), 25–35.

152. *New-York Daily Tribune*, November 7, 1857, 2.

153. Cited in Edward Mack, *Peter Cooper: Citizen of New York* (New York: Duell, Sloan and Pearce, 1949), 191.

154. George Opdyke, *Treatise on Political Economy* (New York: G. P. Putnam, 1851), 327, 330, 331.

155. *Schenectady Democrat*, April 29, 1856; G. Tucker to Isaac Sherman, Albany, February 28, 1859, Isaac Sherman Papers, Huntington Library, Pasadena, Calif.; Isaac Sherman to Thurlow Weed, Champlain Arsenal, Vermont, March 22, 1861, copy in Isaac Sherman Papers, original in Rochester University Library.

156. *Transactions of the American Institute of the City of New-York for the Year 1850* (Albany: L. Van Benthuysen, 1851), 7; *Transactions of the American Institute of the City of New-York for the Year 1856*, 7–8.

157. *Transactions of the American Institute of the City of New-York for the Year 1850*, 9; *Transactions of the American Institute of the City of New-York for the Year 1851* (Albany: C. Van Benthuysen, 1852), 11.

158. Beckert, *Monied Metropolis*, 95.

159. The importance of this split to weakening elite political power is discussed in Beckert, *Monied Metropolis*, 78; Jaher, *Urban Establishment*, 56.

160. For that history, see Beckert, *The Monied Metropolis*, chaps. 5–10.

4. Gilded Age Gospels

1. Henry Adams, *Democracy: An American Novel* (New York: Modern Library, 2003), 1, 6, 8–9.

2. On this point, my interpretation is at odds with historians who, with Lee Benson and Gabriel Kolko, argue that the Gilded Age businessmen actively sought government regulation as a solution to internal structural problems. It is my argument that the businessmen's entry into the political sphere was defensive and reactive, not offensive and voluntary. For discussions of this literature, see Elizabeth Sanders, *Roots of Reform: Farmers, Workers, and the American State, 1877–1917* (Chicago: University of Chicago Press, 1999), 179–181, and Stephen Skowronek, *Building a New American State: The Expansion of National Administrative Capacities, 1877–1920* (New York: Cambridge University Press, 1982), 125–131. For the best one-volume survey of Gilded Age political economy, see Richard Franklin Bensel, *The Political Economy of American Industrialization, 1877–1900* (New York: Cambridge University Press, 2000).

3. The one obvious exception being, of course, the western silver interests.

4. *New York Times*, October 29, 1882, 8.

5. Reprinted in *New York Times*, November 19, 1882, 5.

6. See Daniel T. Rodgers, *The Work Ethic in Industrial America, 1850–1920* (Chicago: University of Chicago Press, 1978), 210–220.

7. This is not to say that others did not do this job for them. Throughout the Gilded Age, there was a profusion of hagiographic portraits and success manuals which proclaimed that the wealth of the new millionaires was founded entirely on their inner virtues, most specifically their diligence, perseverance, discipline, chastity, temperance, and hard, hard work. See, for example, Judy Hilkey, *Character Is Capital: Success Manuals and Manhood in Gilded Age America* (Chapel Hill: University of North Carolina Press, 1997).

8. Jay Gould testimony, United States Congress, Senate, Committee on Education and Labor, *Report upon the Relations between Labor and Capital* (Washington, D.C.: Government Printing Office, 1885), 1088.

9. Though he did not name names, it was clear that the railroad millionaires were the Vanderbilts, that he himself was the model for the iron and steel magnate, Philip Armour or Gustavus Swift the meatpacking king, and William A. Clark the Montana miner.

10. Andrew Carnegie, "Wealth" (1906), in *Problems of To-day: Wealth, Labor, Socialism* (Garden City, N.Y.: Doubleday, Doran, 1908), 13, 17–21.

11. Ibid., 2–3.

12. Ron Chernow, *Titan: The Life of John D. Rockefeller, Sr.* (New York: Random House, 1998), 54–57.

13. Andrew Carnegie, "[Gospel of] Wealth," *North American Review* (June 1889), in *The Andrew Carnegie Reader*, ed. Joseph Frazier Wall (Pittsburgh: University of Pittsburgh Press, 1992), 132–133. The article was originally titled "Wealth"; it was retitled "The Gospel of Wealth" when reprinted in an English edition. Carnegie adopted the latter title.

14. Ibid., 138.

15. Although Irwin Wyllie (*The Self-Made Man in America* [New York: Free Press, 1954], 86–87) claimed that few, if any, Gilded Age businessmen had read or learned anything from Darwin or Spencer, and Robert C. Bannister went a step further to argue that there was, in fact, "no school (or schools) of social Darwinists" in America or anywhere else, and that the term had been invented by its enemies as an epithet or label to "caricature the 'let-alone-philosophy' (as it was termed)" (*Social Darwinism* [Philadelphia: Temple University Press, 1970], xi), neither critic managed to dislodge the social Darwinist ideological edifice from its scholarly pedestal. I have no intention of entering into the larger debate on social Darwinism other than to commend Richard Hofstadter's brilliant exercise in intellectual and cultural history (*Social Darwinism in American Thought* [Boston: Beacon Press, 1955]). Even though he was unable to draw direct lines between individual businessman and social Darwinism, or indeed to meld its multiple doctrines into a coherent theory, he demonstrated forcibly how these doctrines "were used to buttress the conservative outlook" (5–6).

16. Henry Adams, *The Education of Henry Adams: An Autobiography* (Boston: Houghton Mifflin, 1918), 232.

17. Andrew Carnegie, *Autobiography of Andrew Carnegie* (Boston: Northeastern University Press, 1986), 327.

18. Hofstadter, *Social Darwinism*, 33.

19. Adams, *Democracy*, 1.

20. See, on this gathering, *Herbert Spencer on the Americans and the Americans on Herbert Spencer*, comp. Edward L. Youmans (New York: Appleton, 1883).

21. J. D. Y. Peel, *Herbert Spencer: The Evolution of a Sociologist* (New York: Basic Books, 1971), 100.

22. Herbert Spencer, *Social Statics, or The Conditions Essential to Human Happiness* (London: John Chapman, 1851), 42.

23. Ibid., 45.

24. Ibid., 42, 65, 332–333.

25. Ibid., 324–325.

26. John D. Rockefeller, *Random Reminiscences of Men and Events* (New York: Doubleday, Page, 1909), 90–91.

27. Gould testimony, 1081.

28. See Edward Kirkland, *Business in the Gilded Age* (Madison: University of Wisconsin Press, 1951), 45–48.

29. Andrew Carnegie, "The Road to Business Success: A Talk to Young Men" (1885), in *The Empire of Business* (Garden City, N.Y.: Doubleday, Page, 1913), 7.

30. Rockefeller, *Random Reminiscences*, 65.

31. Gould testimony, 1089.

32. Ibid., 1090. It is striking how similar Gould's formulation was to Spencer's. While Spencer was unalterably opposed to trades unions whose only raison d'être was raising the wages of their members—and thereby upsetting the economic laws that governed wage rates—he refused to condemn worker combinations out of hand. They were, he conceded, quite primitive forms of social organization, but they occasionally performed a positive social role. By encouraging laborers to cooperate with one another, they prepared them "for such higher forms of social organization as will probably hereafter arise." Herbert Spencer, *The Principles of Sociology,* vol. 3 (New York: D. Appleton, 1896), 551–552.

33. Andrew Carnegie, "An Employer's View of the Labor Question," *Forum* (April 1886), in *The Gospel of Wealth and Other Timely Essays* (Cambridge, Mass.: Harvard University Press, 1965), 98.

34. Andrew Carnegie, "Results of the Labor Struggle," *Forum* (August 1886), ibid., 109, 111.

35. Ibid., 119–120.

36. Thomas A. Scott, "The Recent Strikes," *North American Review* 125 (September 1877), 360–361.

37. Sven Beckert, *The Monied Metropolis: New York City and the Consolidation of the American Bourgeoisie, 1850–1896* (New York: Cambridge University Press, 2001), 235.

38. Leon Fink, *Workingmen's Democracy: The Knights of Labor and American Politics* (Urbana: University of Illinois Press, 1983), 26–27.

39. Gould testimony, 1075.

40. Gerald Berk, *Alternative Tracks: The Constitution of American Industrial Order, 1865–1917* (Baltimore: Johns Hopkins University Press, 1994), 85.

41. Chauncey Depew, *My Memories of Eighty Years* (New York: Charles Scribner's Sons, 1922), 242–243.

42. Thomas K. McCraw, *Prophets of Regulation: Charles Francis Adams, Louis*

D. Brandeis, James M. Landis, Alfred E. Kahn (Cambridge, Mass.: Harvard University Press, 1984), 67.

43. Andrew Carnegie, "Pennsylvania's Industrial and Railroad Policy" (1889), in *Miscellaneous Writings*, ed. Burton Hendrick, vol. 1 (Garden City, N.Y.: Doubleday, Doran, 1933), 297.

44. Chernow, *Titan*, 292.

45. Beckert, *The Monied Metropolis*, 305–307.

46. Gretchen Ritter, *Goldbugs and Greenbacks: The Antimonopoly Tradition and the Politics of Finance in America, 1865–1896* (New York: Cambridge University Press, 1997), 162.

47. Cited ibid., 79.

48. Richard Hofstadter, *The Age of Reform* (New York: Vintage Books, 1955), 104.

49. Jean Strouse, *Morgan: American Financier* (New York: Random House, 1999), 305.

50. Andrew Carnegie, "The ABC of Money," *North American Review* (June 1891), in *Andrew Carnegie Reader*, 256.

51. Andrew Carnegie, "Popular Illusions about Trusts," *Century Magazine* (May 1900), in *The Gospel of Wealth*, 81, 83.

52. James Livingston, *Origins of the Federal Reserve System: Money, Class, and Corporate Capitalism, 1890–1913* (Ithaca: Cornell University Press, 1986), 55.

53. Ibid., 66.

54. William J. Bryan, "Cross of Gold" speech, in *Documents of American History*, ed. Henry Steele Commager, 6th ed., vol. 2 (New York: Appleton-Century-Crofts, 1958), 176.

55. Ibid., 178–179.

56. Strouse, *Morgan*, 355; Chernow, *Titan*, 388; Mark Hanna to Andrew Carnegie, October 17, 1896, vol. 39, Andrew Carnegie Papers, Manuscript Division, Library of Congress, Washington, D.C.

57. Livingston, *Origins of the Federal Reserve System*, 81–106.

5. The Abortive Rule of Big Money

1. The debate appears to have occurred at a distance in a literary exchange that began with lines from a Fitzgerald short story, "The Rich Boy" (1926), and continued with Hemingway's account of a 1936 conversation in which "someone" had said to Fitzgerald, "Yes, they have more money." It is reported in Matthew J. Bruccoli, *Scott and Ernest* (New York: Random House, 1978), 754n3.

2. If we follow change over time in social relations, then class "happens" in

different ways at different times depending on changing historical circumstances. See Edward Thompson, *The Making of the English Working Class* (London: V. Gollancz, 1963), 9. For that reason, historians have much to contribute to understanding the role of the upper classes in American history. Unfortunately, until very recently they have shied away from studying "the few," looking instead at the working-class "many," the broad middle classes, or the mass mentalities of gender and race. Among the relatively few historical studies of "the few," see Sven Beckert, *The Monied Metropolis: New York City and the Consolidation of the American Bourgeoisie, 1850–1896* (New York: Cambridge University Press, 2001); Frederic Cople Jaher, *The Urban Establishment: Upper Strata in Boston, New York, Charleston, Chicago, and Los Angeles* (Urbana: University of Illinois Press, 1982); Ronald Story, *The Forging of an Aristocracy: Harvard and the Boston Upper Class, 1800–1870* (Middletown, Conn.: Wesleyan University Press, 1980); John Ingham, *The Iron Barons: A Social Analysis of an American Urban Elite, 1874–1965* (Westport, Conn.: Greenwood Press, 1978). While group portraits of the upper class are relatively rare, biographies of prominent figures and their golden dynasties are abundant. See, for examples, Ron Chernow, *The House of Morgan: An American Banking Dynasty and the Rise of Modern Finance* (New York: Atlantic Monthly Press, 1990), and *Titan: The Life of John D. Rockefeller, Sr.* (New York: Random House, 1998); Clarice Stasz, *The Rockefeller Women: Dynasty of Piety, Privacy, and Service* (New York: St. Martin's Press, 1995).

3. There is surprisingly little work on the American upper class as a group and its relation to power. In a society that is arguably more bound up with the capitalist market than any other, the beginning of wisdom in any definition of class starts with material conditions, as expressed in terms such as "capitalist class" or "business class." The nineteenth-century "bourgeoisie," for example, is defined in Beckert, *Monied Metropolis*, 6, as a group whose power is derived "from the ownership of capital rather than birthright, status, or kinship." On the "business class," see Robert Lynd and Helen Lynd, *Middletown: A Study in Modern American Culture* (New York: Harcourt, Brace and Co., 1929). One reason why class is a useful category is that it draws connections between material conditions and other spheres of life. For a working definition, we can say that class pertains to both vertical relations of dominance and subordination and horizontal solidarities of interest and affinity as these take shape around the intertwining relations of property, family, and the state. In Marxist renderings, these relations always involve the exploitation of the laboring many by the propertied few, with an older emphasis on economic factors and a more recent emphasis on cultural modes of domination. Compare, for example, two influential works, Paul Baran and Paul Sweezy, *Mo-*

nopoly Capital: An Essay on the American Economic and Social Order (New York: Monthly Review Press, 1966), and Pierre Bourdieu, *Distinction: A Social Critique of the Judgement of Taste*, trans. Richard Nice (Cambridge, Mass.: Harvard University Press, 1984). In liberal sociology, the study of stratification by wealth or income preserves the economic connection without the connotation of exploitation. A founding text for the liberal idea of class as "the different and unequal faculties of acquiring property" is James Madison, "Number 10" (1787), in *The Federalist* (New York, 1937), 55. In conservative approaches, by comparison, class inequality becomes a positive good. Conservative champions of the virtues of inequality range from Alexis de Tocqueville and William Graham Sumner to E. Digby Baltzell, *Philadelphia Gentlemen: The Making of a National Upper Class* (Glencoe, Ill.: Free Press, 1958).

4. For thoughtful comments on the debilitating effects of American exceptionalism in American scholarship, see Ian Tyrrell, *The Absent Marx: Class Analysis and Liberal History in Twentieth-Century America* (Westport, Conn.: Greenwood Press, 1986); Dorothy Ross, *The Origins of American Social Science* (New York: Cambridge University Press, 1991).

5. Dwight Moody, *The Truth about the Trusts* (New York: Moody Publishing Company, 1904), defended concentrated wealth against populist and other critics of "monopoly"; Alfred Chandler, *The Visible Hand: The Managerial Revolution in American Business* (Cambridge, Mass.: Belknap Press of Harvard University Press, 1977), offered the classic account of oligopoly; Michael Piore and Charles Sabel, *The Second Industrial Divide: Possibilities for Prosperity* (New York: Basic Books, 1984), began a reconsideration of the inevitability of oligopoly, which has more recently been furthered by Naomi Lamoreaux, Daniel Raff, and Peter Temin, "Beyond Markets and Hierarchies: Toward a New Synthesis of American Business History," *American Historical Review*, 108 (April 2003), 404–433.

6. Raymond Fosdick, *Chronicle of a Generation: An Autobiography* (New York: Harper & Bros., 1958).

7. The pioneering work on the separation of ownership and control was Adolf A. Berle and Gardiner C. Means, *The Modern Corporation and Private Property* (1932; New York: Macmillan, 1948). The idea of a managerial revolution was first broached by James Burnham, *The Managerial Revolution: What Is Happening in the World* (New York: John Day Company, 1941); it was accepted by John Kenneth Galbraith, *The New Industrial State* (Boston: Houghton Mifflin, 1967). The subtitle of Chandler, *The Visible Hand*, is *The Managerial Revolution in American Business*.

8. Investigations from the bottom up have produced a more jaundiced view

of "scientific management." See, for examples, Ira Katznelson and Aristide Zolberg, *Working-Class Formation: Nineteenth-Century Patterns in Western Europe and the United States* (Princeton: Princeton University Press, 1986); David Gordon, Richard Edwards, and Michael Reich, *Segmented Work, Divided Workers: The Historical Transformation of Labor in the United States* (New York: Cambridge University Press, 1982); Susan Porter Benson, *Counter Cultures: Saleswomen, Managers, and Customers in American Department Stores, 1890–1940* (Urbana: University of Illinois Press, 1986); Harry Braverman, *Labor and Monopoly Capital: The Degradation of Work in the Twentieth Century* (New York: Monthly Review Press, 1974).

9. The complexity of a given social formation requires other ways of apprehending inequality as well, and so we find other terms in the tool kit of twentieth-century social science. These include "race" and "caste": Oliver Cromwell Cox, *Caste, Class, and Race: A Study in Social Dynamics* (Garden City, N.Y.: Doubleday & Company, 1948); "establishment": E. Digby Baltzell, *The Protestant Establishment: Aristocracy and Caste in America* (New Haven: Yale University Press, 1964), 7–8, which contains a useful distinction between elite, upper class, and "establishment" (or ruling class); in addition, Baltzell, *Philadelphia Gentlemen*, introduced the term "business aristocracy" to connote an economic group that also provides social and political leadership; and "elite": C. Wright Mills, *The Power Elite* (New York: Oxford University Press, 1956), which examines the iron triangle of corporate, military, and presidential power. G. William Domhoff, *Who Rules America* (Englewood Cliffs, N.J.: Prentice-Hall, 1967), 1–11, attempts to synthesize Baltzell's upper class and Mills's power elite in his analysis of the American "governing class."

10. The distinction follows Baltzell, *Protestant Establishment*, 7–8; Baltzell also identifies members of the upper class by the overlap of names between *Who's Who* and *The Social Register*.

11. Works that have emphasized the "financialization" of capitalism in this period include Kevin Phillips, *Wealth and Democracy: A Political History of the American Rich* (New York: Broadway Books, 2002); Giovanni Arrighi, *The Long Twentieth Century: Money, Power, and the Origins of Our Times* (London: Verso, 1994). Others subsume finance under the general trend toward corporate concentration; see Martin Sklar, *The Corporate Reconstruction of American Capitalism* (New York: Cambridge University Press, 1988).

12. Moody, *Truth about the Trusts;* Louis Brandeis, *Other People's Money and How the Bankers Use It* (1914; New York: Harper & Row, 1967).

13. Quote from Thomas Lamont, *Across World Frontiers* (New York: Harcourt,

Brace, 1951), 39; John Garraty, *Right Hand Man: The Life of George W. Perkins* (New York: Harper 1960), 211–215; Chernow, *House of Morgan*, 122–130; Lester Chandler, *Benjamin Strong: Central Banker* (Washington, D.C.: Brookings Institution, 1958), 29. Several of the biggest names in finance over the next generation were present for the late-night meeting at the Morgan library, including Morgan associates George Perkins, Thomas Lamont, and Benjamin Strong, as well as James Stillman of National City Bank (forerunner of CityCorp) and George Baker of First National Bank.

14. Dixon Wecter, *The Saga of American Society: A Record of Social Aspiration, 1607–1937* (New York: C. Scribner's Sons, 1937), 6. See also Cleveland Amory, *Who Killed Society?* (New York: Harper, 1960).

15. Chandler, *Benjamin Strong*, 24–30.

16. Wecter, *Saga*, 6.

17. John H. Glenn et al., *Russell Sage Foundation, 1907–1946* (New York: Russell Sage Foundation, 1947); Raymond Fosdick, *The Story of the Rockefeller Foundation* (New York: Harper, 1952); E. Richard Brown, *Rockefeller Medicine Men* (Berkeley: University of California Press, 1979).

18. Wecter, *Saga*, 6; Lamont, *Across World Frontiers*, 37. See also Stasz, *Rockefeller Women*.

19. Quoted in Amory, *Who Killed Society?* 80. See also Nelson Aldrich, *Old Money: The Mythology of America's Upper Class* (New York: Knopf, 1988).

20. Aldrich, *Old Money*, 275; Baltzell, *Protestant Establishment*, was written, in part, to alert members of the upper class to the inevitable disappearance of any resolutely Protestant Establishment in a society with successful Catholics and Jews.

21. Walter Dean Burnham, *Critical Elections and the Mainsprings of American Politics* (New York: Norton, 1970).

22. On the transition from laissez-faire liberalism to something new, see Stephen Skowronek, *Building a New American State* (New York: Cambridge University Press, 1982); Alan Dawley, *Struggles for Justice: Social Responsibility and the Liberal State* (Cambridge, Mass.: Belknap Press of Harvard University Press, 1991).

23. *World's Work*, 1, no. 1 (November 1900), 1, 4.

24. See Joseph Smith, *The Spanish American War: Conflict in the Caribbean and the Pacific, 1895–1902* (New York: Longman, 1994); David Traxel, *1898: The Birth of the American Century* (New York: Knopf, 1998); Ivan Musicant, *Empire by Default: The Spanish-American War and the Dawn of the American Century* (New York: Henry Holt, 1998); Max Boot, *The Savage Wars of Peace: Small Wars and*

the Rise of American Power (New York: Basic Books, 2002); Kristin Hoganson, *Fighting for American Manhood: How Gender Politics Provoked the Spanish-American and Philippine-American Wars* (New Haven: Yale University Press, 1998).

25. Gail Bederman, *Manliness and Civilization: A Cultural History of Gender and Race in the United State, 1880–1917* (Chicago: University of Chicago Press, 1995).

26. *World's Work,* 1, no. 1 (November 1900), 1; William Howard Taft to Elihu Root, August 18, 1900, ser. 21, 2:131, William Howard Taft Papers, Library of Congress, Washington, D.C.; Robert Rydell, *All the World's a Fair: Visions of Empire at American International Expositions, 1876–1916* (Chicago: University of Chicago Press, 1984).

27. In the "world systems" approach of Immanuel Wallerstein, the stress is on the role of the United States as the global hegemon in maintaining the unequal relation between the world's developed core and underdeveloped periphery. By shifting the axis of class conflict to the transnational plane of core and periphery, the "world systems" concept tends to reduce internal conflicts to secondary importance. See Immanuel Wallerstein, ed., *World Inequality: Origins and Perspectives on the World System* (Montreal: Black Rose Books, 1975), and *The Capitalist World-Economy: Essays* (New York: Cambridge University Press, 1979). In the same vein, see Thomas McCormick, *America's Half Century: United States Foreign Policy in the Cold War* (Baltimore: Johns Hopkins University Press, 1989). Other Marxist analysis, following Lenin, presents imperialism as the outgrowth of the system of monopoly capitalism rather than the result of the specific aims and interests of the bourgeoisie. See Harry Magdoff, *The Age of Imperialism: The Economics of U.S. Foreign Policy* (New York: Monthly Review Press, 1969).

28. The Wisconsin school of historians explains overseas expansion in terms of an effort to resolve (or escape) the internal problems of American society by pushing them out to the frontier, with tragic consequences at home and abroad. William A. Williams, *The Tragedy of American Diplomacy* (Cleveland: World Publishing Company, 1959); Lloyd Gardner, Walter LaFeber, and Thomas McCormick, *Creation of the American Empire* (Chicago: Rand McNally, 1973); Walter LaFeber, *The New Empire: An Interpretation of American Expansion, 1860–1898* (Ithaca, N.Y.: Cornell University Press, 1963). Instead of emphasizing upper-class leadership, the Wisconsin school often stresses systemic causation and popular consensus around empire; see especially William A. Williams, *The Roots of the Modern American Empire: A Study of the Growth and Shaping of Social Consciousness in a Marketplace Society* (New York: Random House, 1969). Charles Berquist, *Labor and the Course of American Democracy: U.S. History in Latin Amer-*

ican Perspective (New York: Verso, 1996), offers a sophisticated view of the incorporation of American labor in imperial expansion.

29. Cesar Ayala, *The American Sugar Kingdom: The Plantation Economy of the Spanish Caribbean, 1898–1934* (Chapel Hill: University of North Carolina Press, 1999), 75, 87, 95.

30. Taft to Root, August 18, 1900.

31. Quoted in Aldrich, *Old Money*, 36.

32. Louis Brandeis, *Other People's Money and How the Bankers Use It* (1914; New York: Harper & Row, 1967), 12.

33. Twain quoted in Phillips, *Wealth and Democracy*, 240.

34. Quoted in John Milton Cooper, *The Warrior and the Priest: Woodrow Wilson and Theodore Roosevelt* (Cambridge, Mass.: Belknap Press of Harvard University Press, 1983), 116.

35. Paul Reinsch, *World Politics at the End of the Nineteenth Century* (1900; New York: Macmillan, 1972), 354.

36. Alan Dawley, *Changing the World: American Progressives in War and Revolution* (Princeton: Princeton University Press, 2003).

37. W. E. B. Du Bois, *The Souls of Black Folk* (1903; New York: Knopf, 1993), 16.

38. Quoted in Harvey O'Connor, *Mellon's Millions: The Biography of a Fortune* (New York: John Day Company, 1933), 113.

39. Michael Conniff, *Black Labor on a White Canal: Panama, 1904–1981* (Pittsburgh: University of Pittsburgh Press, 1985).

40. Similar consequences were played out in slow motion in the Chinese Revolution, 1911–1949. Americans such as Paul Reinsch saw labor as a key to Chinese development. "They have cheap and abundant labor,—the best, the most reliable, and the most frugal in the Orient," observed Reinsch. Given, in addition, China's huge population and rich natural resources, "there is little room for doubt that, when the industrial forces of this region have once been set in motion, China will in truth become 'the realm of the center.'" If America was not to be left behind, it was essential that the door for trade and investment be kept as wide open as possible. See Reinsch, *World Politics*, 248.

41. Pell quoted in Aldrich, *Old Money*, 272; Lodge and Bonaparte quoted in Amory, *Who Killed Society?* 23, 21.

42. O'Connor, *Mellon's Millions*, 113.

43. Charlotte Perkins Gilman, *Women and Economics* (Boston: Small, Maynard & Company, 1898); Thorstein Veblen, *The Theory of the Leisure Class* (New York: Macmillan, 1899).

44. Fernando Fasce, *An American Family: The Great War and Corporate Culture in America,* trans. Ian Harvey (Columbus: Ohio State University Press, 2002).

45. Quoted in Cooper, *The Warrior and the Priest,* 113; Garraty, *Right Hand Man,* deals with Perkins's career.

46. Quote from *www.san.beck.org/WP20-LeagueofNations.html,* September 18, 2003.

47. See James Livingston, *Origins of the Federal Reserve System: Money, Class, and Corporate Capitalism, 1890–1913* (Ithaca: Cornell University Press, 1986); Arthur Link, *Woodrow Wilson and the Progressive Era* (New York: Harper, 1954), 44–53.

48. Sklar, *Corporate Reconstruction of American Capitalism,* is indispensable for understanding the changing relationship between business and government, although the interpretation there differs from the one presented here.

49. Chernow, *House of Morgan,* 188, 200, 617, 618, 627.

50. See David Montgomery, *The Fall of the House of Labor: The Workplace, the State, and American Labor Activism, 1865–1925* (New York: Cambridge University Press, 1987).

51. See Gary Gerstle, *American Crucible: Race and Nation in the Twentieth Century* (Princeton: Princeton University Press, 2001).

52. The overlap of class and ethnic consciousness has long been a staple of social history; for a founding text, see Herbert Gutman, *Work, Culture, and Society in Industrializing America* (New York: Knopf, 1976).

53. Aldrich, *Old Money,* 275; and see Baltzell, *Protestant Establishment.*

54. Berle and Means, *The Modern Corporation and Private Property,* 1, 356.

55. Abundant documentation on the Special Conference Committee can be found in the DuPont Company Records, Presidential Papers, Acc. 1662, Hagley Library, Wilmington, Del.

56. Quoted in Chandler, *Benjamin Strong,* 265. In the end, despite worry about Americans being seen as Shylocks, Strong decided that debts were sacred obligations and outright forgiveness "is not to be contemplated"; Strong to Russell Leffingwell, U.S. Undersecretary of the Treasury, July 25, 1919, quoted in Andrew Boyle, *Montague Norman: A Biography* (London: Cassell, 1967), 151. There is a large literature on the U.S. role in recasting bourgeois Europe in the 1920s. A fresh insight is found in Emily Rosenberg, *Financial Missionaries to the World: The Politics and Culture of Dollar Diplomacy, 1900–1930* (Cambridge, Mass.: Harvard University Press, 1999). See also Carl Parrini, *Heir to Empire: U.S. Economic Diplomacy, 1916–1923* (Pittsburgh: University of Pittsburgh Press, 1969); William C.

McNeil, *American Money and the Weimar Republic: Economics and Politics on the Eve of the Great Depression* (New York: Columbia University Press, 1986); Charles Maier, *Recasting Bourgeois Europe: Stabilization in France, Germany, and Italy in the Decade after World War I* (Princeton: Princeton University Press, 1975); Frank Costiglia, *Awkward Dominion: American Political, Economic, and Cultural Relations with Europe, 1919–1933* (Ithaca: Cornell University Press, 1984); Michael Hogan, *Informal Entente: The Private Structure of Cooperation in Anglo-American Economic Diplomacy, 1918–1929* (Columbia: University of Missouri Press, 1977); Mary Nolan, *Visions of Modernity* (New York: Oxford University Press, 1994).

57. Kees van der Pijl, *The Making of an Atlantic Ruling Class* (London: Verso, 1984).

58. *Vanity Fair*, January 1930, 15; October 1929, 114. Another example from the October 1929 issue: "Why not spend the holidays in North Africa, the latest playground of the international set?" (40). For theoretical discussion, see Edward Said, *Orientalism* (New York: Pantheon Books, 1978); Mary Helms, *Ulysses' Sail: An Ethnographic Odyssey of Power, Knowledge, and Geographical Distance* (Princeton: Princeton University Press, 1988); Mary Helms, *Craft and the Kingly Ideal: Art, Trade, and Power* (Austin: University of Texas Press, 1993) .

59. *New York Times*, October 25, 1929, 38. From the same source: "Mr. and Mrs. Harvey M. Hall and the members of their family, who returned recently from Europe, have left their country place in New Canaan, Conn., and are at 885 Park Avenue for the winter."

60. Quoted in David Kennedy, *Freedom from Fear: The American People in Depression and War, 1929–1945* (New York: Oxford University Press, 1999), 53.

61. Ibid., 82.

62. Stuart Brandes, *American Welfare Capitalism* (Chicago: University of Chicago Press, 1976), 84, 141–142; Sanford Jacoby, *Employing Bureaucracy: Managers, Unions, and the Transformation of Work in American Industry, 1900–1945* (New York: Columbia University Press, 1985), 196–199.

63. Ferdinand Lundberg, *America's Sixty Families* (New York: Vanguard Press, 1937), xv, xvii; Lippmann quoted in Aldrich, *Old Money*, 36.

64. Charles Beard, *The Open Door at Home* (New York: Macmillan, 1934), 302, 303. See also Charles Beard, *A Foreign Policy for America* (New York: Knopf, 1940). Beard was not the only "progressive" historian to draw the connection between domestic and foreign affairs; Carl Becker characterized the American Revolution as a two-sided struggle over "home rule and who should rule at

home." Although Frederick Jackson Turner paid little attention to foreign policy per se, his vision of the frontier centered on the adaptation of European traditions to American conditions. For a pro-empire use of Beard's ideas, see Andrew Bacevich, *American Empire: The Realities and Consequences of U.S. Diplomacy* (Cambridge, Mass.: Harvard University Press, 2002).

6. The Managerial Revitalization of the Rich

1. Thorstein Veblen, *The Theory of the Leisure Class* (New York: Macmillan, 1899), and "The Discipline of the Machine" (1904), reprinted in *The Portable Veblen*, ed. Max Lerner (New York: Viking Press, 1948), 335–348; James Burnham, *The Managerial Revolution* (New York: John Day Company, 1941). The classic text on the separation of ownership and control is Adolf A. Berle and Gardiner C. Means, *The Modern Corporation and Private Property* (1932; New York: Macmillan, 1948). No one could read more than a few paragraphs of this chapter without recognizing my debt to Christopher Lasch's seminal essay "The Moral and Intellectual Rehabilitation of the Ruling Class," in *The World of Nations* (New York: Knopf, 1973), 80–91.

2. Charles Ponce de Leon, *Self-Exposure: Human-Interest Journalism and the Emergence of Celebrity in America, 1890–1940* (Chapel Hill: University of North Carolina Press, 2002), 159; Peter W. Cookson and Caroline Hodges Pursell, *Preparing for Power: America's Elite Boarding Schools* (New York: Basic Books, 1985), 13, 14, 17, 114, 125, 130, 204; James McLachlan, *American Boarding Schools: A Historical Study* (New York: Scribner, 1970), chap. 9.

3. On the revitalization of class hegemony, see T. J. Jackson Lears, *No Place of Grace: Antimodernism and the Transformation of American Culture, 1880–1920* (New York: Pantheon Books, 1981), esp. chap. 3. On Jewish quotas at Harvard, see Kim Townsend, *Manhood at Harvard: William James and Others* (Cambridge, Mass.: Harvard University Press, 1998), 282; and on Ivy admissions more generally, see Marcia Graham Synnott, *The Half-Opened Door: Discrimination and Admissions at Harvard, Yale, and Princeton* (Westport: Greenwood Press, 1979).

4. I discuss this imagery at length in *Fables of Abundance: A Cultural History of Advertising in America* (New York: Basic Books, 1994), esp. chaps. 6, 7.

5. Henry Demarest Lloyd, *Wealth against Commonwealth* (New York: Harper & Brothers, 1894); Ida Tarbell, *The History of the Standard Oil Company* (New York: McClure, Phillips & Co., 1904–5); Ron Chernow, *Titan: The Life of John D. Rockefeller, Sr.* (New York: Random House, 1998), 112–165, 438–439; Daniel T.

Rodgers, *Atlantic Crossings: Social Politics in a Progressive Age* (Cambridge, Mass.: Belknap Press of Harvard University Press, 1998). See also the classic essays collected by Herbert Gutman in *Work, Culture, and Society in Industrializing America* (New York: Knopf, 1976).

6. Lears, *No Place*, 26–32; Cleveland Amory, *The Last Resorts* (New York: Harper, 1952), 432.

7. Townsend, *Manhood*, 17; Frances A. Walker, "College Athletics," *Harvard Graduates' Magazine* 2 (1894), 11, quoted in Clifford Putney, *Muscular Christianity: Manhood and Sports in America, 1880–1920* (Cambridge, Mass.: Harvard University Press, 2001), 39.

8. Robert Grant, *Fourscore: An Autobiography* (Boston: Houghton Mifflin Company, 1934); Myron T. Scudder, "The Value of Recreation in Rural Communities," in *The Rural Church*, vol. 6 of *Messages of the Men and Religion Forward Movement* (New York: Association Press, the YMCA, 1912), 228–229, quoted in Putney, *Muscular Christianity*, 28–29; "The Fate of the Salaried Man," *The Independent*, August 20, 1903, 2002–3.

9. Townsend, *Manhood at Harvard*, 256–258; Kathleen Dalton, *Theodore Roosevelt: A Strenuous Life* (New York: Knopf, 2002), chap. 2.

10. Dalton, *Roosevelt*, 82, 126, 158, 208, 265, 279; William Henry Harbaugh, *The Life and Times of Theodore Roosevelt* (New York: Oxford University Press, 1975), 212–214.

11. "President in California," *New York Times*, May 8, 1903, 3, quoted in Gail Bederman, *Manliness and Civilization: A Cultural History of Gender and Race in the United States, 1890–1917* (Chicago: University of Chicago Press, 1994), 204. On masculine regeneration through imperial adventure, see Kristin L. Hoganson, *Fighting for American Manhood: How Gender Politics Provoked the Spanish-American and Philippine-American Wars* (New Haven: Yale University Press, 1998), and Richard Slotkin, *Gunfighter Nation: The Myth of the Frontier in Twentieth-Century America* (New York: Atheneum, 1992), esp. 29–62.

12. Theodore Roosevelt, *An Autobiography* (New York: Scribner's, 1920), 122, and *The Strenuous Life* (New York: Century Company, 1900), 1–24.

13. Owen Wister, *The Virginian* (1902; New York: Penguin Books, 1988); G. Edward White, *The Eastern Establishment and the Western Experience: The West of Frederic Remington, Theodore Roosevelt, and Owen Wister* (New Haven: Yale University Press, 1968); Townsend, *Manhood*, 265–273.

14. William James, "The Ph.D. Octopus" (1903), in *Writings*, vol. 2, *1902–1910*, Library of America ed. (New York: Viking, 1987), 1111–18; William James,

"The Social Value of the College Bred" (1906), ibid., 1242–49; William James, "The Moral Equivalent of War" (1910), in *The Writings of William James*, ed. John J. McDermott (New York: Random House, 1967), 660–670.

15. Theodore Roosevelt, "College Life" (1907), quoted in Townsend, *Manhood*, 277.

16. Theodore Roosevelt, review of Brooks Adams, *The Law of Civilization and Decay*, *The Forum* 22 (December 1896), 575–579; Alfred Thayer Mahan, *The Interest of America in Sea Power, Present and Future* (Boston: Little, Brown, and Company, 1897), 121, cited in Putney, *Muscular Christianity*, 32. See also Lears, *No Place*, 134–137, and Hoganson, *Fighting for American Manhood*, chaps. 2–4.

17. Henry Cabot Lodge, "Football," *Harvard Graduates Magazine* 5 (September 1896), 67; Eliot, quoted in Townsend, *Manhood*, 96; Thomas J. Schaeper and Kathleen Schaeper, *Cowboys into Gentlemen: Rhodes Scholars, Oxford, and the Creation of an American Elite* (New York: Berghahn Books, 1998), 16–17.

18. Putney, *Muscular Christianity*, 107; McLachlan, *American Boarding School*, chap. 9.

19. George Martin, "Preface to a Schoolmaster's Biography," *Harper's* 188 (January 1944), 161; Ellery Sedgwick, "Three Men of Groton," *Atlantic Monthly* 178 (1946), 68.

20. McLachlan, *American Boarding Schools*, 298.

21. Putney, *Muscular Christianity*, 107; Cookson and Pursell, *Preparing for Power*, 19, 57, 205.

22. Cookson and Pursell, *Preparing for Power*, 199ff.

23. Charles William Eliot, "American Democracy," *Harvard Graduates Magazine* 10 (June 1902), 506–507; Townsend, *Manhood*, 92, 121; Hugh Hawkins, *Between Harvard and America: The Educational Leadership of Charles William Eliot* (New York: Oxford University Press, 1972).

24. Henry A. Yeomans, *Abbott Lawrence Lowell, 1856–1943* (Cambridge, Mass.: Harvard University Press, 1948), 68; Richard Angelo, "The Social Transformation of American Higher Education," in *The Transformation of Higher Learning, 1860–1930*, ed. Konrad H. Jarausch (Chicago: University of Chicago Press, 1983); Donald Meyer, "Early Football," unpublished paper cited in Christopher Lasch, *The Culture of Narcissism* (New York: Norton, 1979), 113.

25. Maureen E. Montgomery, *Displaying Women: Spectacles of Leisure in Edith Wharton's New York* (New York: Routledge, 1998), 63–68.

26. Kathleen McCarthy, *Women's Culture: American Philanthropy and Art, 1830–1930* (Chicago: University of Chicago Press, 1991), 209, 237–239.

27. Amory, *Last Resorts*, 315. See also Kathleen McCarthy, *Noblesse Oblige:*

Charity and Cultural Philanthropy in Chicago, 1849–1929 (Chicago: University of Chicago Press, 1982); Barry Karl and Stanley Katz, "Foundations and Ruling Class Elites," *Daedalus* 116 (Winter 1987), 1–40.

28. Amory, *Last Resorts*, 6–7.

29. Ibid., 48.

30. Gerard quoted ibid., 8; Jean Strouse, *Morgan: American Financier* (New York: Random House, 1999), 672.

31. My account of Taylor is based on Sudhir Kakar, *Frederick Winslow Taylor: A Study in Personality and Innovation* (Cambridge, Mass.: MIT Press, 1970), and Robert Kanigel, *The One Best Way: Frederick Winslow Taylor and the Enigma of Efficiency* (New York: Viking, 1997).

32. Kakar, *Taylor*, 36–38; Kanigel, *One Best Way*, 116–147.

33. Kanigel, *One Best Way*, 145–147, 181–184.

34. Ibid., 162–180, 240–346.

35. Ibid., 315–323, 467–484; Frederick Winslow Taylor, *The Principles of Scientific Management* (1911; New York: Norton, 1967), 43–53.

36. Hugh C. J. Aitken, *Taylorism at Watertown Arsenal* (Cambridge, Mass.: Harvard University Press, 1960); Kanigel, *One Best Way*, 467–484; Samuel Haber, *Efficiency and Uplift: Scientific Management in the Progressive Era* (Chicago: University of Chicago Press, 1964).

37. I discuss the new managerial self in *Fables*, 162–234.

38. John Kasson, *Houdini, Tarzan, and the Perfect Man: The White Male Body and the Challenge of Modernity in America* (New York: Hill and Wang, 2001), 30–76, quotation at 75; Lears, *Fables*, 158, 166–169.

39. Kasson, *Houdini*, 174–175.

40. Ibid., 179–182; Putney, *Muscular Christianity*, 180–200.

41. Roland Marchand, *Advertising the American Dream: Making Way for Modernity, 1920–1940* (Berkeley: University of California Press, 1985); Ponce de Leon, *Self-Exposure*, 154–157.

42. Ponce de Leon, *Self-Exposure*, 141–145.

43. Edith Wharton, *The Age of Innocence* (1920; New York: Scribner's, 1970), 346.

44. Ibid., 353–358.

45. Theodore Dreiser, *An American Tragedy* (1925; New York: Signet, 2000), 43, 202, 173–174.

46. Ibid., 331, 543.

47. F. Scott Fitzgerald, "The Rich Boy" (1926), in *The Stories of F. Scott Fitzgerald*, ed. Malcolm Cowley (New York: Scribner, 1951), 177.

48. Ibid., 200–201.

49. Fitzgerald, "Winter Dreams" (1922), ibid., 130, 134.

50. Ibid., 136ff.

51. F. Scott Fitzgerald, *The Great Gatsby* (New York: Scribner's, 1925), 119.

52. Amory, *Last Resorts*, 310.

53. Peabody quoted in McLachlan, *American Boarding Schools*, 297.

7. The Foreign Policy Establishment

1. This account is from Godfrey Hodgson, *The Colonel: The Life and Wars of Henry L. Stimson* (New York: Alfred A. Knopf, 1990), 7–8, based on Stimson's diary for January 17, 1909.

2. Elihu Root (1845–1937) was a successful corporation lawyer who made a fortune before he was thirty. He went on to become secretary of state (1905–1908) and was awarded the Nobel Prize in 1912 for his work in connection with the Hague conference of 1907.

3. In November 1919 George Herbert Walker, grandfather of President George Herbert Walker Bush and great-grandfather of President George Walker Bush, founded the W. A. Harriman & Co. bank, which in December 1930 merged with the long-established Anglo-American bank Brown Brothers.

4. Walter Isaacson and Evan Thomas, *The Wise Men: Six Friends and the World They Made: Acheson, Bohlen, Harriman, Kennan, Lovett, McCloy* (New York: Simon & Schuster, 1986), 624.

5. "For boys from Groton or St. Paul's of that [1920s] era college meant Harvard, Yale, or Princeton." Ibid., 60.

6. George Wilson Pierson, *History of Yale College* (New Haven: Yale University Press, 1952); Brooks Mather Kelley, *Yale: A History* (New Haven: Yale University Press, 1974); Alexandra Robbins, *Secrets of the Tomb: Skull and Bones, the Ivy League, and the Hidden Paths of Power* (Boston: Little, Brown, 2002).

7. Evan Thomas, *The Very Best Men* (New York: Simon & Schuster, 1995), 92.

8. For example, James Perloff, *The Shadows of Power: The Council on Foreign Relations and the American Decline* (Appleton, Wisc.: Western Island, 1988).

9. Godfrey Hodgson, "The Establishment," *Foreign Policy* 10 (Spring 1973), 3–40.

10. Kennan was raised in Wisconsin, educated at Princeton. His cousin, also named George Kennan, was a famous traveler in nineteenth-century Russia. He

was the author of *Siberia and the Exile System* (1891; Chicago: University of Chicago Press, 1958).

11. Clayton was born in Tupelo, Mississippi, in 1880. He became "the greatest cotton merchant in the world." In 1940 he went to work, unsalaried, for Nelson Rockefeller in inter-American affairs and in 1943 was made undersecretary of state for economic affairs. After the war he was one of the creators of the Marshall Plan for European reconstruction.

12. Thomas, *The Very Best Men*, 55.

13. See *www.theodoreroosevelt.org/life/quotes.htm*.

14. "The President needs help," wrote the Brownlow Committee in 1940, recommending that the president should be given six high-level special assistants to share his workload. Richard P. Nathan, *The Plot That Failed: Nixon and the Administrative Presidency* (New York: Wiley, 1975), 87.

15. The background of both telegram and article are interestingly explained by George Kennan, *Memoirs*, vol. 1 (Boston: Atlantic–Little, Brown, 1967), 290–295, 354–367. The text of the long telegram is published at 547–559.

16. Though he himself, it has astutely been pointed out, used the word to describe to President Johnson the elder statesmen he ought to recruit to his support. Isaacson and Thomas, *The Wise Men*, 644.

17. Ray Stannard Baker, *Woodrow Wilson: Life and Letters*, vol. 7 (Garden City, N.Y.: Doubleday, 1927–1939), 254.

18. See Arno J. Mayer, *The Political Origins of the New Diplomacy, 1917–1918* (New Haven: Yale University Press, 1959), passim.

19. Lawrence E. Gelphand, *The Inquiry: American Preparations for Peace, 1917–1919* (New Haven: Yale University Press, 1963), 47.

20. See William P. Bundy, "About *Foreign Affairs*," *www.foreignaffairs.org/about/history*. See also Whitney H. Shepardson, *Early History of the Council on Foreign Relations* (Stamford, Conn.: Overbrook Press, 1960); Robert F. Byrnes, *Awakening American Education to the World: The Role of Archibald Cary Coolidge, 1866–1928* (South Bend: University of Notre Dame Press, 1982); Robert D. Schulzinger, *The Wise Men of Foreign Affairs: The History of the Council on Foreign Relations* (New York: Columbia University Press, 1984).

21. Ronald Steel, *Walter Lippmann and the American Century* (Boston: Little Brown, 1980).

22. Justus D. Doenecke, *Storm on the Horizon: The Challenge to American Interventionism, 1939–1941* (Lanham, Md.: Rowman & Littlefield, 2000).

23. On America First, see Wayne S. Cole, *America First: The Battle against In-*

tervention, 1940–1941 (Madison: University of Wisconsin Press, 1953); Justus D. Doenecke, ed., *In Danger Undaunted: The Anti-Interventionist Movement of 1940–1941* (Stanford: Hoover Institution Press, 1990).

24. Cole, *America First*, 13.

25. Ibid., 141.

26. Peter Grose, *Gentleman Spy: The Life of Allen Dulles* (Boston: Houghton Mifflin, 1994), 5.

27. Allen W. Dulles and Hamilton Fish Armstrong, *Can We Be Neutral?* (New York: Harper & Brothers, 1936), 117.

28. William G. Hyland, "*Foreign Affairs* at 70," *Foreign Affairs* 71 (Fall 1992), 171–193; Hamilton Fish Armstrong, "Armistice at Munich," *Foreign Affairs* 17 (January 1939), 289.

29. Hamilton F. Armstrong and Allen W. Dulles, "Legislating Peace," *Foreign Affairs* 17 (October 1938), 1–13.

30. Isaacson and Thomas, *Wise Men*, 95.

31. See House-FDR correspondence in the House papers in Department of Manuscripts and Archives, Yale University Library.

32. Gar Alperovitz, *Atomic Diplomacy: Hiroshima and Potsdam: The Use of the Atomic Bomb and the American Confrontation with Soviet Power* (New York: Simon & Schuster, 1965); *Atomic Diplomacy: The Critical Issues*, ed. Barton J. Bernstein (Boston: Little, Brown, 1976).

33. Elting E. Morison, *Turmoil and Tradition: A Study of the Life and Times of Henry L. Stimson* (Boston: Houghton Mifflin, 1960).

34. Kai Bird, *The Color of Truth: McGeorge Bundy and William Bundy, Brothers in Arms* (New York: Simon & Schuster, 1998), 84–85.

35. Two of the scientists who were members of the panel advising the interim committee, J. Robert Oppenheimer and Arthur Compton, stated later that they believed the decision had already been taken. Morison, *Turmoil and Tradition*, 626–627.

36. Bird, *Color of Truth*, 84.

37. Hodgson, *The Colonel*, 350–363.

38. The agency replaced the Central Intelligence Group by the authority of the National Security Act of 1947, which also combined the War and Navy departments into the Department of Defense.

39. Robin W. Winks, *Cloak and Gown: Scholars in the Secret War, 1939–1961* (New York: Morrow, 1987), 35.

40. Ibid., 437.

41. Godfrey Hodgson, *America in Our Time* (Garden City, N.Y.: Doubleday, 1976).

42. Dean Acheson, *Present at the Creation* (New York: Norton, 1987), 219.

43. See, for example, among a large literature, Thomas, *The Very Best Men*, and Winks, *Cloak and Gown*.

44. At Yale, Richard Bissell was actually tapped for Skull and Bones but refused to accept. Robbins, *Secrets of the Tomb*, 187.

45. Evan Thomas writes that "the target for most covert action enthusiasts . . . was no longer liberating the East Bloc, but rather stopping the dominoes from falling in other parts of the world—the Middle East, Asia, Africa, Latin America" (*The Very Best Men*, 107). But this suggests that the change in policy resulted from decisions in Washington. In reality Washington was responding to a change in Soviet strategy and to the communist victory in China in 1949.

46. Though he went out of his way to deny that he was part of "the Groton clique." Ibid., 108.

47. FitzGerald, St. Mark's and Harvard, married Marietta Peabody, granddaughter of the headmaster of Groton. For Lansdale's account, see Edward Geary Lansdale, *In the Midst of Wars: An American Mission to Southeast Asia* (New York: Harper & Row, 1972).

48. See Bradley F. Smith, *The Shadow Warriors: OSS and the Origins of the CIA* (New York: Basic Books, 1983), xiii. See also R. Harris Smith, *OSS: The Secret History of America's First Central Intelligence Agency* (Berkeley: University of California Press, 1972).

49. Smith, *Shadow Warriors*, xv.

50. Roger Hilsman, a graduate of West Point, was wounded while serving with Merrill's Marauders in Burma in 1944. After recovering from his wounds, he stayed in Burma, serving with OSS, and commanded a guerrilla group of three hundred Burmese troops. After the war he received both a master's degree and Ph.D. from Yale University. He headed the State Department's Bureau of Intelligence in the Kennedy administration. To meet the guerrilla threat in South Vietnam, he wrote, "we need reformers to reorganize mass parties and social and political programs that could become the basis of modernization." He was assistant secretary of state for Far Eastern affairs 1963–64. He later served on the faculty of Columbia University. See Lt. Col. James B. Wilkinson, Ret., "A Gazette Retrospective: Counterguerrilla Warfare," *Marine Corps Gazette* (February 2002).

51. Lawrence Freedman, *Kennedy's Wars: Berlin, Cuba, Laos, and Vietnam* (New York: Oxford University Press, 2000), 138.

52. Devious because Kennedy went to great lengths to conceal the fact that his policy depended on a deal, to remove U.S. missiles from Turkey, which he denied making.

53. Thomas Powers, *The Man Who Kept the Secrets: Richard Helms and the CIA* (New York: Knopf, 1979), 180.

54. Freedman, *Kennedy's Wars*, 295–304; Rudy Abramson, *Spanning the Century: The Life of Averell Harriman* (New York: Morrow, 1992), 582–591.

55. Powers, *The Man Who Kept the Secrets*, 181–183. William Colby, who succeeded FitzGerald as head of DDP's Far East division and later became director of central intelligence, subsequently admitted that 20,587 Vietnamese civilians had been killed by Operation Phoenix. South Vietnamese estimates went as high as 40,000 dead.

56. For example, Michael Forrestal, son of James Forrestal, the investment banker and first secretary of defense.

57. Kai Bird, *The Chairman: John J. McCloy and the Making of the American Establishment* (New York: Simon & Schuster, 1992), 570. The president sent Secretary of State Dean Rusk to sound McCloy out.

58. James Chace, *Acheson: The Secretary of State Who Created the American World* (New York: Simon & Schuster, 1998), 420.

59. Bird, *Color of Truth*, 338.

60. Bird, *The Chairman*, 518, citing Armstrong to Arthur Dean, August 9, 1965.

61. Ibid., 598.

62. Bird, *Color of Truth*, 360.

63. Subsequently Chief Justice of the Supreme Court until he resigned after a conflict of interest controversy.

64. Isaacson and Thomas, *Wise Men*, 679–680.

65. Don Oberdorfer, *Tet! The Turning Point in the Vietnam War* (Garden City, N.Y.: Doubleday, 1971).

66. Bird, *Color of Truth*, 366.

67. Chace, *Acheson*, 424.

68. Ibid., 427.

69. Isaacson and Thomas, *Wise Men*, 700.

70. Walter Isaacson, *Kissinger: A Biography* (New York: Simon & Schuster, 1992), 83.

71. Sidney Blumenthal, *The Rise of the Counter-Establishment: From Conservative Ideology to Political Power* (New York: Times Books, 1986).

72. Dan Smoot, *The Invisible Government* (Dallas: Dan Smoot Report, 1962);

Colonel Victor J. Fox [pseud.], *The Welfare Staters* (New York: Freedom Press, 1962); Kent Courtney and Phoebe Courtney, *America's Unelected Rulers: The Council on Foreign Relations* (New Orleans: Conservative Society of America, 1962).

73. For example, Gary Allen, *None Dare Call It Conspiracy* (Rossmoor, Calif.: Concord Press, 1972), sold over 5 million copies.

74. For example, David Halberstam, *The Best and the Brightest* (New York: Random House, 1972); Walter Isaacson and Evan Thomas, *The Wise Men;* Bird, *The Chairman.*

75. Perloff, *The Shadows of Power.*

76. Ibid., 42.

77. Ibid., 168–169.

78. Godfrey Hodgson, "The Establishment."

79. Boulay de la Meurthe, on the execution of the duc d'Enghien in 1804.

8. Conservative Elites and the Counterrevolution against the New Deal

1. Bruce J. Schulman, *From Cotton Belt to Sunbelt: Federal Policy, Economic Development, and the Transformation of the South, 1938–1980* (Durham: Duke University Press, 1994), 218. See also Dewey W. Grantham, *The South in Modern America: A Region at Odds* (New York: HarperCollins, 1994).

2. Michael Lind, *The Next American Nation* (New York: Free Press, 1995). For a similar but not identical argument, see Bruce Ackerman, *We the People: Foundations* (Cambridge, Mass.: Belknap Press of Harvard University Press, 1993).

3. Jordan A. Schwarz, *The New Dealers: Power Politics in the Age of Roosevelt* (New York: Random House, 1993).

4. Theodore Caplow, Louis Hicks, and Ben J. Wattenberg, *The First Measured Century: An Illustrated Guide to Trends in America, 1900–2000* (Washington, D.C.: AEI Press, 2000), 20.

5. For an analysis of the strategies of dissimulation by which American judicial and political elites have sought to camouflage anti-white racial discrimination in the name of affirmative action, see Daniel Sabbagh, "Judicial Uses of Subterfuge: Affirmative Action Reconsidered," *Political Science Quarterly* 118 (Fall 2003), 411–436.

6. DeWayne Wickham, "Racial, Ideological Issues Split Black, White Voters," *USA Today,* November 4, 2002.

7. Ruy Texeira, "Deciphering the Democrats' Debacle," *Washington Monthly*, May 1, 2003.

8. Caplow, Hicks, and Wattenberg, *First Measured Century*, 17.

9. Jack Citrin and Benjamin Highton, "Race, Ethnicity, and Voting: What Accounts for Turnout Differences in California?" research brief, Public Policy Institute of California, December 2002, 2.

10. See Ruy Texeira and Joel Rogers, *America's Forgotten Majority: Why the White Working Class Still Matters* (New York: Basic Books, 2000).

11. In *The Next American Nation*, I used the term "overclass" to distinguish the college-educated, credentialed managerial-professional elite from the hereditary upper class, with which it overlaps to a degree. Like "underclass," "overclass" is a phrase in Swedish that Gunnar Myrdal translated into English and introduced to American public discourse.

12. Jeffrey M. Berry, "Revived, Yet Hardly Recognizable," *Washington Post Outlook*, July 11, 1999, B3.

13. Ibid.

14. Ibid. See also Jeffrey M. Berry, *The New Liberalism: The Rising Power of Citizen Groups* (Washington, D.C.: Brookings Institution Press, 1999).

15. Stephen A. Herzenberg, John A. Alic, and Howard Wial, *New Rules for a New Economy: Employment and Opportunity in Postindustrial America* (Ithaca: Cornell University Press, 1998), 26, 27, table 4.

16. *New York Times*, November 25, 1984, cited in Dennis Gilbert and Joseph A. Kahl, *The American Class Structure: A New Synthesis*, 4th ed. (Belmont, Calif.: Wadsworth Publishing Company, 1993), 215.

17. Ted Halstead and Michael Lind, *The Radical Center: The Future of American Politics* (New York: Doubleday, 2001), 1.

18. Caplow, Hicks, and Wattenberg, *First Measured Century*, 11.

19. Ibid., 21.

20. Fred M. Shelley, J. Clark Archer, Fiona M. Davidson, and Stanley D. Brunn, *Political Geography of the United States* (New York: Guilford Press, 1996), 79.

21. Daniel Henninger, "Blue-State Pols Are Emptying Their Own States," *Wall Street Journal*, August 29, 2003, A8.

22. Thomas Byrne Edsall, *The New Politics of Inequality* (New York: W. W. Norton, 1984), 128–129.

23. *New York Times*, August 4, 1981, cited in Gilbert and Kahl, *American Class Structure*, 262.

24. Caplow, Hicks, and Wattenberg, *First Measured Century*, 49.

25. "International Tax Comparisons, 1965–2001 (Federal, State, and Local)," Citizens for Tax Justice, November 5, 2002.

26. "Texas State and Local Taxes in 1995: Shares of Family Income for Non-elderly Married Couples," Appendix 1, 44, Citizens for Tax Justice, *http://ctj.org/whop/whop_tx.pdf.*

27. For the history of regional divisions over trade, see Peter Trubowitz, *Defining the National Interest: Conflict and Change in American Foreign Policy* (Chicago: University of Chicago Press, 1998).

28. Herman M. Schwartz and Aida A. Hozic, "Who Needs the New Economy?" *Salon*, March 16, 2001.

29. Thomas R. Dye, *Who's Running America? The Bush Era*, 5th ed. (Englewood Cliffs, N.J.: Prentice-Hall, 1990), 236.

30. See Steve Fraser and Gary Gerstle, eds., *The Rise and Fall of the New Deal Order, 1930–1980* (Princeton: Princeton University Press, 1989).

31. Michael Lind, *Made in Texas: George W. Bush and the Southern Takeover of American Politics* (New York: Basic Books, 2003).

Coda

1. Alexis de Tocqueville, *Democracy in America*, trans. Arthur Goldhammer (New York: Library of America, 2004).

Acknowledgments

The editors want to acknowledge a number of people for their help in getting this book from idea to reality. At the outset, we consulted with a fair number of our fellow historians about the nature and shape of this project. We learned a great deal from what they had to say. Special thanks are due to Ira Berlin, Michael Kazin, and Nelson Lichtenstein for their trenchant comments on the whole manuscript. Our contributors took substantial time away from other projects to write for us and then to rework their essays in light of the revisions we requested. Their deep commitment to this project has been one of our greatest satisfactions. It has been a pleasure to work with our editor, Joyce Seltzer, and we have benefited from her energy, enthusiasm, and savvy editorial advice. Nancy Clemente skillfully guided this book through each production stage. Amanda Heller did an excellent job copyediting the manuscript, saving it from various literary infelicities. For that matter, all the people involved with the project at Harvard University Press performed their tasks with talent, efficiency, and professional care, for which we are grateful. Daniel Gerstle expertly checked footnotes and Katarina Keane's critical assistance with the copyeditor's queries got us through a particularly tough bottleneck. James O'Brien's index, as usual, is first-rate. We thank you all.

Contributors

Steve Fraser is a writer and editor who lives in New York City. He is the author of *Every Man a Speculator: A History of Wall Street in American Life* (2005) and *Labor Will Rule: Sidney Hillman and the Rise of American Labor* (1991), winner of the Philip Taft Prize. He is co-editor of *The Rise and Fall of the New Deal Order, 1930–1980* (1989).

Gary Gerstle is Professor of History at the University of Maryland. He is the author of *Working-Class Americanism* (1989) and *American Crucible: Race and Nation in the Twentieth Century* (2001), winner of the Theodore Saloutos Prize. He is co-editor of *The Rise and Fall of the New Deal Order, 1930–1980* (1989).

Sven Beckert, Professor of History at Harvard University, is the author of *The Monied Metropolis: New York City and the Consolidation of the American Bourgeoise* (2001). He is currently writing a global history of cotton.

Alan Dawley is Professor of History at The College of New Jersey. He is the author of *Class and Community: The Industrial Revolution in Lynn* (1976), winner of the Bancroft Prize; *Struggles for Justice: Social Responsibility and the Liberal State* (1991); and *Changing the World: American Progressives in War and Revolution* (2003).

Godfrey Hodgson is a British print, radio, and TV journalist and historian of the United States. His books include *America in Our Time* (1976); *The Colonel: The Life and Wars of Henry Stimson, 1867–1950* (1990); *More Equal Than Others: America from Nixon to the New Century* (2004). He is currently at work on a biography of Woodrow Wilson's key adviser, Colonel House.

Gary J. Kornblith, Professor of History at Oberlin College, is the author of *The Industrial Revolution in America* (1996) and many essays on entrepreneurs, artisans, and political elites in antebellum America.

Jackson Lears is Board of Governors Professor of History at Rutgers University and editor of *Raritan: A Quarterly Review*. He is the author of *No Place of Grace: Antimodernism and the Transformation of American Culture, 1880–1920* (1981), nominated for a National Book Critics Circle Award; *Fables of Abundance: A Cultural History of Advertising in America* (1994), winner of the Los Angeles Times Book Award for History; and *Something for Nothing: Luck in America* (2003).

Michael Lind, Whitehead Senior Fellow at the New America Foundation in Washington, D.C., is the author of a number of books about American politics and history, including *The Next American Nation* (1995) and *What Lincoln Believed* (2004).

John M. Murrin is Professor of History, emeritus, at Princeton University and one of the country's leading scholars of colonial and revolutionary America. He has co-authored *Liberty, Equality, Power: A History of the American People* (2004), and edited or co-edited five books. His own essays on early America range from politics and the law to economics and culture.

David Nasaw is Distinguished Professor of History and Director of the Center for the Humanities at the CUNY Graduate Center. Author of four books, including *The Chief: The Life of William Randolph Hearst* (2000), winner of the Bancroft Prize, the J. Anthony Lukas

Book Prize, and three other prizes, he is currently working on a biography of Andrew Carnegie.

Adam Rothman is Assistant Professor of History at Georgetown University. He is the author of *Slave Country: American Expansion and the Origins of the Deep South* (2005).

Index